CompTIA® A+®
Complete Review Guide

Core 1 Exam 220-1101 and Core 2 Exam 220-1102

Fifth Edition

Troy McMillan

SYBEX®
A Wiley Brand

This book is dedicated to my sweet wife, Heike.

Acknowledgments

I would like to thank Kim Wimpsett for helping to keep me on track, Ken Brown for continuing to publish my work, and Buzz Murphy for his work in making sure I'm technically correct.

About the Author

Troy McMillan writes practice tests, study guides, and online course materials for CyberVista while also running his own consulting and training business. He holds more than 30 industry certifications and also appears in training videos for OnCourse Learning and Pearson Press. Troy can be reached at mcmillantroy@hotmail.com.

About the Technical Editor

George Murphy, (Buzz) is a public speaker, corporate trainer, author, and cybersecurity evangelist who has instructed of thousands of cyber security professionals around the world over the past 25 years with courses, seminars and consulting presentations on a variety of technical and cybersecurity topics. A former Dell technology training executive, he has addressed audiences at RSA, Comdex, Networld, and the National Computer Conference as well as major corporations and educational institutions such as Princeton University. Buzz has earned more than twenty-nine IT and cybersecurity certifications from such prestigious organizations as ISC², CompTIA, PMI, and Microsoft, and other industry certification organizations. He is an ISC² Authorized Instructor.

Contents at a Glance

Contents

Chapter 3   **Hardware**   **95**

Chapter   4   Virtualization and Cloud Computing   197

Introduction

The A+ certification program was developed by the Computing Technology Industry Association (CompTIA) to provide an industry-wide means of certifying the competency of computer service technicians. The A+ certification is granted to those who have attained the level of knowledge and troubleshooting skills that are needed to provide capable support in the field of personal computers. CompTIA is a widely respected industry leader in this area.

CompTIA's A+ exam objectives are periodically updated to keep the certification applicable to the most recent hardware and software. This is necessary because a technician must be able to work on the latest equipment. The most recent revisions to the objectives—and to the whole program—were introduced in 2022 and are reflected in this book.

This book and the Sybex *CompTIA A+ Complete Study Guide* (both the Standard and Deluxe Editions) are tools to help you prepare for this certification—and for the new areas of focus of a modern computer technician's job.

What Is A+ Certification?

The A+ certification program was created to offer a wide-ranging certification, in the sense that it's intended to certify competence with personal computers from many different makers/vendors. Everyone must take and pass two exams: 220-1101 and 220-1102.

You don't have to take the 220-1101 exam and the 220-1102 exam at the same time. The A+ certification isn't awarded until you've passed both tests. For the latest pricing on the exams and updates to the registration procedures, call Pearson VUE at (877) 551-7587. You can also go to Pearson VUE for additional information or to register online at www .pearsonvue.com/comptia. If you have further questions about the scope of the exams or related CompTIA programs, refer to the CompTIA website at www.comptia.org.

Who Should Buy This Book?

If you want to acquire a solid foundation in personal computer basics and your goal is to prepare for the exams by filling in any gaps in your knowledge, this book is for you. You'll find clear explanations of the concepts you need to grasp and plenty of help to achieve the high level of professional competency you need to succeed in your chosen field.

If you want to become certified as an A+ holder, this book is definitely what you need. However, if you just want to attempt to pass the exam without really understanding the basics of personal computers, this guide isn't for you. It's written for people who want to acquire skills and knowledge of personal computer basics.

How to Use This Book

We've included several learning tools in the book. These tools will help you retain vital exam content as well as prepare to sit for the actual exams.

Exam Essentials   Each chapter includes a number of exam essentials. These are the key topics that you should take from the chapter in terms of areas on which you should focus when preparing for the exam.

Chapter Review Questions   To test your knowledge as you progress through the book, there are review questions at the end of each chapter. As you finish each chapter, answer the review questions and then check your answers—the correct answers are in the appendix. You can go back to reread the section that deals with each question you got wrong to ensure that you answer correctly the next time you're tested on the material.

Interactive Online Learning Environment and Test Bank

The interactive online learning environment that accompanies *CompTIA® A+® Complete Review Guide: Core 1 Exam 220-1101 and Core 2 Exam 220-1102, Fifth Edition*, provides a test bank with study tools to help you prepare for the certification exam—and increase your chances of passing it the first time! The test bank includes the following:

Sample Tests   All the questions in this book are provided, including the review questions at the end of each chapter. In addition, there are four practice exams. Use these questions to test your knowledge of the study guide material. The online test bank runs on multiple devices.

Flashcards   Two sets of questions are provided in digital flashcard format (a question followed by a single correct answer). You can use the flashcards to reinforce your learning and provide last-minute test prep before the exam.

Other Study Tools   A glossary of key terms from this book and their definitions is available as a fully searchable PDF.

Tips for Taking the A+ Exams

Here are some general tips for taking your exams successfully:

- Bring two forms of ID with you. One must be a photo ID, such as a driver's license. The other can be a major credit card or a passport. Both forms must include a signature.

- Arrive early at the exam center so that you can relax and review your study materials, particularly tables and lists of exam-related information.

- Read the questions carefully. Don't be tempted to jump to an early conclusion. Make sure you know exactly what the question is asking.

- Don't leave any unanswered questions. Unanswered questions are scored against you.

- There will be questions with multiple correct responses. When there is more than one correct answer, a message at the bottom of the screen will prompt you to either "Choose two" or "Choose all that apply." Be sure to read the messages displayed to know how many correct answers you must choose.

- When answering multiple-choice questions you're not sure about, use a process of elimination to get rid of the obviously incorrect answers first. Doing so will improve your odds if you need to make an educated guess.

- On form-based tests (nonadaptive), because the hard questions will eat up the most time, save them for last. You can move forward and backward through the exam.

- For the latest pricing on the exams and updates to the registration procedures, visit CompTIA's website at www.comptia.org.

CompTIA A+ 1100 Series Exam Objectives

CompTIA goes to great lengths to ensure that its certification programs accurately reflect the IT industry's best practices. The company does this by establishing Cornerstone Committees for each of its exam programs. Each committee consists of a small group of IT professionals, training providers, and publishers who are responsible for establishing the exam's baseline competency level and who determine the appropriate target audience level.

Once these factors are determined, CompTIA shares this information with a group of hand-selected subject-matter experts (SMEs). These folks are the true brainpower behind the certification program. They review the committee's findings, refine them, and shape them into the objectives you see before you. CompTIA calls this process a *job task analysis* (JTA).

Finally, CompTIA conducts a survey to ensure that the objectives and weightings truly reflect the job requirements. Only then can the SMEs go to work writing the hundreds of questions needed for the exam. And, in many cases, they have to go back to the drawing board for further refinements before the exam is ready to go live in its final state. So, rest assured, the content you're about to learn will serve you long after you take the exam.

Exam objectives are subject to change at any time without prior notice and at CompTIA's sole discretion. Please visit the certification page of CompTIA's website at www.comptia.org for the most current listing of exam objectives.

CompTIA also publishes relative weightings for each of the exam's objectives. The following tables list the objective domains and the extent to which they're represented on each exam:

220-1101 Exam Domains	Percent of Exam
1.0 Mobile Devices	15%
2.0 Networking	20%
3.0 Hardware	25%
4.0 Virtualization and Cloud Computing	11%
5.0 Hardware and Network Troubleshooting	29%
Total	100%

220-1102 Exam Domains	Percent of Exam
1.0 Operating Systems	31%
2.0 Security	25%
3.0 Software Troubleshooting	22%
4.0 Operational Procedures	22%
Total	100%

CompTIA A+ Core 1 Exam 220-1101

Chapter

1

Mobile Devices

- Location services
- Mobile device management (MDM)/mobile application management (MAM)
- Mobile device synchronization

This chapter will focus on the exam topics related to mobile devices. It will follow the structure of the CompTIA A+ 220-1101 exam blueprint, objective 1, and cover the four subobjectives that you will need to master before taking the exam. The Mobile Devices domain represents 15 percent of the total exam.

1.1 Given a scenario, install and configure laptop hardware and components

Whether you choose to call them laptops, notebooks, tablets, or something different is mostly a matter of semantics. In this section, I'll discuss some of the basic components of laptops and their installation (when possible and called for). In many cases, the components are the same as in a desktop computer.

The following topics are addressed in exam objective 1.1:

- Hardware/device replacement
- Physical privacy and security components

Hardware/device replacement

Replacing hardware and devices in a laptop can be a challenge because of the size limitations. The best way to determine the proper disassembly method is to consult the documentation from the manufacturer.

 Many laptop manufacturers will consider a warranty void if an unauthorized person opens a laptop case and attempts to repair it.

Some models of notebook PCs require a special T-8 Torx screwdriver. Most PC toolkits come with a T-8 bit for a screwdriver with interchangeable bits, but you may find that the T-8 screws are countersunk in deep holes so that you can't fit the screwdriver into them. In such cases, you need to buy a separate T-8 screwdriver, available at most hardware stores or auto parts stores.

Prepare a clean, well-lit, flat work surface; assemble your tools and manuals; and ensure that you have the correct parts. Shut down the PC, unplug it, and detach any external devices such as an external keyboard, mouse, or monitor. In this section, with these general guidelines for opening the laptop in mind, you'll look at replacing various components of a laptop. Always ensure that you have grounded yourself before working with computer components of any kind. Use an antistatic wristband and attach it to the case.

Battery

Replacing the battery in a laptop is simply a matter of removing the battery storage bay, removing the old battery from the bay, inserting the new battery into the bay, and replacing the bay. Determining the battery type for the replacement will probably take longer than the replacement procedure. In fact, many users carry extra batteries for situations where they know they will need to use the laptop for longer than the battery life (such as a long plane trip) and change the battery as needed.

 WARNING   If BitLocker encryption is enabled, the laptop will not boot after a battery replacement unless the BitLocker encryption key is provided.

Keyboard/keys

When replacing the keyboard, one of the main things you want to keep in mind is *not* to damage the data cable connector to the system board.

1. With the laptop fully powered off and unplugged from the wall, remove the battery. Examine the screws on the back of the laptop. Ideally, icons indicating which screws are attached to the keyboard will be available. If not, look up the model online and determine which of the screws are attached to the keyboard.

2. Remove the screws with a T-8 or Phillips-head screwdriver. With the laptop turned back over, open it. If the keyboard is tucked under any plastic pieces, determine whether those pieces need to have screws removed to get them out of the way; if so, remove the screws and the plastic pieces. In some cases, there may just be clamps that are easily removed.

3. With any plastic covers out of the way, remove any screws at the top and remove the keyboard itself from top to bottom. There should be a thin, but wide, data cable to the system board at the bottom. This is the piece to be careful with!

4. Take a pick and lift the plastic connectors that hold this data cable in place. Remove the data cable. Take the new keyboard and slip the data cable back in between the plastic connectors on the system board. Ensure it's all the way in.

5. Put the plastic connector back into place and make sure it's holding the data cable in. Position the keyboard into place and refasten the keyboard in place at the top, replacing any screws that were there before.

6. Replace any plastic pieces that were covering the keyboard, turn the laptop over, and replace all of the keyboard screws. When you replace the battery and turn it on, check the functionality. If the keyboard doesn't work, the main component to check is the data connector.

Random-access memory (RAM)

There should be a panel used for access to the memory modules. If the panels are not marked (many are not), refer to your laptop instruction manuals to locate the panel on the bottom.

1. Remove any screws holding the panel in place, remove the panel from the laptop, and set it aside. If removing an existing memory module, remove it by undoing the module clamps, gently lifting the edge of the module to a 45-degree angle, and then pulling the module out of the slot.

2. Align the notch of the new module with that of the memory slot and gently insert the module into the slot at a 45-degree angle. With all pins in the slot, gently rotate the module down flat until the clamps lock the module into place.

3. Replace the memory access panel, replace any screws, and power up the system. When the computer is powered back up, it may be necessary to go into the computer BIOS to let the system properly detect the new RAM that has been installed in the computer. Please refer to the user manual for the computer system for any additional information.

HDD/SSD replacement

Before changing a hard drive, you should back up the old hard drive if the data is needed. Then, to change the hard drive, follow these steps:

1. Turn the laptop upside down and look for a removable panel or a hard drive release mechanism. Laptop drives are usually accessible from the bottom or side of the chassis. Release the drive by flicking a lock/unlock button and/or removing a screw that holds the drive in place.

2. You may be required to remove the drive from a caddy or detach mounting rails from its sides. Attach the rails or caddy to the new drive using the same screws and washers. If required, remove the connector attached to the old drive's signal pins and attach it to the new drive. Make sure it's right side up and do not force it. Damaging the signal pins may render the drive useless.

3. Reverse your steps to place the drive (and caddy if present) into the case. Replace the screws and start the laptop. The system should recognize the drive. If you or the user created a bootable backup disc or a complete image disc (before the drive failed, by the way), place it in the optical drive and follow the instructions for restoring the data.

SSD drives

Although many devices still use a magnetic disk hard drive, most laptop vendors are moving to using either solid-state drives or hybrid drives, which are a combination of magnetic disk and solid-state technology.

The advantage of solid-state drives is that they are not as susceptible to damage if the device is dropped, and they are generally faster because no moving parts are involved. They are, however, more expensive, and when they fail, they don't typically display any advanced warning symptoms like a magnetic drive will do.

Hybrid storage products have a magnetic disk and some solid-state memory. These drives monitor the data being read from the hard drive, and they cache the most frequently accessed bits to the high-speed flash memory. These drives tend to cost slightly more than traditional hard drives (but far less than solid-state drives), but the addition of the SSD memory for cached bits creates a surprising improvement in performance. This improvement will not appear initially because the drive must "learn" the most frequently accessed data on the drive.

1.8 in vs. 2.5 in

The 2.5-inch hard drives are small (which makes them attractive for a laptop, where space is at a minimum), but in comparison to 3.5-inch hard drives, they have less capacity and cache, and they operate at a lower speed.

Moreover, whereas 2.5-inch drives operate from 5,400 to 7,200 rpm, 3.5-inch drives can operate from 7,200 to 10,000 rpm. However, 2.5-inch drives use about half the power (again, good for a laptop) of a 3.5-inch drive (2.5 W rather than 5 W).

The 1.8-inch drive is the smallest of the three I'm discussing here. It was originally used in subnotebooks and audio players. It has the least capacity of the three, with the largest up to 320 GB. It has only two platters, each of which can hold 220 GB maximum.

Hard disk drive (HDD)/solid-state drive (SSD) migration

When you have made the decision migrate data from hard disk drives (HDD) to solid-state drives (SDD), the process may be easier than you think.

1. First, ensure both drives are connected to the motherboard. Make sure both the power cable and the data cable are in place.

2. In Windows, open Disk Management, select the SSD drive, and then select Initialize Disk, as shown in Figure 1.1 (this assumes the HDD has already been initialized to the local system).

FIGURE 1.1   Initialize Disk

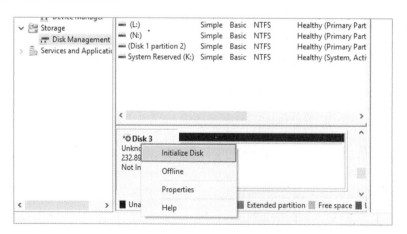

3. Select Control Panel ➤ System And Security ➤ Backup And Restore (Windows 7).

4. Click **Create A System Image** in the left pane. On the **Do You Want To Save Backup** page, from the **On A Hard Disk** drop-down list, choose the SSD drive. After selecting the destination disk or volume, click Next.

5. Make sure both System Reserved (System) and (C:) (System) drives (assuming C: is where the operating system is) are selected. Select any other drives that may hold data as well. Click Next. Confirm the backup settings and click Start Backup.

Wireless cards

Both 802.11 and Bluetooth wireless cards that are built in can be replaced if they go bad. Sometimes they reside near the memory, so you would open the same panel that holds the memory. In other cases (such as a Dell Inspiron), you have to remove the memory, keyboard, optical drive, and hand rest to get to it. The Bluetooth card may be located in the same place, or it may be located at the edge of the laptop with its own small panel to remove. Consult your documentation.

Once you've found either type of wireless card, disconnect the two antenna contacts from the card. Do not pull by the wire; pull by the connector itself. Remove any screws from the wireless card and gently pull out the card from the slot. Insert the replacement card into the slot at a 45-degree angle, replace the screws, and reconnect the antenna to the adapter. Replace the parts you were required to remove to get to the card, reversing your steps carefully.

Cellular card

Changing an external mobile broadband card is as simple as pulling the old USB stick out and plugging in the new one. Because USB is plug and play, you shouldn't have to do anything, but even in the case of an issue the manufacturer usually provides a CD with the drivers or you can obtain them from the vendor website. Changing an internal card is much like the process of changing an internal 802.11 card; follow the instructions indicated in the previous section.

Mini PCIe

Since many of the wireless cards are mini-PCIe, replacing any other card in this format will follow the same procedure, with the exception of removing and reconnecting the antenna cables (present only on the wireless cards). You can find the location of the card in the documentation. Make sure that the new card is firmly inserted into the slot after removing the old card.

Physical privacy and security components

Some features are designed to enhance the privacy of the data on a device and of the transmission of said data by enhancing physical security. In the following section, you'll learn about two concepts that help to provide additional security in this regard.

Biometrics

Most mobile devices now offer the option to incorporate biometrics as an authentication mechanism. The two most common implementations of this use fingerprint scans or facial scans or facial recognition technology. While there can be issues with both false negatives (the denial of a legitimate user) and false positives (the admission of an illegitimate user), they offer much better security than other authentication mechanisms.

A good example is a fingerprint lock that uses the fingerprint of the user as credentials to authenticate the user and, when successful authentication completes, unlocks the screen. Because it relies on biometrics, it is for the most part more secure than using a passcode or a swipe.

To set up fingerprint authentication in Windows 10, follow these steps:

1. Select Start ➢ Settings to open the Settings app.

2. Select Accounts ➢ Sign-in Options page. In the right pane, find the Fingerprint section under Windows Hello and click the Set Up button.

3. On the Welcome screen, click the Get Started button to continue.

4. Authenticate yourself with a PIN or a password to continue.

5. Scan your finger on the fingerprint sensor multiple times. As you scan your finger, you will see a fingerprint animation filling. When you see the All Set screen, you are done.

Near-field scanner features

A near-field scanner allows you to measure and map the EMI that may be leaking from a system or its cables, creating a physical security issue. While these devices are used for much more than detecting EMI, they can be used for that purpose. They can be used to analyze potential circuit designs for flaws as well. These devices are typically handheld.

Exam essentials

List the steps to install or replace laptop components.   This includes but is not limited to keyboards, hard drives, optical drives, wireless cards, mini-PCIe cards, and batteries,

List the steps to configure biometrics.   This includes features that depend on biometrics such as the fingerprint authentication in Windows 10.

1.2 Compare and contrast the display components of mobile devices

The display of a laptop contains more components than you may expect. In this section, I'll discuss these components and, in some cases, cover competing technologies. The following topics are addressed in exam objective 1.2:

- Types
- Mobile display components
- WIFI antenna connector/placement
- Camera/webcam
- Microphone
- Touch screen/digitizer
- Inverter

Types

Laptop displays can use any of several technologies: LCD, LED, or OLED. This section provides a quick survey of these display types and their characteristics as they apply to laptops.

Liquid crystal display (LCD)

LCDs have completely replaced CRTs as the default display type for both laptops and desktops. Two major types of LCDs are used today: active matrix screens and passive matrix screens. Their main differences lie in the quality of the image. Both types use some kind of lighting behind the LCD panel to make the screen easier to view. One or more small fluorescent tubes are used to backlight the screen.

Passive Matrix   A passive matrix screen uses a row of transistors across the top of the screen and a column of them down the side. It sends pulses to each pixel at the intersection of each row and column combination, telling it what to display. Passive matrix displays are becoming obsolete because they're less bright and have poorer refresh rates and image quality than active matrix displays. However, they use less power than active matrix displays.

Active Matrix   An active-matrix screen uses a separate transistor for each individual pixel in the display, resulting in higher refresh rates and brighter display quality. These screens use more power, however, because of the increased number of transistors that must be powered. Almost all notebook PCs today use active matrix. A variant called thin-film transistor (TFT) uses multiple transistors per pixel, resulting in even better display quality.

In-plane switching (IPS)

There are two major LCD technologies used in LCDs. In-plane switching (IPS) is a newer technology that solves the issue of poor quality at angles other than straight on. It also provides better color quality. However, it has much slower response time and is more expensive. Newer versions like Super-IPS (SIPS) make improvements on the response time.

Twisted nematic (TN)

Twisted nematic (TN) is the older of the two major technologies for flat-panel displays. While it provides the shortest response time, has high brightness, and draws less power than competing technologies, it suffers from poor quality when viewed from wide angles. It suffers color distortions when viewed from above or from the sides.

Fluorescent vs. LED backlighting

LCDs can use two kinds of backlighting: LED-based and fluorescent. Fluorescent is an older technology and consists of a fluorescent tube connected to a voltage inverter board that provides power to the backlight. LED-based is a newer technology and uses a matrix of LEDs for the backlighting. Table 1.1 compares the two technologies.

TABLE 1.1   Fluorescent and LED

Characteristic	Fluorescent	LED
Size	Thicker and heavier	Thinner and lighter
Cost	Cheaper	More expensive
Power	High power consumption and heat generation	Lower power consumption and heat generation
Brightness	Lower	Higher
Lifespan	Shorter	Longer

Vertical alignment (VA)

A third type is an LED that uses vertical alignment (VA). In VA, when no electric current is running through the liquid crystal cells, the cells naturally align vertically between two substrate panes of glass, which block the transmission of light from the backlight. This renders the crystals opaque and results in a black display screen. When an electric current is applied, the liquid crystal cells shift to a horizontal position between the substrates, allowing light to pass through and resulting in a white display screen. Monitors with VA LCD panels provide the advantages of wide viewing angles and high-contrast ratios and reproduce colors well. The operation of VA is shown in Figure 1.2

FIGURE 1.2   Vertical alignment

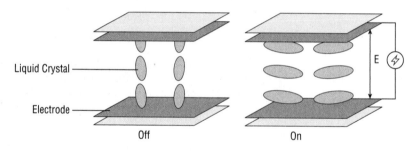

Off   On

Organic light-emitting diode (OLED)

An organic light-emitting diode (OLED) is another type of LED technology. It uses an emissive electroluminescent layer of organic compounds that emit light in response to an electric current. An interesting characteristic of these displays is their flexibility and transparency. This means they can roll up for storage (like a mat), and you can see through the display to objects behind the display. These displays are now available but quite expensive.

Mobile display components

The display of a laptop contains more components than you may expect. In this section, I'll discuss these components.

WIFI antenna connector/placement

The wireless antenna is located in the display. You may recall that when replacing a laptop screen, you encountered a number of wires coming from the screen to the laptop body. One of these is the cable that connects the wireless antenna (located in the display) with the wireless card located in the body of the laptop.

The antennas built into the display usually work quite well. In any specific situation, you may improve your signal by moving the laptop around. This changes the polarization of the antenna and may cause it to line up better to the incoming signal.

Camera/webcam

Many displays today, especially laptop displays, have a webcam built in. They come ready to go with all drivers preinstalled and nothing to configure or set up. If you need to replace the webcam, you will have to disconnect the laptop lid (which holds the display) from the base, remove the screw covers and screws holding the display bezel in place, and remove the bezel. After removing the screws holding the mounting rails to the hinges, remove the LED screen from the lid assembly. Now you can get at the camera, but first carefully remove the tape that holds the camera cable in place and remove it and the camera. Attach the replacement cable to the new camera, install the new camera, and reverse these steps.

Microphone

While many desktop systems lack a built-in microphone, almost all laptops have one. In some cases, this microphone will be located on the laptop bottom, but in many cases, it will be in the display next to the webcam or off to the side. If you need to replace it, you will need to take the same steps to get inside the display that you took for the webcam.

When you unhook the lid from the bottom, you will need to unplug several things from the board, and one of those will be the microphone cable. If the microphone is not working (which it probably isn't or you wouldn't be replacing it), take a moment to inspect the cable. Sometimes the cable can be cut by the constant opening and closing of the case (it shouldn't, but sometimes it does happen). You may be able to repair the cable without replacing the microphone.

If that is not the case, remove the microphone and cable and replace both with the new mic and cable. Reverse the steps to get into the display, reconnect the cables to the board, and put the back on the bottom.

Touch screen/digitizer

Digitizers read pressure applied to the surface of the display and are what make touchscreens work. In some cases, they work with a stylus or small pen-like device; in others, you simply touch the screen with your finger. The digitizer is a thin piece of clear material that fits on top of the display. It has its own cable just as the display itself does. If it gets cracked, which often happens, it can be replaced without replacing the display itself. Typically, when you perform this replacement, you will have to open the display lid, as I covered earlier, and separate the digitizer from the display. It is usually glued to the display, and you can use a hair dryer to heat the glue to make removing it easier. When you put the new digitizer in, you may need to reheat the glue on the display to stick them back together.

Inverter

An inverter is a component that takes DC power and converts it to an AC form that can be used by the LCD screen. It is implemented as a circuit board that is located behind the LCD. If problems with flickering display or dimness occur, the inverter is a prime suspect. If the inverter needs to be replaced, you should be aware that it may contain stored energy, so it may need to be discharged to be safe.

Exam essentials

Differentiate the types of displays available in laptops.   Two major types of LCDs are used today: active matrix screens and passive matrix screens.

Describe the location and operational characteristics of the wireless antenna in a laptop.   The wireless antenna is located in the display. Moving the laptop changes the polarity of the antenna and may result in a better signal.

Identify the location and function of the inverter.   An inverter is a component that takes DC power and converts it to a form that can be used by the LCD screen. It is implemented as a circuit board behind the LCD.

1.3 Given a scenario, set up and configure accessories and ports of mobile devices

Mobile devices can come with a variety of interfaces or ports to which various types of peripherals can be connected. The following topics are addressed in exam objective 1.3:

- Connection methods
- Accessories
- Docking station
- Port replicator
- Trackpad/drawing pad

Connection methods

Many connection methods have come and gone with respect to external ports on devices. In this section you'll learn about the most common ones found in today's mobile devices.

Universal Serial Bus (USB)/USB-C/microUSB/miniUSB

USB is an expansion bus type that is used almost exclusively for external devices. All motherboards today have at least two USB ports. Some of the advantages of USB include hot-plugging and the capability for up to 127 USB devices to share a single set of system resources. A USB port requires only one IRQ (short for interrupt request, an IRQ is a signal sent to the computer processor to stop [interrupt] it momentarily) for all USB devices that are connected to it, regardless of the type or number of devices.

Connector types: A, B, mini, micro

USB connectors come in two types and two form factors or sizes. The type A connector is what is found on USB hubs, on host controllers (cards that are plugged into slots to provide USB connections), and on the front and back panels of computers. Type B is the type of USB connector found on the end of the cable that plugs into the devices.

The connectors also come in a mini version and a micro version. The micro version is used on mobile devices, such as mobile phones, GPS units, and digital cameras, whereas the mini is found in applications described in the previous paragraph. The choice between a standard A and B and a mini A and B will be dictated by what is present on the device. The cables used cannot exceed 5 meters in length. Figure 1.3 shows, from left to right, a standard Type A, a mini Type A, a standard Type B, and a mini Type B. Some manufacturers have chosen to implement a mini connector that is proprietary, choosing not to follow the standard.

FIGURE 1.3   USB connectors

USB-C   The USB-C connectors connect to both hosts and devices, replacing various USB-B and USB-A connectors and cables with a standard. This type is distinguished by its twofold rotationally symmetrical connector. The cable is shown in Figure 1.4 next to USB 3.0 cable.

FIGURE 1.4   USB C and USB

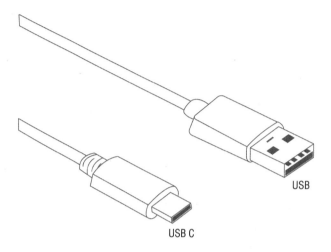

USB 2.0/3.0   USB 1.1 runs at 12 Mbps and USB 2.0 runs at 480 Mbps. USB 3.0 has transmission speeds of up to 5 Gbps, significantly reduces the time required for data transmission, reduces power consumption, and is backward-compatible with USB 2.0. Because USB is a serial interface, its width is 1 bit. It is useful to note, however, that a USB 2.0 device will perform at 2.0 speeds even when connected to a 3.0 port. If you connect a USB 3.0 to a USB 2.0 port, it will also only operate at 2.0 speeds

By utilizing USB hubs in conjunction with the USB ports available on the local machine, you can connect up to 127 of these devices to the computer. You can daisy-chain up to four external USB hubs to a USB port. Daisy chaining means that hubs are attached to each other in a line. A USB hub will not function if it is more than four hubs away from the root port.

Lightning

Apple uses what it calls the Lightning connector for power. Although it makes an adapter to convert this connector to mini-USB (see the next section), Apple doesn't encourage its use because of the limitations the adapter places on the functionality of the proprietary connector.

This is an eight-pin connector that while not standard has advantages over USB, according to Apple. It operates at USB 3.0 speeds of 640 MB. The following are some of these advantages:

- It can supply more power.
- It can be inserted either way.

- It is physically more durable than USB.
- It can detect and adapt to connected devices.

Figure 1.5 shows a Lightning connector next to a USB cable.

FIGURE 1.5   Lightning connector and USB

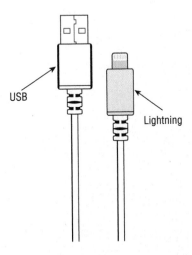

USB

Lightning

Serial interfaces

Although an older cable type, a serial connector may be found connecting some peripherals to the serial connection on the system. This connector is shown in Figure 1.6. The maximum speed is 115,200 bps.

FIGURE 1.6   Serial connector

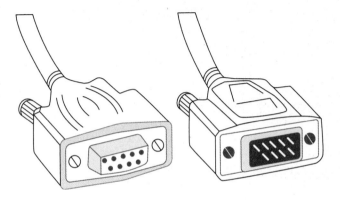

RS-232

The RS-232 standard had been commonly used in computer serial ports. A serial cable (and port) uses only one wire to carry data in each direction; all the rest are wires for signaling and traffic control.

Common bit rates include 1,200; 2,400; 4,800; 9,600; 14,400; 19,200; 38,400; 57,600; and 115,200 bits per second. The connector used for serial is a D-shaped connector with a metal ring around a set of pins. These are named for the number of pins/holes used: DB-25, DB-9, HD-15 (also known as DB-15), and so on. Figure 1.7 shows DB-25, DB-15, and DB-9.

FIGURE 1.7   DB-25, DB-15, and DB-9 ports

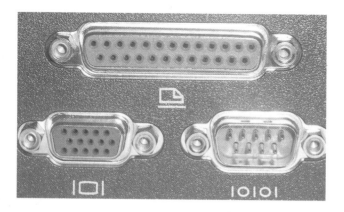

Near-field communication (NFC)

Near-field communication (NFC) is a wireless technology that allows smartphones and other equipped devices to communicate when very near one another or when touching. NFC operates at slower speeds than Bluetooth but consumes far less power and doesn't require pairing. It also does not create a personal area network (PAN) like Bluetooth; rather, the connections are point-to-point. NFC can operate up to 20 cm at a transfer rate of 0.424 Mbps.

NFC is also a standard managed by the ISO and uses tags that are embedded in the devices. NFC components include an initiator and a target; the initiator actively generates an RF field that can power a passive target. This enables NFC targets to take simple form factors such as tags, stickers, key fobs, or cards that do not require batteries.

You may have noticed these small devices in retail outlets. They communicate wirelessly with NFC cards and smartphones. In some cases, it requires tapping the phone on the device, and in other cases that is not required. These devices connect either using USB or in some rare cases a serial connection. Consult the documentation to determine whether you need a special driver installed.

The technology was first used in radio frequency ID (RFID) tagging and was implemented on mobile devices first as a way to share short-range information and later as a method to make payments at a point of sale. It operates by reading tags, which are small microchips with antennas that can in some cases only be read and other cases can be read and written to.

A mobile device must have the support for NFC built in, and many already do. Special applications are available that make it easy to use the technology in various ways.

- Making point-of-sale payments
- Reading information stored in tags in posters and advertisements
- Communication between toys used in gaming
- Communication with peripherals

Bluetooth

Mobile devices also support Bluetooth wireless connections. Bluetooth is a technology that can connect a printer to a computer at a short range; its absolute maximum range is 100 meters (330 feet), and most devices are specified to work within 10 meters (33 feet). When printing with a Bluetooth-enabled device and a Bluetooth-enabled printer, all you need to do is get within range of the device (that is, move closer), select the print driver from the device, and choose Print. The information is transmitted wirelessly through the air using radio waves and is received by the device. Bluetooth speed depends on version. Table 1.2 shows this for the latest versions.

TABLE 1.2 Bluetooth speeds

Version	Speed
2.0	2.1 MB
2.1	2.1 MB
3.0	24 MB (over Wi-Fi connection)
4.0	2.1 MB over Bluetooth and 24 MB over Wi-Fi
4.1	2.1 MB over Bluetooth and 24 MB over Wi-Fi
4.2	2.1 MB over Bluetooth and 24 MB over Wi-Fi
5.0	2.1 MB over Bluetooth and 24 MB over Wi-Fi

Hotspot

Another way that many mobile devices can connect to other devices is through a hotspot or when tethered to another device. Many mobile devices can act as 802.11 hotspots for other wireless devices in the area. There are also devices dedicated solely to performing as mobile hotspots.

Hotspots are publicly provided points of access to an 802.11 wireless network connected to the Internet. They typically have little or no security configured to make it as easy as possible for users to connect. Vendors have also created devices that allow a single device to act as a hotspot for other devices in the area. Sometimes these are called mobile hotspots. Some mobile devices can be turned into mobile hotspots with a software upgrade or an addition to the service plan.

Accessories

Mobile devices require a lot of accessories to take advantage of many of the features they provide. While many of these are also commonly used with desktop and laptop devices, some are much more likely to be used with mobile devices. In this section, you'll take a brief look at the types of accessories you may find attached to a mobile device.

Touch pens

While there is a specific product called the Touch Pen, in many cases this is a synonym for the stylus that comes with a touchscreen system. An example of a stylus or touch pen is shown in Figure 1.8

FIGURE 1.8 Touch pen or stylus

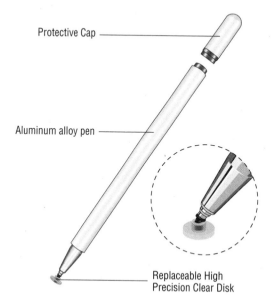

Protective Cap

Aluminum alloy pen

Replaceable High Precision Clear Disk

Headsets

Headsets provide the ability to take your conversation offline or to listen to your music in private. They can be connected both through a wired connection, usually a 3.55 mm audio connector or USB, and by using Bluetooth to pair the device with the headset.

VR/AR headsets

Extended reality is an exciting new field that includes both augmented reality and virtual reality. Both concepts involve wearing special headsets that deliver the visual experience. While reality immerses the user into a virtual environment, much like a four-dimensional game, augmented reality involves glasses that, while permitting a clear vison of the real world, can project graphics and text onto this view using a small side screen. A virtual reality headset is shown in Figure 1.9.

FIGURE 1.9   VR headset

VR headsets are widely used with computer games, but they are also used in other applications, including simulators and trainers. They are worn on the head and cover the eyes with stereo sound and head motion tracking sensors. Most connect to either the USB or HDMI connector, although some are wireless. Several additional types are shown in Figure 1.10.

By now, everyone has heard about and probably seen Google Glass, the most well-known and recognizable computing device worn as glasses. Just in case you haven't, Figure 1.11 shows a drawing of the glasses. This is no longer commercially available as a retail product

FIGURE 1.10   Different types of VR headsets

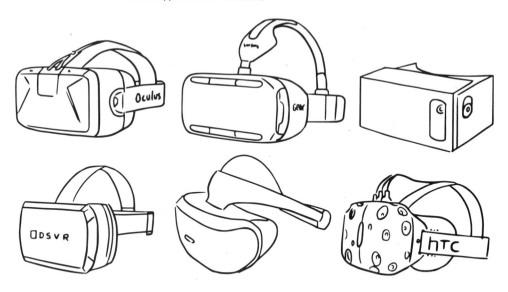

FIGURE 1.11   Google Glass

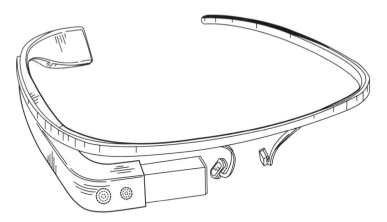

While worn as glasses, they also have a small screen just to the side of one of the eyes that houses the computer screen (think Cyborg). The user can view the screen at any time by just casting a glance at it. Many promising uses have been proposed for the devices, with a number in the healthcare field. Although sale of the devices to individuals was halted, sales to organizations that have or are working to find ways to use the glasses continue.

Another similar device that is not based on glasses but around a headset format is the HC1 headset computer by Zebra. It can respond to voice commands and body movements. One of these is shown in Figure 1.12.

FIGURE 1.12   Headset computer

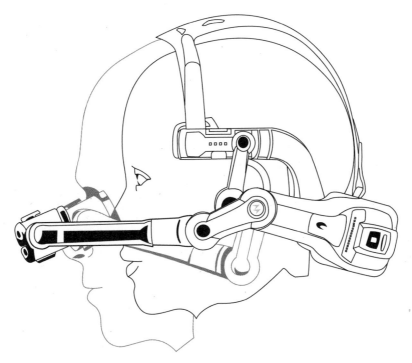

Speakers

Speakers are used in the same fashion as headsets. They can also be connected using the same options that include using USB, using a 3.55 mm audio plug, or by pairing the speakers with the devices using Bluetooth. This includes the speaker systems in many cars, which can now be paired with the devices using Bluetooth as well.

Volume settings

On the top row where the keys labeled F1–F12 are located, there are usually a couple of keys (typically F8 and F9) with icons that look like speakers. These keys can be used to raise and lower the volume of the sound. If the icon is blue, you have to hold down the Fn key. Otherwise, you do not need to use the Fn key to activate them. (As a matter of fact, if you hold down the Fn key and use the F8 key, you may be changing the location of the display output. If these keys are not present, consult the documentation for the key to use in conjunction with Fn to lower and raise the volume. Most laptops also include a mute button marked as such.

Installation

Installing speakers is more a matter of connecting them properly than installing them. Usually, one of the speakers will connect to a power source, and the other will connect to the powered speaker. Once they are connected to a power source, connect the speaker cable to the proper plug in the PC. These plugs will be marked with icons that indicate which is for a microphone and which is for speakers.

Replacement

To replace speakers, first follow the earlier instructions to remove the hard drive, the battery pack, and all the screws holding the body together.

1. Lift the screen up and separate it from the body. Do not remove the wires connecting the screen to the motherboard.

2. Separate the two pieces of plastic body frame to view the inside of the laptop. Locate the speakers, using the documentation if necessary.

3. Unscrew the speakers and note where they connect to the motherboard. Disconnect the old speakers, and connect the new ones to the same location as where the old speakers were removed.

4. Replace all the parts in the reverse order you removed them.

No sound from speakers

When a speaker on a mobile device is not functioning, in most cases it has simply been inadvertently turned off. After checking the settings described later in this section, you can assume that there is a hardware problem. In that case, with smartphones, it is typically advisable to send the device to the manufacturer, but with laptops, it is possible to replace the internal speakers.

To determine whether the settings are the issue, ensure that the speaker volume is up and the speaker is not disabled. On an Android, first test the loudspeaker by following these steps:

1. Go to the Home screen and tap the Phone icon.

2. Type *#7353# into the dialer as though you are dialing a phone number. A list of options will appear.

3. Tap Speaker, and music should start to play. You can tap Speaker again to silence the music.

To test the internal speaker, follow the same steps, but in step 3, tap Melody. Music should start to play from the earpiece on the phone and allow you to see whether the speaker that you hold up to your ear to talk with people is working properly as well.

On an iPhone, follow these steps:

1. Go to Settings ➢ Sounds and drag the Ringer And Alerts slider to turn the volume up.

2. If you can hear sound from the speaker, then the speaker works.

3. If the device has a Ring/Silent switch, make sure it's set to ring. If you can see orange, it's set to silent.

Voice-enabled, smart speaker/digital assistant

Smart speakers that fulfill your commands are an extension of the digital assistants found in many operating systems today. Alexa, Cortana, and other digital assistants are installed in the speaker. Installing one of these is usually just a matter of turning it on and going through some prompts to enter the wireless network's SSID and password. Then you're up and running.

Webcam

Earlier in this chapter you learned about webcams. Digital cameras usually connect to the PC with a USB cable. In many cases, the operating system comes with software that may detect the camera and assist you in accessing the pictures and moving them to the computer. In other instances, you may want to install software that came with the camera. Doing so will often allow you to take fuller advantage of the features the camera offers. SD cards can be used to transfer images from the camera if a cable is not available.

Docking station

Some notebook PCs have optional accessories called docking stations or port replicators. They let you quickly connect/disconnect with external peripherals and may also provide extra ports that the notebook PC doesn't normally have.

A docking station essentially allows a laptop computer to be converted to a desktop computer. When plugged into a docking station, the laptop has access to things it doesn't have stand-alone—the network, a workgroup printer, and so on. The cheapest form of docking station (if it can be called that) is a port replicator. Typically, you slide a laptop into the port replicator, and the laptop can then use a full-sized monitor, keyboard (rather than the standard 84 keys on a laptop), mouse, and so on. Extended, or enhanced, replicators add other ports not found on the laptop, such as PC slots, sound, and more. The most common difference between port replicators and docking stations is that port replicators duplicate the ports the laptop already has to outside devices, and the docking station expands the laptop to include other ports and devices that the laptop does not natively have.

Laptops can support plug and play at three levels, depending on how dynamically they're able to adapt to changes.

Cold Docking   The laptop must be turned off and back on for the change to be recognized.

Warm Docking   The laptop must be put in and out of suspended mode for the change to be recognized.

Hot Docking   The change can be made and is recognized while running normal operations.

Each docking station works a little differently, but there is usually a button you can press to undock the notebook from the unit. There may also be a manual release lever in case you need to undock when the button is unresponsive. Moreover, the docking station must be purchased from the same vendor you purchased the laptop from because docking stations are vendor-and model-specific.

Port replicator

Port replicators are a form of docking station and were discussed in the previous section.

Trackpad/drawing pad

An *optical trackpad* is an input device based on an optical sensor, which detects the movement of a finger that is moving on top of it. The sensor is used typically in smartphones where it replaces the D-pad. The main advantages over a D-pad are:

- It can track movements in 360 degrees and with varying speeds.
- It uses space efficiently, without the need for small buttons that are difficult to press.

    A *drawing pad* is a computer input device that enables a user to hand-draw images, with a special pen-like stylus.

Exam essentials

Describe the various connection methods.   These include Universal Serial Bus (USB), Lightning, serial interfaces, near-field communication (NFC), Bluetooth, and through a hotspot.

Differentiate various mobile device accessories.   Understand the use of touch pens, headsets, speakers, webcams, docking stations, port replicators, and trackpads/drawing pads.

Differentiate between docking stations and port replicators.   A docking station essentially allows a laptop computer to be converted to a desktop computer. Extended, or enhanced, replicators add other ports not found on the laptop, such as PC slots, sound, and more. The most common difference between port replicators and docking stations is whether the peripheral provides network access and expands the laptop's capabilities.

1.4 Given a scenario, configure basic mobile-device network connectivity and application support

For mobile devices to deliver the functionality that most expect, they must be connected to a network. To use email (one of the most important functions to many users), the device must be set up properly. The subobjectives covered in this section include the following:

- Wireless/cellular data network (enable/disable)
- Bluetooth

- Location services
- Mobile device management (MDM)/mobile application management (MAM)
- Mobile device synchronization

Wireless/cellular data network (enable/disable)

Like most computing devices, mobile devices provide more robust functionality when connected to a network (especially if that network is the Internet). Two types of networks can be used to gain access to the Internet: cell phone networks and Wi-Fi networks.

Cell phone networks have in the past been the second choice because the performance is not as good as an 802.11 Wi-Fi connection. With the introduction of 4G Long-Term Evolution (LTE) technologies, however, the performance delivered by the cell network may become more competitive. The latest standard is 5G and promises better performance.

In either case, most mobile devices will have the ability to make an 802.11 connection or use the cell network. If you want to disable the automatic connection to the cell phone network or if it was somehow turned off and needs to be turned back on, you can do this through the settings. One example of the steps to access these settings is Settings ➤ Wireless ➤ Mobile ➤ Enable Data (select or deselect this). This is only one navigational example, and you should consult the documentation that came with the device.

Making a Wi-Fi connection is much like doing so with a laptop. In the settings of the device will be a section for Wi-Fi (in iPhone it's called Wi-Fi, and in Android it's called Wireless And Networks). When you access it, you will see all the Wi-Fi networks within range. Just as you would do with a laptop, select one and attempt to connect to the Wi-Fi network. If the connection requires a password, you will have to supply it. You also can preconfigure a wireless profile for commonly used secure wireless networks as well as those where the service set identifier (SSID) has been hidden.

2G/3G/4G/5G

Cell phone technology has come a long way from its beginnings. There have been four major milestones of data speed and connection resilience. Let's take a look.

2G

2G is also called second-generation cellular. It uses the Global System for Mobile Communications (GSM), a standard developed by the European Telecommunications Standards Institute (ETSI). Three primary benefits of 2G networks over their predecessors were:

- Digitally encrypted phone conversations between the mobile phone and the cellular base station
- More efficient use of the radio frequency spectrum supporting more users
- Data services starting with SMS text messages

3G

Third generation, or 3G, introduced web browsing, email, video downloading, picture sharing, and other smartphone technologies. 3G should be capable of handling around 2 Mbps.

4G

Fourth generation, or 4G, is a later cellular technology that specifies 100 Mbps and up to 1 Gbps to pass as 4G. Outside of the covered areas, 4G phones regress to the 3G standards.

LTE

Long-Term Evolution (LTE) is based on the Global System for Mobile Communications/ Enhanced Data rates for GSM Evolution (GSM/EDGE) and Universal Mobile.

5G

With speeds of up to 100 gigabits per second, 5G is as much as 1,000 times faster than 4G and will provide greater network stability to ensure that business-critical mobile functions do not go offline and have the speed necessary to give employees a fully equipped virtual office almost anywhere. Verizon, Art and T and T-Mobile currently offer 5G broadband Internet in most big cities.

Hotspot

When the devices using the Internet connection on the cellular device are connected wirelessly using 802.11, it is sometimes called a mobile hotspot. This is also the term used for devices that can act as a hotspot for surrounding WiFi devices. The mobile hotspot device may get its Internet access through either cellular or 802.11. To enable connection to a hotspot, follow these steps:

- Click the WiFi icon in the system tray.
- The hotspot will show up as a wireless connection.
- Select it, and enter the password.
- Click Connect.

Global System for Mobile Communications (GSM) vs. code-division multiple access (CDMA)

Mobile devices have made cellular networking popular, though they are not the only devices capable of using networking; for example, a cellular modem can also be quickly added to a laptop. Cellular networks use a central access point (a cell tower) in a mesh network design. For a long time, two competing standards were the Global System for Mobile Communications (GSM) and code-division multiple access (CDMA); the latest technology is 5G, discussed earlier.

The basic difference between GSM and CDMA is that GSM is specific to a SIM card that is used with the mobile phone. On the other hand, the CDMA is handset specific. GSM uses time division multiple access (TDMA) and frequency division multiple access (FDMA). In TDMA multiuser access is provided by slicing the channel into different time slices. In FDMA multiple user access is made possible by separating the frequencies in the channel. As GSM is used and accepted worldwide, there is no problem of roaming in GSM mobile phones.

The technology used in CDMA is code-division multiplexing (CDM). In CDM multiple users in a channel are separated by the code they use to send the signal. Because CDMA is not used or accepted worldwide, it has limited roaming accessibility.

Preferred Roaming List (PRL) updates

The Preferred Roaming List (PRL) is a list of radio frequencies residing in the memory of some kinds of digital phones. It lists frequencies the phone can use in various geographic areas. Each area is ordered by the bands the phone should try to use first. Therefore, it's a priority list for which towers the phone should use. When roaming, the PRL may instruct the phone to use the network with the best roaming rate for the carrier, rather than the one with the strongest signal at the moment. As carrier networks change, an updated PRL may be required.

The baseband is the chip that controls all radio functions. An update makes the code in the chip current.

All mobile devices may require one or more of these updates at some point. In many cases, these updates will happen automatically, or "over the air." In other cases, you may be required to disable WiFi and enable data for these to occur.

PRL updates

In Android phones, the location of the PRL update option will differ, but you'll generally find it in one of a few places in the Settings menu.

- Settings ➤ System Updates ➤ Update PRL
- Settings ➤ Sprint System Updates ➤ Update PRL
- Settings ➤ About Phone ➤ Update PRL

In iOS, there is no separate PRL update command on iOS devices, but running a software update will force an update of the PRL.

Bluetooth

Bluetooth is a short-range wireless technology that is used to create a wireless connection between digital devices. One of its applications is to create connections between mobile devices and items such as speakers, headphones, external GPS units, and keyboards. Before you can take advantage of this technology, the devices must be configured to connect to one another. This section will discuss how to configure a Bluetooth connection.

Enable Bluetooth

On Android mobile devices, follow these steps:

1. From the Home screen, select the Menu button. From the menu, choose Settings ➤ Connections ➤ Bluetooth.

2. Once Bluetooth is selected, wait until a check mark appears next to Bluetooth. Bluetooth is now enabled.

On iOS mobile devices, follow these steps:

1. On the main page, choose Settings ➤ Bluetooth.
2. Tap the slider to enable Bluetooth.

Enable pairing

Pairing a mobile device with an external device (speaker, headphone, and so forth) will enable the two devices to communicate. The first step is to enable pairing. This is much simpler than it sounds. For either mobile operating system, simply turn the external device on, and you are ready for the next step. In some cases, you may need to make the external device discoverable. Check the documentation for the external device to see whether this is the case and how you do this.

Find a device for pairing

Now that the external device is on and transmitting a signal, the mobile device is ready for pairing.

On an Android mobile device, follow these steps:

1. Swipe up on an empty spot on the Home screen to open the Apps tray.
2. Select Settings and then Connections.
3. Turn on the Bluetooth switch by tapping it.
4. If the mobile device stops scanning before the Bluetooth device is ready, tap Scan again.
5. In the list of available devices, tap the Bluetooth device to pair it with the phone.
6. Follow any on-screen instructions.
7. If a password is required, consult the documentation or try either 0000 or 1234 (common passcodes).

On an iOS mobile device, when Bluetooth is enabled, it automatically starts scanning for Bluetooth devices. When your device appears in the list, select it. If a PIN is required, move on to the next step.

Enter the appropriate pin code

Many external devices will ask for a PIN when you select the external device from the list of discovered devices. In many cases, the PIN is 0000, but you should check the manual for the external device.

Test connectivity

Once the previous steps are complete, test communication between the two devices. If you're using a headset, turn on some sound and see whether you can hear it in the headphones.

No Bluetooth connectivity

Bluetooth is also enabled and disabled with a key combination and can be disabled easily. The first thing to try is to reenable it. The second thing to try is to reseat the antenna cable. If all else fails, try a new antenna. This can also be a hardware switch on the side, front, or back of the case.

In smartphones and laptops, the problem also can occur after an upgrade or update of some sort. In these cases, it can be that the proper driver is missing from the upgrade or was somehow corrupted or overwritten during the upgrade process. Here are some additional things you might try on a smartphone:

1. Power-cycle the device.

2. Remove the battery and put it back in.

3. Clear the Bluetooth cache. While each device is different, a common way to access this setting and clear the cache on Android is to open the phone's Settings, tap the More tab, tap Application Manager, select to view all, select Bluetooth Share, and tap Clear Cache.

4. Clear the Bluetooth data. While each device is different, a common way to access this setting and clear the data is to go to Settings, tap the More tab, tap Application Manager, select to view all, select Bluetooth Share, and select Clear Data.

5. Reboot the device in safe mode.

6. Make sure the device to which you are pairing has no issues.

7. As a last resort, perform a hard reset, which resets the device to factory defaults.

Unintended Bluetooth pairing

Unintended Bluetooth connections or pairings can also occur with mobile devices. This is also a security issue because several wireless attacks are made through a Bluetooth connection. Many users leave their Bluetooth settings in a state that makes connections to their peripheral devices easier to make. However, leaving them in a discoverable state also makes it easier for malicious individuals to create a Bluetooth pairing with your mobile device that makes wireless attacks through the Bluetooth connection possible.

Even though it adds a step to the process of pairing a new device to the mobile device, users should make their mobile devices undiscoverable as a default setting and enable this setting only when they need to create a new pairing with a trusted device. Many new devices (for example, iPhone 6) unfortunately don't have a setting to turn off discovery without disabling Bluetooth entirely. While the logic behind this is that the iPhone automatically prevents access to personal data through the Bluetooth connection, on any devices that make turning off discovery possible, it should be done.

Given all this, if a device that is supposedly secured makes an unintended Bluetooth connection, it could be a clue that the device has been compromised through either malware or social engineering.

Location services

Location services making use of GPS services can track the geographic location of your device. In this section you'll learn about these two related services.

Global Positioning System (GPS) services

A global positioning system (GPS) uses satellite information to plot the global location of an object and use that information to plot the route to a second location. GPS devices are integrated into many of the mobile devices discussed already and are used for many things, but when I use the term for a stand-alone device, I am usually referring to a navigation aid.

These aids have grown in sophistication over time and now not only can plot your route but also help you locate restaurants, lodging, and other services along the way. Another use for these devices is tracking delivery vehicles and rental cars.

GPS not functioning

When location services do not appear to be working (these are the services that make the GPS feature work), keep the following principles in mind:

- Make sure GPS is turned on!

- Keep in mind it always works best outdoors rather than indoors.

- Check for Internet access. If you don't have that, you won't have GPS services.

- The first time you use the GPS service, it will take longer because it must find the GPS location.

- As always, the first thing to try is restarting the device.

The GPS performance on some mobile devices can also be affected by the position of your hand on the device. If your hand covers the antenna used for GPS, performance can be negatively affected. It also has been reported that certain UV-protected windshields can block GPS.

Cellular location services

Location services allows the device to determine your location for the purpose of tailoring search results. Location tracking can be disabled on a mobile device. In most cases, disabled location tracking is the default, and users will be asked by certain applications if they want to enable it. When a user has never enabled this feature or has disabled this feature and it suddenly begins to track the location of the device, it is another indication that the device has been compromised.

Mobile device management (MDM)/mobile application management (MAM)

Centralized mobile device management tools are becoming the fastest-growing solution for both organization issues and personal devices. Some solutions leverage the messaging server's management capabilities, and others are third-party tools that can manage multiple brands of devices. Systems Manager by Cisco is one example that integrates with their Cisco Meraki cloud services. Another example for iOS devices is the Apple Configurator. One of the challenges with implementing such a system is that not all personal devices may support native encryption and/or the management process.

Typically, centralized mobile device management tools handle company-issued and personal mobile devices differently. For organization-issued devices, a client application typically manages the configuration and security of the entire device. If the device is a personal device allowed through a bring-your-own-device (BYOD) initiative, the application typically manages the configuration and security of itself and its data only. The application and its data are sandboxed from the other applications and data. The result is that the organization's data is protected if the device is stolen, while the privacy of the user's data is also preserved.

Mobile device management (MDM) policies can be created in Active Directory (AD), or they can be implemented through MDM software. This software allows you to exert control over the mobile devices, even those you do not own if they have the software installed. These policies can force data encryption and data segregation, and they can be used to wipe a stolen device remotely.

Corporate email configuration

Email is one of the most important functions that people access on their mobile devices. This section will discuss how to configure email on a mobile device. The following procedures are common examples, and your specific device may differ slightly. Please consult the documentation for your device.

Before you can access email on your mobile device, you must know the settings for the email server of your email provider. There are two protocols that can be used to access email accounts: Post Office Protocol (POP) 3 and Internet Message Access Protocol (IMAP). If your account offers the use of IMAP, you should select it in the following steps because IMAP accounts have more functionality. You will need the following information to complete this setup:

- The fully qualified domain name (FQDN) of your POP3 server or IMAP server (this server receives the emails sent to you, so it's sometimes called incoming)
- The FQDN of your Simple Mail Transfer Protocol (SMTP) server (this server sends your email to the recipient's email server, so it's sometimes called outgoing)
- The port numbers used for both server types
- The security type used (if any)

POP3

On an Android mobile device, follow these steps:

1. In Settings, select Clouds And Accounts and then Accounts.
2. In Accounts, select Add An Account and select Email as the type.

3. Enter the email address and password and select Sign In.

4. After your account is recognized and set up, select Pop3 as the account type.

5. Enter the name of the incoming POP3 server, and if desired, select to enable encryption.

6. Enter **110** as the incoming port, and if desired, select Delete Email Off The Server.

7. Enter the name of the outgoing PO3 server and enter port number 25.

8. Finally, if desired, turn on SMTP authentication.

On an iOS mobile device, follow these steps:

1. Select Settings ➢ Accounts And Passwords ➢ Add Account.

2. Select Other.

3. Select Add Mail Account. Fill in your name, your email address, your password, and a description. Click Next.

4. Select POP. Verify that the name, address, and description carried over from the last page.

5. Under Incoming Email Server, enter the FQDN of the POP3 server, your email address, and your password.

6. Under Outgoing Mail Server, enter the FQDN of the SMTP server and your email address.

7. Click Next. Click Save in the upper-right corner.

IMAP

On an Android mobile device, follow these steps:

1. In Settings, select Accounts, then Add An Account.

2. Click the appropriate account type.

3. If prompted for an account subtype, select the type.

4. After entering the email address, tap Next.

5. After entering the password, tap Next.

6. If prompted, enter the username, password, or server.

7. After configuring any account options desired (Sync Frequency, Inbox Download Size, and so on), click Next.

8. Complete any account options based on the account type chosen.

9. Enter the account name and, if prompted, the name for outgoing messages.

On an iOS mobile device, follow these steps:

1. Select Settings ➢ Accounts And Passwords ➢ Add Account.

2. Select Other.

3. Select Add Mail Account. Fill in your name, your email address, your password, and a description. Click Next.

4. Select IMAP. Verify that the name, address, and description are carried over from the last page.

5. Under Incoming Email Server, enter the FQDN of the IMAP server, your email address, and your password.

6. Under Outgoing Mail Server, enter the FQDN of the SMTP server and your email address.

7. Click Next. Click Save in the upper-right corner.

Port and SSL settings

With either operating system, you can (and should) select to use security if your email server supports it. This will encrypt all traffic between the mobile device and the email server. The choices offered are usually SSL or TLS, so you will need to know which of these is in use.

Two-factor authentication

Authentication factors describe the method used to verify the user's identity. There are three available authentication factors:

- Something you know (such as a password)
- Something you are (such as a fingerprint)
- Something you have (such as a smartcard)

When two different types of factors are required (such as something you know and something you have), it is called two-factor authentication. It is important to understand that using two or more of the same type of factors (such as a password and a PIN, both something you know) is not multifactor authentication. However, when multifactor authentication is used for mobile devices, the level of security is significantly increased.

Corporate applications

Authenticator applications, such as Google Authenticator, make it possible for a mobile device to use a time-based one-time password (TOTP) algorithm with a site or system that requires such authentication. In the setup operation, the site provides a shared secret key to the user over a secure channel to be stored in the authenticator app. This secret key will be used for all future logins to the site. The user will enter a username and password into a website or other server, generate a one-time password for the server using TOTP running locally, and type that password into the server as well. The server will then also run TOTP to verify the entered one-time password. While Google makes versions for multiple mobile platforms, there are also other third-party solutions.

Trusted sources vs. untrusted sources

Applications and utilities for mobile devices can come from both trusted and untrusted sources. An example of a trusted source is the official Google Play site or the Apple Store. That doesn't mean these are the only trusted sources, but users should treat this issue with the same approach they have been taught with regard to desktop and laptop computers.

Any piece of software, be it an application, tool, or utility, can come with malware attached. Users should be trained to regard any software downloads with suspicion. It may be advisable to use an enterprise mobility management system to prevent users from downloading any software to a company-owned mobile device. You also may want to deselect the setting shown in Figure 1.13, which is an Android device setting. Apple devices warn users with a pop-up message when they download from an unknown source.

FIGURE 1.13   Allowing applications from unknown sources

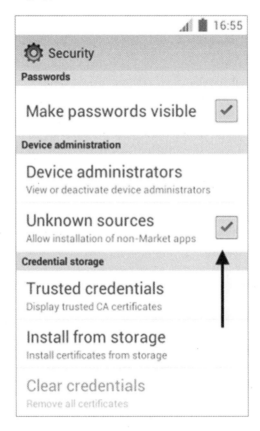

Mobile device synchronization

Keeping information in sync between your desktop or laptop and your mobile device is one of the features that many users want to take advantage of. There are many types of information that can be synced, applications that can be installed to perform the synchronization, and connection methods that can be used to do this. This section discusses mobile device synchronization.

Synchronization methods

When synchronizing the various data types we will discuss shortly, there are three basic ways to make this happen: you can synchronize to the cloud, a desktop, or an automobile's computer system. In this section, you'll look at all three approaches.

SYNCHRONIZE TO THE CLOUD

One synchronization method that is gaining in popularity (along with all things "cloud") is synchronizing all your devices to a cloud server. This provides a central location for your data, settings, and all other items This can be set up such that all devices update with the cloud as soon as they attain Internet access.

SYNCHRONIZE TO THE DESKTOP

Another approach is to set up a sync process directly between two devices such as a smartphone and a desktop computer. In this case, the two devices will sync with each other any time they find themselves on the same network, such as a home wireless network.

SYNCHRONIZE TO THE AUTOMOBILE

Yes, cars have computing systems and as such can be synced to the mobile device either by using Bluetooth or by using cables designed by the vendors to connect to the car system.

Recognizing data caps

Many smartphone accounts have a data cap. Regulating data use is complicated, because most users have no idea how much data they're using by streaming a video or getting turn-by-turn directions. To identify the current use, follow these steps:

iPhone

1. Open Settings. It's a gray app with gears that you'll likely find on the Home screen.
2. Tap Cellular. This option is near the top of the Settings page. On phones that use a UK English keyboard, tap Mobile Data.
3. Scroll down to view the Cellular Data Usage section.

Data listed under Current Period does not automatically reset for your billing cycle. You can reset your data usage statistics by tapping Reset Statistics at the bottom of the page.

Data may be listed differently on different cellular carriers and data plans. If you do not see Current Period, tap Usage below the header with your carrier's name to view your data usage.

ANDROID

1. Open your Androids Settings, typically found on the Home screen or in the app drawer.
2. Tap Data Usage. You should now see at the top of the screen the total amount of mobile data used in the current month.

Microsoft 365

In April 2017, Microsoft announced the ending of mainstream support for Office 2016 in October 2020. Today enterprises use a subscription-based product, first called Office 365 and later changed to Microsoft 365 since it incorporates many services that are not a part of Office.

ActiveSync

ActiveSync allowed a mobile device to be synchronized with either a desktop PC or a server running a compatible software product. Starting with Windows Vista, ActiveSync has been replaced with the Windows Mobile Device Center, which is included as part of the operating system.

Calendar

The calendar is a critical application for both work and play. All mobile devices support syncing the calendar between devices. In some cases, it may require a small application, especially when the email system of which the calendar is part is in a different ecosystem (for example, Google Mail and an iPhone).

Contacts

No one wants to enter a long list of contacts into a mobile device when that same list already exists in your email account. Using push synchronization (*push* means it's automatic and requires no effort on the part of the user), you ensure that any changes made to the contact list either on the mobile device or on the desktop will be updated on the other device the next time you make a connection to the email account from the other device. It will also update if the mobile device makes a direct connection to the desktop.

Commercial mail application

You probably also want to set up your personal email on a device from a commercial provider. This section will look at some of the major email systems you may encounter.

iCloud

To set up iCloud email on an Android device, follow these instructions:

1. Swipe up or down in the Home screen to access the Apps screen.
2. In Settings, select Accounts, then Add An Account.
3. Select the account type.
4. If prompted, select the account subtype.
5. After entering the email address, select Next.
6. After entering the password, select Next.

7. If promoted for the username, password, or server name, enter them and select Next.

8. Enter the SMTP server, port number, and outgoing server, and select Next.

9. After configuring any account options desired (Sync Frequency, Inbox Download Size, and so on), click Next.

10. Address any additional options you encounter and select Next.

11. Enter an account name for outgoing messages.

As you can imagine, setting up iCloud email on an iOS device is simple because the applications all reside in the Apple ecosystem. First set up an iCloud email account. If you have an email address that ends with @ *mac.com* or @ *me.com*, you already have an equivalent address that's the same except it ends with *@icloud.com*. On your iOS device, go to Settings, tap your name, and then select iCloud. Choose the apps—such as Photos, Contacts, Calendars, and third-party apps—that you want to use with iCloud.

GOOGLE/INBOX

On an Android mobile device, follow these steps:

1. Select the Gmail icon.

2. Select Already Have A Google account.

3. In the Sign In With Your Google Account field, enter your username and password and select Sign In.

On an iOS mobile device, follow these steps:

1. Select Settings ➢ Accounts & Passwords ➢ Add Account.

2. Select Gmail.

3. Fill in your name, address, password, and description if desired. Click Next.

4. Verify that the address carried over from the last page. Click Next.

5. Select the items you want to sync automatically with the email server and click Done.

EXCHANGE ONLINE

To set up Outlook on Android, first, if required, install Outlook for Android. Follow these steps:

1. On the Android device, select the Email icon.

2. After entering the email address and password, select Manually Setting.

3. Complete the Domain\Username field.

4. After entering the password for the Exchange Server, select Use Secure Connection (SSL) and then Next.

5. In the Account Options interface, select a frequency for checking email and click Next.

6. Finally, if desired, enter a name for the account in the Give This Account A Name field and select Done.

On iOS, follow these steps:

1. Add your Exchange account by tapping Settings ➤ Passwords & Accounts ➤ Add Account ➤ Exchange.

2. Enter your address.

3. Choose either Configure Manually or Sign In to connect to your Exchange Server.

If you select Configure Manually, you can set up an Exchange account with Basic authentication. Enter your email password. You might also be prompted to enter additional server information.

If you select Sign In, your email address is sent to Microsoft to discover your Exchange account information. If your account uses multifactor authentication, you'll be guided through a custom authentication workflow.

YAHOO

Because Yahoo recommends using IMAP as an email client, these are the instructions for setting up IMAP on Android systems:

1. Swipe up or down on the Home screen to access the Apps screen.

2. In Settings, select Accounts and then add an account.

3. After selecting the account type, select the subtype if required.

4. Enter the email address and then select Next.

5. After entering the password, select Next.

6. If prompted, enter the username, password, or server and click Next.

7. Configure the SMTP server, port number, and outgoing server and click Next.

8. Select any account options desired, such as Sync Frequency, Inbox Download Size, and so on, and select Next.

9. If prompted, enter an account name and an account for outgoing messages.

On an iOS device, use these instructions:

1. Tap Select Settings ➤ Accounts & Passwords.

2. Tap Add Account.

3. Tap Yahoo.

4. Enter your name, your email address, your email password, and a description; then tap Next.

5. Optionally, disable aspects of Yahoo Mail from syncing.

6. Tap Save.

Exam essentials

Enable Bluetooth and pair a Bluetooth device with a mobile network.   Describe the process for both the iOS and Android operating systems.

Configure email on a mobile device.   Describe the process of configuring email, including both Exchange and Gmail for both the iOS and Android operating systems.

Review Questions

You can find the answers in the appendix.

1. Which email client does Yahoo recommend when you are setting up Yahoo email?
    A. SMTP
    B. IMAP
    C. POP3
    D. S/MIME

2. Which action can invalidate a laptop warranty?
    A. Reinstalling the OS
    B. Opening the case
    C. Flashing the BIOS
    D. Performing a remote wipe

3. What special screwdriver is typically required to work on a notebook?
    A. Phillips head
    B. T-8 Torx
    C. Hex
    D. Metric

4. If you have an email address that ends with *@mac.com* or *@me.com*, you already have an equivalent address that's the same except that it ends with which of the following?
    A. @iapple
    B. @icloud
    C. @iemail
    D. @istorage

5. Which component if damaged can render the hard drive useless?
    A. The caddy
    B. The rails
    C. The signal pins
    D. The chassis

6. What tool replaced ActiveSync?
    A. iSync
    B. MS Mobile Wizard
    C. Windows Mobile Device Center
    D. Office 365

7. Which is *not* an advantage of solid-state drives?

    A. Cheaper

    B. Not as susceptible to damage

    C. Faster

    D. No moving parts

8. Which of the following makes it possible for a mobile device to use a time-based one-time password (TOTP) algorithm with a site or system that requires such authentication?

    A. Hardware security modules

    B. Non-transitive trust

    C. Authenticator applications

    D. In-plane switching

9. Which display is a newer technology that solves the issue of poor quality at angles other than straight on?

    A. Passive matrix

    B. Active matrix

    C. Twisted nematic

    D. In-plane switching

10. Which of the following will you *not* need to set up corporate email?

    A. FQDN of your SMTP server

    B. IP address of your SMTP server

    C. FQDN of your POP3 server or IMAP server

    D. Port numbers used for both server types

11. In what mode of plug and play must the laptop be turned off and back on for the change to be recognized?

    A. Hot docking

    B. Warm docking

    C. Cold docking

    D. Open docking

12. Which of the following is *not* an example of two-factor authentication?

    A. Smartcard and password

    B. Smartcard and iris scan

    C. Password and PIN

    D. Voice recognition and password

13. Which of the following uses satellite information to plot the global location of an object and uses that information to plot the route to a second location?

   A. GPS

   B. Geofencing

   C. Remote wipe

   D. Local wipe

14. Which of the following provides centralized device management for company-issued and personal mobile devices?

   A. MDM

   B. DFS

   C. PCM

   D. PS/2

15. Which is the most common PIN code when selecting discovered Bluetooth devices?

   A. 0000

   B. 5555

   C. 1111

   D. 0135

16. When setting up POP3, which of the following port numbers should you enter?

   A. 25

   B. 53

   C. 110

   D. 443

17. Which of the following storage system monitors the data being read from the hard drive and caches the most frequently accessed bits to the high-speed flash memory?

   A. SSD

   B. HDD

   C. Hybrid drive

   D. Virtual

18. Which of the following is the use of physical factors of authentication?

   A. Mutual authentication

   B. SSO

   C. Multifactor authentication

   D. Biometrics

Chapter

2

Networking

COMPTIA A+ CERTIFICATION EXAM CORE 1 (220-1101) OBJECTIVES COVERED IN THIS CHAPTER:

✓ **2.1 Compare and contrast Transmission Control Protocol (TCP) and User Datagram Protocol (UDP) ports, protocols, and their purposes.**

- Ports and protocols
    - 20/21 – File Transfer Protocol (FTP)
    - 22 – Secure Shell (SSH)
    - 23 – Telnet
    - 25 – Simple Mail Transfer Protocol (SMTP)
    - 53 – Domain Name System (DNS)
    - 67/68 – Dynamic Host Configuration Protocol (DHCP)
    - 80 – Hypertext Transfer Protocol (HTTP)
    - 110 – Post Office Protocol 3 (POP3)
    - 137/139 – Network Basic Input/Output System (NetBIOS)/ NetBIOS over TCP/IP (NetBT)
    - 143 – Internet Mail Access Protocol (IMAP)
    - 161/162 – Simple Network Management Protocol (SNMP)
    - 389 – Lightweight Directory Access Protocol (LDAP)
    - 443 – Hypertext Transfer Protocol Secure (HTTPS)
    - 445 – Server Message Block (SMB)/Common Internet File System (CIFS)
    - 3389 – Remote Desktop Protocol (RDP)
- TCP vs. UDP
    - Connectionless
    - DHCP
    - Trivia File Transfer Protocol (TFTP)

- Connection-oriented
    - HTTPS
    - SSH

✓ **2.2 Compare and contrast common networking hardware.**

- Routers
- Switches
    - Managed
    - Unmanaged
- Access points
- Patch panel
- Firewall
- Power over Ethernet (PoE)
    - Injectors
    - Switch
    - PoE standards
- Hub
- Cable modem
- Digital subscriber line (DSL)
- Optical network terminal (ONT)
- Network Interface Card (NIC)
- Software-defined networking (SDN)

✓ **2.3 Compare and contrast protocols for wireless networking.**

- Frequencies
    - 2.4GHz
    - 5GHz
- Channels
    - Regulations
    - 2GHz vs. 5GHz

- Bluetooth
- 802.11
  - a
  - b
  - g
  - n
  - ac (WIFI 5)
  - ax (WIFI 6)
- Long-range fixed wireless
  - Licensed
  - Unlicensed
  - Power
  - Regulatory requirements for wireless power
- NFC
- Radio-frequency identification (RFID)

✓ **2.4 Summarize services provided by networked hosts.**

- Server roles
  - DNS
  - DHCP
  - Fileshare
  - Print servers
  - Mail servers
  - Syslog
  - Web servers
  - Authentication, authorization, and accounting (AAA)
- Internet appliances
  - Spam gateways
  - Unified threat management (UTM)

- Load balancers
- Proxy servers
- Legacy/embedded systems
  - Supervisory control and data acquisition (SCADA)
  - Internet of Things (IoT) devices

✓ **2.5 Given a scenario, install and configure basic wired/wireless small office/home office (SOHO) networks.**

- Internet Protocol (IP) addressing
- IPV4
  - Private addresses
  - Public addresses
- IPV6
- Automatic Private IP Addressing (APIPA)
- Static
- Dynamic
- Gateway

✓ **2.6 Compare and contrast common network configuration concepts.**

- DNS
  - Address
  - A
  - AAAA
  - Mail exchanger (MX)
  - Text (TXT)
  - Spam management
    - DomainKeys Identified Mail (DKIM)
    - Sender Policy Framework (SPF)
    - Domain-based Message Authorization, Reporting, and Compliance (DMARC)

- DHCP
    - Leases
    - Reservations
    - Scope
- Virtual LAN (VLAN)
- Virtual private network (VPN)

✓ **2.7 Compare and contrast Internet connection types, network types, and their features.**

- Internet connection types
    - Satellite
    - Fiber
    - Cable
    - DSL
    - Cellular
    - Wireless Internet service provider (WISP)
- Network types
    - Local area network (LAN)
    - Wide area network (WAN)
    - Personal area network (PAN)
    - Metropolitan area network (MAN)
    - Wireless local area network (WLAN)

✓ **2.8 Given a scenario, use networking tools.**

- Crimper
- Cable stripper
- WIFI analyzer
- Toner probe
- Punchdown tool
- Cable tester
- Loopback plug
- Network tap

CompTIA offers a number of other exams and certifications on networking (Network+, Server+, and so on), but to become A+ certified, you must have good knowledge of basic networking skills. Not only do you need to know the basics of cabling and connectors, but you also need to know how to install and configure a wireless/wired router, apply appropriate settings, and use some basic tools. There are eight objectives for this domain.

2.1 Compare and contrast Transmission Control Protocol (TCP) and User Datagram Protocol (UDP) ports, protocols, and their purposes

Communication across a TCP/IP-based network takes place using various protocols, such as FTP to transfer files, HTTP to view web pages, and POP3 or IMAP to work with email. Each of these protocols has a default port associated with it, and CompTIA expects you to be familiar with them for this exam.

Both Transport Control Protocol (TCP) and User Diagram Protocol (UDP) use port numbers to listen for and respond to requests for communication using various protocols. There are a number of protocols and their port numbers that you must know for this exam, as well as the differences between TCP and UDP.

Ports and protocols

There are two transport layer protocols in the TCP/IP stack. TCP provides guaranteed, connection-oriented delivery, whereas UDP provides nonguaranteed, connectionless delivery. Each protocol or service uses one of the two transport protocols (and in some cases both). There will be additional information later in this chapter on TCP and UDP.

TCP and UDP both use port numbers to listen for and respond to requests for communications. RFC 1060 defines *common ports* for a number of services routinely found in use, and these all have low numbers—up to 1,024. You can, however, reconfigure your service to use another port number (preferably much higher) if you're concerned about security and you don't want your site to be available to anonymous traffic.

20/21 – File Transfer Protocol (FTP)

File Transfer Protocol is both a TCP/IP protocol and software that permits the transferring of files between computer systems. Because FTP has been implemented on numerous types of computer systems, files can be transferred between disparate systems (for example, a personal computer and a minicomputer). It uses ports 20 and 21 by default. It can be configured to allow or deny access to specific IP addresses and can be configured to work with exceptions. While the protocol can be run within most browsers, a number of FTP applications are available; FileZilla (`http://filezilla-project.org`) is one of the most popular.

It is valuable to note the FTP is not secure, and if confidentiality is required, you should use either SFTP (FTP encrypted with SSH) or FTPS (encrypted with SSL).

22 – Secure Shell (SSH)

Secure Shell is a remote administration tool that can serve as a secure alternative to using Telnet to remotely access and configure a device like a router or switch. Although it requires a bit more setup than Telnet, it provides an encrypted command-line session for managing devices remotely.

23 – Telnet

Telnet is a protocol that functions at the application layer of the OSI model, providing terminal-emulation capabilities. Telnet runs on port 23 but has lost favor to SSH because Telnet sends data—including passwords—in plain-text format.

25 – Simple Mail Transfer Protocol (SMTP)

Simple Mail Transfer Protocol (SMTP) is a protocol for sending email between SMTP servers. Clients typically use either IMAP or POP to access their email server and use SMTP to send email. SMTP uses port 25 by default.

53 – Domain Name System (DNS)

DNS is the Domain Name System, and it is used to translate hostnames into IP addresses. DNS is an example of a protocol that uses both UDP and TCP.

67/68 – Dynamic Host Configuration Protocol (DHCP)

Dynamic Host Configuration Protocol (DHCP) serves the useful purpose of issuing IP addresses and other network-related configuration values to clients to allow them to operate on the network. It uses ports 67 and 68.

80 – Hypertext Transfer Protocol (HTTP)

Hypertext Transfer Protocol (HTTP) is the protocol used for communication between a web server and a web browser. It uses port 80 by default.

110 – Post Office Protocol (POP) 3 (POP3)

The Post Office Protocol (POP) is a protocol for receiving email from a mail server. It runs on port 110. The current version of the protocol is 3 (POP3), and the alternative to it is Internet Message Access Protocol (IMAP).

137/139 – Network Basic Input/Output System (NetBIOS)/NetBIOS over TCP/IP (NetBT)

NetBIOS/NetBT is an early networking protocol that used a flat namespace, unlike the hierarchal one found in DNS. Computers register their services with the other devices and locate one another using NetBIOS names. NetBIOS/NetBT uses ports 137–139.

143 – Internet Mail Access Protocol (IMAP)

Internet Message Access Protocol (IMAP) is a protocol with a store-and-forward capability. It can also allow messages to be stored on an email server instead of downloaded to the client. The current version of the protocol is 4 (IMAP4), and the alternative to it is Post Office Protocol (POP). IMAP runs on port 143.

161/162 – Simple Network Management Protocol (SNMP)

Simple Network Management Protocol (SNMP) is a protocol that facilitates network management functionality. It is not, in itself, a network management system (NMS); it is simply the protocol that makes NMS possible. It uses ports 161 and 162.

389 – Lightweight Directory Access Protocol (LDAP)

Lightweight Directory Access Protocol (LDAP) is a protocol that provides a mechanism to access and query directory services systems. These systems are most likely to be Microsoft's Active Directory but could also be Novell Directory Services (NDS). Although LDAP supports command-line queries executed directly against the directory database, most LDAP interactions are via utilities such as an authentication program (network logon) or a search engine that locates a resource in the directory. LDAP uses port 389.

443 – Hypertext Transfer Protocol Secure (HTTPS)

Hypertext Transfer Protocol over Secure Sockets Layer (HTTPS) is a protocol used to make a secure connection. It uses port 443 by default.

445 – Server Message Block (SMB)/Common Internet File System (CIFS)

Server Message Block (SMB) is an application layer protocol used to provide shared access to resources. The Common Internet File System (CIFS) protocol is a dialect of SMB. It is primarily used in Windows systems. The latest version is 3.1.1, which was released to support Windows 10 and Windows Server 2016. It operates as a client-server application. It uses port 445.

3389 – Remote Desktop Protocol (RDP)

Remote Desktop Protocol (RDP) is used in a Windows environment to make remote desktop communications possible. It presents the user with the graphical interface of the remote device rather than a command line as in Telnet or SSH.

TCP vs. UDP

Operating at the transport layer of the TCP/IP stack are two key protocols: Transmission Control Protocol and User Datagram Protocol. The biggest difference between these two is that one is connection based (TCP) and the other works in the absence of a dedicated connection (UDP). Both are needed and serve key roles.

If you are sending credit card information to a website, you need a dedicated connection between your host and the server, so TCP handles that task. An example of UDP is DHCP. When a client sends a request for any DHCP server listening to give it an address, it is not requiring a dedicated communication.

Connectionless

Connectionless protocols are those that use UDP as the transport protocol and therefore do not go through the establishment of a connection prior to sending data. In this section you'll learn about two such protocols.

DHCP

Earlier in this chapter you learned about DHCP. This protocol forgoes the overhead of TCP and gives up error recovery in the process. However, like DNS it has its own mechanisms for recovering from errors. So if a response is not forthcoming, the DHCP client will make multiple attempts to contact the DHCP server.

Trivial File Transfer Protocol (TFTP)

Trivial File Transfer Protocol (TFTP) is a version of FTP that uses UDP instead of TCP and is thus called the lightweight version of FTP since it doesn't generate the overhead from establishing a connection. It is used in any scenario where speed of the process is key. Some typical uses are:

- To transfer operating systems and images to routers and switches
- To send configuration files to IP phones

Connection-oriented

Connection-oriented protocols are those that use TCP as the transport protocol and therefore do go through the establishment of a connection prior to sending data. In this section you'll learn about two such protocols.

HTTPS

Hypertext Transfer Protocol (HTTP) is the protocol used on the web to transmit website data between a web server and a web client. With each new address that is entered into the web browser, whether from initial user entry or by clicking a link on the page displayed, a new connection is established because HTTP is a stateless protocol.

HTTP Secure (HTTPS) is the implementation of HTTP running over the SSL/TLS protocol, which establishes a secure session using the server's digital certificate. SSL/TLS keeps the session open using a secure channel. HTTPS websites will always include the *https://* designation at the beginning.

Although it sounds very similar, Secure HTTP (S-HTTP) protects HTTP communication in a different manner. S-HTTP encrypts only a single communication message, not an entire session (or conversation). S-HTTP is not as common as HTTPS.

SSH

If you don't need access to the graphical interface and you just want to operate at the command line, you have two options: Telnet and SSH. While Telnet works just fine, it transmits all of the data in clear text, which obviously is a security issue. Therefore, the connection tool of choice has become Secure Shell (SSH). It's not as easy to set up, because it encrypts all of the transmissions, and that is not possible without an encryption key.

While the commands will be somewhat different based on the operating system, you must generate a key, which is generated using some unique information about the server as seed information so that the key will be unique to the server (the encryption algorithm will be well known). Once configured, the connection process will be similar to using Telnet, with the exception of course that the transmissions will be protected.

Exam essentials

Know the default ports.   There are a number of protocols whose default ports you need to know: FTP (20/21), Telnet (23), SMTP (25), DNS (53), HTTP (80), POP3 (110), IMAP (143), HTTPS (443), and RDP (3389).

Know what the protocols do.   In addition to the protocols for which ports are given, know the purpose of DHCP, DNS, LDAP, SNMP, and SSH.

2.2 Compare and contrast common networking hardware

To make a network, you need a number of devices. The most common of those devices are tested on the A+ exam and discussed in this section. Networks are built using multiple devices. For those covered in this section, you should know enough to be able to answer questions about their functions and features on the exam.

Routers

A router is used to connect LANs; you can even use a router to connect dissimilar topologies that use the same protocol, because physical specifications don't apply. A router can be a dedicated hardware device or a computer system with more than one network interface and the appropriate routing software. All modern network operating systems include the functionality to act as a router.

Switches

Like routers, switches are the connectivity points of an Ethernet network. Devices connect to switches via twisted-pair cabling, one cable for each device. The difference between hubs and switches is in how the devices deal with the data they receive. Whereas a hub forwards the data it receives to all the ports on the device, a switch forwards it to only the port that connects to the destination device. It does this by learning the Media Access Control (MAC) address of the devices attached to it and then matching the destination MAC address in the data it receives.

Managed

Managed switches are those used in an enterprise network. These switches can be configured with advanced features such as virtual LANs (VLANs), discussed under objective 2.6 later in this chapter, and EtherChannel links. They are managed remotely, using either a command-line interface or in some cases a GUI management interface.

Unmanaged

Unmanaged switches are those that cannot be managed remotely. While they can provide basic switching services (full duplex service and the like), they cannot be configured with the more advanced services of a managed switch.

Access points

Access points (APs) are transmitter and receiver (transceiver) devices used to create a wireless LAN (WLAN). An AP is typically a separate network device with a built-in antenna, transmitter, and adapter. APs use the wireless infrastructure network mode to provide a connection point between WLANs and a wired Ethernet LAN. APs also typically have several ports, giving you a way to expand the network to support additional clients.

Depending on the size of the network, one or more APs might be required. Additional APs are used to allow access to more wireless clients and to expand the range of the wireless network. Each AP is limited by a transmission range—the distance a client can be from an AP and still obtain a usable signal. The actual distance depends on the wireless standard being used and the obstructions and environmental conditions between the client and the AP.

Patch panel

A *patch panel* is a device to which the cables running through the walls from the hosts are connected. Then shorter cables called *patch cables* run from the patch panel to the switch or hub. Figure 2.1 shows three types of patch panels.

FIGURE 2.1   Patch panels

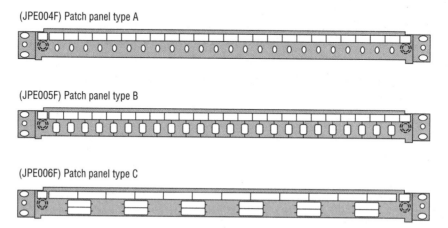

(JPE004F) Patch panel type A

(JPE005F) Patch panel type B

(JPE006F) Patch panel type C

Firewall

A firewall is a server that sits between the internal network and the rest of the world (or between a public and private network) and filters what goes between the two. While the filtering can be done on programs, most filtering is performed on ports since applications and protocols use ports that are recognized. *Open* ports are those that allow traffic, whereas *closed* ports are those that block traffic. The firewall can be software- or hardware-based, and most incorporate both. The firewall may incorporate a proxy, a gateway, and a filter.

Power over Ethernet (PoE)

Many times when installing devices, the device needs to be located far from an available power outlet. On switches that support Power over Ethernet (PoE), the switch can supply power using an adjacent pair of wires in the same data cable used to connect to the device. So if you get the device within 100 meters of a switch, you can eliminate the need to install costly power outlets.

Injectors

A PoE injector is a device that can be used to provide PoE to a device when the switch does not support PoE. It plugs into the wall; then a line providing data and PoE is run to the device, and another cable runs to the switch, as shown in Figure 2.2.

FIGURE 2.2   Power over Ethernet

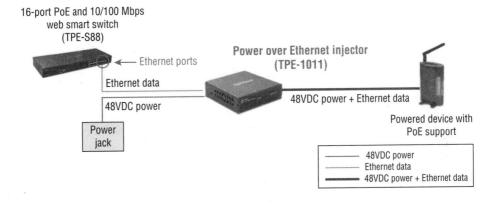

Switch

Enterprise-grade switches such as Cisco switches can also come equipped with PoE ports. These ports can be set to provide power to the devices connected.

PoE standards

There have been a number of standards created for providing power over a data cable. These standards differ in several ways.:

- Minimum power per port provided to the device
- Maximum power per port provided by the power-sourcing device
- Required cable category
- Power over pairs
- Released date

The standards and their characteristics are shown in Table 2.1.

TABLE 2.1   PoE standards

Type	Standard	PD min. power per port	PSE max. power per port	Cable category	Power over pairs	Released date
Type 1	IEEE 802.3af	12.95W	15.4W	Cat5e	2 pairs	2003
Type 2	IEEE 802.3at	25W	30W	Cat5e	2 pairs	2009
Type 3	IEEE 802.3bt	51–60W	60W	Cat5e	2 or 4 pairs classes 0–4, 4 pairs classes 5–6	2018
Type 4	IEEE 802.3bt	71–90W	100W	Cat5e	4 pairs classes 7–8	2018

Hub

Hubs are used in networks that use twisted-pair cabling to connect devices, and they can be used to join segments into larger networks. A hub directs data packets to all devices connected to it, regardless of whether the data package is destined for the device. This makes them inefficient by nature and can create a performance bottleneck on busy networks. In its most basic form, a hub does nothing except provide a pathway for the electrical signals to travel along. Such a device is called a *passive* hub. Far more common nowadays is an *active* hub, which, as well as providing a path for the data signals, regenerates the signal before it forwards it to all the connected devices. In addition, an active hub can buffer data before forwarding it. However, a hub does not perform any processing on the data it forwards, nor does it perform any error checking.

Cable modem

A modem, short for "modulator/demodulator," is a device that converts the digital signals generated by a computer into analog signals that can travel over conventional phone lines. The modem at the receiving end converts the signal back into a format that the computer can understand. Modems can be used to connect to an ISP or as a mechanism for dialing up a LAN.

Digital subscriber line (DSL)

Digital Subscriber Line (DSL) uses existing phone lines with a DSL modem and a network card. A standard RJ-45 connector is used to connect the network card to the DSL modem, and a phone cord with RJ-11 connectors is used to connect the DSL modem to the phone jack. Multiple types of DSL exist; the most popular are high bit-rate DSL (HDSL), symmetric DSL (SDSL), very high bit-rate DSL (VHDSL), rate-adaptive DSL (RADSL), and asymmetric DSL (ADSL). The latter provides slower upload than download speeds and is the most common for home use.

Optical network terminal (ONT)

In the same way that a cable modem provides Internet access from an Ethernet network, optical network terminals (ONT) provide Internet access from a fiber network. ONTs can be provided by an ISP. The positioning of the INT is shown in Figure 2.3. In the fiber line running to the multi-dwelling unit, each unit will have a splitter, such as the one in the fiber line running to a single-family home. This splits the data signal from the phone line.

FIGURE 2.3   Optical network terminal (ONT)

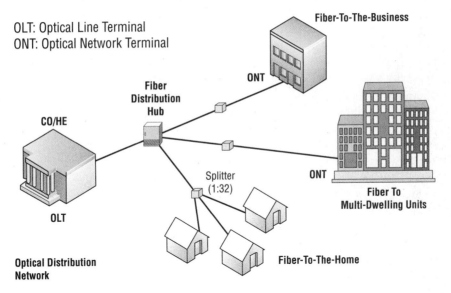

Network interface card (NIC)

Network interface cards (NICs) are expansion cards that are installed into slots in a desktop computer. These cards connect the computer to a network. In most cases today, devices large and small have integrated or built-in network interfaces.

Software-defined networking (SDN)

In a network, three planes typically form the networking architecture:

- Control plane: This plane carries signaling traffic originating from or destined for a router. This is the information that allows routers to share information and build routing tables.

- Data plane: Also known as the forwarding plane, this plane carries user traffic.

- Management plane: This plane administers the router.

Software-defined networking (SDN) has been classically defined as the decoupling of the control plane and the data plane in networking. In a conventional network, these planes are implemented in the firmware of routers and switches. SDN implements the control plane in software, which enables programmatic access to it.

This definition has evolved over time to focus more on providing programmatic interfaces to networking equipment and less on the decoupling of the control and data planes. An example of this is the provision of application programming interfaces (APIs) by vendors into the multiple platforms they sell.

One advantage of SDN is that it enables very detailed access into, and control over, network elements. It allows IT organizations to replace a manual interface with a programmatic one that can enable the automation of configuration and policy management.

An example of the use of SDN is using software to centralize the control plane of multiple switches that normally operate independently. (While the control plane normally functions in hardware, with SDN it is performed in software.) This concept is shown in Figure 2-4.

FIGURE 2.4   Centralized and decentralized SDN

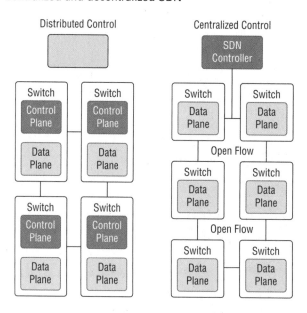

Exam essentials

Know the two types of hubs.   Hubs can be passive or active. If the hub does nothing except provide a pathway for the electrical signals to travel along, it is passive. If it regenerates the signal, it is considered active.

Be able to recognize a firewall.   A firewall is a server that sits between the internal network and the rest of the world and filters what goes between the two.

2.3 Compare and contrast protocols for wireless networking

More and more, networks are using wireless as the medium of choice. It is much easier to implement, reconfigure, upgrade, and use than wired networks. Unfortunately, there can be downsides; security is one of the largest.

The 802.11 standard applies to wireless networking, and there have been many versions/types of it released; the main ones are a, b, g, and n. Encryption has gone from very weak (WEP) to much stronger with increments along the way, including WPA, WPA2, and implementations of TKIP and AES.

The IEEE 802.11x family of protocols provides for wireless communications using radio frequency transmissions. The frequencies in use for 802.11 standards are the 2.4 GHz and 5 GHz frequency spectrums. Several standards and bandwidths have been defined for use in wireless environments, and they aren't compatible with each other.

Frequencies

WLAN operates in two frequency ranges or bands. In this section you'll learn what standards operate in these two frequencies and a bit about the standards.

2.4GHz

Four standards operate in this frequency, 802.11b, 802.11g, 802.11n and 802.11ax You will learn more about these standards later in this chapter.

5GHz

Four standards operate in this frequency range, 802.11a, 802.11n, 802.11ac and 802.11ax.

Table 2.2 compares the speed, distance, and frequency of some of the 802.11 standards.

TABLE 2.2   Comparison of 802.11 standards

STANDARD	SPEED	DISTANCE (INDOORS)	FREQUENCY
802.11a	Up to 54 Mbps	Up to 115 feet	5 GHz
802.11b	Up to 11 Mbps	Up to 115 feet	2.4 GHz
802.11g	Up to 54 Mbps	Up to 125 feet	2.4 GHz
802.11n	Up to 600 Mbps	Up to 380 feet	2.4 GHz/5 GHz
802.11ac	Up to 6.9 Gbps	Up to 115 feet	5 GHz

Channels

Wireless routers can be set to use different channels, which are numbered 1 through 11 (1, 6, and 11 are those commonly used in the United States) for the 2.4 GHz band.

Each channel represents a different frequency. You can change the channel to avoid interference—either from another network nearby or from devices also using that frequency.

The channel change is made only on the router because each client should automatically detect and change to the new channel. If you locate APs close to one another, they should be on different channels to prevent them from interfering with one another.

Regulations

Every country has their own set of regulations regarding the frequencies or channels that can be used for 802.11 transmission. While the focus here has thus far been on the 2.4 GHz and 5.0 GHz frequencies, they are not the only ones allowed in the United States. There are 14 channels designated in the 2.4 GHz range spaced 5 MHz apart (with the exception of a 12 MHz spacing before Channel 14). As the protocol requires 25 MHz of channel separation, adjacent channels overlap and will interfere with one another. Consequently, using only channels 1, 6, 11, and 14 is recommended to avoid interference. In North America, while use of Channel 14 is not allowed, use of 12 and 13 is actually allowed under low-powered conditions

2.4GHz vs. 5GHz

While both the 2.4Ghz and the 5.0 GHz frequencies are both in use, there are some operational and performance differences between them.

The 2.4 GHz band can transmit over longer distances but offers slower speeds due to the data modulation methods in use, the more crowded nature of the frequency and the greater susceptibility of 2.4 stations to interference. On the other hand, the 5 GHz band transmits for shorter distances but provides the users with faster speeds.

Bluetooth

In Chapter 1, "Mobile Devices," you learned about Bluetooth. Please review that section.

802.11

There have been several amendments that apply to 802.11 technology. Each amendment describes some improvement in the design or operation of 802.11 networks. In this section you'll learn about the major amendments.

a

The 802.11a standard provides wireless LAN bandwidth of up to 54 Mbps in the 5 GHz frequency spectrum. The 802.11a standard also uses orthogonal frequency-division multiplexing (OFDM) for encoding rather than frequency-hopping spread spectrum (FHSS) or direct sequence spread spectrum (DSSS).

b

The 802.11b standard provides for bandwidths of up to 11 Mbps (with fallback rates of 5.5, 2, and 1 Mbps) in the 2.4 GHz frequency spectrum. This standard is also called WiFi or 802.11 high rate. The 802.11b standard uses only DSSS for data encoding.

g

The 802.11g standard operates in the 2.4 GHz frequency spectrum. This offers a maximum rate of 54 Mbps and is backward compatible with 802.11b. To achieve 54 Mbps, it also uses OFDM for encoding rather than FHSS or DSSS.

n

The goal of the 802.11n standard is to significantly increase throughput in both the 2.4 GHz and 5 GHz frequency ranges. The baseline goal of the standard was to reach speeds of 100 Mbps, but given the right conditions, it is estimated that the 802.11n speeds might be able to reach 600 Mbps. In practical operation, 802.11n speeds will be much slower.

802.11n achieves some of the higher speeds by using multiple antennas on the AP and station, a feature called multiple in/multiple out (MIMO).

ac (WIFI 5)

The 802.11ac standard builds on the features of 802.11n and improves on them in the following ways:

- Wider channels (40 MHz, 80 MHz, and 160 MHz)
- New modulation (256 quadrature amplitude modulation [QAM], which has the potential to provide a 30 percent increase in speed)

- More spatial streams (up to eight spatial streams)
- Improved MIMO and beamforming with the use of multiuser MIMO, allowing an AP to transmit a signal to multiple client stations on the same channel simultaneously if the client stations are in different physical areas

With 802.11ac, which operates only in the 5 GHz frequency range, it is possible to achieve a data rate of almost 2 Gbps if the AP and the station have enough antennas.

ax (WIFI 6)

802.11ax, or WiFi 6 as it also called, is designed to operate in license-exempt bands between 1 and 7.125 GHz, including the 2.4 and 5 GHz bands already in common use as well as the much wider 6 GHz band (5.925–7.125 GHz in the United States).

It focuses on improving performance in high-density areas, and it is estimated that ax improves performance over 802.11ac by 37 percent. Over an entire network, however, the improvement can be up to 400 percent. This is accomplished by using OFDM, deploying power-control methods to avoid interference with neighboring networks, and the introduction of the higher-order 1024 QAM modulation.

Long-range fixed wireless

It is also possible to implement 802.11 in a point-to-point configuration using long-range antennas that are perfectly aligned to one another. You may have seen this on occasion as small dishes at the tops of telephone poles. The antennas used are not like the ones used in a WLAN. Unlike those antennas, which tend to transit in multiple directions, these antennas are highly directional, meaning they focus the transmission in a tight beam, which makes it transmit a much longer distance. Because of this, the alignment of the two antennas on either end is critical.

Licensed/Unlicensed

Since there is a limit to the number of frequencies in the radio spectrum, governmental bodies referee the use of these frequency bands. In the United States, that body is the FCC. While some bands (such as those described above used for 802.11) are free to use by anyone (while also abiding by the limits controlling transmission power covered in the next section), others such as the bands used by AM and FM radio stations require a license. By requiring a license for the exact frequency used by an entity, the FCC is able to ensure that entities using the exact same frequency are geographically separated from one another to eliminate interference issues.

Power

It is also becoming possible to transit power over long distances. In this arrangement, a coil of wire generates a magnetic field, a metal plate generates an electric field, an antenna radiates radio waves, or a laser generates light.

Using the same fields and waves as wireless communication devices, only a fraction of what is transmitted will be received, which explains why wireless power technologies are likely to be more limited by distance than wireless communication technologies.

Regulatory requirements for wireless power

The amount of power that can be applied to the radio transmission is also regulated by the FCC. There are two sets of rules: those for a point-to-multipoint network as you would find in a WLAN, and those for a point-to-point connection such as described in the previous section, long-range fixed wireless. For more information on the specifics, see www.air802.com/fcc-rules-and-regulations.html.

NFC

In Chapter 1, you learned about near-field communication (NFC). Please review that section.

Radio-frequency identification (RFID)

Radio frequency identification (RFID) is a wireless, no-contact technology that uses radio frequency chips and readers to manage inventory, track animals, and many other uses. The chips are placed on individual pieces or pallets of inventory. RFID readers are placed throughout the location to communicate with the chips. Identification and location information are collected as part of the RFID communication. Organizations can customize the information that is stored on an RFID chip to suit their needs.

Two types of RFID systems can be deployed: active reader/passive tag (ARPT) and active reader/active tag (ARAT). In an ARPT system, the active reader transmits signals and receives replies from passive tags. In an ARAT system, active tags are awakened with signals from the active reader.

RFID chips can be read only if they are within a certain proximity of the RFID reader. Different RFID systems are available for different wireless frequencies. If your organization decides to implement RFID, it is important that you fully research the advantages and disadvantages of different frequencies.

Exam essentials

Identify the frequencies used in 802.11 networks.   The frequencies in use for 802.11 standards are the 2.4 GHz and 5 GHz frequency spectrums.

Describe the characteristics of the 802.11 amendments.   These include 802.11a, 802.11b, 802,11g, 802.11n, 802.11ac, and 802.11ax.

2.4 Summarize services provided by networked hosts

To configure and provide service to a network, you must be versed in the various roles that servers may play in the network. Armed with this knowledge, you can better ensure the proper function of these servers.

Server roles

Servers are computers that provide some type of shared service to the hosts on the network. There are many roles that servers can play, but this section will discuss some of the more common server roles, focusing on those you are most likely to find in your network.

DNS

DNS servers resolve device and domain names (website names) to IP addresses, and vice versa. They make it possible to connect to either without knowing the IP address of the device or of the server hosting the website. Clients are configured with the IP address of a DNS server (usually through DHCP) and make requests of the server using what are called queries. The organization's DNS server will be configured to perform the lookup of IP addresses for which it has no entry in its database by making requests of the DNS servers on the Internet, which are organized in a hierarchy that allows these servers to more efficiently provide the answer. When they have completed their lookup, they return the IP address to the client so that the client can make a direct connection using the IP address.

DHCP

DHCP servers are used to automate the process of providing an IP configuration to devices in the network. These servers respond to broadcast-based requests for a configuration by offering an IP address, subnet mask, and default gateway to the DHCP client. While these options provide basic network connectivity, many other options can also be provided, such as the IP address of a TFTP server that IP phones can contact to download a configuration file.

Fileshare

File servers are used to store files that can be accessed by the users in the network. Typically, users are encouraged or even required to store any important data on these servers rather than on their local hard drives because these servers are typically backed up on a regular basis, whereas the user machines typically are not. These servers will have significant amounts of storage space and may even have multiple hard drives configured in a RAID (redundant array of independent disks) system to provide quicker recovery from a drive crash than could be provided by recovering with the backup.

Print servers

Print servers are used to manage printers, and in cases where that is their only role, they will manage multiple printers. This type of server provides the spooler service to the printers that it manages, and when you view the print queue, you are viewing it on the print server. Many enterprise printers come with a built-in print server, which makes using a dedicated machine for the role unnecessary.

Mail servers

Mail servers run email server software and use SMTP to send and receive email on behalf of users who possess mailboxes on the server. Those users will use a client email protocol to retrieve their email from the server. Two of the most common are POP3, which is a retrieve-only protocol, and IMAP4, which has more functionality and can be used to manage the email on the server.

Syslog

All infrastructure devices such as firewalls, routers, and switches have logs where events of various types are recorded. These logs can contain information valuable for troubleshooting both security and performance of systems. You can direct these event messages to a central server, called a syslog server. By doing so, you create a single system for access to all event logs. A syslog server also makes it easier to correlate events on various devices by combining the events into a single log. To ensure proper sequencing of events, all devices should have their time synchronized from a single source using a Network Time Protocol (NTP) server.

Web servers

Web servers are used to provide access to information for users connecting to the server using a web browser, which is the client part of the application. The browser uses HTTP as its transfer mechanism. These servers can be either contained within a network and available only within the network (called an intranet server) or connected to the Internet, where they can be reached from anywhere. To provide security, a web server can be configured to require and use HTTPS, which uses SSL/TLS to encrypt the connection with no effort on the part of the user.

Authentication, authorization, and accounting (AAA)

An authentication, authorization, and accounting (AAA) server is one that centralizes the authentication process, while providing the additional services of managing the authorization of rights and the accounting of all that takes place. The server accepts authentication and authorization requests that are relayed from entry devices such as access points and VPN servers, performs the process, and returns the result to the entry devices.

Internet appliances

Beyond the roles that you can assign to servers by installing server software, there are network appliances that are dedicated to performing particular functions. In many cases, they perform better than a similar product that is software based. This section will look at several of the most common ones.

Spam gateways

A spam gateway is an appliance through which all email is examined and all spam is removed or at least segregated from non-spam items. These small rack-mounted devices are connected to the network and email is routed through the appliance prior to being delivered to mailboxes. Software bundled with the appliance lets you manage and customize the process to meet organizational needs.

Unified threat management (UTM)

Unified threat management (UTM) is an approach that involves performing multiple security functions within the same device or appliance. The functions may include the following:

- Network firewalling
- Network intrusion prevention
- Gateway antivirus
- Gateway antispam
- VPN
- Content filtering
- Load balancing
- Data leak prevention
- On-appliance reporting

UTM makes administering multiple systems unnecessary. However, some feel that UTM creates a single point of failure and instead favor creating multiple layers of devices as a more secure approach.

Load balancers

A form of fault tolerance that focuses on providing high availability of a resource is load balancing. In load balancing a frontend device or service receives work requests and allocates the requests to a number of backend servers. This type of fault tolerance is recommended for applications that do not have long-running in-memory state or frequently updated data. Web servers are good candidates for load balancing. The load-balancing device or service can use several methods to allocate the work, including round-robin, DNS delegation, and random.

Proxy servers

A proxy server is one that makes Internet connections on behalf of users in a network. In doing so, it prevents them from making direct connections to the Internet and provides a point of exit at which you can control their access in a variety of ways. For example, you may allow certain users to have complete access to the Internet with no restrictions, whereas other groups of users may be restricted in the sites they can visit and the activities in which they may participate.

An additional feature of these servers is their role in web caching. Web caching is the process of retrieving a web page for a user and then caching that web page so that another request for the page by the same users or other users can be served locally without returning to the Internet to retrieve the page. It results in faster page retrievals in cases where the page has been cached.

Legacy/embedded systems

An embedded system is a computer system with a specific function within a larger device. Embedded systems are present in many Internet-connected devices, such as VoIP phones and routers, but they are also increasingly found in devices such as home appliances and automobiles. Legacy embedded systems are those that have been handed down from one version of a system to another with no major revision.

Supervisory control and data acquisition (SCADA)

Industrial control systems (ICSs) is a general term that encompasses several types of control systems used in industrial production. The most widespread is supervisory control and data acquisition (SCADA). SCADA is a system operating with coded signals over communication channels so as to provide control of remote equipment. ICS includes the following components:

- Human interface: Such an interface presents data to the operator.

- Programmable logic controllers (PLCs): PLCs connect to the sensors and convert sensor data to digital data; they do not include telemetry hardware.

- Remote terminal units (RTUs): RTUs connect to the sensors and convert sensor data to digital data, including telemetry hardware.

- Sensors: Sensors typically have digital or analog I/O and are not in a form that can be easily communicated over long distances.

- Telemetry system: Such a system connects RTUs and PLCs to control centers and the enterprise.

Internet of Things (IoT) devices

If you don't already have an Internet of Things (IoT) device in your home or office, you probably will soon. These are any devices that can be connected to the SOHO network and managed from a smartphone or desktop application.

Thermostat

When IoT-enabled thermostats are installed, they connect to the local wireless network. At some point during their configuration, you will enter the SSID of the network and the password or key. For example, Nest, one of the most popular systems, will display a home screen after the first time you power the system on after wiring it up. (Be sure to follow the manufacturer's directions.) The system will prompt you for language, wireless information, and other settings covering how high and how low you want the temperature to range and whether you want heat, air conditioning, or auto. When the installation is complete, install the app on your phone and follow the directions there for connecting to your thermostat.

Light switches

Lighting systems can also be IoT-enabled. Many of today's systems can be controlled by your personal assistant (Alexa, Cortana, and similar devices). Kasa is a company that makes plugs you introduce between the light and the power outlet that communicate wirelessly with your wireless network. You install a smartphone app and use that to control the light from anywhere you have the Internet.

Security cameras

Security camera systems that can be managed over the Internet are also available, and they use a smartphone app much like the light switch and thermostat. These systems come with a video recorder to record video for later viewing. After the wireless cameras are physically placed and installed, they typically link up with the video system upon startup. After installing the smartphone app, you can manage and view the cameras from anywhere you have the Internet. Follow the specific directions from your system.

Door locks

Smart door locks replace the manual lock system in doors and can be managed remotely. They communicate wirelessly with your network and in some cases may be part of a total package that includes security system and lights. After physical installation of the lock assembly in the doors, follow the directions in the system to install the smartphone app, connect to the doors, and manage the locks.

Exam essentials

Identify examples of Internet of Things (IoT) devices.   These include thermostats, door locks, cameras, light switches, and heating and cooling systems.

Know the major roles played by servers.   These include DNS, DHCP, mail, file, AAA, and print servers.

2.5 Given a scenario, install and configure basic wired/wireless small office/home office (SOHO) networks

The protocol of the Internet is TCP/IP, and because of this, TCP/IP has become the de facto protocol of most networks as well. Far from the only networking protocol available, TCP/IP meets the needs of most organizations and is becoming more and more the one protocol suite that administrators must understand in order to do their jobs. In this section, we'll cover the common configurations and settings required to get TCP/IP up and running.

Internet Protocol (IP) addressing

A host is any machine or interface that participates in a TCP/IP network—whether as a client or a server. Every interface on a TCP/IP network that must be issued an IP address is considered a host. Those addresses can be manually entered or provided dynamically to the host by a DHCP server. (If IPv4 is in use, the addresses fall into three classes—A, B, and C.) The other values needed, besides the IP address, are the subnet mask (identifying the scope of the network on which the host resides) and the default gateway (the router interfacing with the outside world). A default gateway is the address of the local router and serves as the gateway to other networks. Since memorizing complex numerical addresses can be difficult to do, DNS is used to translate hostnames into IP addresses as needed. In this section you'll learn about both IPv4 and IPv6 IP addressing.

IPv4

Although there is no official IP class objective, it is helpful to understand IP classes in the real world, and knowing about them also enriches your understanding of various CompTIA objectives.

IPv4 addresses (IPv6 is discussed later) are 32-bit binary numbers. Because numbers of such magnitude are difficult to work with, they're divided into four octets (8 bits) and converted to decimal. Thus, 01010101 becomes 85. This is important because the limits on the size of the decimal number exist because they are representations of binary numbers. The range must be from 0 (00000000) to 255 (11111111) per octet, making the lowest possible IP address 0.0.0.0 and the highest 255.255.255.255. Many IP addresses aren't available because they're reserved for diagnostic purposes, private addressing, or some other function.

Three classes of IP addresses are available for assignment to hosts; they're identified by the first octet. Table 2.3 shows the class and the range the first octet must fall into to be within that class. The entire 127.0.0.0 network is missing because that network has been set aside or reserved for diagnostics.

TABLE 2.3   IP address classes

Class	Range
A	1–126
B	128–191
C	192–223

 Five classes exist. Class D (multicast) and Class E (experimental) are not assigned to hosts.

Class A   If you're given a Class A address, then you're assigned a number such as 125. With a few exceptions, this means you can use any number between 0 and 255 in the second field, any number between 0 and 255 in the third field, and any number between 0 and 255 in the fourth field. This gives you a total number of hosts that you can have on your network in excess of 16 million. The default subnet mask is 255.0.0.0.

Class B   If you're given a Class B address, then you're assigned a number such as 152.119. With a few exceptions, this means you can use any number between 0 and 255 in the third field and any number between 0 and 255 in the fourth field. This gives you a total number of hosts that you can have on your network in excess of 65,000. The default subnet mask is 255.255.0.0.

Class C   If you're given a Class C address, then you're assigned a number such as 205.19.15. You can use any number between 1 and 254 in the fourth field, for a total of 254 possible hosts (0 and 255 are reserved). The default subnet mask is 255.255.255.0.

The class, therefore, makes a tremendous difference in the number of hosts your network can have. In most cases, the odds of having all hosts at one location are small. Assuming you have a Class B address, will there be 65,000 hosts in one room, or will they be in several locations? Most often, it's the latter.

Private addresses

Within each of the three major classes of IP addresses, there is a range set aside for private addresses. These are addresses that do not communicate directly with the Internet (often using a proxy server or network address translation to do so), so each host's address needs to be unique only within the realm of that network. Table 2.4 lists the private address ranges for Class A, B, and C addresses.

TABLE 2.4   Private address ranges

Class	Range
A	10.0.0.0 to 10.255.255.255
B	172.16.0.0 to 172.31.255.255
C	192.168.0.0 to 192.168.255.255

Public addresses

Public addresses are those that are allowed to be routed to the Internet. These addresses must be obtained from the Network Information Center (NIC) or the Internet Assigned Number Authority (IANA). Issuance by a central body ensures there are no duplicates. These addresses come from the ranges depicted in Table 2.5.

TABLE 2.5   Public IP addresses

Class	Public IP ranges
Class A	1.0.0.0 to 9.255.255.255 to 11.0.0.0 to 126.255.255.255
Class B	128.0.0.0 to 171.255.255.255 173.0.0.0 to 191.255.255.255
Class C	192.0.0.0 to 195.255.255.255 197.0.0.0 to 223.255.255.255
Class D	224.0.0.0 to 247.255.255.255 Multicast Addresses
Class E	248.0.0.0 to 255.255.255.254 Experimental Use

Subnet mask

Subnetting your network is the process of taking the total number of hosts available to you and dividing it into smaller networks. When you configure TCP/IP on a host, you typically need give only three values: a unique IP address, a default gateway (router) address, and a subnet mask. Table 2.6 shows the default subnet mask for each class of network.

TABLE 2.6   Default subnet values

Class	Default subnet mask
A	255.0.0.0
B	255.255.0.0
C	255.255.255.0

 Purists may argue that you don't need a default gateway. Technically this is true if your network is small and you don't communicate beyond it. For all practical purposes, though, most networks need a default gateway.

When you use the default subnet mask, you're allowing all hosts to be at one site and not subdividing your network. This is called *classful* subnetting. Any deviation from the default signifies that you're dividing the network into multiple subnetworks, which is called *classless* subnetting.

The problem with classful subnetting is that it allows for only three sizes of networks: Class A (16,777,216 hosts), Class B (65,536 hosts), and Class C (254 hosts). Two of these are too large to operate efficiently in the real world, and when enterprises were issued public network IDs that were larger than they needed, many public IP addresses were wasted. For this reason and simply to allow for the creation of smaller networks that operate better, the concept of classless routing, or Classless Interdomain Routing (CIDR), was born.

Using CIDR, administrators can create smaller networks called *subnets*, by manipulating the subnet mask of a larger classless or major network ID. This allows you to create a subnet that is much closer in size to what you need, thus wasting fewer IP addresses and improving performance in each subnet, as a result of the reduced broadcast traffic generated in each subnet.

CIDR notation is another way to represent the IP address and the subnet mask. The number of bits in the mask is shown after the address and preceded by a slash. For example, the address 192.168.5.5 with a mask of 255.255.255.0 can be written as 192.168.5.5/24.

IPv4 configuration

If you're not using DHCP on the router/switch, you'll have to configure the IP addresses of the computers manually. When you do this, ensure the following:

▪ Each wired interface needs to have an IP address in the same network with the address of the router Ethernet address. Also, the default gateway needs to be set to the address of the router. Finally, configure the IP address of the DNS server so that name resolution can occur.

- Each wireless interface needs to have an IP address in the same network with the address of the router/switch wireless interface. Also, the default gateway should be set to that same address. Finally, configure the IP address of the DNS server so that name resolution can occur.

Note that the requirements are the same for wired and wireless interfaces.

NIC configuration

The end user device will need to have the network interface, either wired or wireless, configured to operate on the network. The most common configuration dialog box is that in Windows 10, shown in Figure 2.5. Other operating systems are quite similar.

FIGURE 2.5   The Windows 10 dialog box for configuring a NIC

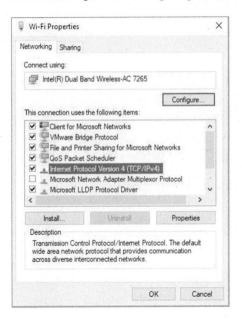

Wired

As a representative procedure, you would take the following steps to configure a NIC in Windows 10:

1. Start by navigating to Control Panel ➤ Network And Internet ➤ Network And Sharing Center ➤ Change Adapter Settings.

2. Right-click the interface you would like to configure and select Properties. You will see the dialog box in Figure 2.5.

3. Select Internet Protocol Version 4 and select Properties. You will see the dialog box in Figure 2.6.

FIGURE 2.6 TCP/IP Properties dialog box

4. If you're using a DHCP server, leave both selections as shown in Figure 2.6 to obtain IP and DNS server addresses automatically.

   If you're using static IP addressing, select the radio button Use The Following IP Address and enter the IP address, subnet mask, and default gateway. The gateway address should be the IP address of the router.

5. In the bottom section, select Use The Following DNS Server Address and enter the IP address of the DNS server. In a SOHO, this will probably be the address of the router/switch.

6. Click OK in all dialog boxes as you close them.

Wireless

Configuring the IP configuration on the wireless NIC will be the same as just described for the wired NIC.

IPv6

IPv4 uses a 32-bit addressing scheme that provides for more than 4 billion unique addresses. Unfortunately, there are a lot of IP-enabled devices added to the Internet every day—not to mention, not all of the addresses that can be created are used by public networks (many are reserved in classes D and above and are unavailable for public use). This reduces the number of addresses that can be allocated as public Internet addresses.

IPv6 offers a number of improvements, the most notable of which is its ability to handle growth in public networks. IPv6 uses a 128-bit addressing scheme, allowing a huge number of possible addresses: 340,282,366,920,938,463,463,374,607,431,768,211,456. Table 2.7 compares IPv4 to IPv6.

TABLE 2.7   IPv4 vs. IPv6

Feature	IPv4	IPv6
Loopback address	127.0.0.1	0:0:0:0:0:0:0:1 (::1)
Private ranges	10.0.0.0 172.16.0.0 to 172.31.0.0 192.168.0.0	FEC0:: (proposed)
Autoconfigured addresses	169.254.0.0	FE80::

In IPv6 addresses, repeating zeros can be left out so that colons next to each other in the address indicate one or more sets of zeros for that section.

Link local

In IPv6, there is a type of address called a *link local address* that in many ways is like an APIPA address in that the device will generate one of these addresses for each interface with no intervention from a human, as is done with APIPA. The scope of the address is also the same in that it is not routable and is good only on the segment the device is located on.

However, as is the case with APIPA addresses, if two devices connected to the same segment generate these addresses, they will be in the same network, and the two devices will be able to communicate. This is because the devices always generate the address using the same IPv6 prefix (the equivalent of a network ID in IPv4), which is FE80::/64. The remainder of the address is created by spreading the 48-bit MAC address across the last 64 bits, yielding an IPv6 address that looks like the example shown here:

```
FE80::2237:06FF:FECF:67E4/64
```

Automatic Private IP Addressing (APIPA)

Within each of the three major classes of IP addresses, there is a range set aside for private addresses. These are addresses that do not communicate directly with the Internet (often using a proxy server or network address translation to do so), so each host's address needs to be unique only within the realm of that network. Table 2.8 lists the private address ranges for Class A, B, and C addresses.

TABLE 2.8   Private address ranges

Class	Range
A	10.0.0.0 to 10.255.255.255
B	172.16.0.0 to 172.31.255.255
C	192.168.0.0 to 192.168.255.255

Automatic Private IP Addressing (APIPA) is a TCP/IP feature Microsoft added to its operating systems. If a DHCP server cannot be found and the clients are configured to obtain IP addresses automatically, the clients automatically assign themselves an IP address, somewhat randomly, in the 169.254.*x.x* range with a subnet mask of 255.255.0.0. This allows them to communicate with other hosts that have similarly configured themselves, but they are unable to connect to the Internet. If a computer is using an APIPA address, it will have trouble communicating with other clients if those clients do not use APIPA addresses.

CIDR notation is another way to represent the IP address and the subnet mask. The number of bits in the mask is shown after the address and preceded by a slash. For example, the address 192.168.5.5 with a mask of 255.255.255.0 can be written as 192.168.5.5/24.

Static vs. Dynamic

The two methods of entering address information for a host are static and dynamic. *Static* means that you manually enter the information for the host and it does not change. *Dynamic* means that DHCP is used for the host to lease information from.

While DHCP can be a godsend, a SOHO network is small enough that you can get by without it issuing IP addresses to each host. The advantage to assigning the IP addresses statically is that you can make certain which host is associated with which IP address and then utilize filtering to limit network access to only those hosts.

Although static IP addressing may not be scalable in a wired network with many devices, in a small network, using static IP addressing will make it impossible for someone to just plug into your network without knowing your IP address scheme.

Gateway

A gateway can have two meanings. In TCP/IP, a gateway is the address of the machine to send data to that is not intended for a host on the network (in other words, a default gateway). A gateway is also a physical device operating between the transport and application layers of the OSI model that can send data between dissimilar systems. The best example of the latter is a mail gateway—it doesn't matter which two networks are communicating; the gateway allows them to exchange email.

A gateway, as it is tested on the exam, is the server (router) that allows traffic beyond the internal network. Hosts are configured with the address of a gateway (called the default gateway), and if they need to correspond with a host outside the internal network, the data is sent to the gateway to facilitate this. When you configure TCP/IP on a host, one of the fields that should be provided is a gateway field, which specifies where data not intended for this network is sent in order to be able to communicate with the rest of the world.

Exam essentials

Identify the private IP address ranges in IPv4.   The three ranges are 10.0.0.0 to 10.255.255.255, 172.16.0.0 to 172.31.255.255, and 192.168.0.0 to 192.168.255.255.

Describe the purpose of a default gateway.   A gateway, as it is tested on the exam, is the server (router) that allows traffic beyond the internal network. Hosts are configured with the address of a gateway (called the default gateway), and if they need to correspond with a host outside the internal network, the data is sent to the gateway to facilitate this.

2.6 Compare and contrast common network configuration concepts

Earlier in this chapter you learned about configuring IP addressing on a system. In this section, we'll cover additional common configurations and settings required to get a system up and running.

DNS

As stated earlier, every computer, interface, or device on a TCP/IP network is issued a unique identifier known as an IP address that resembles 192.168.12.123. Because of the Internet, TCP/IP is the most commonly used networking protocol today. You can easily see that it's difficult for most users to memorize these numbers, so hostnames are used in their place. Hostnames are alphanumeric values assigned to a host; any host may have more than one hostname.

For example, the host 192.168.12.123 may be known to all users as Gemini, or it may be known to the sales department as Gemini and to the marketing department as Apollo9. All that is needed is a means by which the alphanumeric name can be translated into its IP address. There are a number of methods of doing so, but for this exam, you need to know only one: the Domain Name System. On a large network, you can add a server to be referenced by all hosts for the name resolution. The server runs DNS and resolves a fully qualified domain name (FQDN) like www.entrepreneurshipcamp.com into its IP address. Multiple DNS servers can serve an area and provide fault tolerance for one another. In all cases, the DNS servers divide their area into zones; every zone has a primary server and any number of secondary servers. DNS works with any operating system and any version.

DNS records are organized by type. The following sections cover some of the key record types; Table 2.9 shows DNS record types.

TABLE 2.9   DNS record types

Record type	Function
A	A host record that represents the mapping of a single device to an IPv4 address
AAAA	A host record that represents the mapping of a single device to an IPv6 address
CNAME	An alias record that represents an additional hostname mapped to an IPv4 address that already has an A record mapped
NS	A name server record that represents a DNS server mapped to an IPv4 address
MX	A mail exchanger record that represents an email server mapped to an IPv4 address
SOA	A Start of Authority record that represents a DNS server that is authoritative for a DNS namespace

Address (A)

(A) records are also called host records and make up the hostname IPv4 address mapping.

IPv6 address (AAAA)

(AAAA) records are also called host records and make up the hostname IPv6 address mapping.

Mail exchanger (MX)

An (MX) record is one that maps a mail exchanger server to an IPv4 address. This allows others to contact your DNS server for name resolution.

Text (TXT)

(TXT) records provide text information for sources outside of your domain. You add these records to your domain settings. You can use TXT records for various purposes. For example, some use them to verify domain ownership and to ensure email security. Let's investigate these record types more closely.

Spam management

TXT records can be part of the campaign to mitigate email security issues. For example, it can be used to reduce spam, which often contains attractive phishing emails.

DomainKeys IDENTIFIED MAIL (DKIM)

DomainKeys Identified Mail (DKIM) allows you to verify the source of an email. It provides a method for validating a domain name identity that is associated with a message through cryptographic authentication. The email server verifies the domain name (called the DKIM signature) with the DNS server first before delivering the email. DKIM works by digitally signing each email using a public-private key pair. The public key is hosted in a TXT record associated with the domain.

SENDER POLICY FRAMEWORK (SPF)

Another possible mitigation technique is to implement a Sender Policy Framework (SPF). An SPF is an email validation system that works by using DNS to determine whether an email sent by someone has been sent by a host sanctioned by that domain's administrator. If it can't be validated, it is not delivered to the recipient's box. SPF TXT records list all the servers that are authorized to send email messages from a domain.

DOMAIN-BASED MESSAGE AUTHENTICATION REPORTING, AND CONFORMANCE (DMARC)

Domain-based Message Authentication, Reporting & Conformance (DMARC) is an email authentication and reporting protocol that improves email security within federal agencies. All federal agencies are required to implement this standard, which improves email security. Protocols (SPF, DKIM) authenticate emails to ensure they are coming from a valid source. DMARC TXT records can be set up once DKIM and SPF are configured. A DMARC TXT record should be stored under the title _dmarc.*example.com* with *example.com* representing the actual domain name. The value of the record is the domain's DMARC policy.

DHCP

You learned about the function of a DHCP server earlier in this chapter. Rather than an administrator having to configure a unique IP address for every host added on a network (and a default gateway and a subnet mask), they can use a DHCP server to issue these values.

DHCP is built on the older Bootstrap Protocol (BOOTP) that was used to allow diskless workstations to boot and connect to a server that provided them with an operating system and applications. The client uses broadcasts to request the data and thus—normally—can't communicate with DHCP servers beyond their own subnet (broadcasts don't route). A DHCP relay agent, usually installed on the router, however, can be employed to allow DHCP broadcasts to go from one network to another.

While the primary purpose of DHCP is to lease IP addresses to hosts, when it gives the IP address, it also often includes the additional configuration information as well: DNS server, router information, and so on.

Leases

The server takes one of the numbers it has available and leases it to the client for a length of time. If the client is still using the configuration data when 50 percent of the lease has expired, it requests a renewal of the lease from the server; under normal operating conditions, the request is granted. When the client is no longer using the address, the address goes back in the scope and can be issued to another client.

Reservations

Although by default DHCP randomly assigns IP addresses, it is possible to reserve a dynamic IP address for a device. This is advisable when you want the device to keep the same IP address all the time but you still want the device to participate in DHCP so that you can keep the device abreast of any changes in the address of the DNS server or the default gateway address.

Scope

The DHCP server is given a number of addresses in a range that it can supply to clients called a scope. For example, the server may be given the IP range 192.168.12.1 to 192.168.12.200. When a client boots, it sends out a request for the server to issue it an address (and any other configuration data) from that scope.

Virtual LAN (VLAN)

Virtual local area networks (VLANs) are logical subdivisions of a switch that segregate ports from one another as if they were in different LANs. VLANs offer another way to add a layer of separation between sensitive devices and the rest of the network. For example, if only one device should be able to connect to the finance server, the device and the finance server could be placed in a VLAN separate from the other VLANs. As traffic between VLANs can occur only through a router, access control lists (ACLs) can be used to control the traffic allowed between VLANs.

These VLANs can also span multiple switches, meaning that devices connected to switches in different parts of a network can be placed in the same VLAN regardless of physical location.

VLANs have many advantages and only one disadvantage. The disadvantage is managerial overhead securing the VLANs. The advantages are:

- Cost: Switched networks with VLANs are less costly than routed networks, since routers cost more than switches.

- Performance: By creating smaller broadcast domains (each VLAN is a broadcast domain), performance improves.

- Flexibility: Removes the requirement that devices in the same LAN (or in this case VLAN) be in the same location.

- Security: Provides one more layer of separation at layers 2 and 3.

Virtual private network (VPN)

Virtual private network (VPN) connections are remote access connections that allow users to securely connect to the enterprise network and work as if they were in the office. These connections use special tunneling protocols that encrypt the information being transferred between the user and the corporate network. Anywhere users, business partners, or vendors are allowed remote access to the network, VPN connections should be used.

VPN connections use an untrusted carrier network but provide protection of the information through strong authentication protocols and encryption mechanisms. While we typically use the most untrusted network—the Internet—as the classic example, and most VPNs do travel through the Internet, a VPN can be used with interior networks as well whenever traffic needs to be protected from prying eyes.

In VPN operations, entire protocols wrap around other protocols when this process occurs. They include the following:

- A LAN protocol (required)

- A remote access or line protocol (required)

- An authentication protocol (optional)

- An encryption protocol (optional)

A device that terminates multiple VPN connections is called a VPN concentrator. VPN concentrators incorporate the most advanced encryption and authentication techniques available.

VPN connections can be used to provide remote access to teleworkers or traveling users (called remote access VPNs) and can also be used to securely connect two locations (called site-to-site VPNs). The implementation process is conceptually different for these two. In the former, the tunnel that is created has as its endpoints the user's computer and the VPN concentrator. In this case, only traffic traveling from the user computer to the VPN concentrator uses this tunnel.

In the case of two office locations, the tunnel endpoints are the two VPN routers, one in each office. With this configuration, all traffic that goes between the offices will use the tunnel, regardless of the source or destination. The endpoints are defined during the creation of the VPN connection and thus must be set correctly according to the type of remote access link being used.

Exam essentials

Know the capabilities and limitations of VLANs.   Virtual local area networks (VLANs) are logical subdivisions of a switch that segregate ports from one another as if they were in different LANs. VLANs offer another way to add a layer of separation between sensitive devices and the rest of the network.

Know the capabilities and limitations of the 802.11x network standards.   The current standards for wireless protocols are 802.11, 802.11a, 802.11b, 802.11g, 802.11n, and 802.11ac.

2.7 Compare and contrast Internet connection types, network types, and their features

Your network can connect to the Internet in a number of ways. These can range from the slow dial-up connection that is established only when you need it to be established to a high-speed fiber connection that is always on. This section looks at many of the options available and all that you need to know for this objective on the A+ exam.

Internet connection types

When discussing ways to connect to the Internet, most of the focus is on broadband network techniques. It is imperative that you understand the various types of networks, including broadband. The sections that follow will focus on the key issues associated with connecting to the Internet.

Satellite

Whereas the other broadband technologies discussed require the use of physical wiring, with satellite broadband the service provider sends a microwave signal from a dish to an orbiting satellite and back. One satellite can service many receivers, so this is commonly known as point-to-multipoint technology. As a general rule, satellite connections are slower than the other broadband technologies you need to know for the exam, and they are adversely affected by weather and atmospheric conditions.

 With satellite, download speed is much faster than upload speed.

Fiber

Fiber-optic cabling provides excellent speed and bandwidth but is expensive. Not only are the cables that you use costly, but the light-emitting/receiving hardware costs also make this an expensive undertaking. Because of the cost involved, fiber is often an option for businesses only when it comes to broadband access.

Fiber to the Home (FTTH) is an attempt some communities are undertaking to offer high-speed connectivity to residential dwellings as well. Verizon FiOS, a similar implementation, runs single-mode optical fiber to homes and includes phone and television service along with Internet access.

Cable/DSL

Two of the most popular methods of connecting to the Internet today are using DSL and cable. DSL and cable were covered earlier in this chapter.

Cellular

Smartphones have made cellular networking popular, though they are not the only devices capable of using networking; for example, a cellular modem can also be quickly added to a laptop. Cellular networking was covered in Chapter 1.

Wireless Internet service provider (WISP)

Wireless Internet service providers provide Internet access to regions where running cables is not cost effective, such as in mountainous areas. Some use 802.11 standards, whereas others use proprietary technologies.

Network types

You should know the terminology used for networking as well as the major topologies that are available. Networks consist of servers and clients. A server is a dedicated machine offering services such as file and print sharing. A client is any individual workstation accessing the network. A workstation is a client machine that accesses services elsewhere (normally from a server).

Networks differ in size and scope. The size of the network on which servers and clients operate can range significantly.

Local area network (LAN)

A local area network is a network that is geographically confined within a small space—a room, a building, and so on. Because it's confined and does not have to span a great distance, it can normally offer higher speeds.

With Ethernet, you can often use the network type to compute the required length and speed of your cabling. For example, 100BaseT tells you three things.

- 100: The speed of the network, 100 Mbps.

- Base: The technology used (either baseband or broadband).

- T: Twisted-pair cabling. In the case of 10BaseT, it's generally UTP.

When you configure a network, one of the first places to turn your attention is the routers and access points—they are the hardware components on which network access can rely. Because it must always be possible to find these devices, I suggest that you not use DHCP to issue them addresses but configure their addresses statically.

To increase security, devices should be behind a firewall, and you should always change the administrative username and password that comes preconfigured with these devices to ones that adhere to stringent password policies (a mixture of uppercase and lowercase alphabet, numbers, and special characters), and you should keep the firmware updated.

With wireless access points, you should change the SSID from its default value (if one is preconfigured) and disable broadcasts. MAC filtering can be used on a wireless network, for example, to prevent certain clients from accessing the Internet. You can choose to deny service to a set list of MAC addresses (and allow all others) or allow service only to a set of MAC addresses (and deny all others).

Wide area network (WAN)

A wide area network (WAN) is a collection of two or more LANs, typically connected by routers and dedicated leased lines (not to mention complicated implementations). The geographic limitation is removed, but WAN speeds are traditionally less than LAN speeds.

Personal area network (PAN)

A personal area network (PAN) is a LAN created by personal devices. Often, personal devices include networking capabilities and can communicate directly with one another. Wireless technologies have introduced a new term: wireless personal area network (WPAN). This refers to the technologies involved in connecting devices in close proximity to exchange data or resources. An example is connecting a laptop with a PDA to synchronize an address book. Because of their small size and the nature of the data exchange, WPAN devices lend themselves well to ad hoc wireless networking. Ad hoc wireless networks are those that have devices connect to each other directly, not through a wireless access point.

Metropolitan area network (MAN)

Occasionally, a WAN will be described as a metropolitan area network (MAN) when it is confined to a certain geographic area, such as a university campus or city. No formal guidelines dictate the differences between a MAN and a WAN; technically, a MAN is a WAN. Perhaps for this reason, the term *MAN* is used less frequently than *WAN*. If any distinction exists, it's that a MAN is smaller than a WAN. A MAN is almost always bigger than a LAN and usually is smaller than or equal to a WAN. MANs utilize an ISP or telecommunications (telco) provider.

Storage area network (SAN)

Storage area networks (SAN) consist of high-capacity storage devices that are connected by a high-speed private network (separate from the LAN) using storage-specific switches. This storage information architecture addresses the collection of data, management of data, and use of data. In a SAN, only devices that can use the Fibre channel Small Computer System Interface (SCSI) network can access the data, so it is typically done through a server.

Wireless local area network (WLAN)

A wireless local area network (WLAN) is simply one that uses one of the 802.11 standards. The use of 802.11 is discussed earlier in this chapter.

Exam essentials

Differentiate the types networks.   These include local area networks (LANs), wide area networks (WANs), personal area networks (PANs), metropolitan area networks (MANs), storage area networks (SANs), and wireless local area networks (WLANs).

Describe Internet connection types.   These include satellite, fiber, cable, DSL, cellular, and wireless Internet service provider (WISP).

2.8 Given a scenario, use networking tools

To create a network and solve problems with it, you need a toolbox. While some of the tools you use will be in the form of software, many others are hardware, and those are the focus of this objective.

No networking administrators worth their pay would try to troubleshoot a problem without a set of tools. The tools that should be readily on hand include a crimper for fixing connectors, a multimeter for checking signals, a toner probe to find breaks in a cable, a cable tester, a loopback plug, and a punchdown tool, among others.

Crimper

Wire crimpers look like pliers but are used to attach media connectors to the ends of cables. For instance, you use one type of wire crimper to attach RJ-45 connectors on an unshielded twisted-pair (UTP) cable. You use a different type of wire crimper to attach Bayonet Neill-Concelman (BNCs) to coaxial cabling.

Cable stripper

A cable stripper is used to remove the outer covering of the cable to get to the wire pairs within. You place the end of the cable in the mouth of the device, close the mouth, and then circle the cable, cutting away the outer sheath without damaging the wire pairs within. Figure 2.7 shows a cable stripper.

WiFi analyzer

A WiFi analyzer is a tool that gathers information of all sorts about the RF medium in the area. These may be handheld hardware devices or software that is installed on a laptop that uses the wireless card in the laptop to gather information. These analyzers vary widely in what type of information they are capable of generating and the price point.

FIGURE 2.7   Cable stripper

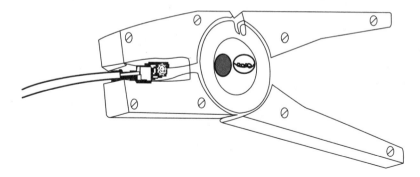

The following are among the functions that these analyzers offer:

- Noise and inference detection and location
- Channel information
- Signal strength
- List of APs in the area

Toner probe

A toner probe has two parts: the tone generator (called the toner) and the tone locator (called the probe). The toner sends the tone, and at the other end of the cable, the probe receives the toner's signal. This tool makes it easier to find the beginning and end of a cable.

The purpose of the toner probe is to generate a signal that is transmitted on the wire you are attempting to locate. At the other end, you press the probe against individual wires. When it makes contact with the wire that has the signal on it, the locator emits an audible signal or tone.

   A toner probe can be used to find breaks in a cable.

Punchdown tool

Punchdown tools are used to attach twisted-pair network cables to connectors within a patch panel. Specifically, they connect twisted-pair wires to the insulation displacement connector (IDC).

Cable tester

Cable testers (sometimes called media testers) are used to verify that the cable you are using is good. Commonly used with network cabling, they enable you to perform many of the same tests as a multimeter. Any tool that facilitates the testing of a cable can be deemed a cable tester, but a media tester allows administrators to test a segment of cable, looking for shorts, improperly attached connectors, or other cable faults. All media testers have a way of telling you whether the cable is working correctly and where the problem in the cable might be.

Loopback plug

Also called wrap plugs, loopback plugs take the signal going out and essentially echo it back. This allows you to test ports to make certain they're working correctly.

To simply test an implementation of TCP/IP on a host, you can always use the loopback address of 127.0.0.1. This is often used with ping (discussed in Chapter 6, "Operating Systems").

Network tap

A network tap is a hardware device with (at least) three ports: an input port, an output port, and a monitor port. The tap is inserted between the input and output and passes all traffic (send and receive data streams) through unimpeded in real time, but also copies that same data to its monitor port, enabling you to capture all traffic for inspection. The copied traffic can then be directed from the network tap to security devices such as an IPS for examination.

Exam essentials

Know the tools for working with networks.   A good administrator's toolbox will include wire crimpers, a multimeter, a toner probe, cable tester, loopback plugs, and a punchdown tool.

Know the two parts of a toner probe.   A toner probe has two parts: the tone generator (the toner) and the tone locator (the probe).

Review Questions

You can find the answers in the appendix.

1. Which of the following uses port 110?

    A. FTP

    B. SSH

    C. Telnet

    D. POP3

2. Which of the following uses two ports?

    A. FTP

    B. SSH

    C. Telnet

    D. POP3

3. Which of the following uses port 22?

    A. FTP

    B. SSH

    C. Telnet

    D. POP3

4. Which device operates at layer 2?

    A. Router

    B. Switch

    C. Repeater

    D. Hub

5. Which device operates at layer 1?

    A. Router

    B. Switch

    C. Bridge

    D. Hub

6. Which device operates at layer 2?

    A. Router

    B. Switch

    C. Repeater

    D. Hub

7. Which of the following is *not* a private IP address range?

   A. 10.0.0.0–10.255.255.255

   B. 172.16.0.0–172.16.255.255

   C. 192.168.0.0–192.168.255.255

   D. 192.168.5.5–192.168.255.255

8. Which of the following delivers an upload speed equal to the download speed?

   A. SDSL

   B. VDSL

   C. VHDSL

   D. RADSL

9. Which of the following is a system operating with coded signals over communication channels so as to provide control of remote equipment?

   A. NAT

   B. DMZ

   C. SCADA

   D. IPS

10. Which of the following operates in the 5.0 GHz range?

    A. 802.11a

    B. 802.11b

    C. 802.11g

    D. 802.11

11. Which of the following operates at a maximum of 2 MB?

    A. 802.11a

    B. 802.11b

    C. 802.11g

    D. 802.11

12. Which of the following has the largest cell size?

    A. 802.11a

    B. 802.11b

    C. 802.11g

    D. 802.11

13. Which type of server resolves IP addresses to hostnames?

    A. HTTP

    B. DNS

    C. DHCP

    D. SQL

14. Which type of server provides automatic IP configurations?

   A. HTTP

   B. DNS

   C. DHCP

   D. SQL

15. Which type of server is a database server?

   A. HTTP

   B. DNS

   C. DHCP

   D. SQL

16. Which of the following is a Class B address?

   A. 192.168.5.5

   B. 10.6.6.3

   C. 172.6.8.9

   D. 201.69.3.2

17. Which of the following is a Class A address?

   A. 192.168.5.5

   B. 10.6.6.3

   C. 172.6.8.9

   D. 201.69.3.2

18. Which of the following is a Class C address?

   A. 192.168.5.5

   B. 10.6.6.3

   C. 172.6.8.9

   D. 224.69.3.2

19. When personal devices include networking capabilities and can communicate directly with one another, they create which type of network?

   A. WAN

   B. MAN

   C. PAN

   D. WMN

20. Which of the following is a collection of two or more LANs, typically connected by routers and dedicated leased lines and is confined to a certain geographic area, such as a university campus or city?

   A. WAN

   B. MAN

   C. PAN

   D. WMN

21. Which of the following is a form of an ad hoc WLAN?

   A. WAN

   B. MAN

   C. PAN

   D. WMN

22. Which of the following is used to attach media connectors to the ends of cables?

   A. Crimper

   B. Cable stripper

   C. Multimeter

   D. Tone generator

23. Which of the following includes a voltmeter, an ohmmeter, and an ammeter?

   A. Crimper

   B. Cable stripper

   C. Multimeter

   D. Tone generator

24. Which of the following makes it easier to find the beginning and end of a cable?

   A. Crimper

   B. Cable stripper

   C. Multimeter

   D. Tone generator

Chapter

3

Hardware

COMPTIA A+ CERTIFICATION EXAM CORE 1 (220-1101) OBJECTIVES COVERED IN THIS CHAPTER:

✓ **3.1 Explain basic cable types and their connectors, features, and purposes.**

  ■ **Network cables**

    ■ Copper

      ■ Cat 5

      ■ Cat 5e

      ■ Cat 6

      ■ Cat 6a

      ■ Coaxial

      ■ Shielded twisted pair

      ■ Direct burial

      ■ Unshielded twisted pair

    ■ Plenum

    ■ Optical

    ■ Fiber

    ■ T568A/T568B

  ■ **Peripheral cables**

    ■ USB 2.0

    ■ USB 3.0

    ■ Serial

    ■ Thunderbolt

  ■ **Video cables**

    ■ High-Definition Multimedia Interface (HDMI)

    ■ DisplayPort

- Digital Visual Interface (DVI)
- Video Graphics Array
- **Hard drive cables**
  - Serial Advanced Technology Attachment (SATA)
  - Small Computer System Interface (SCSI)
  - External SATA (eSATA)
  - Integrated Drive Electronics (IDE)
- **Adapters**
- **Connector types**
- **RAM types**
  - RJ11
  - RJ45
  - F type
  - Straight tip (ST)
  - Subscriber connector (SC)
  - Lucent connector (LC)
  - Punchdown block
  - microUSB
  - miniUSB
  - USB-C
  - Molex
  - Lightning port
  - DB9

✓ **3.2 Given a scenario, install the appropriate RAM.**

- Virtual RAM
  - **Small outline dual inline memory module (SODIMM)**
  - **Double Data Rate 3 (DDR3)**
  - **Double Data Rate 4 (DDR4)**

- Double Data Rate 5 (DDR5)
- Error correction code (ECC) RAM
- Single-channel
- Dual-channel
- Triple-channel
- Quad-channel

✓ 3.3 Given a scenario, select and install storage devices

- **Hard drives**
  - Speeds
    - 5,400rpm
    - 7,200rpm
    - 10,000rpm
    - 15,000rpm
  - Form factor
    - 2.5
    - 3.5
- **SSDs**
  - Communications interfaces
    - Non-volatile Memory Express (NVMe)
    - SATA
    - Peripheral Component Interconnect Express (PCIe)
  - Form factors
    - M.2
    - mSATA
- **Drive configurations**
  - Redundant Array of Independent (or Inexpensive) Disks (RAID) 0, 1, 5, 10

Removable storage

- **Flash drives**
- **Memory cards**
- **Optical drives**

✓ **3.4 Given a scenario, install and configure motherboards, central processing units (CPUs), and add-on cards**

Motherboard form factor

- Advanced Technology eXtended (ATX)
- Information Technology eXtended (ITX)

Motherboard connector type

- Peripheral Component Interconnect (PCI)
- PCI Express (PCIe)
- Power connectors
- SATA
- eSATA
- SAN
- Headers
- M.2

Motherboard compatibility

- CPU sockets
  - Advanced Micro Devices, Inc. (AMD)
  - Intel
- Server
- Multisocket
- Desktop
- Mobile

Basic Input/Output System (BIOS)/Unified Extensible Firmware Interface (UEIF) settings

- **Boot options**
- **USB permissions**

- Trusted Platform Module (TPM) security features
- Fan considerations
- Secure Boot
- Boot password

Encryption

- TPM
- Hardware security module (HSM)

CPU architecture

- X64/x86
- Advanced RISC Machine (ARM)
- Single-core
- Multicore
- Multithreading
- Virtualization support

Expansion cards

- Sound card
- Video card
- Capture card
- NIC

Cooling

- Fans
- Heat sink
- Thermal paste/pads
- Liquid

✓ **3.5 Given a scenario, install or replace the appropriate power supply**

- 115V vs. 220V
- Output 3.3V vs. 5V vs. 12V
- 20-pin to 24-pin motherboard adapter

- **Redundant power supply**

- **Modular power supply**

- **Wattage rating**

✓ **3.6 Given a scenario, deploy and configure multi-function devices/printers and settings**

- **Properly unboxing a device – setup location considerations**

- **Use appropriate drivers for a given OS**

  - Printer Control Language (PCL) vs. PostScript

- **Device connectivity**

  - USB

  - Ethernet

  - Wireless

- **Public/shared devices**

  - Printer share

  - Print server

- **Configuration settings**

  - Duplex

  - Orientation

  - Tray settings

  - Quality

- **Security**

  - User authentication

  - Badging

  - Audit logs

  - Secured prints

- **Network scan services**

  - Email

  - SMB

  - Cloud services

- **Automatic document feeder (ADF)/flatbed scanner**

✓ 3.7 Given a scenario, install and replace printer consumables

Laser

- Imaging drum, fuser assembly, transfer belt, transfer roller, pickup rollers, separation pads, duplexing assembly

- Imaging process: processing, charging, exposing, developing, transferring, fusing, and cleaning

- Maintenance: Replace toner, apply maintenance kit, calibrate, clean

- Inkjet
  - Ink cartridge, print head, roller, feeder, duplexing assembly, carriage belt
  - Calibration
  - Maintenance: Clean heads, replace cartridges, calibrate, clear jams

- Thermal
  - Feed assembly, heating element
  - Special thermal paper
  - Maintenance: Replace paper, clean heating element, remove debris
  - Heat sensitivity of paper

- Impact
  - Print head, ribbon, tractor feed
  - Impact paper
  - Maintenance: Replace ribbon, replace print head, replace paper

- 3-D printer
  - Filament
  - Resin
  - Print bed

This chapter will focus on the exam topics related to PC hardware. It will follow the structure of the CompTIA A+ 220-1101 exam blueprint, objective 3, and it will explore the eight subobjectives that you will need to master before taking the exam.

3.1 Explain basic cable types and their connectors, features, and purposes

You're expected to know the basic concepts of networking as well as the different types of cabling that can be used. For the latter, you should be able to identify connectors and cables from figures even if those figures are crude line art (think shadows) appearing in pop-up boxes. This chapter covers cables and connectors of all types.

Network cables

For this exam you must know the three specific types of network cables (fiber, twisted pair, and coaxial) and the connectors associated with each. Fiber is the most expensive of the three and can run the longest distance. A number of types of connectors can work with fiber, but three you must know are the subscriber connector (SC), straight tip (ST), and Lucent connector (LC).

Twisted-pair is commonly used in office settings to connect workstations to hubs or switches. It comes in two varieties: unshielded (UTP) and shielded (STP). The two types of connectors commonly used are RJ-11 (four wires; popular with telephones) and RJ-45 (eight wires; used with xBaseT networks—100BaseT, 1000BaseT, and so forth). Two common wiring standards are T568A and T568B. Coaxial cabling is not as popular as it once was, but it's still used with cable television and some legacy networks. The two most regularly used connectors are F-connectors (television cabling) and BNC (10Base2, and so on).

Copper

Ethernet is a popular method of networking computers in a local area networks (LANs) using copper cabling. It is used in a variety of scenarios, such as connecting patch panels to switches in the form of patch cables, connecting a wall outlet to a desktop, and connecting infrastructure devices such as routers and switches. In this section we'll look at its various implementations.

Cat 5

Cat 5 transmits data at speeds up to 100 Mbps and was used with Fast Ethernet (operating at 100 Mbps) with a transmission range of 100 meters. It contains four twisted pairs of copper wire to give the most protection. Although it had its share of popularity (it's used primarily for 10/100 Ethernet networking), it is now an outdated standard. Newer implementations use the 5e standard.

Cat 5e

Cat 5e transmits data at speeds up to 1 Gbps (1000 Mbps). Category 5e cabling can be used up to 100 meters, depending on the implementation and standard used and provides a minimum of 100 MHz of bandwidth. It also contains four twisted pairs of copper wire, but they're physically separated and contain more twists per foot than Cat 5 to provide maximum interference protection.

Cat 6

Cat 6 transmits data at speed up to 10 Gbps, has a minimum of 250 MHz of bandwidth, and specifies cable lengths up to 100 meters (using Cat 6a). It contains four twisted pairs of copper wire and is used in 10GBaseT networks. Cat 6 cable typically is made up of four twisted pairs of copper wire, but its capabilities far exceed those of other cable types. Category 6 twisted pairs uses a longitudinal separator, which separates each of the four pairs of wires from each other and reduces the amount of crosstalk possible.

Cat 6a

Cat 6A cable has improved alien crosstalk characteristics, allowing 10GBaseT to be run for the same 100 meter (330′) maximum distance as previous Ethernet variants.

Coaxial

Coaxial cable, or coax, is one of the oldest media used in networks. Coax is built around a center conductor or core that is used to carry data from point to point. The center conductor has an insulator wrapped around it, a shield over the insulator, and a nonconductive sheath around the shielding. This construction, depicted in Figure 3.1, allows the conducting core to be relatively free from outside interference. The shielding also prevents the conducting core from emanating signals externally from the cable.

 Before you read any further, accept the fact that the odds are slim that you will ever need to know about coax for a new installation in the real world (with the possible exception of RG-6, which is used from the wall to a cable modem). That said, you do need to know about coax for this exam.

FIGURE 3.1 Coax

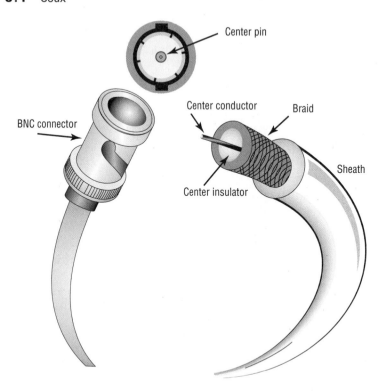

Center pin

Center conductor

Braid

BNC connector

Sheath

Center insulator

Shielded twisted pair

Shielded twisted pair (STP) differs from unshielded twisted pair (UTP) only in the presence of the shielding, which resembles aluminum foil directly beneath the outer insulation. The shielding adds to the cost of the cable and eliminates interference from outside the cable. As a rule of thumb based on current prices, STP is 30 percent more expensive than UTP for the same length of cable.

DIRECT BURIAL

Direct burial cabling (DBC), typically used for coaxial of fiber runs, is cable made to be buried with no outer covering. DBC consists of multiple layers of heavy, metallic-banded sheathing, reinforced by heavy rubber covers and shock-absorbing gel, wrapped in thread-fortified waterproof tape, and stiffened by a heavy metal core. A cross-section of a DBC cable is shown in Figure 3.2.

Unshielded twisted pair

Unshielded twisted pair (UTP) is the most popular twisted-pair cabling in use and should be used in any scenario where external interference is not an issue.

FIGURE 3.2   DBC cable

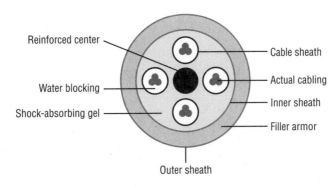

Plenum

Plenum cable is a specific type of cable that is rated for use in plenum spaces—those spaces in a building used for heating and air-conditioning systems. Most cable cannot be used in the plenum because of the danger of fire (or the fumes the cables give off as they burn). While it is more expensive, plenum cable is fire-rated and meets the necessary standards, which makes it acceptable to use in these locations. It replaces PVC with a Teflon-like material.

Optical

Optical transmission of data using either lasers or LEDs offers a secure and speedy way to move traffic. In this section you'll learn about the cables used in optical transmission.

Fiber

Fiber-optic cabling provides excellent speed and bandwidth but is expensive. Not only are the cables that you use costly, but the light-emitting/receiving hardware costs also make this an expensive undertaking.

Because of the cost involved, fiber is often an option for businesses only when it comes to broadband access. Fiber to the Home (FTTH) is an attempt some communities are undertaking to offer high-speed connectivity to residential dwellings as well. Verizon's FiOS, a similar implementation, runs single-mode optical fiber to homes and includes phone and television service along with Internet access.

Fiber-optic cabling has a glass core within a rubber outer coating and uses beams of light rather than electrical signals to relay data (see Figure 3.3). Because light doesn't diminish over distance the way electrical signals do, this cabling can run for distances measured in kilometers with transmission speeds from 1 Gbps up to 100 Gbps or higher.

FIGURE 3.3   Fiber-optic cable

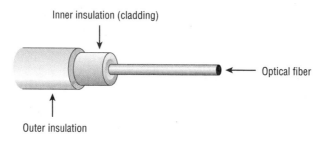

T568A/T568B

Two wiring standards are commonly used with twisted-pair cabling: T568A and T568B (sometimes referred to simply as 568A and 568B). These are telecommunications standards from TIA and EIA that specify the pin arrangements for the RJ-45 connectors on UTP or STP cables. The number 568 refers to the order in which the wires within the Cat 5 cable are terminated and attached to the connector. The signal is identical for both.

T568A was the first standard, released in 1991. Ten years later, in 2001, T568B was released. Figure 3.4 shows the pin number assignments for the 568A and 568B standards. Pin numbers are read left to right, with the connector tab facing down. Notice that the pin-outs stay the same, and the only difference is in the color coding of the wiring.

FIGURE 3.4   Pin assignments for T568A and T568B

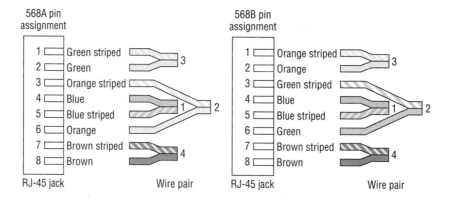

The bottom line here is that if the same standard is used on each end, the cable will be a crossover cable, and if a different standard is used on either end, it will be a straight-through cable. Crossover cables are used to connect like systems such as two computers or two switches or two routers.

 Mixing cable types can cause communication problems on the network. Before installing a network or adding a new component, make sure the cable being used is in the correct wiring standard.

Peripheral cables

The following cable is used specifically for peripherals.

USB 2.0/USB 3.0

USB 1.1 runs at 12 Mbps, and USB 2.0 runs at 480 Mbps.

USB 3.0 has transmission speeds of up to 5 Gbps, significantly reduces the time required for data transmission, reduces power consumption, and is backward-compatible with USB 2.0. Because USB is a serial interface, its width is 1 bit. It is useful to note, however, that a USB 2.0 device will perform at 2.0 speeds even when connected to a 3.0 port.

By utilizing USB hubs in conjunction with the USB ports available on the local machine, you can connect up to 127 of these devices to the computer. You can daisy-chain up to four external USB hubs to a USB port. Daisy chaining means that hubs are attached to each other in a line. A USB hub will not function if it is more than four hubs away from the root port.

Serial

Although an older cable type, a serial connector may be found connecting some peripherals to the serial connection on the system. This cable is shown in Figure 3.5. The maximum speed is 115200 bps.

FIGURE 3.5   Serial cable

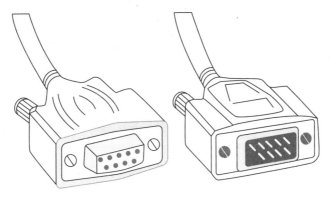

Thunderbolt

Thunderbolt ports are most likely to be found on Apple laptops, but they are now showing up on others as well. Figure 3.6 shows a Thunderbolt port on an HP laptop. Notice the "thunderbolt" icon next to the port. Thunderbolt has a maximum speed of 10 Gbps, Thunderbolt 2 has a maximum speed of 20 Gbps, and Thunderbolt 3 has a maximum speed of 40 Gbps, compared to 800 Mbps for Firewire 800, 5 Gbps for USB 3.0, and 10 Gbps for USB 3.1.

FIGURE 3.6 Thunderbolt port

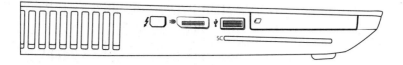

The Thunderbolt cable is shown in Figure 3.7.

FIGURE 3.7 Thunderbolt cable

Video cables

You may require one of a variety of cable types for video or display. In this section, we'll survey the types you may encounter.

High-Definition Multimedia Interface (HDMI)

High-Definition Multimedia Interface (HDMI) connectors are used to connect compatible digital items (DVD players and conference room projectors, for example). The Type A connector has 19 pins and is backward-compatible with DVI (discussed later in this chapter).

Type B connectors have 29 pins and aren't backward compatible with DVI, but they support greater resolutions. Type C connectors are a smaller version of Type A for portable devices. Type D is an even smaller micro version that resembles a micro-USB connector. Type E is planned for use in automotive applications. HDMI has a theoretical cable length limit of 45 feet, or 15 meters. Figure 3.8 shows all HDMI types.

FIGURE 3.8   HDMI connectors

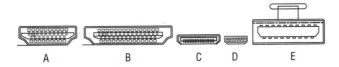

A   B   C   D   E

There are several versions of HDMI, as described in Table 3.1.

TABLE 3.1   HDMI versions

Version	1.0	1.1	1.2	1.3	1.4	2.0
Maximum throughput (Gbps)	3.96	3.96	3.96	10.2	10.2	6
Maximum color depth (bit/px)	24	24	24	48	48	48
Maximum audio throughput (Mbps)	36.86	36.86	36.86	36.86	36.86	49.152

Mini-HDMI

A Mini-HDMI port is used on digital single-lens reflex (DSLR) cameras and standard-sized tablets. It differs only in the physical size of the connector. Both are shown in Figure 3.9.

FIGURE 3.9   Mini and regular HDMI

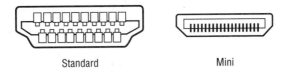

Standard   Mini

DisplayPort

DisplayPort is a digital interface standard produced by the Video Electronics Standards Association (VESA) and is used for audio and video. The interface is primarily used to connect a video source to a display device such as a computer monitor or television set. It resembles a USB connector (see Figure 3.10). Its supports a 1.62, 2.7, 5.4, or 8.1 Gbps data rate per lane; 1, 2, or 4 lanes; (effective total 5.184, 8.64, 17.28, or 25.92 Gbps for 4-lane link); and 1 Mbps or 720 Mbps for the auxiliary channel.

FIGURE 3.10   DisplayPort

Digital Visual Interface (DVI)

There are several types of Digital Video Interface (DVI) pin configurations, but all connectors are D-shaped. The wiring differs based on whether the connector is single-linked or dual-linked (extra pins are used for the dual link). DVI differs from everything else in that it includes both digital and analog signals at the same time, which makes it popular for LCD and plasma TVs. The maximum cable length is 16 feet (5 meters).

DVI connectors can come in several forms, known as DVI-D, DVI-I, and DVI-A. DVI can sometimes do analog and digital at the same time. Figure 3.11 shows the various types of DVI plugs discussed in this section.

FIGURE 3.11   DVI connectors

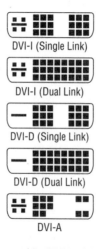

The single link maximum data rate including 8b/10b overhead is 4.95 Gbps at 165 MHz. With the 8b/10b overhead subtracted, the maximum data rate is 3.96 Gbps.

Dual link maximum data rate is twice that of single link. Including 8b/10b overhead, the maximum data rate is 9.90 Gbps at 165 MHz. With the 8b/10b overhead subtracted, the maximum data rate is 7.92 Gbps.

DVI-D

DVI-D (the D stands for digital) connectors supply digital signals only. These can also come in a single- or a dual-link format. A dual-link format allows for a second data link.

DVI-I

A DVI-I connector (the I stands for integrated) has pins that can provide analog and digital. These can also come in a single- or a dual-link format.

DVI-A

A DVI-A connector (the A stands for analog) has pins that can provide analog and digital. This type comes in a single-link format only.

Video Graphics Array (VGA)

This is the traditional connector for the display of a computer, and it is shaped like a D. It has three rows of five pins each, for a total of 15 pins. This is also often called the HD-15 (also known as DB-15) connector. A VGA cable carries analog signals. The cable length utilized will affect the resolution achieved: 1024×768 would operate more effectively with 30 feet or less of cable length. As the need for resolution increases, the allowable maximum cable length decreases. Figure 3.12 shows a VGA port.

FIGURE 3.12   VGA port

Hard drive cables

When drives are connected internally, there are several options, and the options available on your PC will be a function of how old it is and, in the case of SCSI, whether it is a computer designed to operate as a server.

Serial Advanced Technology Attachment (SATA)

Serial AT Attachment (SATA) drives are AT Attachment (ATA) drives that use serial transmission as opposed to parallel. They use a different cable because of this. It is not a ribbon cable but a smaller cable. Both implementations can operate up to 16 GB. Figure 3.13 shows the data cable and its connector.

FIGURE 3.13   Serial ATA data cable and connector

SATA   Internal SATA storage devices have 7-pin data cables and a 15-pin power cable.

eSATA   eSATA cables may be either flat or round and can be only 2 meters (6 feet) in length. An eSATA connector is shown in Figure **3.14**.

FIGURE 3.14   eSATA cable

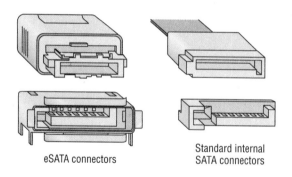

eSATA connectors

Standard internal
SATA connectors

Small Computer System Interface (SCSI)

Small Computer System Interface (SCSI) is most commonly used for hard disks and tape drives, but it can connect a wide range of other devices, including scanners and CD drives. These devices reside on a single bus, which must be terminated on either end. Eight or 16 devices can be attached to a single bus (with number one taken by the host bus controller), depending on whether the SCSI bus is wide (0–15) or narrow (0–7) bus. There also is a host bus controller, which is usually plugged into a slot in the computer or can be integrated into the motherboard. Figure 3.15 shows an internal SCSI connector.

FIGURE 3.15   Internal SCSI connector

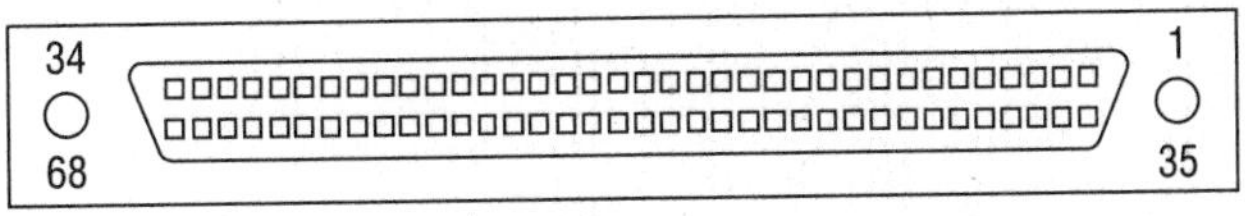

SCSI IDs (0–15)

The devices are identified by a unique SCSI ID. The SCSI ID of a device in a drive enclosure that has a backplane is set either by jumpers or by the slot in the enclosure the device is installed into, depending on the model of the enclosure. In the latter case, each slot on the enclosure's backplane delivers control signals to the drive to select a unique SCSI ID. It is important that all devices have unique IDs. The bootable hard disk should be set with an ID of 0, and the host controller should be set at 7 or 15 in the case of a 16-bit SCSI (it will be the highest number possible based on the SCSI width). Each end of the chain must be terminated.

In some cases, a single SCSI target (as they are called) may contain multiple drives within the unit. In these cases, the drives are differentiated with a second number called a logical unit number (LUN).

External SATA (eSATA)

As introduced and illustrated earlier in the chapter, connections for storage devices can be either SATA or IDE. IDE was the only option early on, and then SATA came on the scene. SATA came out as a standard and was first adopted in desktops and then laptops. Whereas ATA had always been an interface that sends 16 bits at a time, SATA sends only one bit at a time. The benefit is that the cable used can be much smaller, and faster cycling can actually increase performance. SATA uses a seven-wire cable that can be up to 1 meter in length. eSATA cables can be up to 2 meters. Figure 3.13 earlier shows the SATA connector, and Figure 3.14 shows the eSATA connector.

Table 3.2 lists the speeds of the options.

TABLE 3.2   SATA speeds

STANDARD	TRANSFER SPEED
SATA 1.0	150 MBps
SATA 2.0	300 MBps
SATA 3.0	600 MBps
SATA 3.2	1,969 MBps
eSATA	6 GBps

Integrated Drive Electronics (IDE)

Integrated Drive Electronics (IDE) drives are the most common type of hard drive found in computers. But IDE is much more than a hard drive interface; it's also a popular interface for many other drive types, including CD-ROM, DVD, and Zip drives. IDE drives are easy to install and configure, and they provide acceptable performance for most applications. Their ease of use relates to their most identifiable feature—the controller is located on the drive itself. The IDE drive along with its data and power cables is shown in Figure 3.16.

FIGURE 3.16   IDE drive

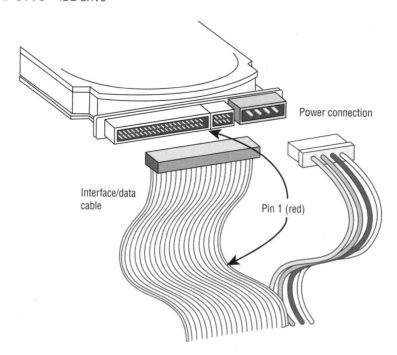

The design of the IDE is simple: build the controller right on the drive and use a relatively short ribbon cable to connect the drive/controller to the IDE interface. This offers the benefits of decreasing signal loss (thus increasing reliability) and making the drive easier to install. The IDE interface can be an expansion board, or it can be built into the motherboard, as is the case on almost all systems today.

IDE generically refers to any drive that has a built-in controller. The IDE you know today is more properly called AT IDE; two previous types of IDE (MCA IDE and XT IDE) are obsolete and incompatible with it.

There have been many revisions of the IDE standard over the years, and each one is designated with a certain AT attachment (ATA) number—ATA-1 through ATA-8. Drives that support ATA-2 and higher are generically referred to as enhanced IDE (EIDE). Here are some of the highlights: With ATA-3, a technology called ATA Packet Interface (ATAPI) was introduced to help deal with IDE devices other than hard disks. ATAPI enables the BIOS to recognize an IDE CD-ROM drive, for example, or a tape backup or Zip drive. Starting with ATA-4, a new technology was introduced called UltraDMA, supporting transfer modes of up to 33 Mbps. ATA-5 supports UltraDMA/66, with transfer modes of up to 66 Mbps. To achieve this high rate, the drive must have a special 80-wire ribbon cable. The drive in Figure 3.16 shows the 40-pin cable, and the motherboard or IDE controller card must support ATA-5. ATA-6 supports UltraDMA/100, with transfer modes of up to 100 Mbps.

 If an ATA-5 or ATA-6 drive is used with a normal 40-wire cable or is used on a system that doesn't support the higher modes, it reverts to the ATA-4 performance level.

ATA-7 supports UltraDMA/133, with transfer modes of up to 150 Mbps and SATA. ATA-8 made only minor revisions to ATA-7 and also supports UltraDMA/133, with transfer modes of up to 600 Mbps and SATA.

Table 3.3 lists the ATA standards and their details.

TABLE 3.3 ATA standards

STANDARD	SPEED	CABLE TYPE	NEW FEATURE
ATA 1	8.3 Mbps	40 wire	Multiword Direct Memory Access (DMA)
ATA 2	16.6 Mbps	40 wire	Programmed Input/Output (PIO) mode
ATA 3	16.6 Mbps	40 wire	ATAPI
ATA 4	33 Mbps	40 or 80 wire	UltraDMA
ATA 5	66 Mbps	40 or 80 wire	UltraDMA 66
ATA 6	100 Mbps	40 or 80 wire	UltraDMA 100
ATA 7	150 Mbps	40 or 80 wire	UltraDMA 133
ATA 8	600 Mbps	40 or 80 wire	Hybrid drive capability

IDE configuration and setup (primary, secondary, cable select)

The primary benefit of IDE is that it's nearly universally supported. Almost every mother-board has IDE connectors.

A typical motherboard has two IDE connectors, and each connector can support up to two drives on the same cable. That means you're limited to four IDE devices per system unless you add an expansion board containing another IDE interface. In contrast, with SCSI (covered in the next section), you can have up to seven drives per interface (or even more on some types of SCSI).

Performance also may suffer when IDE devices share an interface. When you're burning CDs, for example, if the hard drive you are reading from is on the same cable as the CD drive you are writing to, errors may occur. SCSI drives are much more efficient with this type of transfer.

To install an IDE drive, do the following:

1. Set the primary/secondary jumper on the drive.

2. Install the drive in the drive bay.

3. Connect the power-supply cable.

4. Connect the ribbon cable to the drive and to the motherboard or IDE expansion board. Ensure that the primary device is closest to the connection to the motherboard.

5. Configure the drive in BIOS Setup if it isn't automatically detected.

6. Partition and format the drive using the operating system.

Each IDE interface can have only one primary drive on it. If there are two drives on a single cable, one of them must be the secondary drive. This setting is accomplished via a jumper on the drive. Some drives have a separate setting for Single (that is, primary with no secondary) and Primary (that is, primary with a secondary); others use the Primary setting generically to refer to either case. The Cable Select setting will assume you have the primary drive first and secondary drive second on the cable. Figure 3.17 shows a typical primary/secondary jumper scenario, but different drives may have different jumper positions to represent each state. Today, the need for jumper settings has decreased because many drives can autodetect the primary/secondary relationship.

FIGURE 3.17   Primary/secondary jumpers

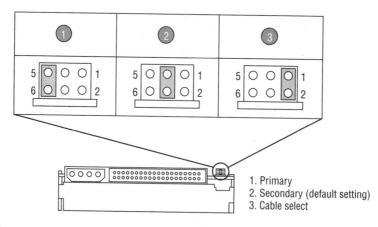

1. Primary
2. Secondary (default setting)
3. Cable select

Most BIOS Setup programs today support plug and play, so they detect the new drive automatically at startup. If this doesn't work, the drive may not be installed correctly, the jumper settings may be wrong, or the BIOS Setup may have the IDE interface set to None rather than Auto. Enter BIOS Setup and find out. All you usually have to do is set the IDE interface to Auto and allow the BIOS to detect the drive.

In BIOS Setup for the drive, you might have the option of selecting a Direct Memory Access (DMA) channel or Programmed Input/Output (PIO) setting for the drive. Both are methods for improving drive performance by allowing the drive to write directly to RAM, bypassing the CPU when possible. For modern drives that support Ultra-Direct Memory Access (UltraDMA), neither of these settings is necessary nor desirable. The Ultra DMA interface is the fastest method used to transfer data through the ATA controller, usually between the computer and an ATA device.

When the drive is installed, you can proceed to partition and format it for the operating system you've chosen. Then, you can install your operating system of choice.

For a Windows 10 system, allow the Windows Setup program to partition and format the drive (when installing the operating system), or use the Disk Management utility in Windows to perform those tasks. To access Disk Management, from the Control Panel choose Administrative Tools and then Computer Management.

Adapters

In many cases, you will need to attach a device to a computer on which the correct connectors are not present. In these cases, there are adapters (converters) and connectors that can be used to connect the device to a connector type for which it was not designed. In this section you'll look at some of the more common of these.

DVI to HDMI

These adapters connect from HDMI to DVI and come in a number of gender combinations (Dom DVI to Sub HDMI, Dom DVI to Dom HDMI, Sub DVI to Dom HDMI, and so on) and as either a cable or simply an inline connector. Figure 3.18 shows an inline connector.

USB to Ethernet

These converters allow you to use a USB port as a network interface. They come both as cables and as inline connectors. Figure 3.19 shows an example of a USB-to-Ethernet adapter.

DVI to VGA

In cases where you need to convert DVI to VGA, you can use a DVI-to-VGA adapter. These come as cable or inline connectors and also come in a variety of gender combinations. Figure 3.20 shows an example of the ends of this adapter.

FIGURE 3.18   HDMI to DVI

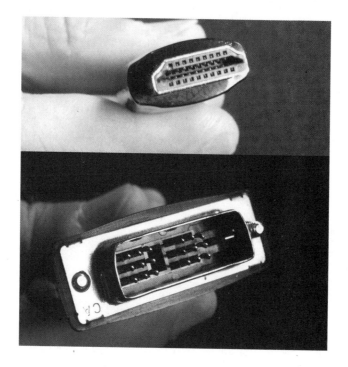

FIGURE 3.19   USB to Ethernet

FIGURE 3.20   DVI to VGA

Connector types

A computer's peripheral ports are the physical connectors outside the computer. Cables of various types are designed to plug into these ports and create a connection between the PC and the external devices that may be attached to it. A successful IT technician should have an in-depth knowledge of ports and cables.

Because the peripheral components need to be upgraded frequently, either to keep pace with technological change or to replace broken devices, a well-rounded familiarity with the ports and their associated cabling is required. In this section you'll learn about connector types.

RJ45

A registered jack (RJ) is a plastic plug with small metal tabs, like a telephone cord plug. Numbering is used in the naming: RJ-11 has two metal tabs, and RJ-14 has four. RJ-45 has eight tabs and is used for Ethernet 10 BaseT/100 BaseT, 1000Base, and 10GBase networking. The maximum cable length is 100 meters but can vary slightly based on the category of cabling used. Figure 3.21 shows RJ-11 (left) and RJ-45 (right) connectors.

FIGURE 3.21   RJ-11 and RJ-45

RJ11

An RJ-11, as described above and shown in Figure 3.21, is a standard connector for a telephone line and is used to connect a computer modem to a phone line. It looks much like an RJ-45 but is noticeably smaller.

F type

The RG-59 connector, also called an F type connector, is used with a coaxial cable and normally used to generate low-power video connections. This cable cannot be used over long distances because of its high-frequency power losses. In such cases, RG-6 cables are used instead.

RG-6 is another connector normally used with coaxial cabling. It is often used for cable TV and cable modems. It can run longer distances than RG-59 and support digital signals.

Straight tip (ST)

A straight tip (ST) is used with fiber cables and are spring loaded, which means they are easily inserted and removed, but you also have to make sure that they are seated properly to ensure that there is no light loss.

Subscriber connector (SC)

Subscriber connector (SC) is a standard-duplex fiber-optic connector with a square molded plastic body and push-pull locking features.

Lucent connector (LC)

The LC connector was first developed by Lucent Technology for TelCo uses. These LC connectors utilize traditional components of the standard connector but with a 1.25 mm ceramic ferrule. All three fiber connector types are shown in Figure 3.22. From top to bottom they are SC, LC, and ST.

FIGURE 3.22   SC, LC, and ST

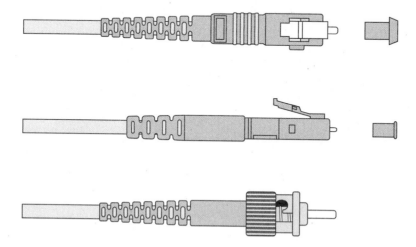

Punchdown block

A punchdown block is a panel owned by the telco where solid copper wires are "punched down" into short, open-ended slots, which are a type of insulation-displacement connector. You learned about the tool used to do this back in Chapter 2, "Networking." Figure 3.23 shows the relationship of the punchdown block to the computers and to the Intermediate Distribution Frame (IDF) in the server room.

FIGURE 3.23   Punchdown block

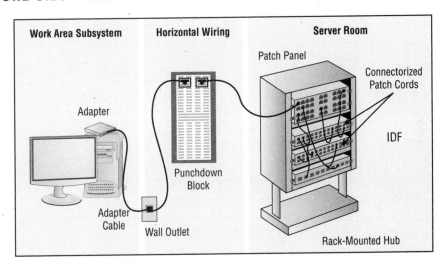

USB

USB connectors come in two types and two form factors, or sizes. The type A connector is what is found on USB hubs, on host controllers (cards that are plugged into slots to provide USB connections), and on the front and back panels of computers. Type B is the type of USB connector found on the end of the cable that plugs into the devices.

MicroUSB/MiniUSB

USB connectors also come in a mini version and a micro version. The micro version is used on mobile devices, such as mobile phones, GPS units, PDAs, and digital cameras, whereas the mini version of the connector is found in applications described in the previous paragraph. The choice between a standard A and B and a mini A and B will be dictated by what is present on the device. The cables used cannot exceed 5 meters in length. Figure 3.24 shows, from left to right, a standard Type A, a mini Type A, a standard Type B, and a mini Type B.

Some manufacturers have chosen to implement a mini-connector that is proprietary, choosing not to follow the standard.

FIGURE 3.24   USB connectors

USB-C

The USB-C connectors connect to both hosts and devices, replacing various USB-B and USB-A connectors and cables with a standard connection. This connector type was discussed and illustrated earlier in Chapter 1, "Mobile Devices."

Molex

Connectors usually used for computer fans are called Molex connectors, and there can be several types. The following are some examples:

- A three-pin Molex connector is used when connecting a fan to the motherboard or other circuit board. Figure 3.25 shows the three-pin Molex.

- A four-pin Molex connector includes an additional pin used for a pulse-width modulation signal to provide variable speed control. These connectors can be plugged into three-pin headers but will lose their fan speed control. Figure 3.26 shows the four-pin Molex connector.

FIGURE 3.25   Three-pin Molex

FIGURE 3.26   Four-pin Molex

Lightning port

The Lightning connector from Apple is an eight-pin connector that, though not standard, has advantages over USB, according to Apple. The following are some of these advantages:

- It can supply more power than USB.
- It can be inserted either way.
- It is physically more durable than USB.
- It can detect and adapt to connected devices.
- It operates at USB 3.0 speeds.

Figure 3.27 shows a Lightning connector next to a USB cable.

FIGURE 3.27   Lightning connector and USB

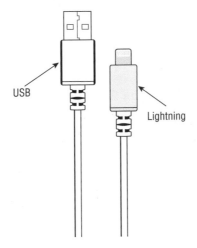

DB9

A DB9 cable is one of several form factors for serial connections. It is shown in Figure 3.28.

FIGURE 3.28   Serial cable

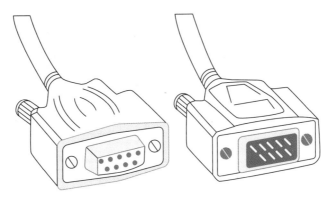

Exam essentials

Identify display connectors, their associated cables, and the maximum cable lengths. This includes but is not limited to DVI in all variants: DisplayPort, RCA, HD-15 (or DB-15), BNC, miniHDMI, and miniDIN-6.

Identify hard drive cables and adapters. These include SATA, eSATA, IDE, and SCSI. It also includes adapters like DVI to HDMI, USB to Ethernet, and DVI to VGA.

3.2 Given a scenario, install the appropriate RAM

RAM slots contain the memory chips. There are many and varied types of memory for PCs today, which I'll outline in this section.

PCs use memory chips arranged on a small circuit board. These circuit boards are called single inline memory modules (SIMMs) or dual inline memory modules (DIMMs). DIMMs utilize connectors on both sides of the board, whereas SIMMS utilize single connectors that are mirrored on both sides. DIMM is 64-bit and SIMM is 32-bit.

RAM types

Physically, RAM is a collection of integrated circuits that store data and program information as patterns of 1s and 0s (on and off states) in the chip. Most memory chips need constant power (also called a constant refresh) to maintain those patterns of 1s and 0s. If power is lost, all those tiny switches revert to the off position, effectively erasing the data from memory. Some memory types, however, don't require a refresh.

Along with chip placement, memory modules also differ in the number of conductors, or pins, that the particular module uses. The number of pins used directly affects the overall size of the memory slot. Slot sizes include 30-pin, 72-pin, 168-pin, and 184-pin. Laptop memory comes in smaller form factors known as small outline DIMMs (SODIMMs).

Figure 3.29 shows the form factors for the most popular memory chips. Notice that they basically look the same but that the memory module sizes are different.

Virtual RAM

Virtual RAM, also called virtual memory, is a location on the hard drive used temporarily for storage when memory space is low. At times when there is insufficient memory for the task at hand, some of the contents of memory are moved (a process called swapping or paging) to the drive to free up memory. This process is shown in Figure 3.30.

FIGURE 3.29 Various memory module form factors

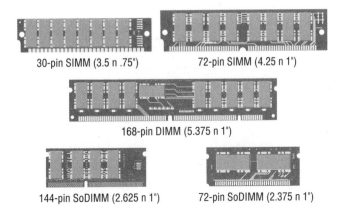

30-pin SIMM (3.5 n .75")   72-pin SIMM (4.25 n 1")

168-pin DIMM (5.375 n 1")

144-pin SoDIMM (2.625 n 1")   72-pin SoDIMM (2.375 n 1")

FIGURE 3.30 Virtual memory

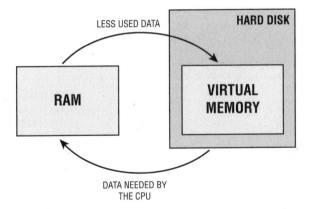

Small outline dual inline memory module (SODIMM)

Portable computers (notebooks and subnotebooks) require smaller sticks of RAM because of their smaller size. One of the two types used is small outline DIMM (SODIMM), which can have 72, 144, or 200 pins, whereas desktops use a full-size DIMM. Figure 3.29 earlier shows the form factors for 72- and 144-pin SODIMMs.

Double Data Rate 3 (DDR3)

Double Data Rate (DDR) is clock-doubled SDRAM. The memory chip can perform reads and writes on both sides of any clock cycle (the up, or start, and the down, or ending), thus doubling the effective memory executions per second. So, if you're using DDR SDRAM with a 100 MHz memory bus, the memory will execute reads and writes at 200 MHz and transfer the data to the processor at 100 MHz. The advantage of DDR over regular SDRAM is increased throughput and thus increased overall system speed.

DDR SDRAM is Double Data Rate 2 (DDR2). This allows for two memory accesses for each rising and falling clock and effectively doubles the speed of DDR. DDR2-667 chips work with speeds at 667 MHz and are also referred to as PC2-5300 modules.

The primary benefit of DDR3 over DDR2 is that DDR3 transfers data at twice the rate of DDR2 (eight times the speed of its internal memory arrays), enabling higher bandwidth or peak data rates. By performing two transfers per cycle of a quadrupled clock, a 64-bit-wide DDR3 module may achieve a transfer rate of up to 64 times the memory clock speed in megabytes per second. In addition, the DDR3 standard permits chip capacities of up to 8 GB.

Double Data Rate 4 (DDR4)

DDR4 SDRAM is an abbreviation for double data rate fourth-generation synchronous dynamic random access memory. DDR4 is not compatible with any earlier type of RAM. The DDR4 standard allows for DIMMs of up to 64 GB in capacity, compared to DDR3's maximum of 8 GB per DIMM. Higher bandwidths are achieved by sending more read/write commands per second. To allow this, the standard divides the DRAM banks into two or four selectable bank groups so that transfers to different bank groups may be done more rapidly. Table 3.4 lists the selected memory standards, speeds, and formats.

TABLE 3.4   Selected memory details

MODULE STANDARD	SPEED	FORMAT
DDR500	4,000 MBps	PC4000
DDR533	4,266 MBps	PC4200
DDR2-667	5,333 MBps	PC2-5300
DDR2-750	6,000 MBps	PC2-6000
DDR2-800	6,400 MBps	PC2-6400
DDR3-800	6,400 MBps	PC3-6400
DDR3-1600	12,800 MBps	PC3-12800
DDR4-1866M	14,933 MBps	PC4-14900
DDR4-2133P	17,066.67 MBps	PC4-17000
DDR4-2400R	19,200 MBps	PC4-19200
DDR4-2666U	21,333 MBps	PC4-21333
DDR4-2933W	23,466 MBps	PC4-23466
DDR4-3200W	25,600 MBps	PC4-25600

Double Data Rate 5 (DDR5)

DDR5 has several improvements over DDR4, among them:

- Reduces memory voltage to 1.1 V, thus reducing power consumption
- Supports a speed of 51.2 GB/s per module and 2 memory channels per module
- A slightly extended addressing range

Error correction code (ECC) RAM

A type of RAM error correction is Error Correction Code (ECC). RAM with ECC can detect and correct errors. As with parity RAM, additional information needs to be stored and more processing needs to be done, making ECC RAM more expensive and a little slower than nonparity and parity RAM. Both ECC and parity memory work in ECC mode. However, ECC memory does not work in plain parity checking mode because the extra bits cannot be individually accessed when ECC memory is used. This type of parity RAM is now obsolete. Most RAM today is non-ECC.

Single-channel/Dual-channel

Utilizing multiple channels between the RAM and the memory controller increases the transfer speed between these two components. Single-channel RAM does not take advantage of this concept, but dual-channel memory does and creates two 64-bit data channels. Do not confuse this with DDR, or double data rate. DDR doubles the rate by accessing the memory module twice per clock cycle.

This strategy requires a motherboard that supports it and two or more memory modules. The modules go in separate color-coded banks, as shown in Figure 3.31.

FIGURE 3.31   Dual-channel memory slots

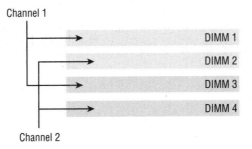

Triple Channel

Triple-channel architecture adds a third memory module and reduces memory latency by interleaving or accessing each module sequentially with smaller bits of data rather than completely filling up one module before accessing the next one. Data is spread among the modules alternatingly, with the potential to triple bandwidth as opposed to storing the data all on one module.

Quad-channel

As you might expect from the name, this type possesses four channels for moving data. The architecture can be used only when all four memory modules (or a multiple of four) are identical in capacity and speed and are placed in quad-channel slots.

Eight modules can be used on motherboards with eight memory sockets, and each group of four modules can have different capacities, but the modules inside the same group must be identical. This arrangement is shown in Figure 3.32.

FIGURE 3.32   Quad channel with eight modules

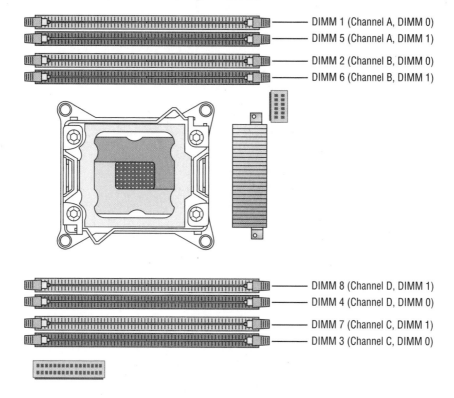

DIMM 1 (Channel A, DIMM 0)
DIMM 5 (Channel A, DIMM 1)
DIMM 2 (Channel B, DIMM 0)
DIMM 6 (Channel B, DIMM 1)

DIMM 8 (Channel D, DIMM 1)
DIMM 4 (Channel D, DIMM 0)
DIMM 7 (Channel C, DIMM 1)
DIMM 3 (Channel C, DIMM 0)

Exam essentials

Identify the types of memory.   Types of memory include single data rate (SDRAM) and D double data rate (DDR), DDR2, DDR3, DDR4 and DDR5). These types differ in their data rate. Memory can also differ in packaging. There are SIMMS (single module) and DIMMs (double modules). They also can use either parity or ECC for error checking and can be single, dual, triple channel, or quad channel, with multiple channels widening the path between the memory and the memory controller.

Follow RAM speed and compatibility guidelines.   Faster memory can be added to a PC with slower memory installed, but the system will operate only at the speed of the slowest module present. RAM types cannot be mixed.

3.3 Given a scenario, select and install storage devices

Storage media hold the data being accessed, as well as the files the system needs to operate and the data that needs to be saved. The various types of storage differ in terms of capacity, the access time, and the physical media being used. This section covers the installation and configuration of various storage devices.

Hard drives

Before the development and use of SSDs, magnetic drives were—and are still as of this writing—the main type of hard drive used. The drive itself is a mechanical device that spins a number of disks or platters and uses a magnetic head to read and write data to the surface of the disks. One of the advantages of SSDs (discussed in the next section) is the absence of mechanical parts that can malfunction. Figure 3.33 shows the parts of a magnetic hard drive.

FIGURE 3.33   Magnetic hard drive

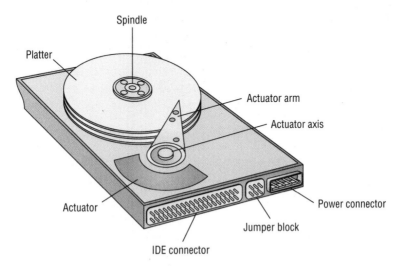

The basic hard disk geometry consists of three components: the number of sectors that each track contains, the number of read/write heads in the disk assembly, and the number of cylinders in the assembly. This set of values is known as CHS (for cylinders/heads/sectors). A *cylinder* is the set of tracks of the same number on all the writable surfaces of the assembly. It is called a cylinder because the collection of all same-number tracks on all writable surfaces of the hard disk assembly looks like a geometric cylinder when connected vertically. Therefore, cylinder 1, for instance, on an assembly that contains three platters consists of six tracks (one on each side of each platter), each labeled track 1 on its respective surface. Figure 3.34 illustrates the key terms presented in this discussion.

FIGURE 3.34   Cylinders, heads, and sections

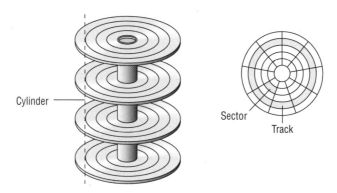

Speeds

The rotational speed of the disk or platter has a direct influence on how quickly the drive can locate any specific disk sector on the drive. This locational delay is called *latency* and is measured in milliseconds (ms). The faster the rotation, the smaller the delay will be. The most common speeds are discussed in the following sections.

5,400rpm

A drive operating at 5,400 rpm will experience about 5.5 ms of this delay.

7,200rpm

Drives that operate at 7,200 rpm will experience about 4.16 ms of latency. A typical 7,200 rpm desktop hard drive has a sustained data transfer rate up to 1,030 Mbps. This rate depends on the track location, so it will be higher for data on the outer tracks and lower toward the inner tracks.

10,000rpm

At 10,000 rpm, the latency will decrease to about 3 ms. Data transfer rates also generally go up with a higher rotational speed but are influenced by the density of the disk (the number of tracks and sectors present in a given area).

15,000rpm

Drives that operate at 15,000 rpm are higher-end drives and suffer only 2 ms of latency. These drives also generate more heat, requiring more cooling to the case. They also offer faster data transfer rates for the same area density.

Form factor/2.5/3.5

Form factor describes the size of the drive enclosure. Magnetic hard drives come in two sizes: 2.5 inch and 3.5 inch. Smaller drives are for laptops, whereas the larger size is for desktop computers.

SSDs

Solid-state drives (SSDs) retain data in nonvolatile memory chips and contain no moving parts. Compared to electromechanical hard disk drives (HDDs), SSDs are typically less susceptible to physical shock, are silent, have lower access time and latency, use less power, but are more expensive per gigabyte.

Communications interfaces

Drives can use various interface types to connect to the system. This sections looks at these communication interface technologies.

Non-volatile Memory Express (NVMe)

NVM Express (NVMe) or Non-Volatile Memory Host Controller Interface Specification (NVMHCIS) is an open logical device interface specification for accessing nonvolatile storage media attached via a PCI Express (PCIe) bus. It allows host hardware and software to fully exploit the levels of parallelism possible in modern SSDs. The latest version is 2.0a.

SATA

Earlier in this chapter you learned about the SATA drive interface. SATA 3, also known as SATA 6 Gbit/s, is the most recent generation of SATA; the full version was released in 2009. SATA 3 communicates at the rate of up to 6 Gbit/s, and its bandwidth throughput is 4.8 Gbit/s (600 MB/s), which doubles that of SATA 2. SATA 3 is backward compatible with both SATA 1 and SATA 2.

Peripheral Component Interconnect Express (PCIe)

PCI Express (PCIE, PCI-E, or PCIe) uses a network of serial interconnects that operate at high speed. It's based on the PCI system; you can convert a PCIe slot to PCI using an adapter plug-in card, but you cannot convert a PCI slot to PCIe. Intended as a replacement for AGP and PCI, PCIe has the capability of being faster than AGP while maintaining the flexibility of PCI. There are five versions of PCIe: Version 1 is up to 8 GBps, version 2 is up to 16 GBps, version 3 is up to 32 GBps, version four is up to 64 GBps, and version five up to 128 GBps. Figure 3.46 shows the slots discussed so far in this section.

Form factors

Solid-state drives come in two form factors, covered in the following sections.

M.2

M.2, formerly known as the Next Generation Form Factor (NGFF), is a specification for internally mounted computer expansion cards and associated connectors. It replaces the mSATA standard. M.2 modules are rectangular, with an edge connector on one side and a semicircular mounting hole at the center of the opposite edge. They can use PCI-Express, Serial ATA, and USB 3 connectors The M.2 standard allows module widths of 12, 16, 22, and 30 mm, and lengths of 16, 26, 30, 38, 42, 60, 80, and 110 mm.

mSATA

This type of SSD has a smaller form factor than SATA SSDs. Apart from having a small form, this drive also features low power consumption. The capacity of mSATA SSD is up to 1TB. M.2 replaces mSATA.

Drive configurations

There are some special configuration scenarios that you should also understand. These forms include a Redundant Array of Independent (or Inexpensive) Disks (RAID). In this section, you'll learn about 4 forms of RAID.

Redundant Array of Independent (or Inexpensive) Disks (RAID) 0, 1, 5, 10

RAID stands for Redundant Array of Independent (or Inexpensive) Disks. It's a way of combining the storage power of more than one hard disk for a special purpose such as increased performance or fault tolerance. RAID is more commonly done with SCSI drives, but it can be done with IDE or SATA drives. This section outlines the most common types of RAID. Because of the methods used to provide fault tolerance, the total amount of usable space in the array will vary, as discussed for each type.

> **RAID 0**   RAID 0 is also known as *disk striping*. This is technically not RAID because it doesn't provide fault tolerance. Data is written across multiple drives, so one drive can be reading or writing while the next drive's read/write head is moving. This makes for faster data access. However, if any one of the drives fails, all content is lost. In RAID 0, since there is no fault tolerance, the usable space in the drive is equal to the total space on all the drives. So if the two drives in an array have 250 GB each of space, 500 GB will be the available drive space. RAID 0 is shown in Figure 3.35.

FIGURE 3.35 RAID 0

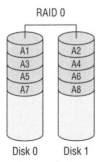

RAID 1   RAID 1 is also known as *disk mirroring*. This is a method of producing fault tolerance by writing all data simultaneously to two separate drives. If one drive fails, the other drive contains all the data and may also be used as a source of the data. However, disk mirroring doesn't help access speed, and the cost is double that of a single drive. Since RAID 1 repeats the data on two drives, only one half of the total drive space is available for data. So if two 250 GB drives are used in the array, 250 GB will be the available drive space. RAID 1 is shown in Figure 3.36.

FIGURE 3.36 RAID 1

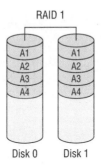

RAID 5   RAID 5 combines the benefits of RAID 0 and RAID 1 and is also known as *striping with parity*. It uses a parity block distributed across all the drives in the array, in addition to striping the data across them. That way, if one drive fails, the parity information can be used to recover what was on the failed drive. A minimum of three drives is required. RAID 5 uses $1/n$ (n = the number of drives in the array) for parity information (for example, one-third of the space in a three-drive array), and only 1 ($1/n$) is available for data. So if three 250 GB drives are used in the array (for a total of 750 GB), 500 GB will be the available drive space. RAID 5 is shown in Figure 3.37.

FIGURE 3.37   RAID 5

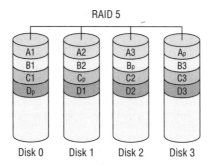

RAID 10   RAID 10 is also known as RAID 1+0. Striped sets are mirrored (a minimum of four drives, and the number of drives must be even). It provides fault tolerance and improved performance but increases complexity. Since this is effectively a mirrored stripe set and a stripe set gets 100 percent use of the drive without mirroring, this array will provide half of the total drive space in the array as available drive space. For example, if there are four 250 GB drives in a RAID 10 array (for a total of 1 TB), the available drive space will be 500 GB. RAID 10 is shown in Figure 3.38.

FIGURE 3.38   RAID 10

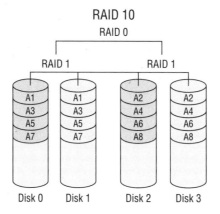

Removable storage

Drives that connect as peripherals are called removable storage. In this section you'll learn about these devices.

Flash drives

Thumb drives are USB flash drives that have become extremely popular for transporting files. Figure 3.39 shows three thumb drives (also known as keychain drives) next to a pack of gum for size comparison.

FIGURE 3.39   USB flash

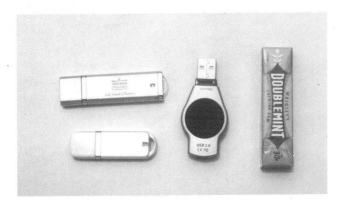

Flash drives (which are solid-state) have been growing in popularity for years and completely replaced floppy disks because of their capacity and small size.

Memory cards

Flash technology is ideally suited for use not only with computers but also with many other things—digital cameras, MP3 players, and so on. The next section discusses various forms of these drives.

SD card

Secure Digital (SD) cards are just one type of flash; there are many others. The maximum capacity of a standard SD card is 512 GB, and there are two other standards that go beyond this: Secure Digital High Capacity (SDHC) can go to 32 GB and Secure Digital Extra Capacity (SDXC) to 2 TB. Figure 3.40 shows a CompactFlash card (the larger of the two) and an SD card along with an eight-in-one card reader/writer. The reader shown connects to the USB port and then interacts with CompactFlash, CompactFlash II, Memory Stick, Memory Stick PRO, SmartMedia, xD-Picture cards, SD, and MultiMediaCards. The SD card specification defines three physical sizes, discussed in the following sections.

FIGURE 3.40 SD and CompactFlash

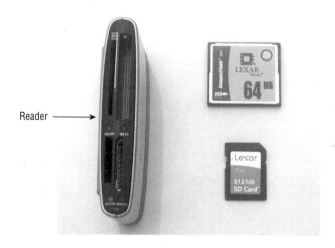

CompactFlash

CompactFlash (CF) cards are a widely used form of solid-state storage. There are two main subdivisions of CF cards: Type I (3.3 mm thick) and the thicker Type II (CF2) cards (5 mm thick). CF cards can be used directly in a PC card slot with a plug adapter, used as an ATA (IDE) or PCMCIA storage device with a passive adapter or with a reader, or attached to other types of ports such as USB or FireWire. Figure 3.40 shows a CF card.

Micro-SD card

Micro-SD is the smallest of the three. It is 11 mm × 15 mm × 1 mm.

Mini-SD card

Mini-SD is the middle child of the three SD form factors shown in Figure 3.41. It is 20 mm × 21.5 mm × 1.4 mm.

xD

xD-Picture card is a flash memory card format, used mainly in older digital cameras. xD stands for Extreme Digital. xD cards are available in capacities from 16 MB up to 2 GB. Pictures are transferred from a digital camera's xD card to a PC by plugging the camera into the USB or IEEE 1394 (FireWire) cable or by removing the card from the camera and inserting it into a card reader. Figure 3.42 shows an xD card.

FIGURE 3.41   SD, micro-, and mini-SD

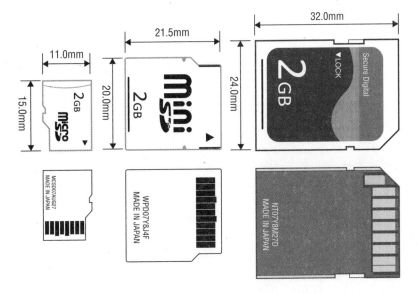

FIGURE 3.42   xD card

Optical drives

Optical drives work by using a laser rather than magnetism to change the characteristics of the storage medium. This is true for CD-ROM drives, DVD drives, and Blu-ray, all of which are discussed in the following sections.

CD-ROM/CD-RW

CD-ROM stands for Compact Disc Read-Only Memory. The CD-ROM media is used for long-term storage of data. CD-ROM media is read-only, meaning that once information is written to a CD, it can't be erased or changed. Access time for CD-ROM drives is considerably slower than for a hard drive. Standard CDs normally hold 650 MB to 700 MB of data and use the ISO 9660 standard, which allows them to be used on multiple platforms.

Compact Disc-ReWritable (CD-RW) media is a rewritable optical disc. A CD-RW drive requires more sensitive laser optics. It can write data to the disc but also has the ability to erase that data and write more data to the disc. It does this by liquefying the layer where the data resides (removing the reflectivity placed there by the writing process used to create the old data) and then creating new reflectivity in the same layer upon writing again that represents the new data. Two states of reflectivity are used to represent the 0s and 1s for the data.

DVD-ROM/DVD-RW/DVD-RW DL

Because DVD-ROM drives use slightly different technology than CD-ROM drives, they can store up to 4.7 GB of data in a single-layer configuration. This makes DVDs a better choice than CDs for distributing large software bundles. Many software packages today are so huge that they require multiple CDs to hold all the installation and reference files. A single DVD, in a double-sided, double-layered configuration, can hold as much as 17 GB (as much as 26 regular CDs).

As you might expect, the primary advantage of DVD-RW drives over DVD-R drives is the ability to erase and rewrite to a DVD-RW disc. In these drives, a layer of metal alloy on the disk is manipulated to erase and write the data, rather than burning into the disc itself, similar to the operation of CD-RW.

A dual-layer DVD-RW disc employs a second physical layer within the disc itself. The drive with dual-layer capability accesses the second layer by shining the laser through the first semitransparent layer.

Blu-ray

Blu-ray recorders have been available since 2003, and they have the ability to record more information than a standard DVD using similar optical technology. In recent years, Blu-ray has been more synonymous with recording television and movie files than data, but the Blu-ray specification (1.0) includes two data formats: BD-R for write-once and BD-RE for rewritable media (more later in this section). BD-J is capable of more sophisticated bonus features than provided by standard DVD, including network access, picture-in-picture, and access to expanded local storage. With the exception of the Internet access component, these features are called Bonus View. The addition of Internet access is called BD Live.

 In the official specification, as noted on the Blu-ray Disc Association website (http://us.blu-raydisc.com), the *r* is lowercase. CompTIA favors the uppercase *R*.

The current capacity of a Blu-ray is 100 GB. As a final note, there was a long-running battle between Blu-ray and HD DVD to be the format of the future, and Blu-ray won.

BD-R

Blu-ray players have two data formats: BD-R for recording computer data and BD-RE for rewritable media. BD-R can be written to only one time.

BD-RE

Blu-ray Disc Recordable Erasable (BD-RE) can be erased and written to multiple times. Disc capacities are 25 GB for single-layer discs, 50 GB for double-layer discs, 100 GB for triple-layer discs, and 128 GB for quad-layer discs.

Exam essentials

Identify and differentiate the optical drive options for the long-term storage of data.   Those options include CD-ROM, DVD-ROM, and Blu-ray. When the ability to erase and rewrite to the disk is required, the options include CD-RW, DVD-RW, dual-layer (DL) DVD-RW, and Blu-ray Disc Recordable Erasable (BD-RE).

Describe the types of interfaces to connect a drive to the system.   Drives can be connected externally using USB, FireWire (IEEE 1394), eSATA, and Ethernet. Internally the connection types are SATA, IDE, and SCSI.

Appreciate the importance of the Primary/Secondary settings for IDE.   Each IDE interface can have only one primary drive on it. If there are two drives on a single cable, one of them must be the secondary drive. This setting is accomplished via a jumper on the drive.

3.4 Given a scenario, install and configure motherboards, central processing units (CPUs), and add-on cards

When working with motherboards, CPUs, and add-on cards, you are working with the basic components of a PC. In this section we'll look at installing and configuring these basic components.

Motherboard form factor

The motherboard is the physical platform through which all the connected components communicate. The motherboard provides basic services needed for the machine to operate and provides communication channels through which connected devices such as the processor, memory, disk drives, and expansion devices communicate.

The figures in this section are representative of what can be expected. Minor variations depend on the motherboard manufacturer. Consult the documentation for your motherboard.

The spine of the computer is the *system board*, or *motherboard*. This component is made of green or brown fiberglass and is placed in the bottom or side of the case. It's the most important component in the computer because it connects all the other components of a PC together. On the system board you'll find the central processing unit (CPU), underlying circuitry, expansion slots, video components, RAM slots, and a variety of other chips. There are a number of different sizes or *form factors* of motherboards, which will be discussed in this section.

Advanced Technology eXtended (ATX)

An older but still used form factor, Advanced Technology Extended (ATX), provided many design improvements over the previous version, the AT. These improvements include I/O ports built directly into the side of the motherboard, the CPU positioned so that the power-supply fan helps cool it, and the ability for the PC to be turned on and off via software. It can use a PS/2-style connector for the keyboard and mouse, but that is rarely used today because USB keyboards are used. Newer ATX models have removed PS/2 connectors. The expansion slots are parallel to the narrow edge of the board. See Figure 3.43.

FIGURE 3.43 An ATX-style motherboard

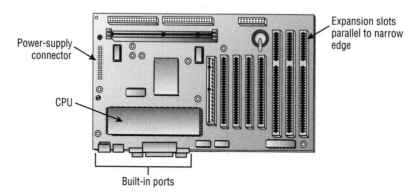

mATX

The mini-ATX has dimensions of 15 cm × 15 cm (5.9 in × 5.9 in) and is slightly smaller than the mini-ITX (discussed in the next section). It was originally part of the ATX specification but was removed after the introduction of micro-ATX. It uses less power, generates less heat, and fits into a single DIN space.

Information Technology eXtended (ITX)

The Information Technology Extended (ITX) motherboards—the mini-ITX, nano-ITX, and pico-ITX—were proposed by VIA Technologies. The mini-ITX fits in the same case as the micro-ATX; uses low power, which means it can be passively cooled (no fan); and has one expansion slot. The nano-ITX is even smaller; it is used for set-top boxes, media centers, and car computers. The pico-ITX is even smaller again, half the size of the nano-ITX. It uses daughter cards (extensions of the motherboard) to supply additional functionality.

Figure 3.44 compares common motherboard types and their sizes.

FIGURE 3.44 Motherboard sizes

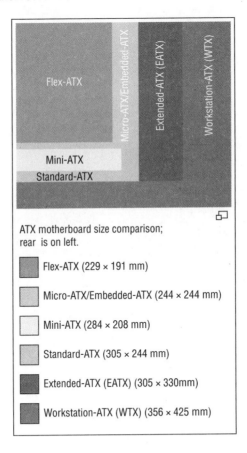

mITX

Mini-ITX is a 17 cm × 17 cm (6.7 in × 6.7 in) motherboard. It is commonly used in small-configured computer systems.

Motherboard connector types

Expansion slots exist on a motherboard to allow for the addition of new interfaces to new technologies without replacing the motherboard. If expansion slots did not exist, you would have to buy a new motherboard every time you wanted to add a new device that uses an interface to the board that does not currently exist on the board. This section reviews various types of expansion slots as well as connecters on the board for components such as drives, and panel lights.

Peripheral Component Interconnect (PCI)

The Peripheral Component Interconnect (PCI) bus is a fast (33 MHz), wide (32-bit or 64-bit) expansion bus that was a modern standard in motherboards for general-purpose expansion devices. Its slots are typically white. PCI devices can share interrupt requests (IRQs) and other system resources with one another in some cases. You may see two PCI slots, but most motherboards have gone to newer standards. Figure 3.45 shows some PCI slots.

FIGURE 3.45   PCI bus connectors

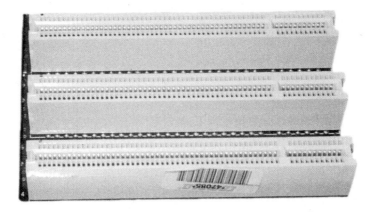

PCI cards that are 32-bit with 33 MHz operate up to 133 MBps, whereas 32-bit cards with 64 MHz operate up to 264 MBps. PCI cards that are 64-bit with 33 MHz operate up to 266 MBps, whereas 64-bit cards with 66 MHz operate up to 538 MBps.

PCI Express (PCIe)

PCI Express (PCIE, PCI-E, or PCIe) uses a network of serial interconnects that operate at high speed. It's based on the PCI system; you can convert a PCIe slot to PCI using an adapter plug-in card, but you cannot convert a PCI slot to PCIe. Intended as a replacement for AGP and PCI, PCIe has the capability of being faster than AGP while maintaining the flexibility of PCI. There are five versions of PCIe: Version 1 is up to 8 GBps, version 2 is up to 16 GBps, version 3 is up to 32 GBps, version 4 is up to 64 GBps, and version 5 is up to 128 GBps. Figure 3.46 shows the slots discussed so far in this section.

FIGURE 3.46 PCI slots

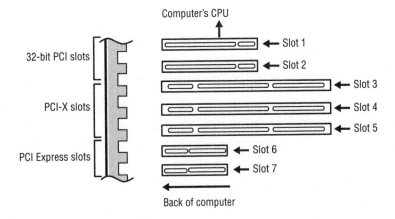

miniPCI

Laptops and other portable devices utilize an expansion card called the miniPCI. It has the same functionality as the PCI but has a much smaller form factor. Unlike portable PCM-CIA cards, which are inserted externally into a slot, these are installed inside the case. Figure 3.47 shows a miniPCI card alongside a miniPCI Express card. Table 3.5 lists the specifications of all the slot types discussed in this section.

TABLE 3.5 Slot types and speeds

TYPE	SPEEDS
PCI 33 MHz 32-bit	133 MBps
PCI 33 MHz 64-bit	266 MBps
PCI 66 MHz 32-bit	264 MBps
PCI 66 MHz 64-bit	538 MBps
PCI-X version 1	1.06 GBps
PCI-X version 2	4.26 GBps

FIGURE 3.47 miniPCI

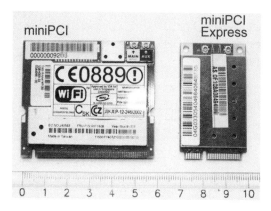

Power connectors

Various components in the case must receive power from the power supply. While you'll learn about power supplies later in this chapter, in this section you'll learn about the cables that run from the power supply to each component.

SATA

The SATA power connector has 15 pins, with 3 pins designated for 3.3V, 5V, and 12V and with each pin carrying 1.5 amps. This results in a total draw of 4.95 watts + 7.5 watts + 18 watts, or about 30 watts. Figure 3.48 shows the SATA power connector.

FIGURE 3.48 SATA power connector

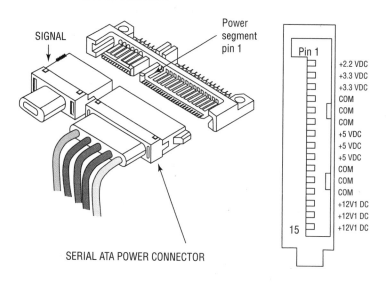

Molex

A Molex connector is used to provide power to drives of various types. It has four pins, two of which have power (one 12V and the other 5V). These are standard for IDE (PATA) or older SCSI drives. The total power demands are from 5 to 15 watts for IDE and 10 to 40 watts for SCSI. The four-pin Molex connector was shown in Figure 3.26 earlier.

Four/eight-pin 12V

With the introduction of the Pentium 4, motherboards began to require more power. Supplemental power connections were provided to the motherboard in 4-, 6- (discussed later in this section), or 8-pin formats. These were in addition to the 20-pin connector (also discussed later) that was already provided.

There is a four-pin square mini version of the ATX connector, which supplies two pins with 12V, and an eight-pin version (two rows) that has four 12V leads. These connect to other items, such as the processor, or to other components, such as a network card that may need power that exceeds what can be provided with the ATX connection to the board. Figure 3.49 shows the eight-pin version and the four-pin square mini version.

FIGURE 3.49 Eight-pin and four-pin 12V

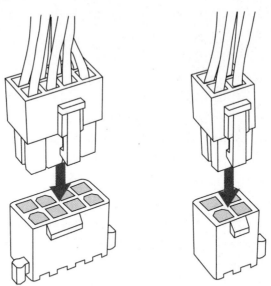

PCIe six/eight-pin

PCIe slots also draw more power and require power in addition to the main 20-pin connector (discussed next). These additional connectors can be six pins and may also contain an additional two-pin connector on the side for cases where the connection required is eight-pin.

20-pin

The main ATX connector, referenced earlier, is a 20-pin connector. The four pins carrying power are 3.3V, 3.3V, 5V, and 5V. This allows the motherboard to pull about 20 to 30 watts. Figure 3.50 shows the 20-pin ATX.

FIGURE 3.50   20-pin ATX

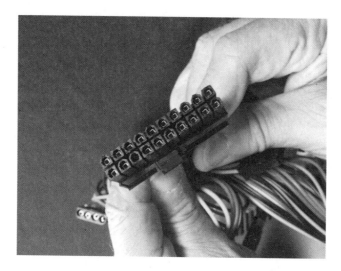

24-pin

The 24-pin ATX connector is simply the 20-pin connector discussed earlier along with the extra 4-pin connector on the side. This provides the four pins carrying power as discussed earlier plus an additional four pins with 5V standby, 12V, 12V, and 3.3. Figure 3.51 shows the 24-pin ATX.

FIGURE 3.51   24-pin ATX

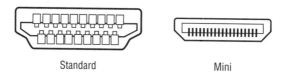

Standard   Mini

eSATA

eSATA provides a form of SATA meant for external connectivity. SATA (discussed more completely earlier in the section "eSATA") is used for drive connections internally on many PCs. eSATA uses a more robust connector, longer shielded cables, and stricter (but backward-compatible) electrical standards. The interface resembles that of USB and IEEE

1394 (FireWire), but the cable cannot be as long, and the cable does not supply power to the device. The advantage it has over the other technologies is speed—it is approximately three times as fast as either FireWire or USB 2.0 (although USB 3.0 is faster).

SAN

You learned about storage area networks (SANs) in Chapter 2. When a server is connected to SAN, a cable connects to a host adapter through a host bus adapter. The connections for the fiber cables can be seen on the end of the card shown in Figure 3.52.

FIGURE 3.52   SAN HBA

Wikipedia Commons

Headers

Headers is simply another name for the contention or plugs found on a motherboard. So a USB connector might be also be called a USB header and a fan power connector might also be called a fan header.

M.2

You learned about the M.2 form factor for drives earlier in this chapter. They can interface to the motherboard using either SATA, PCI, or PCIe slots.

Motherboard compatibility

When adding or replacing components on a motherboard, you must ensure that the components are compatible with the board. In some cases, the slot will make it obvious, but in other scenarios you may need to consult documentation. In this section you'll learn about components where compatibility is a key issue.

CPU sockets

Processors must be compatible with the sockets in which you install them. Let's take a closer look at sockets, compatibility, and the two major CPU types.

The CPU slot permits the attachment of the CPU to the motherboard, allowing the CPU to use the other components of the system. There are many different types of processors, meaning there are many types of CPU connectors.

The CPU slot can take on several different forms. In the past, the CPU slot was a rectangular box called a pin grid array (PGA) socket, with many small holes to accommodate the pins on the bottom of the chip. With the release of new and more powerful chips, additional holes were added, changing the configuration of the slot and its designator or number. Figure 3.53 shows a typical PGA-type CPU socket.

FIGURE 3.53   A PGA CPU socket

With the release of the Pentium II, the architecture of the slot went from a rectangle to more of an expansion-slot style of interface called a *single-edge contact cartridge* (SECC). This style of CPU slot includes Slot 1 and Slot 2 for Intel CPUs and Slot A for Athlon (AMD)

CPUs. This type of slot looks much like an expansion slot, but it's located in a different place on the motherboard from the other expansion slots. Figure 3.54 shows an SECC.

FIGURE 3.54   SECC

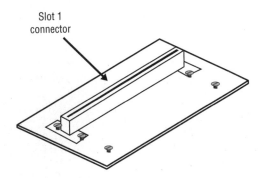

Slot 1
connector

To see which socket type is used for which processors, examine Table 3.6. This list is not exhaustive. Some of the slots may fit processors that are not specifically listed.

Sockets are the interface with which CPUs are plugged into the motherboard. These sockets have evolved over the years along with the changes in CPU architecture and design. There are three form factors for CPU chips: pin grid array (PGA), single-edge contact cartridge (SECC), and land grid array (LGA). The PGA style is a flat square or rectangular ceramic chip with an array of pins in the bottom. The actual CPU is a silicon wafer embedded inside that ceramic chip. The SECC style is a circuit board with the silicon wafer mounted on it. The circuit board is then surrounded by a plastic cartridge for protection; the circuit board sticks out of the cartridge along one edge. This edge fits into a slot in the motherboard.

Advanced Micro Devices, Inc. (AMD)

Advanced Micro Devices (AMD) is one of two major processor vendors in the world. Athlon models are AMD processors. See Table 3.6 for models and socket compatibility.

TABLE 3.6   Socket types and the processors they support

CONNECTOR TYPE	PROCESSOR
Socket 1	486 SX/SX2, 486 DX/DX2, 486 DX4 Overdrive
Socket 2	486 SX/SX2, 486 DX/DX2, 486 DX4 Overdrive, 486 Pentium Overdrive
Socket 3	486 SX/SX2, 486 DX/DX2, 486 DX4 486 Pentium Overdrive
Socket 4	Pentium 60/66, Pentium 60/66 Overdrive

(continues)

TABLE 3.6 Socket types and the processors they support *(continued)*

CONNECTOR TYPE	PROCESSOR
Socket 5	Pentium 75-133, Pentium 75+ Overdrive
Socket 6	DX4, 486 Pentium Overdrive
Socket 7	Pentium 75-200, Pentium 75+ Overdrive
Socket 8	Pentium Pro
Socket 370	Pentium III
Socket 423	Pentium 4
Socket 478	Pentium 4 and Celeron 4
SECC (Type I), Slot 1	Pentium II
SECC2 (Type II), Slot 2	Pentium III
Slot A	Athlon
Socket 603	Xeon
Socket 754	AMD Athlon 64
Socket 939	Some versions of Athlon 64
Socket 940	Some versions of Athlon 64 and Opteron
Socket LGA 775	Core 2 Duo/Quad
Socket AM2	Athlon 64 family (replacing earlier socket usage)
Socket F	Opteron
Socket AM2+	AMD Athlon64, X2, Phenom, and Phenom II
Socket P	Intel Core2
Socket 441	Intel Atom
Socket LGA 1366/B	Intel Core i7, Xeon (35xx, 36xx, 55xx, 56xx series)
G1/G2/rPGA 988A/B	Intel Core i7, i5, i3, P6000, P4000

CONNECTOR TYPE	PROCESSOR
Socket AM3	AMD Phenom, Athlon II, Sempron
Socket H/LGA 1156	Intel Core i7, i5, Xeon, Pentium G5000, G1000
Socket G34	AMD Opteron 6000 series
Socket C32	AMD Opteron 4000 series
LGA 1150	Intel Haswell, Haswell Refresh, and Broadwell
Socket AM3+	AMD FX Vishera, AMD FX Zambezi, AMD Phenom II, AMD Athlon II, AMD Sempron
Socket FM2	AMD Trinity Processors
Socket FM2+	AMD Kaveri
LGA 1248	Intel Titanium 9300 series
LGA 1567	Intel Xeon 6500/7500 series
Socket H2/LGA 1155	Intel Sandy Bridge-DT
Socket R/LGA 2011	Intel Sandy Bridge B2 (also referred to as Xeon E5)
Socket FM1	AMD Llano (also referred to as A-series)

Intel

The market leader in chip manufacturing is Intel Corporation, with Advanced Micro Devices (AMD) gaining a market share in the home PC market. Here's a quick list of socket types from both manufacturers you may encounter:

Intel: LGA 775, 1155, 1156, 1366, 1150, 2011   Earlier in this chapter, Table 3.7 lists the various Intel CPU slots and sockets you may find in a motherboard and explains which CPUs will fit into them.

AMD: AM3, AM3+, FM1, FM2, FM2+   Table 3.7 also lists the various AMD CPU slots and sockets you may find in a motherboard and which CPUs will fit into them. These later-generation AMD sockets were launched as the successor to Socket AM2+. In 2009, AMD3 was released alongside the initial grouping of Phenom II processors designed for it. The principal change from AM2+ to AM3 is support for DDR3 SDRAM. The AM3+ socket has been designed for the AMD FX series Zambezi processors based on the Bulldozer architecture. Socket FM2 is a CPU socket launched in September 2012. Motherboards using the FM2 utilize AMD's new A85X chipset. The FM2+ uses three PCI Express cores: one 2×16 core and two 5×8 cores, for a total of 64 lanes.

Server

Boards for servers will typically be capable of hosting more powerful processers and in some cases multiple processors. In the next section you'll learn about multisocket boards, which are required to host multiple processors.

Multisocket

CPUs can have a single core, or they can be dual-core, quad-core, or even dual-quad-core (eight CPUs total). When multiple cores exist, they operate as individual processors, so the more the better. The largest boost in performance will likely be noticed in improved response time while running CPU-intensive processes, such as virus scans, ripping/burning media (requiring file conversion), or file searching.

The addition of more cores does not have a linear effect on performance. The potential impact of multiple cores also depends on the amount of cache or memory present to serve the CPU. When a computer is designed for the processor, this will have been taken into consideration, but when adding a multicore processor to a PC, it is an issue to consider.

Dual-Core Processors

Dual-core processors, available from Intel as well as AMD, essentially combine two processors into one chip. Instead of adding two processors to a machine (making it a multiprocessor system), you have one chip splitting operations and essentially performing as if it is two processors in order to get better performance. A *multicore* architecture simply has multiple, completely separate processor dies in the same package, whether it's dual core, triple core, or quad core. The operating system and applications see multicore processors in the same way that they see multiple processors in separate sockets. Both dual-core and quad-core processors are common cases for the multicore technology. Most multicore processors from Intel come in even numbers, whereas AMD's Phenom series can contain odd numbers (such as the triple-core processor).

Desktop

While server motherboards have a variety of connector and slot types, a desktop board will typically be much less capable. Of course, all the basic connectors for power and data will be there, but the choice of internal and external card slots headers may be limited. When this is the case, you can make use of external devices that connect through USB.

Mobile

Motherboards in mobile devices are proprietary in nature. There is typically no way to connect anything internally to this board. Therefore, you will be limited to the external connection that appears on the side or edge of the device.

Basic Input/Output System (BIOS)/Unified Extensible Firmware Interface (UEFI) settings

PCs and other devices that use an operating system usually also contain firmware that provides low-level instructions to the device even in the absence of an operating system. This firmware, called either the Basic Input/Output System (BIOS) or the Unified Extensible Firmware Interface (UEFI), contains settings that can be manipulated as well as diagnostic utilities that can be used to monitor the device. This section discusses those settings and utilities.

Boot options

Each system has a default boot order, which is the order in which it checks the drives for a valid operating system to which it can boot. Usually, this order is set for the hard disk and then CD-ROM, but these components can be placed in any boot order. For example, you might set CD-ROM first to boot from a disk that already contains an operating system. If you receive an error message when booting, always check the CD-ROM, and if a nonsystem disk is present, remove it and reboot.

USB permissions

One of the more difficult security measures to enforce is a restriction of use of USB devices. While the reason for this is clear—prevention of the introduction of malware to the network—users don't have a good track record for complying. One step you can take is to disable the USB ports in the BIOS. As you can see in Figure 3.55 it's simply a matter of disabling them in the settings.

FIGURE 3.55 Disabling USB ports

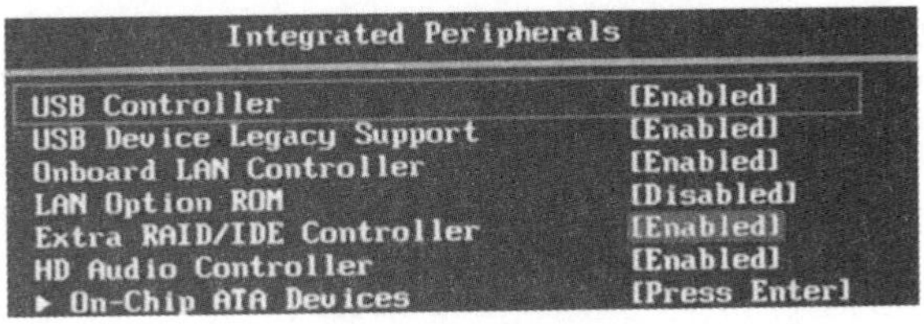

Trusted Platform Module (TPM) security features

Many operating systems provide the ability to encrypt an entire volume or drive, protecting a mobile device's data in the event of theft. A good example of this is BitLocker, which is available in Windows 10. The drives are encrypted with encryption keys, and the proper keys are required to boot the device and access the data.

BitLocker can be used with a TPM chip (discussed in the next paragraph), but it is not required. When this feature is in effect with no TPM chip, the keys are stored on a USB drive that must be presented during startup to allow access to the drives. Without the USB drive holding the key, the device will not boot.

TPM Chips

When the device has a TPM chip present on the motherboard, additional security and options become available. First the chip contains the keys that unlock the drives. When the computer boots, the TPM chip unlocks the drive only after it compares hashes of the drive to snapshots of the drive taken earlier. If any changes have been made or tampering has been done to the Windows installation, the TPM chip will not unlock the drives.

Moreover, you can (and should) combine this with a PIN entered at startup or a key located in a USB drive. In this scenario, the computer will not start unless the hashes pass the test and the PIN or key is provided.

Fan considerations

As you will learn later in this book, overheating causes significant issues with many of the components inside the box, especially the CPU. The BIOS has settings that impact the fan operations. Some BIOS menus allow you to specify the speed or percentage at which the fan operates. In some cases, you may be able to specify at what temperature different fan speeds or power percentages activate. You may find that by altering the fan settings, you suffer fewer overheating issues.

Secure Boot

Secure Boot is a standard adopted by many vendors that requires the operating system to check the integrity of all system files before allowing the boot process to proceed. By doing so, it protects against the alteration or corruption of these system files. As with any emerging technology, issues have already been discovered that can enable a hacker to not only bypass Secure Boot but to also change a key value in the settings that will "brick" the device (render it useless).

Boot password

While you can set a boot password when using a TPM chip (as explained earlier) in most CMOS setup programs, you can also set a supervisor password. Doing so requires a password to be entered in order to use the CMOS setup program, effectively locking out users from making changes to it. You may also be able to set a user password, which restricts the PC from booting unless the password is entered.

To reset a forgotten password, you can remove the CMOS battery to reset everything. There also may be a reset jumper on the motherboard. The CMOS battery is shown in Figure 3.56.

FIGURE 3.56   CMOS battery

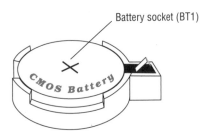

Battery socket (BT1)

Encryption

A number of security features are built into most BIOSs. As you've learned, these features include drive encryption. In this section you'll learn about performing encryption without placing an additional strain on the system CPU.

TPM

TPM chips and their use are covered earlier in this chapter.

Hardware security module (HSM)

A hardware security module (HSM) is an appliance that safeguards and manages digital keys used with strong authentication and provides cryptoprocessing. It attaches directly to a computer or server. Among the functions of an HSM are:

- Onboard secure cryptographic key generation
- Onboard secure cryptographic key storage and management
- Use of cryptographic and sensitive data material
- Offloading of application servers for complete asymmetric and symmetric cryptography

There are some drawbacks to an HSM, including the following:

- High cost
- Lack of a standard for the strength of the number generator
- Difficulty in upgrading

CPU architecture

Computer architecture describes the set of rules and methods and physical structures used in the CPU. There have been many different architectures over the years. In this section you'll learn about them.

x64/x86

CPUs can be either 32 bit or 64 bit. This value describes what is called the *word size* of the processor. Having 64 bits offers two important benefits. Data can be processed in larger chunks, which also means with greater precision. Moreover, the system can point to or address a larger number of locations in physical memory. A key consideration is the operating system. If the operating system is not 64 bit, you cannot take advantage of the 64-bit processor.

Advanced RISC Machine (ARM)

The Advanced RISC Machine (ARM) architecture uses a reduced set of CPU instructions and will only run an operating system designed to support it. They come on both 32-bit and 64-bit versions.

Single-core/Multicore

You learned about single and multi-core processors earlier in this chapter.

Multithreading

Work done by the CPU for a component or application is called a *process*, and these processes are subdivided into *threads* of work. Multithreading is the ability of the CPU to perform work on multiple threads at a time. One of the improvements offered since the Pentium 4 is hyperthreading technology. This feature enables the computer to multitask more efficiently between CPU-demanding applications. An advantage of hyperthreading is improved support for multithreaded code, allowing multiple threads to run simultaneously and thus improving reaction and response time.

Virtualization support

When using virtualization technology, a fuller realization of its benefits can be achieved when the processor supports this concept. The benefit derived from this support is to allow the virtualization product (also called a hypervisor) to use hardware-assisted virtualization. This allows the hypervisor to dynamically allocate CPU to the virtual machines (VMs) as required. Both AMD and Intel offer CPUs that support hardware virtualization.

Expansion cards

Expansion cards allow you to add functionality to the PC. In this section, I'll discuss the types of cards and the functionality they provide. I'll also talk about installing them and configuring them properly.

Newer cards will install in the PCI or PCIe slots and will probably be detected by the operating system. If the operating system already contains the driver for the device in its preinstalled driver library, the process will be done as soon as you restart the PC. If it is not present in the driver cache, you will have to install the driver that came with it.

Sound card

Most computers these days come with an integrated sound card, but for more robust sound or advanced features, you may need to install a sound card. Sound cards can be either internal or external. Internal cards require opening the case and installing the card in a slot. External cards plug into the USB socket.

In some cases, an audio cable will be connected from the card to the CD-ROM. This is rarely required these days. Figure 3.57 shows the connectors present on most sound cards today.

FIGURE 3.57   Sound card connectors

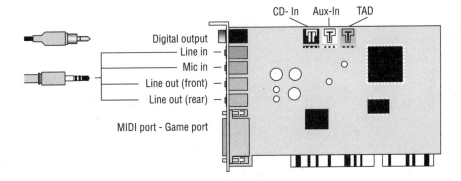

Video card

PCs today also contain internal video cards, but as with sound cards, you can achieve better video quality with more expensive video cards. This is especially true when the video card has its own dedicated memory.

Onboard

In earlier times, most internal cards were vastly inferior to the cards you could buy, but that is much less the case today when users have learned to expect better video quality.

Newer operating systems, like Windows 10, have helped raise the bar for internal cards as well in that they require a card with a minimum set of features and a minimum amount of dedicated RAM to appreciate the visual capabilities of the operating system.

 If you decide to install an add-on card in a system that has an onboard card, the technician will need to disable the onboard card (using the UEFI).

Add-on card

Video cards can be installed in the AGP, PCI, and PCIe slots. At one point, the best choice was clear, and that was the AGP slot. However, the newer PCIe slots provide more bandwidth. AGP provides a wider data path because it's parallel, whereas PCIe is serial. But PCIe now goes up to 16,000 MBps as compared to AGP, which is 2,000 MBps. Figure 3.58 shows the AGP slot next to some slots you have already learned about.

FIGURE 3.58   AGP and PCI slots

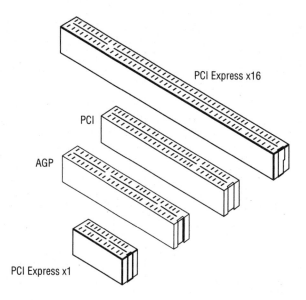

Some of the special functions you may get with a more expensive video card are 3D imaging, MPEG decoding (decoding simply means it can interpret this file type), and TV output. The ability to use multiple monitors is also built into many cards.

Capture card

Many video- and audio-editing software packages come with a special capture card that works in concert with the accompanying software to provide ease of use. For example, it might be an internal PCI card that captures video from any analog or DV source. You can also output video to a VCR or an analog or DV camcorder from this card. They require a high-end audio and video card as well and plenty of memory and a processor that may not have quite the requirements of CAD/CAM but still should be 2.4 GHz or higher.

NIC

Network cards do exactly what you would think; they provide a connection for the PC to a network. In general, network interface cards (NICs) are added to a PC via an expansion slot or they are integrated into the motherboard, but they may also be added through a USB or PCMCIA slot (also known as PC card). The most common issue that prevents network connectivity is a bad or unplugged patch cable.

Network cards are made for Ethernet, fiber-optic, token ring (rarely used now), and 802.11 (wireless) connections. The Ethernet, token ring, and fiber-optic cards accept the appropriate cable, and the wireless cards have radio transmitters and antennas.

The most obvious difference between network cards is the speed of which they are capable. Most networks today operate at 100 MBps or 1 GBps. Regardless of other components, the PC will operate at the speed of the slowest component, so if the card is capable of 1 GBps but the cable is capable of only 100 MBps, the PC will transmit only at 100 MBps.

Another significant feature to be aware of is the card's ability to perform autosensing. This feature allows the card to sense whether the connection is capable of full duplex and to operate in that manner with no action required.

There is another type of autosensing, in which the card is capable of detecting what type of device is on the other end and changing the use of the wire pairs accordingly. For example, normally a PC connected to another PC requires a crossover cable, but if both ends can perform this sensing, that is not required. These types of cards are called auto-MDIX.

Cooling

CPUs produce heat, and the more powerful the CPU, the more heat it produces. Heat is an enemy to the PC in general because it causes problems such as random reboots. Methods of cooling the CPU and in turn the overall interior of the case have evolved with the increasing need to remove this heat. This section covers options that are used.

Among methods of cooling, technology that transfers heat away from components uses thermoelectric cooling, and components that perform this function are called Peltier components. Heat sinks, cooling fans, and cooling fins are Peltier components. Liquid cooling, on the other hand, cools not by transferring heat away from components but by circulating a cool liquid around them.

Fans

Active heat sinks have a fan that sits atop the heat sink. It pulls the heat out of the heat sink and away from it. Then the case fan shunts the heat out the back or side of the case.

Heat sink

The cooling can be either active or passive. A *passive heat sink* is a block of heat-conductive material that sits close to the CPU and wicks away the heat into the air. An *active heat sink* contains a fan that pulls the hot air away from the CPU. The heat sink sits atop the CPU, in many cases obscuring it from view entirely.

Thermal paste/pads

Most *passive heat sinks* are attached to the CPU using a glue-like thermal compound (called *thermal glue*, *thermal compound*, or *thermal paste*). This makes the connection between the heat sink and the CPU more seamless and direct. Thermal compound can be used on active heat sinks, too, but generally it isn't because of the possibility that the fan may stop working and need to be replaced. Thermal compound improves thermal transfer by eliminating tiny air pockets between the heat sink and CPU (or other device like a north bridge or video chipset). Thermal compound provides both improved thermal transfer and adds bonding for heat sinks when there are no mounting holes to clamp the heat sink to the device to be cooled.

Liquid

Liquid-based cooling cases are available that use circulating water rather than fans to keep components cool. These cases are typically more expensive than standard ones and may be more difficult for a technician untrained in this technology to work on, but they result in an almost completely silent system.

Issues with liquid-based cooling machines can include problems with hoses or fittings, the pump, or the coolant. A failure of the pump can keep the liquid from flowing and cause the system to overheat. A liquid-based cooling system should also be checked every so often for leaks or corrosion on the hoses and fittings, and the reservoir should be examined to make sure it is full and does not contain contaminants. Liquid-based cooling is more expensive, less noisy, and more efficient than Peltier components.

Exam essentials

Differentiate the motherboard form factors.   The ATX is the oldest and largest of the motherboard sizes still being manufactured. The micro-ATX is for smaller and cheaper systems. The smaller ITX motherboards come in three sizes: the mini-ITX, the nano-ITX, and the pico-ITX.

Identify expansion slot types.   PCI slots are the standard for general-purpose cards. The PCI-X provides higher bandwidth for servers. PCIe is a newer high-speed slot based on the PCI system. MiniPCI slots are used in laptops.

Locate the CPU socket on the motherboard.   The CPU socket can take on several different forms. In the past, the CPU socket was a rectangular box called a PGA socket, with many small holes to accommodate the pins on the bottom of the chip. With the release of the Pentium II, the architecture of the socket went from a rectangle to more of an expansion-slot style of interface called an SECC.

3.5 Given a scenario, install or replace the appropriate power supply

The power supply provides a number of connectors for various devices as well as a plug for the motherboard. It is important to understand these connector types and to appreciate the power drawn by various devices. Knowledge of the power needs of the devices can allow the technician to choose a power supply that provides the total power needs of the PC.

Input 115V vs. 220V

Most power supplies have a recessed, two-position slider switch (often a red one) on the rear that is exposed through the case. Selections read 110 and 220, 115 and 230, or 120 and 240. This voltage selector switch is used to select the voltage level used in the country where the computer is in service. For example, in the United States, the power grid supplies anywhere from 110 VAC to 120 VAC. However, in Europe, for instance, the voltage supplied is double, ranging from 220 VAC to 240 VAC.

Output 3.3V vs. 5V vs. 12V

In 2004, the ATX 12V 2.0 (now 2.03) standard was passed, changing the main connector from 20 pins to 24. The additional pins provide +3.3V, +5V, and +12V (the fourth pin is a ground) for use by PCIe cards. When a 24-pin connector is used, there is no need for the optional four- or six-pin auxiliary power connectors.

20-pin to 24-pin motherboard adapter

A power connector allows the motherboard to be connected to the power supply. On an ATX, there is a single power connector consisting of a block of 20 holes (in two rows). On an AT, there is a block consisting of 12 pins sticking up; these pins are covered by two connectors with six holes each.

Figure 3.59 shows a versatile motherboard that has both kinds so you can compare them. The upper connector is for ATX, and the lower one is for AT.

FIGURE 3.59 Power connectors on a motherboard

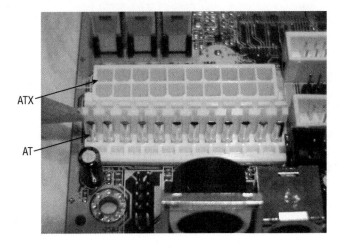

When using the AT power connector, the power cable coming from the power supply will have two separate connectors, labeled P8 and P9. When you are attaching the two parts to the motherboard, the black wires on one should be next to the black wires on the other for proper function.

Redundant power supply

Datacenters usually deploy redundant power sources to maintain constant power. Redundancy can be provided in several ways:

- Parallel redundancy or the N+1 option describes an architecture where there is always a single extra UPS available (that's the +1) and the N simply indicates the total number of UPSs required for the datacenter. Because the system runs in two feeds and there is only one redundant UPS, this system can still suffer failures.

- 2N redundancy means the datacenter provides double the power it requires by providing two power supplies, with one as backup. This ensures that the system is fully redundant.

Redundancy also refers to using redundant power supplies on the devices. Many servers come with two supplies, and you can buy additional power supplies as well. Always ensure that the power supply you buy can accommodate all the needs of the server.

Modular power supply

A modular power supply differs from a non-modular one in that cables or wires that run from the supply to each component on the board are not permanently attached. This allows you to use only the cable you need. The presence of such a unit will allow you to install it even in a miniATX case without losing space in the system unit. Typically, the cost of a modular power supply for a computer is more expensive than the price of a regular one. This is the biggest drawback of a full modular power supply unit.

Wattage rating

When the wattage needs of each device and of the motherboard and CPU are totaled, you will know the wattage that the power supply must provide. A power supply has a rated output capacity in watts, and when you fill a system with power-hungry devices, you must make sure that maximum capacity isn't exceeded. Otherwise, problems with power can occur, creating lockups or spontaneous reboots. Most power supplies provide between 250 watts and 1,200 watts. It's always a good idea to have more than the minimum required for the devices that are present so that additional devices can be added in the future.

Exam essentials

Identify common power connector types and their voltages. These include but are not limited to SATA, Molex, 4- to 8-pin 12V, PCIe 6- to 8-pin, 20-pin, 24-pin, and floppy connectors.

Understand the specifications of power supplies. Differentiate power supplies by wattage, size, number of connectors, and design (ATX or mini-ATX).

Describe a dual-wattage power supply. This is a supply that can be set to accept either 110 volts or 220 volts.

3.6 Given a scenario, deploy and configure multifunction devices/printers and settings

Printers are one of the most common elements in any computing environment, from home to office. The range they cover is phenomenal—everything from a free printer included by a vendor with the purchase of a PC up to a monolith in a large office churning out hundreds of pages a minute. Regardless of where a printer falls in that spectrum, they are all the same in that they must be installed and properly configured to be of use. Moreover, most printing devices today are multifunction devices. They print, scan, and fax in various combinations.

Properly unboxing a device – setup location considerations

When a new a new printer arrives, the setup starts with proper unboxing of the unit. Keep in mind that the device may not function properly and may have to be returned. Until acceptable operation is validated, you should keep all packing materials so that you can reuse them. Also, be very careful using knives and such to cut into the packaging. You don't want to cut a cable or damage a component.

The location of the print device is also an important consideration. You should make it convenient for the bulk of the users rather than making it convenient for yourself or for any single person. Also keep the paper, toner cartridges, and other maintenance items in the same location.

Use appropriate drivers for a given OS

Besides understanding the printer's operation, for the exam you need to understand how these devices talk to a computer. The driver software controls how the printer processes the print job. When you install a printer driver for the printer you are using, it allows the computer to print to that printer correctly (assuming you have the correct interface configured between the computer and printer). Also keep in mind that drivers are specific to the operating system, so you should select the one that is both for the correct printer and for the correct operating system.

An interface is the collection of hardware and software that allows the device to communicate with a computer. Each printer, for example, has at least one interface, but some printers have several to make them more flexible in a multiplatform environment. If a printer has several interfaces, it can usually switch between them on the fly so that several computers can print at the same time.

Printer Control Language (PCL) vs. PostScript

For a printer to work with a particular operating system, a driver must be installed for it. This driver specifies the page description language (PDL) the printer understands, as well as information about the printer's characteristics (paper trays, maximum resolution, and so on). For laser printers, there are two popular PDLs: Adobe PostScript (PS) and Hewlett-Packard Printer Command Language (PCL). Almost all laser printers use one or both of these.

Device connectivity

The forms of connection this exam tests on are USB, Ethernet, and wireless. Each is addressed in the sections that follow.

USB

The most popular type of printer interface as this book is being written is USB. It's the most popular interface for just about every peripheral. The benefits for printers are that it has a higher transfer rate than either serial or parallel, and it automatically recognizes new devices. USB is also fully plug and play, and it allows several printers to be connected at once without adding ports or using up additional system resources.

Ethernet

Most large-environment printers (primarily laser and LED printers) have a special interface that allows them to be hooked directly to a network. These printers have a NIC and ROM-based software that let them communicate with networks, servers, and workstations.

Wireless

The wireless forms of connection included on this exam are Bluetooth, 802.11x, and Infrared (IR). Each is addressed in the sections that follow.

Bluetooth

Bluetooth is an infrared technology that can connect a printer to a computer at a short range; its absolute maximum range is 100 meters (330 feet), and most devices are specified to work within 10 meters (33 feet). When printing with a Bluetooth-enabled device (like a PDA or mobile phone) and a Bluetooth-enabled printer, all you need to do is get within range of the device (that is, move closer), select the print driver from the device, and choose Print. The information is transmitted wirelessly through the air using radio waves and is received by the device.

802.11(a, b, g, n, ac)

A network-enabled printer that has a wireless adapter can participate in a wireless Ethernet (IEEE 802.11b, a, g, n, or ac) network, just as it would as a wired network client.

Infrastructure vs. ad hoc

The architecture of the wireless network may affect the way you set up a wireless printer. In ad hoc mode, all devices communicate directly in a peer-to-peer fashion. This means that each user who accesses the wireless printer will establish their own connection to the wireless printer, and they need to ensure they are in the same IP network with the printer as well as the same WLAN. In infrastructure mode, the wireless network is using an access point (AP), and all communication goes through the AP. In this case, the printer must be set up to automatically connect to.

Public/shared devices

All operating systems allow you to share a local printer or connect over the network to one that has been shared. To connect to a printer in Windows 10, choose Start➢ Control Panel➢ Hardware And Sound ➢ Devices And Printers, and it will show the currently recognized printers (see Figure 3.60) and allow you to add new ones.

FIGURE 3.60   The Devices And Printers window in Windows 10

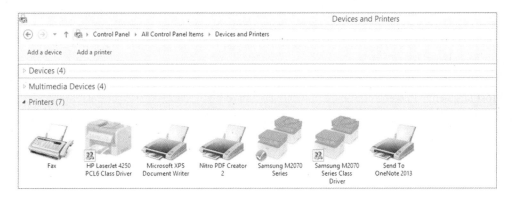

The image of a check box on the first instance of the Samsung M 2070 shows that it is the current default printer, and the image of two people on the second instance of the device means that it is the wizard shown in Figure 3.61.

FIGURE 3.61   Adding a printer

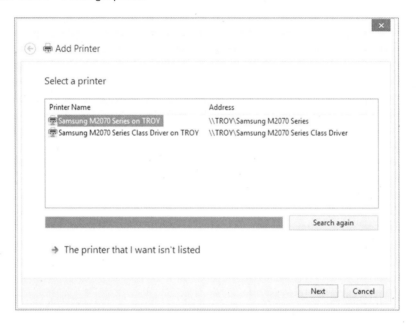

Printer share

To share a local/networked printer via the Windows operating systems, right-click the icon for the printer (beneath Devices And Printers or Printers And Faxes, depending on your operating system) and choose Printer Properties. Next, click the Sharing tab.

Select Share This Printer and provide a name that the printer will be known by on the network. This is the name that will appear when adding a new network printer on a client, and it can also be referenced by the entire qualified name using the syntax \\host\share_name.

TCP/Bonjour/AirPrint

A TCP printer is one that is not shared by a computer but one that has its own network card and IP address. To share one, you must create a TCP port on the computer from which you would like to print, pointing to the IP address of the printer. Then, when adding the printer, select the TCP port you created instead of selecting a local port (USB, and so on) as you would do if setting up a printer that is connected locally.

Bonjour is an Apple technology that discovers devices on a network. It can also be used to facilitate the sharing of a printer in the network. While it can work with Windows, the steps for using it on a Mac are as follows:

1. Click the System Preferences icon in the Dock to open the System Preferences window.

2. Click Print And Scan in the Hardware section to open the Print And Scan window.

3. Click the + button under the Printers list box to open the Add window.

4. Click the Default tab to display the list of available printers. Choose the name of the network printer from the list of printers. The system automatically searches for and installs the appropriate driver for the printer.

5. If the system cannot find a printer driver, click the Use box and manually select it from the pop-up menu. Click Add to automatically make the printer available in the printer queue.

AirPrint is the Apple technology for printing wirelessly to a printer in the network. Many printers come ready to support AirPrint. One important thing to note is that AirPrint does not support printing directly to the wireless printer; it must be done through an access point. This means that you can use this technology only in a WLAN where an access point is present.

Print server

A print server is a popular option for adding a printer to the network and not adding a host computer. To be a print server, the NIC in the printer differs from a NIC in a computer in that it has a processor on it to perform the management of the NIC interface, and it is made by the same manufacturer as the printer.

For a printer to qualify as a print server, when someone on the network prints, the print job must go directly to the printer and not through any third-party device. This tends to make printing to that printer faster and more efficient—that NIC is dedicated to receiving print jobs and sending printer status to clients.

Configuration settings

You need to be familiar with the various settings that are available and what these settings do. This section covers the more common settings, features, and characteristics of printers.

Duplex

An optional component that can be added to printers (usually laser but also inkjet) is a duplexer. This can be an optional assembly added to the printer, or built into it, but the sole purpose of duplexing is to turn the printed sheet over so it can be run back through the printer and allow printing on both sides.

Orientation

The orientation of a document refers to how the printed matter is laid out on the page. In the landscape orientation, the printing is written across the paper turned on its long side, whereas in portrait the paper is turned up vertically and printed top to bottom.

Tray settings

Many printers can hold multiple types and sizes of paper in multiple trays. Tray settings allow you to choose the type of paper and then the printer will use paper found in that tray. Of course, for this system to work, users must be trained to load the proper paper in the proper tray when reloading the machine.

Quality

Print quality is a description of the look of the printing, its sharpness, and its color depth. It is impacted by the quality of the paper, the speed of the printing process, and the resolution settings. It can also be affected by the DPI setting. This setting controls the size of objects on the page and therefore their sharpness. As you increase the size of an object, its quality will usually decrease a bit.

Security

Printers can be a source of data exfiltration if not secured properly. In this section, you'll learn security concepts and best practices regarding printers.

User authentication

While nearly all enterprise-grade multifunction devices support user authentication, it may be easier and make more sense in a large network to perform this on the print server and use domain credentials to take advantage of single sign-on. In any case, user authentication forms the bedrock for auditing.

Badging

Badging can be used to demonstrate the knowledge and skill required to manage a particular printer type. This may be extremely important for specialty printers such as 3D printers or printers that print ID badges.

Audit logs

As you have learned, all devices have a log listing all that has occurred. These logs can be very useful in identifying issues that need to be solved. Also, issues regarding access can be solved by examining the Windows security log.

Secured prints

In some cases you are printing a document that is so secure that you don't want random users visiting the printer to pick up their print jobs to see it. Many printers have the ability to hold the print job until you enter a PIN that releases the job to be printed while you physically monitor the process. These are called secure prints.

Network scan services

Many multifunction devices can also scan documents of various types. In this section you'll learn about scanning of emails and about connection methods used to access the scanner.

Email

Many multifunction devices can scan a document and then send that scan file as an attachment to an email. To do so you typically must use the printer control panel (one you may have to install and use to manage the printer) to create an email account for each user who will be doing this. For example, the HP LaserJet MFP M72625 can do this. When the device is set up properly, there will be a Scan To Email option available.

SMB

Print jobs can also be submitted through the SMB protocol. The SMB printing function is used to print data by directly specifying this machine on the computer. From an application that has the ability to print from within the application, this is done at the command line. For example, to print a document where *FILE* is a local file containing print job data, *SERVER* is the name of the server, and *PRINTQ* is the name of a shared print queue, the command would be:

```
copy /b FILE \\SERVER\PRINTQ
```

Keep in mind that you may need to enable SMB printing and configure some other settings for this to function properly.

Cloud services

Using cloud services to print can follow one of two paradigms. One is the user who uses cloud services to access a printer at home from anywhere. The other is the professional printing service done using cloud technologies to tie together multiple facilities to carry out a print job. For example, the service might be the printing, binding, and boxing of books to sell.

Automatic document feeder (ADF)/flatbed scanner

Scanners are used to convert paper documents or photographs to digital files so that they can be stored on a PC and transmitted as files across the network. The installation process is much like a print device. Because so many of these now are USB, plugging them in will install the driver. In cases where that does not work (usually when it is a new model and the operating system is older), use the installation disc to install the driver. To make functions such as collating and organizing sets of documents possible, the device must have an automatic document feeder that performs these actions. Printing on both sides is another function that requires a feeder that supports it.

Exam essentials

Identify the available printer languages.   This print driver specifies the page description language (PDL) the printer understands. For laser printers, there are two popular PDLs: Adobe PostScript (PS) and Hewlett-Packard Printer Command Language (PCL).

Describe the printer interface types.   These include Ethernet, wireless, and USB.

Identify printer configurations.   These include duplex, orientation, tray settings, and quality.

3.7 Given a scenario, install and replace printer consumables

This objective tests your knowledge of five types of printers: laser, inkjet (sometimes called ink dispersion), thermal, impact, and virtual. Make certain that you understand the imaging process associated with each of these printer types and—in particular—that you can name the steps in the laser imaging process. The A+ certification exams have traditionally focused heavily on laser printers, but you can expect to also see questions about other printer types.

Laser

Laser printers are referred to as *page printers* because they receive their print job instructions one page at a time. They're sheet-fed, nonimpact printers. Another name for a laser printer is an *electrophotographic* (EP) printer.

 LED printers are much like laser printers except they use light-emitting diodes (LEDs) instead of lasers. Their process is similar to that of laser printers.

Imaging drum, fuser assembly, transfer belt, transfer roller, pickup rollers, separation pads, duplexing assembly

First let's discuss the major components used in the laser printing process and then discuss the process steps. An EP (laser) printer consists of the following major components:

Printer Controller   This is a large circuit board that acts as the motherboard for the printer. It contains the processor and RAM to convert data coming in from the computer into a picture of a page to be printed.

Imaging Drum   The toner cartridge and drum are typically packaged together as a consumable product that contains the toner. Toner is a powdery mixture of plastic resin and iron oxide. The plastic allows it to be melted and fused to the paper, and the iron oxide allows it to be moved around via positive or negative charge. Toner comes in a cartridge, like the one shown in Figure 3.62.

FIGURE 3.62   An EP toner cartridge

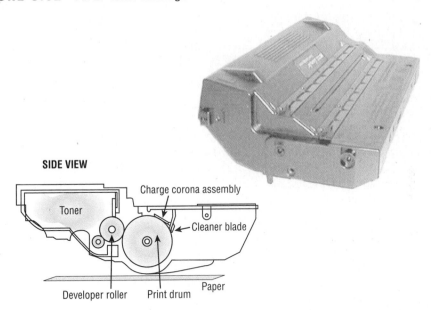

The drum is light sensitive; it can be written to with the laser scanning assembly. The toner cartridge in Figure 3.62 contains the print drum, so every time you change the toner cartridge, you get a new drum. In some laser printers, the drum is a separate part that lasts longer, so you don't have to change it every time you change the toner.

Primary Corona (Charge Corona)   This applies a uniform negative charge (around −600V) to the drum at the beginning of the printing cycle.

Laser Scanning Assembly   This uses a laser beam to neutralize the strong negative charge on the drum in certain areas, so toner will stick to the drum in those areas. The laser scanning assembly uses a set of rotating and fixed mirrors to direct the beam, as shown in Figure 3.63.

FIGURE 3.63   The EP laser scanning assembly (side view and simplified top view)

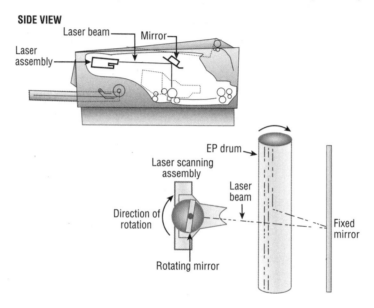

Paper Transport Assembly (Transfer Belt, Transfer Rollers)   This assembly moves the paper through the printer. The assembly consists of a motor and several rubberized rollers and transfer belts. These rollers are operated by an electronic stepper motor. See Figure 3.64 for an example.

FIGURE 3.64   Paper transport rollers

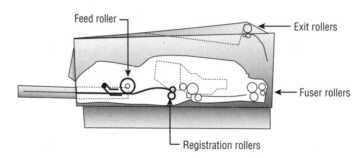

Pickup Rollers   Pickup rollers are rubber wheels that grab the paper and feed it in. When these parts get old, they lose their ability to grip the paper, so they should be checked and changed regularly.

Separation Pads   These pads are used to separate sheets in a stack of printing paper. It does this as the paper passes over them by creating friction that separates the paper. These pads are usually 2 to 3 inches wide, and when they start to wear out, they lose their ability to create friction, and you start getting two and three sheets at a time pulled through.

Transfer Corona   This applies a uniform positive charge (about +600V) to the paper. When the paper rotates past the drum, the toner is pulled off the drum and onto the paper. Then the paper passes through a static eliminator that removes the positive charge from it (see Figure 3.65). Some printers use a transfer corona wire; others use a transfer corona roller.

FIGURE 3.65   The transfer corona assembly

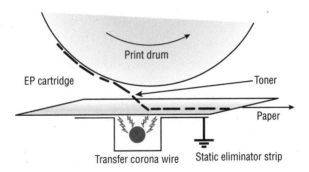

High-Voltage Power Supply (HVPS)   This delivers the high voltages needed to make the printing process happen. It converts ordinary 120V household AC current into high-DC voltages used to energize the primary and transfer corona wires (discussed later).

DC Power Supply   This delivers lower voltages to components in the printer that need much lower voltages than the corona wires (such as circuit boards, memory, and motors).

Fusing Assembly   This melts the plastic resin in the toner so that it adheres to the paper. The fusing assembly contains a halogen heating lamp, a fusing roller made of Teflon-coated aluminum, and a rubberized pressure roller. The lamp heats the fusing roller, and as the paper passes between the two rollers, the pressure roller pushes the paper against the hot fusing roller, melting the toner into the paper (see Figure 3.66).

FIGURE 3.66   The fusing assembly

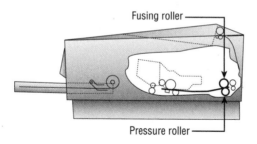

Duplex Assembly   Duplex assemblies were discussed in the section "Duplex" under objective 3.6 earlier in this chapter.

Imaging process: processing, charging, exposing, developing, transferring, fusing, and cleaning

The laser (EP) print process consists of seven steps. Here are the steps in the order you'll see them on the exam:

Step 1: Processing   In this step the data is received by the printer software and the images are rendered for the next step.

Step 2: Charging   In the *conditioning* step (Figure 3.67), a special wire (called a *primary corona* or *charge corona*) within the EP toner cartridge (above the photosensitive drum) gets a high voltage from the HVPS. It uses this high voltage to apply a strong, uniform negative charge (around –600VDC) to the surface of the photosensitive drum.

FIGURE 3.67   The charging or conditioning step of the EP process

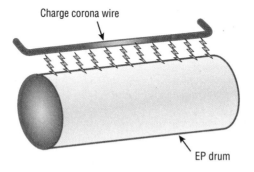

Step 3: Exposing   In the *writing* step of the EP process, the laser is turned on and scans the drum from side to side, flashing on and off according to the bits of information the printer controller sends it as it communicates the individual bits of the image. In each

area where the laser touches the photosensitive drum, the drum's charge is severely reduced from –600VDC to a slight negative charge (around –100VDC). As the drum rotates, a pattern of exposed areas is formed, representing the image to be printed. Figure 3.68 shows this process.

FIGURE 3.68 The exposing step of the EP process

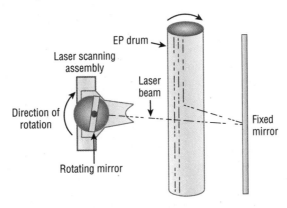

At this point, the controller sends a signal to the pickup roller to feed a piece of paper into the printer, where it stops at the registration rollers.

Step 4: Developing Now that the surface of the drum holds an electrical representation of the image being printed, its discrete electrical charges need to be converted into something that can be transferred to a piece of paper. The EP process's *developing* step accomplishes this (Figure 3.69). In this step, toner is transferred to the areas that were exposed in the writing step.

FIGURE 3.69 The developing step of the EP process

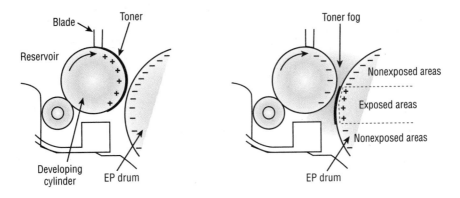

A metallic *developing roller* or *cylinder* inside an EP cartridge acquires a –600VDC charge (called a *bias voltage*) from the HVPS. The toner sticks to this roller because there is a magnet located inside the roller and because of the electrostatic charges between the toner and the developing roller. While the developing roller rotates toward the photosensitive drum, the toner acquires the charge of the roller (–600VDC). When the toner comes between the developing roller and the photosensitive drum, the toner is attracted to the areas that have been exposed by the laser (because these areas have a lesser charge of –100VDC). The toner also is repelled from the unexposed areas (because they're at the same –600VDC charge and like charges repel). This toner transfer creates a fog of toner between the EP drum and the developing roller.

The photosensitive drum now has toner stuck to it where the laser has written. The photosensitive drum continues to rotate until the developed image is ready to be transferred to paper in the next step.

Step 5: Transferring   At this point in the EP process, the developed image is rotating into position. The controller notifies the registration rollers that the paper should be fed through. The registration rollers move the paper underneath the photosensitive drum, and the process of transferring the image can begin with the *transferring* step.

The controller sends a signal to the corona wire or corona roller (depending on which one the printer has) and tells it to turn on. The corona wire/roller then acquires a strong *positive* charge (+600VDC) and applies that charge to the paper. The paper, thus charged, pulls the toner from the photosensitive drum at the line of contact between the roller and the paper because the paper and toner have opposite charges. Once the registration rollers move the paper past the corona wire, the static-eliminator strip removes all charge from that line of the paper. Figure 3.70 details this step. If the strip didn't bleed this charge away, the paper would attract itself to the toner cartridge and cause a paper jam.

FIGURE 3.70   The transferring step of the EP process

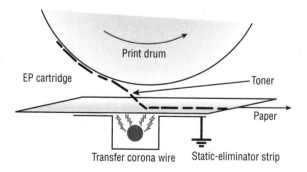

The toner is now held in place by weak electrostatic charges and gravity. It won't stay there, however, unless it's made permanent, which is the reason for the fusing step.

Step 6: Fusing In the next step, *fusing*, the toner image is made permanent. The registration rollers push the paper toward the fuser rollers. Once the fuser grabs the paper, the registration rollers push for only a short time more. The fuser is now in control of moving the paper.

As the paper passes through the fuser, the fuser roller melts the polyester resin of the toner, and the rubberized pressure roller presses it permanently into the paper (Figure 3.71). The paper continues on through the fuser and eventually exits the printer.

FIGURE 3.71 The fusing step of the EP process

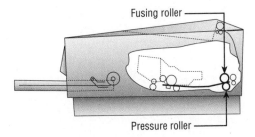

Step 7: Cleaning In the last part of the laser print process, a rubber blade inside the EP cartridge scrapes any toner left on the drum into a used-toner receptacle inside the EP cartridge, and a fluorescent lamp discharges any remaining charge on the photosensitive drum (remember that the drum, being photosensitive, loses its charge when exposed to light). See Figure 3.72.

FIGURE 3.72 The cleaning step of the EP process

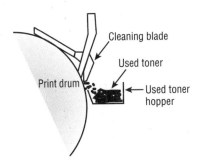

A color laser is much like a regular laser printer except that multiple passes over the page are made, one for each ink color. Consequently, the printing speed is rather low.

The EP cartridge is constantly cleaning the drum. It may take more than one rotation of the photosensitive drum to make an image on the paper. The cleaning step keeps the drum fresh for each use. If you didn't clean the drum, you would see ghosts of previous pages printed along with your image.

 The actual amount of toner removed in the cleaning process is quite small. The cartridge will run out of toner before the used toner receptacle fills up.

Putting it all together

Figure 3.73 summarizes all the EP process printing steps. First, the printer uses a rubber scraper to clean the photosensitive drum. Then the printer places a uniform –600VDC charge on the photosensitive drum by means of a charge corona. The laser paints an image onto the photosensitive drum, discharging the image areas to a much lower voltage (–100VDC). The developing roller in the toner cartridge has charged (–600VDC) toner stuck to it. As it rolls the toner toward the photosensitive drum, the toner is attracted to (and sticks to) the areas of the photosensitive drum that the laser has discharged. The image is then transferred from the drum to the paper at its line of contact by means of the corona wire (or corona roller) with a +600VDC charge. The static-eliminator strip removes the high, positive charge from the paper, and the paper, now holding the image, moves on. The paper then enters the fuser, where the fuser roller and the pressure roller make the image permanent. The paper exits the printer, and the printer starts printing the next page or returns to its ready state.

FIGURE 3.73 The EP print process

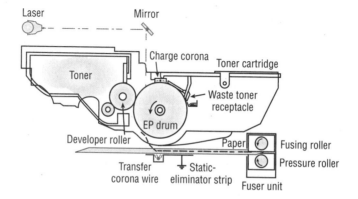

An optional component that can be added to printers (usually laser but also inkjet) is a duplexer. This can be an optional assembly added to the printer, or built into it, but the sole purpose of *duplexing* is to turn the printed sheet over so it can be run back through the printer and allow printing on both sides.

Maintenance: Replace toner, apply maintenance kit, calibrate, clean

Just as laser printers are the most complicated of the types (and offer the most capabilities), they also have the most things that can go awry. A thermal fuse is included to keep the system from overheating, and if it becomes faulty, it can prevent the printer from printing. Many high-capacity laser printers also include an ozone filter to prevent the corona's ozone output from reaching too high a level. On these printers, the filter should be changed as part of regular maintenance.

Other common problems and solutions are as follows:

Paper Jams   While paper jams can be caused by numerous problems, two common ones are the paper not feeding correctly and moisture. To correct improper feeds, make sure you set the alignment guides for the paper you are using and verify that the paper is feeding in straight. Keep the paper from getting any moisture before feeding into the printer because moisture often causes pages to stick together and bind. Paper jams can also be caused by using paper that is not approved for the printer—particularly thick cardstock.

One employee routinely had problems with a printer each time he went to print on high-quality paper—a problem experienced by no one else. Upon close examination, it turned out that each time he chose to print to the expensive paper, he counted the number of sheets he loaded into the printer—counting that involved licking his finger and then touching each page. A simple directive to stop doing this solved the problem.

Regardless of the cause of a paper jam, you need to always fully clear the printer of any traces of paper (torn or whole) before attempting to print again.

Error Codes   Many laser printers include LCDs for interaction with the printer. When error codes appear, refer to the manufacturer's manual or website for information on how to interpret the codes and solve the problem causing them.

Out-of-Memory Error   While PCs now may need a minimum of 1 GB of RAM to run at a base level, it is not uncommon to find printers that still have only 4 MB or 8 MB of memory. If you are routinely running out of memory on a printer, add more memory if possible, and replace the printer when it is no longer possible to do so.

Lines and Smearing   Lines and smearing can be caused by the toner cartridge or the fuser. Try replacing the toner first (and cleaning any that may have spilled). If this does not fix the problem, replace the fuser.

Blank Pages Print   Verify that there is toner in the cartridge. If it's an old cartridge, you can often shake it slightly to free up toner once before replacing. If it's a new cartridge, make sure the sealing tape has been removed from the cartridge prior to placing it in the printer.

Be careful when doing this operation. Someone who has asthma or who is sensitive to microfine particles could be adversely affected by the toner.

Dark Spots Print   The most likely culprit is too much toner. Run blank pages through the printer to clean it.

Garbled Pages Print   Make sure you're using the right printer driver in your application.

Ghosted Images Print   Ghosting—repeating text or images on the page—is usually caused by a bad cartridge. There can be damage to the drum or charging roller, and if there is, replacing the cartridge will help with the problem.

No Connectivity   If a network printer is not able to receive jobs, the issue may be with the IP address that it has (or, more correctly, does not have). Often the printer will need to be manually assigned an IP address to make sure that it has the same one each time. Read the manufacturer's documentation for assigning an IP address to the printer and walk through the steps to do so.

Never overlook the obvious. Connectivity problems also occur when the printer is turned off.

Print-Quality Problems   See whether your printer has the ability to turn resolution enhancement technology (RET) on and off. This is what allows the printer to use partial-sized dots for images that are rounded. If it's turned off, turn it back on. If there are small marks or defects in the same spot on every page printed, the most likely culprit is a scratch on the drum.

Replacing Toner   Toner represents the consumable within the laser printer. Toner cartridges are used by laser printers to store toner. Use toner that is recommended for your printer. Using bad supplies could ruin your printer and void your warranty. Remove the toner before moving or shipping a printer to avoid spills.

Applying a Maintenance Kit   Maintenance kits are marketed by the manufacturer. Each kit varies in contents based on the printer in question but typically consists of a fuser, transfer roller, and feed/separation rollers. A counter on the laser printer often identifies when the maintenance kit is needed, and you can reset the counter after applying the new kit.

Calibration   With laser printers and inkjets, there is often a need to calibrate. Calibration is the process by which the result produced matches what was created. All the hardware, including the monitor, scanner, and printer, need to match on color, margins, and so forth.

The calibration process is different for each manufacturer but is usually similar to the following:

1. During installation of the software, you are asked (by the installation wizard) if you want to calibrate now (say Yes).

2. The printer prints multiple sets of numbered lines. Each set of lines represents an alignment instance, and you are asked which set looks the best.

3. You enter the set number and click OK. In some cases, the alignment ends here. In other cases, the alignment page is reprinted to verify that the settings are correct, and you are given a chance to change.

4. You exit the alignment routine.

Cleaning   It is important to keep the printer and the area around it clean. Each time you replace the toner or perform any maintenance, be sure to clean the debris.

Inkjet

Inkjet printers are one of the most popular types in use today. This type of printer sprays ink on the page to print text or graphics. It's a nonimpact, sheet-fed printer. Figure 3.74 shows an ink cartridge.

FIGURE 3.74   A typical ink cartridge

There are two kinds of inkjet printers: *thermal* and *piezoelectric*. These terms refer to the way the ink is sprayed onto the paper. A thermal inkjet printer heats the ink to about 400 degrees Fahrenheit, creating vapor bubbles that force the ink out of the cartridge. Thermal inkjets are also sometimes called *bubble jets*. A piezoelectric printer does the same thing but with electricity instead of heat.

Inkjet printers are popular because they can print in color and are inexpensive. However, their speed isn't quite as good as that of a laser printer, and the per-page cost of ink can be higher than for a laser printer. Therefore, most businesses prefer laser printers for their main printing needs, perhaps keeping one or two inkjet printers around for situations requiring color printing.

Ink cartridge, print head, roller, feeder, duplexing assembly, carriage belt

Components of an inkjet printer are covered in the following sections.

Ink cartridge

These cartridges contain the ink. Some cartridges contain the printhead for that color of ink; you get a new printhead each time you replace the cartridge. On other printer models, the ink cartridge is just an ink reservoir, and the heads don't need replacing.

Print head

The printhead has a series of nozzles from which the ink is sprayed onto the paper. They may be attached to the ink cartridge, or those two components may be separate. In cases where they are one piece, you will be getting a new printhead each time you get a new ink cartridge.

Roller

Just as on a laser printer, rollers are used to pull the paper in from the tray or feeder and advance the paper when the printhead assembly is ready for another pass. As is the case with any rollers, they will need to be replaced when they lose their ability to "grab" the paper.

Feeder

The feeder looks like a tray and is where you load paper. It is from here that it is pulled into the printer when a new sheet is required. These feeders do not usually hold as much paper as a tray in a printer will.

Duplexing assembly

A duplexing assembly performs the same function on an inkjet printer that it does on a laser printer, which is to flip a sheet over to print on the back side.

Carriage belt

The carriage holds the ink cartridges, and it uses a belt to move the entire piece across the paper as it is printing. As it prints, it uses ink from the various cartridges in whatever proportion is necessary to create the desired colors.

Calibration

Calibrating an inkjet printer is the process of ensuring that there is proper alignment of the cartridges to one another and to the paper so that high quality is maintained. When a printer gets out of calibration, the print quality will decline. When a new cartridge is loaded, the printer will usually perform a calibration, but you may need to do this manually from time to time, especially on printers that are not used often enough to require a cartridge change as often as a calibration may be required.

On an inkjet printer, calibration is more commonly known as *head alignment*. The printer will automatically try to align ink cartridges each time they are replaced (or installed). If you want to make sure they are in the right place, most printers allow you to print an alignment page from the maintenance menu.

If characters are not properly formed or are appearing as straight lines along the margin (usually the left), you can use the maintenance menu settings to align the ink cartridges.

Maintenance: Clean heads, replace cartridges, calibrate, clear jams

While inkjet printers use a different technology to print, they require many of the same maintenance procedures. These are discussed briefly in this section.

Clean Heads   Two maintenance tasks apply to the printheads. If your colors don't look the same or your blacks are getting a bronze look, you need to clean the nozzles. This can be done with the head cleaning cycle, which will clear out the nozzles. The second task is head alignment. If you see white repeating lines or a grid-like pattern in the printing, the head is misaligned. Although some newer printers have an automatic alignment and cleaning function, you may need to do this manually using the printer documentation.

Replace Cartridges   When ink runs low (and most printers will alert you before you run out), you must remove the old cartridge and replace it with a new one. The procedure is as follows:

1. Open the printer cover and locate the button that is used to place the cartridge in the replacement position.
2. Open the cover that is over the cartridge, if one exists.
3. Grasp and remove the empty cartridge.
4. Take the new cartridge out of its packaging.
5. Place the new cartridge in the empty position left by the old cartridge. It should click into place.
6. Replace the cartridge cover.
7. Use the same button you used to place the cartridge into the replacement position to move it back to the home position.

Calibrate   Calibration is a task usually performed by accessing the properties of the printer and looking for the calibration function either on the General tab or on the Advanced tab. Just select it, and the printer will perform a calibration. It is also useful to know that in most cases a calibration is done whenever you replace one of the cartridges.

Clear Jams   While keeping in mind that many paper jams are a result of using poor-quality paper, there will be times you suffer jams with good paper. To clear a jam, do the following:

1. Check the paper tray. If you see a piece protruding from where the paper is picked up, pull it out gently.

2. If there is still a jam, remove the rear access door and look into the printer. If you see any paper stuck inside, pull it out, making sure you get all the pieces out.

3. Check the front door of the printer and see whether any pieces are stuck in that section; if so, gently pull them out.

4. At any point in this process you can select the Resume button, and if you have cleared the jam, the print process will resume.

Thermal

Thermal printers can be found in many older fax machines (most newer ones use either ink-jet or laser printing) that print on a waxy paper that comes on a roll; the paper turns black when heat passes over it. These are also found on many handheld package tracking and point-of-sale (POS) devices such as credit card terminals. These printers should not be used for documents that need long-term storage since the printed image quickly degrades (disappears) and you are just left with a blank sheet of paper. This is especially true of receipts that need to be retained for tax purposes.

Feed assembly, heating element

Thermal printers work by using a printhead the width of the paper. When it needs to print, the printhead heats and cools spots on the printhead. The paper below the heated printhead turns black in those spots. As the paper moves through the printer, the pattern of blackened spots forms an image on the page of what is being printed.

Another type of thermal printer uses a heat-sensitive ribbon instead of heat-sensitive paper. A thermal printhead melts wax-based ink from the ribbon onto the paper. These are called *thermal transfer* or *thermal wax-transfer* printers.

Thermal direct printers typically have long lives because they have few moving parts. However, the paper is somewhat expensive, doesn't last long, and produces poorer-quality images (that tend to fade over time) than most of the other printing technologies.

There are some variations of thermal printing that exist. They're all high-end color graphics printers designed for specialty professional usage. Here are four popular ones:

Thermal Wax Transfer   This is a color, nonimpact printer that uses a solid wax. A heater melts the wax and then sprays it onto the page, somewhat like an inkjet. The quality is very high, but so is the price.

Dye Sublimation   This is another color, nonimpact line printer. This one converts a solid ink into a gas that is then applied to the paper. Color is applied in a continuous tone, rather than individual dots, and the colors are applied one at a time. The ink comes on film rolls. The paper is expensive, as is the ink. Print speeds are low. The quality is extremely high.

Feed Assembly   Feed assemblies, commonly called *feeders*, are available to allow you to feed in the media you are printing on (paper, cards, and so on). Some feeders allow you to switch between multiple feeds, which is helpful if you need to alternate printing on different types of stock.

Heating Element   The heating element for a thermal printer is what generates the heat and does the actual printing. It is often the most expensive component.

Special thermal paper

To print with a thermal printer, you need to use heat-sensitive paper designed for the thermal printer as opposed to paper for any other type of printer. Rolls of thermal paper are available in a variety of sizes and colors.

Maintenance: Replace paper, clean heating element, remove debris

The amount of maintenance required on a thermal printer pales in comparison to laser since there are no moving parts to speak of. The following sections look at the key items to be aware of related to thermal printers as you study for the exam.

Replace Paper   Replace the thermal paper as needed; be sure to keep the feed area clean of paper slivers and other debris.

Clean Heating Element   Before even looking at a heating element, always unplug the printer and make certain it is cool. Thermal printer cleaning cards, cleaning pens, and kits are available and recommended for cleaning.

Remove Debris   Keep the printer free of dust and debris. Any particulates that get into the printer can interfere with the paper feeding properly or can affect the print quality. Use compressed air or a computer vacuum to remove any debris.

Heat sensitivity of paper

When selecting paper for a thermal printer one must be mindful of the heat sensitivity of the paper. A high sensitivity paper will create a better image than a low sensitivity paper when given less heat or energy. Images that need to be rich and dark require a high sensitivity thermal paper.

Impact

A dot-matrix printer is an impact printer; it prints by physically striking an inked ribbon, much like a typewriter. It's an impact, continuous-feed printer.

The printhead on a dot-matrix printer consists of a block of metal pins that extend and retract. These pins are triggered to extend in patterns that form letters and numbers as the printhead moves across the paper. Early models, known as near letter-quality (NLQ), printed using only nine pins. Later models used 24 pins and produced much better letter-quality (LQ) output.

The main advantage of dot matrix is its impact (physical striking of the paper). Because it strikes the paper, you can use it to print on multipart forms. Nonimpact printers can't do that. Dot-matrix printers aren't commonly found in most offices these days because of their disadvantages, including noise, slow speed, and poor print quality.

 NOTE   Dot-matrix printers are still found in many warehouses and other businesses where multipart forms are used or where continuous feed is required.

Print head, ribbon, tractor feed

Key elements of an impact printer are discussed in the sections that follow.

Print Head   The pins in the printhead are wrapped with coils of wire to create a solenoid and are held in the rest position by a combination of a small magnet and a spring. To trigger a particular pin, the printer controller sends a signal to the printhead, which energizes the wires around the appropriate print wire. This turns the print wire into an electromagnet, which repels the print pin, forcing it against the ink ribbon and making a dot on the paper.

Ribbon   The ribbon is like that on an old typewriter. Most impact printers have an option to adjust how close the printhead rests from the ribbon. So if your printing is too light, you may be able to adjust the printhead closer to the ribbon. If it's too dark or you get smeared printing, you may be able to move the printhead back.

Tractor Feed   The tractor feed unit feeds in the continuous feed paper. This paper has holes running down both edges.

Impact paper

An impact printer uses continuous feed paper fed to it by the tractor feed unit.

Maintenance: Replace ribbon, replace print head, replace paper

A dot-matrix printhead reaches high temperatures, and care must be taken to avoid a user or technician touching it and getting burned. Most dot-matrix printers include a temperature sensor to tell whether the printhead is getting too hot. The sensor interrupts printing to let the printhead cool down and then allows printing to start again. If this sensor becomes faulty, it can cause the printer to print a few lines, stop for a while, print more, stop, and so on. The following sections look at the key items to be aware of related to impact printers as you study for the exam.

Replace ribbon.   A common culprit with poor printing is the ribbon. A tight ribbon, or one that isn't advancing properly, will cause smudges or overly light printout. To solve this problem, replace the ribbon.

Replace printhead.   The printhead should never be lubricated, but you can clean off debris with a cotton swab and denatured alcohol. Print pins missing from the printhead will cause incomplete images or characters or white lines running through the text. This can be remedied by replacing the printhead.

If the printhead isn't at fault, make certain it's close enough to the platen (the surface on which typing occurs) to make the right image. The printhead can be moved closer and farther from the platen depending on the thickness of the paper and other considerations.

Replace paper.   Preventive maintenance includes not only keeping the printhead dry and clean but also vacuuming paper shreds from inside the machine. This should be done more often if needed but always when you replace the paper.

3-D printer

3D printers create objects or parts by joining or solidifying materials under computer control to create a three-dimensional object. Some versions use a data source such as an additive manufacturing file (AMF) file (usually in sequential layers).

Filament

3D printers use rolls of special plastic filament as the material source. This filament comes in various colors and is shown in Figure 3.75 with objects created from the filament.

FIGURE 3.75   3D filament

Resin

Resin printers use a different material to form the objects than filament printers. Resin printers can create smooth surfaces that the filament printers cannot. Filaments are used with the fused deposition modeling (FDM) technology in 3D printing, while resins are the materials for stereolithography apparatus (SLA) technology. Resins typically come in a liquid form.

Print bed

The print bed is the area where the material is formed into the eventual shape. Figure 3.76 shows the print bed and an object being formed using FDM technology. The print bed is marked with an "e."

Exam essentials

Identify the components of laser printers.   These include the imaging drum, fuser assembly, transfer belt, transfer roller, pickup rollers, separate pads, and duplexing assembly.

Describe the function of the components of an inkjet printer.   These include the ink cartridge, printhead, roller, feeder, duplexing assembly, and carriage belt.

FIGURE 3.76   The print bed

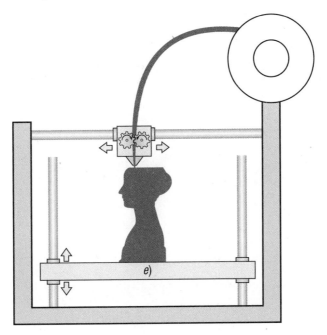

Review Questions

You can find the answers in the appendix.

1. Which cable type comes in two varieties: unshielded and shielded?
   A. Fiber optic
   B. Coaxial
   C. Twisted pair
   D. Serial

2. Which cable type transmits data at speeds up to 100 Mbps and was used with Fast Ethernet (operating at 100 Mbps) with a transmission range of 100 meters?
   A. Cat 4
   B. Cat 5
   C. Cat 5e
   D. Cat 6

3. Which cable type has a glass core within a rubber outer coating?
   A. Fiber optic
   B. Coaxial
   C. Twisted pair
   D. Serial

4. Which connector is used for telephone cord?
   A. RJ-11
   B. RJ-45
   C. RS-232
   D. BNC

5. Which standard has been commonly used in computer serial ports?
   A. RJ-11
   B. RJ-45
   C. RS-232
   D. BNC

6. Which connectors are sometimes used in the place of RCA connectors for video electronics?
   A. RJ-11
   B. RJ-45
   C. RS-232
   D. BNC

7. Which RAM type is used in laptops?

   A. DIMM

   B. SODIMM

   C. Rambus

   D. BNC

8. Which RAM type allows for two memory accesses for each rising and falling clock?

   A. DIMM

   B. SODIMM

   C. DDR3

   D. DDR2

9. Which RAM type is not compatible with any earlier type of random access memory?

   A. DDR5

   B. DDR4

   C. DDR3

   D. DDR2

10. Which of the following is a rewritable optical disc?

    A. CD

    B. CD-RW

    C. DVD

    D. CD-ROM

11. Which of the following is a specification for internally mounted computer expansion cards and associated connectors that replaces the mSATA?

    A. M.2

    B. NVME

    C. SATA

    D. SATA 2.5

12. At what speed will latency on a magnetic drive decrease to about 3 ms?

    A. 5400 rpm

    B. 7200 rpm

    C. 10,000 rpm

    D. 15,000 rpm

13. Laptops and other portable devices utilize which expansion card?

    A. MiniPCI

    B. PCIe

    C. PCI

    D. SATA

14. Which of the following is a standard firmware interface for PCs, designed to replace BIOS?

    A. UEFI

    B. NVRAM

    C. CMOS

    D. CHS

15. Which type of printer has pins in the printhead?

    A. Impact

    B. 3D

    C. Thermal

    D. Laser

16. What is the most expensive part of a thermal printer?

    A. Feed assembly

    B. Heating element

    C. Printhead

    D. Print bed

17. Which of the following is the process of ensuring that there is proper alignment of the cartridges to one another and to the paper so that high quality is maintained?

    A. Orientation

    B. Alignment

    C. Calibration

    D. Tuning

18. Ghosting—repeating text or images on the page—is usually caused by which of the following?

    A. Wrong paper

    B. Wrong driver

    C. No connectivity

    D. Bad cartridge

19. In 2004, the ATX 12V 2.0 (now 2.03) standard was passed, changing the main connector from 20 pins to how many?

    A. 16

    B. 22

    C. 24

    D. 28

20. Which of the following is a subdivision of a process?

A. thread

B. task

C. module

D. string

21. The SATA power connector has how many pins?

A. 8

B. 12

C. 15

D. 18

22. Which of the following causes blank pages in a laser printer?

A. Empty toner cartridge

B. No connectivity

C. Scratched drum

D. Wrong paper

23. What is the last step in the printing process of a laser printer?

A. Fusing

B. Cleaning

C. Transferring

D. Developing

24. Which laser printer component applies a –600V charge to the paper?

A. High-voltage power supply

B. DC power supply

C. Transfer corona

D. Fusing assembly

25. To submit an SMB print job, where *FILE* is a local file containing print job data, *SERVER* is the name of the server, and *PRINTQ* is the name of a shared print queue, what command would you use?

A. copy /b *FILE* *PRINTQ*/*SERVER*

B. copy /b *FILE* *SERVER**PRINTQ*

C. copy *FILE* *SERVER**PRINTQ*

D. copy /b *SERVER**PRINTQ*

26. What type of printing process holds the print job until you enter a PIN that releases the job to be printed while you physically monitor the process?

   A. Locked prints

   B. Printer hold

   C. Secure prints

   D. Privileged print

27. Which of the following is a technology that can connect a printer to a computer at a short range; its absolute maximum range is 100 meters (330 feet), and most devices are specified to work within 10 meters (33 feet)?

   A. 802.11

   B. RFID

   C. Bluetooth

   D. Ethernet

28. What software controls how the printer processes the print job?

   A. Driver

   B. Interface

   C. Network

   D. Line

29. What printer component turns the printed sheet over so it can be run back through the printer and allow printing on both sides?

   A. Driver

   B. Duplexer

   C. Orientation

   D. Collator

30. Which of the following refers to how the printed matter is laid out on the page?

   A. Driver

   B. Duplex

   C. Orientation

   D. Collate

31. Which of the following feeds through the printer using a system of sprockets and tractors?

   A. Continuous feed

   B. Sheet fed

   C. Impact

   D. Thermal

32. Which of the following should not be used more than once?

   A. Toner

   B. Paper

   C. Cable

   D. Inkjets

33. Which of the following is a large circuit board that acts as the motherboard for the printer?

   A. Printer controller

   B. Imaging drum

   C. Toner cartridge

   D. Maintenance kit

Chapter

4

Virtualization and Cloud Computing

COMPTIA A+ CERTIFICATION EXAM CORE 1 (220-1101) OBJECTIVES COVERED IN THIS CHAPTER:

✓ **4.1 Summarize cloud-computing concepts.**

- **Common cloud models**
  - **Private cloud**
  - **Public cloud**
  - **Hybrid cloud**
  - **Community cloud**
  - **Infrastructure as a service (IaaS)**
  - **Software as a service (SaaS)**
  - **Platform as a service (PaaS)**
- **Cloud characteristics**
  - **Shared resources**
  - **Metered utilization**
  - **Rapid elasticity**
  - **High availability**
  - **File synchronization**
- **Desktop virtualization**
  - **Virtual desktop infrastructure (VDI) on premises**
  - **VDI in the cloud**

✓ **4.2 Summarize aspects of client-side virtualization**

- **Purpose of virtual machines**
  - **Sandbox**
  - **Test development**

- **Application virtualization**
  - Legacy software/OS
  - Cross-platform virtualization
- **Resource requirements**
- **Security requirements**

This chapter will focus on the exam topics related to virtualization. It will follow the structure of the CompTIA A+ 220-1101 exam blueprint, objective 4, and it will explore the two subobjectives that you will need to master before taking the exam.

4.1 Summarize cloud computing concepts

Cloud computing and its underlying technology, virtualization, have moved beyond the "new" stage and are now becoming ubiquitous. This chapter will focus on the exam topics related to virtualization.

Common cloud models

Increasingly, organizations are utilizing cloud-based storage instead of storing data in local datacenters. The advantages to this approach include the ability to access the data from anywhere, the ability to scale computing resources to meet demand, and robust fault tolerance options. This section will look at various cloud models and some of the concepts that make it a viable option for the enterprise.

Public vs. private vs. hybrid vs. community

When a company pays another company to host and manage a cloud environment, it is called a public cloud solution. If the company hosts this environment itself, it is a private cloud solution.

There is a trade-off when a decision must be made between the two architectures. The private solution provides the most control over the safety of your data but also requires the staff and the knowledge to deploy, manage, and secure the solution. A public cloud puts your data's safety in the hands of a third party, but that party is often more capable and knowledgeable about protecting data in this environment and managing the cloud environment.

When the solution is partly private and partly public, the solution is called a hybrid solution. It may be that the organization keeps some data in the public cloud but may keep more sensitive data in a private cloud, or the organization may have a private cloud that when overtaxed may utilize a public cloud for additional storage space or additional compute resources.

Finally, a community cloud is one that is shared by multiple organizations for some common purpose. This could be to share data for a joint project, for example.

Infrastructure as a service (IaaS)

Infrastructure as a service (IaaS) means that the vendor provides the hardware platform and the company installs and manages its own operating systems and application systems. The vendor simply provides access to the datacenter and maintains that access.

Software as a service (SaaS)

When an enterprise contracts with a third party to provide cloud services, there is a range of options, differing mostly in the division of responsibilities between the vendor and the client. Software as a service (SaaS) involves the vendor providing the entire solution. This includes the operating system, the infrastructure software, and the application. The company may provide you with an email system, for example, and hosts and manages everything for you.

Platform as a service (PaaS)

Platform as a service (PaaS) means the vendor provides the hardware platform or datacenter and the software running on the platform. This includes the operating systems and infrastructure software. The customer is still involved in managing the system.

Cloud characteristics

There are certain aspects to using a cloud environment that are unique to virtualization. In this section you'll learn about these characteristics.

Shared resources

Devices in a cloud datacenter are virtual machines (VMs) that share the resources of the underlying host. Virtual machines represent virtual instances of an operating system that exist as files on the physical host. Technicians can appropriate these resources in whichever relative percentages they are comfortable. One of the benefits of hypervisor-driven virtualization is the ability of the hypervisor to recognize momentary needs for more resources by one of the VMs and react by shifting some percentage of the resource in contention to the overloaded VM.

Metered utilization

Metered utilization, sometimes called pay-as-you-go, means that you pay for only what you use. Usage metering tracks information about CPU, GPU, TPU, memory, storage, and optionally network egress usage.

This is as compared to services that are prepaid. The fixed price of nonmetered services means that your price won't fluctuate, regardless of your cloud usage, but you may not use all that you pay for.

Rapid elasticity

One of the advantages of a cloud environment is the ability to add resources as needed on the fly and release those resources when they are no longer required. This makes for more efficient use of resources, allocating them where needed at any particular point in time. These include CPU and memory resources. This is called rapid elasticity because it occurs automatically according to the rules for resource sharing that have been deployed.

High availability

Due to the use of rapid elasticity and shared resources the cloud is a highly available environment. You can even have a new VM spun up to address capacity issues, or in cases where a system is down, another can easily be brought up without users losing connections or data.

File synchronization

Most cloud storage services come with an application that can be used to keep the files in the cloud synchronized with the files as they exist in local storage. These apps can automate the synchronization process for you. They typically provide versioning services as well, allowing you to recover from any accidental edits or deletions.

Desktop virtualization

Virtual desktop infrastructures (VDIs) host desktop operating systems within a virtual environment in a centralized server. Users access the desktops and run them from the server. There are three models for implementing VDI.

Virtual desktop infrastructure (VDI) on premises

When hosted on-site there are two approaches to VDI:

- **Centralized** All desktop instances are stored in a single server, requiring significant processing power on the server.
- **Remote Virtual Desktops** An image is copied to the local machine, making a constant network connection unnecessary.

VDI in the cloud

Also called hosted desktops, these are maintained by a service provider in a cloud environment. This model eliminates capital cost and is instead subject to operation cost.

Exam essentials

Describe the cloud service models.   These include SaaS, PaaS, and IaaS. Differentiate the models with respect to the various responsibilities of the vendor and the customer.

Differentiate cloud architectures.   Describe the architectural differences in the private, public, hybrid, and community cloud models.

Identify basic terms describing some of the benefits of cloud computing.   These include rapid elasticity, on-demand computing, and measured service.

4.2 Summarize aspects of client-side virtualization

A client-side virtualized computer is an instance of an operating system that is managed centrally on a server and executed locally. One key feature of this approach is that while a constant connection to the server is not required for the system to function, the operating system disk image is updated and backed up by synchronizing regularly with a server. This section will look at the setup of a client-side virtualization scenario.

Purpose of virtual machines

Traditionally, workstations can have multiple operating systems installed on them but run only one at a time. By running virtualization software, the same workstation can be running Window 10 along with Windows Server 2016 and Red Hat Enterprise Linux (or almost any other operating system) at the same time, allowing a developer to test code in various environments as well as cut and paste between VMs.

From a networking standpoint, each of the VMs will typically need full network access, and configuring the permissions for each can sometimes be tricky.

Sandbox

Sandboxing is the segregation of virtual environments for security proposes. Sandboxed appliances have been used in the past to supplement the security features of a network. These appliances are used to test suspicious files in a protected environment.

Malware sandboxing aims to detect malware code by running it in a computer to analyze it for behavior and traits that indicate malware. One of its goals is to spot zero-day malware, which is malware that has not yet been identified by commercial antimalware systems and for which currently there is no cure.

Test development

Another great use of a virtual environment is in the development of applications or in the testing of network configurations. Using a virtual version of your infrastructure issues that may occur when rolling out any of the following changes can be done safely without impacting the production environment:

- New security devices
- New applications
- Automation scripts
- Updates
- Security patches

Application virtualization

Just as operating systems can be provided on demand with technologies like VDI, applications can also be provided to users from a central location. Two models can be used to implement this:

- Server-based application virtualization (terminal services): In server-based application virtualization, an application runs on servers. Users receive the application environment display through a remote client protocol, such as Microsoft Remote Desktop Protocol (RDP) or Citrix Independent Computing Architecture (ICA). Examples of terminal services include Remote Desktop Services and Citrix Presentation Server.
- Client-based application virtualization (application streaming): In client-based application virtualization, the target application is packaged and streamed to the client PC. It has its own application computing environment that is isolated from the client OS and other applications. A representative example is Microsoft Application Virtualization (App-V). Figure 4.1 compares these two approaches.

FIGURE 4.1   Application streaming and Remote Desktop Services

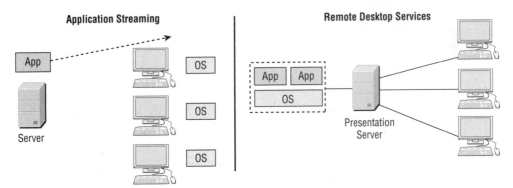

Legacy software/OS

In many cases the organization may use an application that only runs on a certain operating system. In many cases, that operating system is a legacy system, meaning it is no longer supported by the vendor. Moreover, all other workstations in the network may have already been upgraded to another operating system.

In this scenario you can configure a VM with the legacy operating system and use that to run the application. Since legacy operating systems no longer receive security patches from the vendor, you can also take advantage of sandboxing (covered earlier) to isolate the system from the Internet.

Cross-platform virtualization

Another scenario in which virtualization can solve a problem is when an application runs on an operating system that you currently don't use in the network. Perhaps your environment is Windows and an application requires Linux or Apple. You can configure a VM with that system installed and use it to run the application.

Resource requirements

The resource requirements for virtualization are largely based on what environments you are creating. The hardware on the machine must have enough memory, hard drive space, and processor capability to support the virtualization. You also need the software to make virtualization possible (discussed in the next section).

Emulator requirements

XP Mode is a free emulator from Microsoft that you can download and use as a virtual emulator. A number of others are also available. In most cases, the motherboard and associated BIOS settings need no modification to provide services to these VMs. Some of the virtualization products, however (such as Microsoft's Hyper-V, Windows 7 Virtual PC, and Windows 10 Client Hyper-V), require that the motherboard support hardware-assisted virtualization. The benefit derived from using hardware-assisted virtualization is that it reduces overhead and improves performance.

VMware Player allows you to work in multiple environments on one system. For more information, go to www.vmware.com/products/player.

Security requirements

Tales of security woes that can occur with attackers jumping out of one VM and accessing another have been exaggerated. Although such threats are possible, most software solutions include sufficient protection to reduce the possibility to a small one.

Most virtualization-specific threats focus on the hypervisor (the software that allows the VMs to exist). If the hypervisor can be successfully attacked, the attacker can gain root-level access to all virtual systems. While this is a legitimate issue—and one that has been demonstrated to be possible in most systems (including VMware, Xen, and Microsoft Virtual Machine)—it is one that has been patched each time it has appeared. The solution to most virtualization threats is to always apply the most recent patches and keep the systems up-to-date.

It is much easier to attack a virtual machine than a hypervisor because admins do not think about the security of each individual VM. It is also important to ensure that all VMs are updated with patches for both the OS and all applications. If VMs are allowed to run with outdated OS or software, known vulnerabilities will exist that attackers will take advantage of.

Keep in mind that in any virtual environment, each virtual server that is hosted on the physical server must be configured with its own security mechanisms. These mechanisms include antivirus and antimalware software and all the latest service packs and security updates for all the software hosted on the virtual machine.

Exam essentials

Be familiar with virtualization terminology.   The hypervisor is the software that allows the VMs to exist. VMs are separate instances of an operating system, and they function independently of one another on a host physical machine.

Know security concerns related to virtualization.   Most virtualization-specific threats focus on the hypervisor. If the hypervisor can be successfully attacked, the attacker can gain root-level access to all virtual systems.

Review Questions

You can find the answers in the appendix.

1. Which of the following involves the vendor providing the entire solution?
    A. IaaS
    B. SaaS
    C. PaaS
    D. SIEM

2. When a company pays another company to host and manage a cloud environment, it is called what?
    A. Public cloud
    B. Hybrid cloud
    C. Community cloud
    D. Private cloud

3. Which of the following is the ability to add resources as needed on the fly and release those resources when they are no longer required?
    A. On-demand
    B. Rapid elasticity
    C. Virtual sharing
    D. Stretched resources

4. In which VDI model are all desktop instances stored in a single server, requiring significant processing power on the server?
    A. Centralized
    B. Hosted
    C. Remote
    D. Local

5. Which of the following involves the vendor providing the hardware platform and the software running on the platform?
    A. IaaS
    B. SaaS
    C. PaaS
    D. DaaS

6. What is the benefit derived from using hardware-assisted virtualization?
    A. Better performance
    B. Better security
    C. Less power consumption
    D. Easier troubleshooting

7. Which of the following is the software that allows the VMs to exist?

   A. DIMM

   B. Hypervisor

   C. Azureware

   D. NAT

8. Which of the following is a free emulator from Microsoft that you can download and use as a virtual emulator?

   A. XP Mode

   B. Virtual Box

   C. vWindows

   D. Hypervisor

9. Which of the following hosts desktop operating systems within a virtual environment in a centralized server?

   A. VDI

   B. RDP

   C. SSH

   D. OVC

10. Which of the following is the segregation of virtual environments for security proposes.?

    A. VPN

    B. VLAN

    C. DMZ

    D. sandbox

Chapter

5

Hardware and Network Troubleshooting

COMPTIA A+ CERTIFICATION EXAM CORE 1 (220-1101) OBJECTIVES COVERED IN THIS CHAPTER:

✓ **5.1 Given a scenario, apply the best practice methodology to resolve problems.**

- ▪ **Always consider corporate policies, procedures, and impacts before implementing changes.**

    - ▪ 1. Identify the problem

        - ▪ Gather information from the user, identify user changes, and, if applicable, perform backups before making changes

        - ▪ Inquire regarding environmental or infrastructure changes

    - ▪ 2. Establish a theory of probable cause (question the obvious)

        - ▪ If necessary, conduct external or internal research based on symptoms

    - ▪ 3. Test the theory to determine the cause

        - ▪ Once the theory is confirmed, determine the next steps to resolve the problem

        - ▪ If the theory is not confirmed, re-establish a new theory or escalate

    - ▪ 4. Establish a plan of action to resolve the problem and implement the solution

        - ▪ Refer to the vendor's instructions for guidance

    - ▪ 5. Verify full system functionality and, if applicable, implement preventive measures

    - ▪ 6. Document the findings, actions, and outcomes

✓ **5.2 Given a scenario, troubleshoot problems related to motherboards, RAM, CPU, and power**

- **Common symptoms**
  - Power-on self-test (POST) beeps
  - Proprietary crash screens (blue screen of death [BSOD]/pinwheel)
  - Black screen
  - No power
  - Sluggish performance
  - Overheating
  - Burning smell
  - Intermittent shutdown
  - Application crashes
  - Grinding noise
  - Capacitor swelling
  - Inaccurate system date/time

✓ **5.3 Given a scenario, troubleshoot and diagnose problems with storage drives and RAID arrays**

- **Common symptoms**
  - Light-emitting diode (LED) status indicators
  - Grinding noises
  - Clicking sounds
  - Bootable device not found
  - Data loss/corruption
  - RAID failure
  - Self-monitoring, Analysis, and Reporting Technology (S.M.A.R.T.) failure
  - Extended read/write times
  - Input/output operations per second (IOPS)
  - Missing drives in OS

✓ **5.4 Given a scenario, troubleshoot video, projector, and display issues**

- ▪ **Common symptoms**
  - ▪ Incorrect data source
  - ▪ Physical cabling issues
  - ▪ Burned-out bulb
  - ▪ Fuzzy image
  - ▪ Display burn-in
  - ▪ Dead pixels
  - ▪ Flashing screen
  - ▪ Incorrect color display
  - ▪ Audio issues
  - ▪ Dim image
  - ▪ Intermittent projector shutdown

✓ **5.5 Given a scenario, troubleshoot common issues with mobile devices**

- ▪ **Common symptoms**
  - ▪ Poor battery health
  - ▪ Swollen battery
  - ▪ Broken screen
  - ▪ Improper charging
  - ▪ Poor/no connectivity
  - ▪ Liquid damage
  - ▪ Overheating
  - ▪ Digitizer issues
  - ▪ Physically damaged ports
  - ▪ Malware
  - ▪ Cursor drift/touch calibration

✓ **5.6 Given a scenario, troubleshoot and resolve printer issues**

- **Common symptoms**
  - Lines down the printed pages
  - Garbled print
  - Toner not fusing to paper
  - Paper jams
  - Faded print
  - Incorrect paper size
  - Paper not feeding
  - Multipage misfeed
  - Multiple prints pending in queue
  - Speckling on printed pages
  - Double/echo images on the print
  - Incorrect chroma display
  - Grinding noise
  - Finishing issues
    - Staple jams
    - Hole punch
  - Incorrect page orientation

✓ **5.7 Given a scenario, troubleshoot problems with wired and wireless networks**

- **Common symptoms**
  - Intermittent wireless connectivity
  - Slow network speeds
  - Limited connectivity
  - Jitter
  - Poor Voice over Internet Protocol (VoIP) quality
  - Port flapping
  - High latency
  - External interference

This chapter will focus on the exam topics related to troubleshooting. It will follow the structure of the CompTIA A+ 220-1101 exam blueprint, objective 5, and it will explore the seven subobjectives that you will need to master before taking the exam.

5.1 Given a scenario, apply the best practice methodology to resolve problems

Most of those employed in the IT field who will be seeking CompTIA's A+ certification are regularly in positions where they need to know how to troubleshoot, repair, and maintain computer systems. In this section you'll learn about a best practice methodology to resolve problems.

Always consider corporate policies, procedures, and impacts before implementing changes

When implementing the steps in the troubleshooting theory discussed in this section, always keep in mind that before you make any changes or take any actions, you should ensure the changes are consistent with your corporate policies. You should also determine whether a particular change you are considering has an established procedure defined in the corporate guidelines. Finally, have a clear understanding of the potential impact of any change you make, and always ensure that a rollback plan has been established in advance. Whenever you determine that a change has the potential to cause widespread issues, try to make the change in a test environment or on a small, low-impact section of the network. Technicians should check to see whether there is already a defined solution for the stated problem. Often the help desk documentation will include notes of a previous instance of a problem. Going to that documentation first should be a standard practice.

1. Identify the problem

Although it may sound obvious, you can't troubleshoot a problem without knowing what the problem is. In some cases, the problem will be obvious. But in others, especially when relying on the description of the problem by the user, it will appear to be one thing on the surface when in actuality the issue the user is experiencing is a symptom of a different, possibly larger problem. In this section, processes that can help bring clarity to the situation are discussed, and a cautionary note about this step is covered as well.

Gather information from the user, identify user changes, and, if applicable, perform backups before making changes

Identify the problem by questioning the user and identifying user changes to the computer. Before you do anything else, ask the user the following:

1. What the problem is

2. When the last time was that the problem didn't exist

3. What has changed since

Be sure that you do a backup before you make any changes so that all your actions can be undone, if necessary.

When performing this step, be wary of accepting the user's diagnosis of the problem at face value. For example, a user may start the conversation with the statement "The email server is down." At this point, ask the question, "Is there anything else you cannot do besides open your email?" Ask them to try accessing a shared folder or the Internet. If either of those tasks fails, the problem is probably not the email server but basic network connectivity of their computer. At this point, determine the scope of the issue—that is, how many users are experiencing the issue.

Inquire regarding environmental or infrastructure changes

Make note of everything that has or may have changed recently in the immediate environment of the system. Question the user about what recent changes have been made to the device, and also question the team about recent infrastructure changes. Has construction/maintenance been performed to the building/facilities/utilities that could have caused this? Have there been HVAC issues recently? Storms? Power go out?

2. Establish a theory of probable cause (question the obvious)

As you get answers to your initial questions, theories will begin to evolve as to the root of the problem. Analyze the problem, including potential causes, and make an initial determination of whether it's a software or a hardware problem. As you narrow down the problem, determine whether it is hardware or software related so that you can act accordingly.

Once you have developed a list of possible causes, create a list of tests you can perform to test each possibility to narrow the list by eliminating each theory one by one. Don't forget to consider the obvious and make no assumptions. Just because the cable has worked every day for the last five years doesn't mean the person cleaning the office may not have caught the vacuum cleaner on the cable and damaged its connector last night.

If necessary, conduct external or internal research based on symptoms

You are not expected to immediately know the solution to every issue the user may have. You are, however, expected to perform whatever research is required to solve the issue. That can include using the Internet, calling trusted fellow technicians, and contacting vendors for assistance. Later in this section you will learn that when a resolution is found, you should always document these lessons learned in a form that you can use later to solve the same or similar issues.

3. Test the theory to determine cause

Test related components, including connections and hardware and software configurations. Also use Device Manager and consult vendor documentation. Whatever the problem may be, the odds are good that someone else has experienced it before. Use the tools at your disposal—including manuals and websites—to try to zero in on the problem as expeditiously as possible.

Once the theory is confirmed, determine the next steps to resolve the problem

If your theory is confirmed, then determine the next steps you need to take to resolve the problem. In cases where you have determined the device where the problem lies but you have no expertise in that area, escalate the problem to someone as needed. For example, if you have narrowed down the problem to the router and you don't understand or manage the router, escalate the problem to the router administrator.

If the theory is not confirmed, re-establish a new theory or escalate

If your theory is not confirmed, then come up with a new theory or bring in someone with more expertise (escalate the problem). If you make changes to test one theory, make sure you reverse those changes before you test another theory. Making multiple changes can cause new problems and make the diagnostic process even more difficult.

4. Establish a plan of action to resolve the problem and implement the solution

Evaluate the results and develop an action plan of steps to fully resolve the problem. Keep in mind that it's possible that more than one thing is causing the problem. If that is the case, you may need to solve one problem and then turn your attention to the next.

Once you have planned your work, work your plan. Methodically make the required changes while always having a backout plan if your changes cause a larger problem.

5. Verify full system functionality and, if applicable, implement preventive measures

When the problem is believed to be resolved, verify that the system is fully functional. If there are preventive measures that can be put in place to keep this situation from recurring, take those measures on this machine and all others where the problem may exist. Also keep in mind that times like this are great learning moments to teach users what role they may have played and what actions they may be able to take on their own in the future to prevent the problem, if that is appropriate.

6. Document the findings, actions, and outcomes

Document your activities and outcomes. Experience is a wonderful teacher, but only if you can remember what you've done. Documenting your actions and outcomes will help you (or a fellow administrator) troubleshoot a similar problem when it crops up in the future.

In some cases, you may think you have solved a problem only to find it occurs again later because you only treated the symptom of a larger problem. When this type of thing occurs, documentation of what has occurred in the past can be helpful in seeing patterns that otherwise would remain hidden.

Exam essentials

Know the six main steps in the troubleshooting process.   The six steps are as follows: identify the problem; establish a theory of probable cause; test the theory to determine the cause; establish a plan of action to resolve the problem and implement the solution; verify full system functionality and, if applicable, implement preventive measures; and document findings, actions, and outcomes.

5.2 Given a scenario, troubleshoot problems related to motherboards, RAM, CPU, and power

While problems can occur with the operating system with little or no physical warning, that is rarely the case when it comes to hardware problems. Your senses will often alert you that something is wrong based on what you hear, smell, or see. This section discusses common issues with the main players.

Common symptoms

Once you have performed troubleshooting for some time, you will notice a pattern. With some exceptions, the same issues occur over and over and usually give you the same warnings each time. This section covers common symptoms or warning signs. When you learn what these symptoms are trying to tell you, it makes your job easier.

Power-on self-test (POST) beeps

During the bootup of the system, a power-on self-test (POST) occurs, and each device is checked for functionality. If the system boots to the point where the video driver is loaded and the display is operational, any problems will be reported with a numeric error code.

If the system cannot boot to that point, problems will be reported with a beep code. Although each motherboard manufacturer's set of beep codes and their interpretation can be found in the documentation for the system or on the website of the BIOS/UEFI manufacturer, one short beep always means everything is okay. Examples of items tested during this process are:

- RAM
- Video card
- Motherboard

To interpret the beep codes in the case where you cannot read the error codes on the screen, use the chart provided at www.computerhope .com/beep.htm.

During startup, problems with devices that fail to be recognized properly, services that fail to start, and so on are written to the system log and can also be viewed with Event Viewer in Windows or in the Console in macOS. If no POST error code prevents a successful boot, this utility provides information about what's been going on system-wise to help you troubleshoot problems. Event Viewer shows warnings, error messages, and records of things happening successfully. You can access it through Computer Management, or you can access it directly from the Administrative Tools. In Windows 11 it is available through Control Panel or by searching for Event viewer.

Proprietary crash screens (blue screen of death [BSOD]/pinwheel)

Some operating systems have a proprietary method of notifying the user that the worst may have just happened. In this section you'll look at two of the most widely known methods.

BSOD

Once a regular occurrence when working with Windows, blue screens (also known as the Blue Screen of Death) have become much less frequent since Windows 2000. Occasionally, systems will lock up, and you can usually examine the log files to discover what was happening when this occurred and then take the necessary steps to correct it. For example, if you see that a driver or application was loading before the crash, you can begin to isolate it as a possible problem. The details included in the BSOD error that comes up can help in troubleshooting the problem. It is often easy to query Microsoft's Knowledge Base with the first part of the BSOD error to discover the component causing the problem. Often, the Knowledge Base article gives a detailed explanation of how to fix the problem as well.

In more recent versions of Windows, such as Windows 10, information from such crashes is written to XML files by the operating system. When the system becomes stable, a prompt usually appears asking for approval to send this information to Microsoft. The goal that Microsoft has in collecting this data is to be able to identify drivers that cause such problems and work with vendors to correct these issues.

Better-known error messages include the following:

Data_Bus_Error   This error is described on the Microsoft website: "The most common cause of this error message is a hardware problem. It usually occurs after the installation of faulty hardware, or when existing hardware fails. The problem is frequently related to defective RAM, L2 RAM cache, or video RAM. If hardware has recently been added to the system, remove it and test to see if the error still occurs."

Unexpected_Kernel_Mode_Trap   This error is described on the Microsoft website: "If hardware was recently added to the system, remove it to see if the error recurs. If existing hardware has failed, remove or replace the faulty component. Run hardware diagnostics supplied by the system manufacturer, especially the memory scanner, to determine which hardware component has failed. For details on these procedures, see the owner's manual for your computer. Setting the CPU to run at speeds above the rated specification (known as overclocking the CPU) can also cause this error."

Page_Fault_in_nonpaged_area   This error is described on the Microsoft website: "This Stop message usually occurs after the installation of faulty hardware or in the event of failure of installed hardware (usually related to defective RAM, either main memory, L2 RAM cache, or video RAM). If hardware has been added to the system recently, remove it to see if the error recurs. If existing hardware has failed, remove or replace the faulty component. Run hardware diagnostics supplied by the system manufacturer. For details on these procedures, see the owner's manual for your computer."

irq1_not_less_or_equal   This error is described on the Microsoft website: "This Stop message indicates that a kernel-mode process or driver attempted to access a memory address to which it did not have permission to access. The most common cause of this error is an incorrect or corrupted pointer that references an incorrect location in memory. A pointer is a variable used by a program to refer to a block of memory. If the variable has an incorrect value in it, the program tries to access memory that it should not. When this occurs in a user-mode application, it generates an access violation. When it occurs in kernel mode, it generates a STOP 0x0000000A message. If you encounter this error while upgrading to a newer version of Windows, it might be caused by a device driver, a system service, a virus scanner, or a backup tool that is incompatible with the new version."

Pinwheel

While Microsoft users have the BSOD to deal with, Apple users have similarly come to have the same negative feelings about the Pinwheel of Death (PWOD). This is a multicolored pinwheel mouse pointer (shown in Figure 5.1) that signifies a temporary delay while the system "thinks." In the death scenario, waiting until doomsday will yield no relief to the user.

FIGURE 5.1   The Apple PWOD

In many cases, the situation may not be as dire as it appears. It can be that a single application is holding the device captive. If this is the case, either clicking the desktop or bringing another application to the front will return control to the user. While that will solve the issue for the moment, there was some reason why that application caused the lockup, and it will probably occur again. Two things can be done to prevent a problem from recurring.

First, it could be that the system permissions associated with the application and the files it uses have gotten corrupted. You can use Disk Utility to perform a "permissions repair," which restores file or folder permissions to the state the OS and applications expect them to be in.

Second, it may help to clear the dynamic link editor cache. This is a cache of recently used entry points to the dynamic link library. If this cache gets corrupted, it can cause the PWOD. To clear the cache, follow these steps:

1.   Launch Terminal, located at /Applications/Utilities/.

2.   At the Terminal prompt, enter the following command. Please note this is a single line; some browsers may show this command spanning multiple lines.

     sudo update_dyld_shared_cache -force

3. Press Enter or Return.

4. Enter the administrator account password.

5. Terminal may display warnings about mismatches in the dlyd cache. These are normal, and you can proceed.

On the other hand, if you are experiencing this spinning wheel at startup, the problem is more severe. It means that the system is corrupted. The recovery options will be found by booting to the recovery hard drive, which is a partition created for this purpose in OS X 10.13.4. To do this, start the device, and after the chime, press and hold Command+R until a menu appears. Then select to boot to the recovery partition. Figure 5.2 shows the menu that will appear. You have four options:

- Restore the system from a Time Machine backup by selecting Restore From Time Machine Backup. Then use a backup to restore the system.

- Boot to the Apple servers, which can be done only on newer systems. To do this, select Reinstall macOs. Of course, this will require an Internet connection to be working.

- Get Help Online, which will allow you to use Safari to browse to the Apple support site. This will require an Internet connection to be working as well. To do this, select Get Help Online.

- Repair the hard drive and permissions, in which you select Disk Utility from the menu. Click the First Aid tab and select Repair.

FIGURE 5.2 OS X Utilities

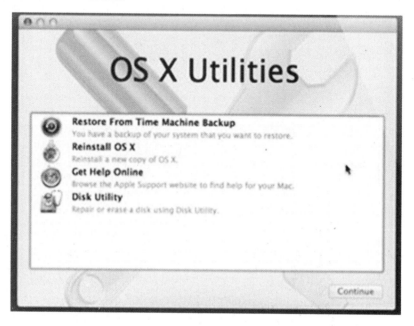

If none of the options discussed so far works, you may need to delete the recovery partition. Take the following steps to do that:

1. Confirm the presence of the recovery partition. Open Terminal.app and enter **diskutil list** to do that.

2. Assuming you see a recovery partition listed on the screen that appears, go back to Terminal.app and enter the following:

   `defaults write com.apple.DiskUtility DUDebugMenuEnabled 1`

3. Open the Disk Utility app. Now, in the menu bar at the top, select Debug ➤ Show Every Partition.

4. Select Recovery HD and click the Mount icon to make it active.

5. Once the option Recovery HD is no longer grayed out, you can right-click to delete it or use Control+click and select Erase.

6. There is still an empty partition, so select the Partition tab and click the Recovery HD partition to select it. Then click the minus sign to remove it.

Black screen

When the screen is blank after bootup and there are signs that the system has power and some functionality (perhaps you can hear the fan or see lights on the system), the problem could lie in several areas. Consider these possibilities:

- Make sure the monitor is on. It has a power switch, so check it.
- If you hear the fan but the system doesn't boot, it could be the power to the motherboard. Check and reseat the power cable to the motherboard.
- Make sure the cable from the monitor to the system is connected properly and try changing it out with a known good cable.
- Try a known good video card to rule out a bad card.
- Ensure that the brightness setting is set high enough.
- In cases where a laptop has been used to direct output to a second display, ensure that the image is being sent to the main display and not just to the external monitor.
- As a last solution, try replacing the monitor.

No power

Power problems usually involve the following issues and scenarios:

- Check the power cord, and if it's plugged into a power strip or UPS, ensure that the strip is plugged in (and if it has a breaker, check to see whether it was tripped by a surge or whether the switch that turns off the entire strip has been inadvertently turned to the off position). In the case of a UPS, check whether the UPS battery is dead. If the cord and UPS are okay, also try a second wall outlet.
- Try replacing the power supply with a known good unit to see whether the power supply failed.

Sluggish performance

Sluggish performance can be caused by many different issues. Among them are:

- Malware consumes resources and may cause this.
- A full system drive can cause slow performance.
- Drive fragmentation will slow performance.
- Insufficient RAM can cause slow performance.
- Overheating will cause the system to slow.
- Drivers or software may be outdated.
- Software may be pirated.

Overheating

Under normal conditions, the PC cools itself by pulling in air. That air is used to dissipate the heat created by the processor (and absorbed by the heat sink). When airflow is restricted by clogged ports, a bad fan, and so forth, heat can build up inside the unit and cause problems. Chip creep—the unseating of components—is one of the more common by-products of a cycle of overheating and cooling of the inside of the system.

Since the air is being pulled into the machine, excessive heat can originate from outside the PC as well because of a hot working environment. The heat can be pulled in and cause the same problems. Take care to keep the ambient air within normal ranges (approximately 60–90 degrees Fahrenheit) and at a constant temperature.

Replacing slot covers is vital. Computers are designed to circulate air with slot covers in place or cards plugged into the ports. Leaving slots on the back of the computer open alters the air circulation and causes more dust to be pulled into the system.

Finally, note whether the fan is working; if it stops, that is a major cause of overheating.

Burning smell

A burning smell usually accompanies smoke but could be present after the smoke has ended because the burning component is now dead. Try to identify the damaged component through a visual inspection; if that is not possible, try to determine the damaged component by replacing parts one by one until functionality returns.

Intermittent shutdown

Among the most vexing issues to troubleshoot is any that comes and goes. When presented with this type of behavior, consider the following possibilities:

- Try replacing the problem component with a known good one.
- A bad motherboard can cause these types of problems when there are issues with its circuitry. Try replacing the motherboard with a known good motherboard.

Application crashes

Application crashes can be an issue with software, but hardware issues can also cause applications to crash. Among the culprits are:

- Voltage spikes or transients
- Heat buildup around a faulty component
- Faulty (partly) memory
- Surface of a hard disk platter hit by the read/write head(s)

Grinding noise

A grinding noise can be one of two things:

- Blades on the fans in the PCs could be hitting each other as they do not necessarily spin at an even pace, therefore resulting in a grinding noise.
- A grinding noise from the hard drive is a symptom of failure in the future. This indicates that components in the hard drive have turned faulty.

Capacitor swelling

A swollen or distended capacitor on the motherboard does not always indicate a failed or failing capacitor, but at the least it indicates one that is in poor health and should be replaced. A distended capacitor will look normal on the side, but the top of it will be swollen a bit, and there may be brown residue coming out of the top of the capacitor. This is caused by gassing of the electrolyte, meaning the electrolyte has been broken down into gas and no longer contributes to the capacitance of the capacitor. The symptoms of this are a system that reboots intermittently and will start only intermittently or not at all.

While replacing a failed capacitor is not easy and in some cases not worth the time and effort compared with replacing the motherboard, to replace a failed capacitor, follow these steps:

1. Locate the failed capacitor. Look for those that exhibit any of the physical symptoms shown in Figure 5.3.
2. Procure a replacement capacitor. It should have the following:
   - The same voltage
   - The same or larger capacity
   - The same external size

   While you can use a capacitor that has a higher voltage or a larger capacity, it is best to use one that matches the one you are replacing.
3. Remove the battery from the board.
4. Use a soldering iron to heat the connection to the board until you can remove the old capacitor. Be careful not to heat the board so much that you damage the connections of other components.

FIGURE 5.3   Failed capacitors

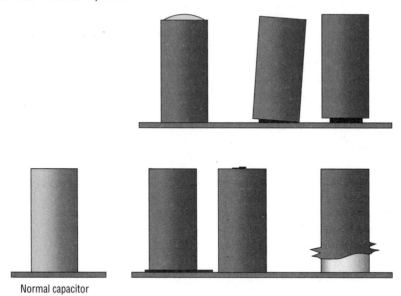

Normal capacitor

5. Clean the remaining hole, and if necessary, use a pin to enlarge the hole for the new capacitor.

6. Insert the new capacitor. Heat some solder and allow it to flow into the hole to seal. Try to keep the remaining drop on the outside as small as possible. This should be performed only by an experienced technician. Soldering incorrectly can ruin the motherboard.

Inaccurate system date/time

If you find that you are continually resetting the system time, it could be that the CMOS battery is dying. Sometimes a symptom of this is that the hard drive and other settings stored in the BIOS are lost. In the absence of an external time source, the time in the BIOS is where the system gets its cue for the date and time. Change the CMOS battery and the problem should be solved.

Exam essentials

Describe the common symptoms of hardware problems.   These symptoms include unexpected shutdowns, lockups, and reboots; POST code beeps; blank screens on bootup; loss of system timekeeping; attempts to boot to an incorrect device; overheating; loss of power; loud noises; intermittent device failures; smoke; a burning smell; and BSODs.

5.3 Given a scenario, troubleshoot and diagnose problems with storage drives and RAID arrays

Common symptoms

Hard drives and RAID arrays typically exhibit symptoms before they fail. Learning to read these clues is critical to troubleshooting. The following are the most common of these clues and symptoms.

Light-emitting diode (LED) status indicators

Most storage devices have LEDs on them that indicate certain things. Every device is different, and referring to the documentation is the best way to learn to interpret these indictors. Just as an example, Table 5.1 shows the meaning of the front-panel LEDs on a My Cloud Mirror storage device from Western Digital.

TABLE 5.1   My Cloud Mirror front-panel indicators

State	Color	Appearance	Description
Power Down	Not Lit	N/A	Device is off.
Powering Up	Blue	Blinking	Device is powering on or in the process of updating firmware.
Power Up	Blue	Solid	Device is powered up and ready.
System Failure	Red	Blinking	System Fault (e.g., firmware update failed, system hang, fan not working, etc.).
Standby	Blue	Pulsing (slowly on and off)	System is in Standby.
User Attention Required	Red	Solid	Device is powered up but user attention is needed.

Grinding noises

A grinding noise will be produced if the read head hits the platter without freezing its rotation. This can be caused by a number of things:

- Power failure that causes the head to stay still over the platter and collapse on it. The friction produced by the moving platter and the stuck head may produce grinding noise.

- Jerks or falls may cause the head to stick to the platter, resulting in grinding noise.

- The hard drive arm is so thin that overheating may deform it. Due to this deformity, the head that is attached to the arm may get in contact with the platter.

Clicking sounds

A loud clicking noise, sometimes referred to as the *click of death*, is caused by the read/write heads making contact with the platters. After that happens, both the heads and the platters become damaged, and the system becomes unable to establish a successful starting point to read the drive. This is serious damage and cannot be repaired. Back up all the data if that's still possible. If the drive is no longer readable, the only option to recover the data is with the help of a professional data recovery service. At that point, you must balance the cost of the recovery with the value of the data. This is a case where performing regular backups saves the day!

Bootable device not found

A failure of the system to boot can be caused by a number of issues:

- Failure of the system to locate the "boot files."

- If you are presented with an "IDE drive not ready" message at startup, the drive may not be spinning fast enough to be read. Enable or increase the hard disk predelay time.

- If you receive the message "Immediately back up all your data and replace your hard drive. A fault may be imminent," take it seriously. This means the drive is using Self-Monitoring, Analysis, and Reporting Technology (SMART) to predict a failure.

- The hard drive data cable or power cable may have become unseated. Sometimes even if the cable appears to be seated fine, reseating it can have a positive effect. Also ensure that the data cable has not been reversed.

OS not found

When you receive the "operating system not found" message, it's usually a software error rather than a hardware error. It could be that the master boot record cannot be located or the active partition cannot be located. These issues can be corrected in Windows by rebooting the computer into Recovery mode and executing one of several commands at the command line of the Recovery environment.

Data loss/corruption

Read/write failures occur when areas of the hard drive require repeated attempts before successful reads or writes occur. This is because these areas are at least partially damaged, although perhaps not enough to be marked as bad sectors. You should perform a hard drive scan using an OS utility to determine whether there are lots of bad sectors. If over time the bad sectors increase, it is an indication that drive failure is imminent and the drive should be replaced. Make sure to back up the system as soon as you discover bad sectors.

RAID failure

RAID can be either software- or hardware-based. When hardware-based RAID is implemented, a RAID controller card is installed into a slot, and the RAID drives connect to that controller card. When the RAID array cannot be located, usually it's a problem with the controller card.

One item to check after you first install the RAID controller card is that RAID is set in the BIOS. It is also possible that the computer has a built-in RAID controller. If that is the case, there will be ports for the drives in the motherboard. Ensure that the two hard drives (or three) are connected to the same port group.

If the RAID system has been operational, check all the cables connecting the drives to the motherboard, reseating them to ensure a good connection. Also ensure that the BIOS/UEFI is still set to RAID.

If there is no integrated RAID controller and the controller card is installed in a slot, ensure that the card is seated properly (maybe even try reseating it). Also ensure that all the drives are securely connected to the ribbon cable coming from the controller card.

RAID stops working

In some cases, one of the drives in the RAID array will cease to function and, depending on the type of RAID, can cause the entire array to be unavailable.

If this is a RAID 1 or a mirrored set, you should still be able to access the other drive. To determine which drive is bad, remove each drive one by one and reboot until you have identified the bad drive. Replace the bad drive and use the RAID software to rebuild the array.

If this is a RAID 5 array, follow the same procedure. The bad news is that if more than one drive has failed, you will not be able to rebuild the array. You will need to create the array again after replacing the bad drives and then restore the data from backup.

Once the bad drives have been replaced, the system may rearrange the drives such that the system cannot locate the drive with the operating system. Use the RAID setup program that you access during bootup to set the boot order of the drives in the array with the drive with the operating system first in the list.

Self-monitoring, Analysis, and Reporting Technology (S.M.A.R.T.) failure

SMART (Self-Monitoring, Analysis, and Reporting Technology; often written as S.M.A.R.T.) is a system included in hard drives and solid-state drives that detects and reports on drive reliability, with a goal of anticipating hardware failures. It requires software on the computer to read the data from the drives and performs its analysis during startup.

Errors reported by SMART should be accepted as predictions that the drive will soon fail, and you should back up all the data as soon as possible, even if the drive appears to be performing normally and passes other disk checks you may run. One error that you may be able to mitigate is overheating. If you can increase ventilation so that the error disappears, you are probably safe to continue using the drive.

Extended read/write times

Another symptom of hard drive issues is slow access to the drive. Oddly, one of the potential causes of this is insufficient memory. When this is the case, it causes excessive paging. Another cause can be a drive that needs to be defragmented. When a drive is fragmented, it takes much longer for all the parts of a file to be located before the file will open. Other issues that cause slow performance are controller cards that need updating, improper data cables, and slower devices sharing the same cable with the hard drive. Finally, insufficient drive space alone will slow performance.

Input/output operations per second (IOPS)

Disk input/output operations per second (IOPS) represents the number of reads and writes that can be done in a second. One of the advantages of newer solid-state drives (SSDs) is that they exhibit much higher IOPS values than traditional hard disk drives. For example, a 15,000 rpm SATA drive with a 3 Gb/s interface is listed to deliver approximately 175–210 IOPS, whereas an SSD with a SATA 3 Gb/s interface is listed at approximately 8,600 IOPS (and that is one of the slower SSD drives).

Missing drives in OS

If the system does not recognize the drive, the problem could be one of the following:

- The hard drive data cable or power cable may have become unseated.
- If you just added a drive, ensure that both drives have not been set to primary or secondary and that the boot drive is set as primary on the first channel.
- If the system uses SATA and you just added a drive, ensure that all the onboard SATA ports are enabled.
- If you just added a drive, ensure that there is no conflict between the new drive and another device.
- If you receive the "No boot device available, strike F1 to retry boot, F2 for setup utility" message, the cause could be incorrect drive geometry (probably not the case if this drive has been functioning properly before), bad CMOS battery, or inability to locate the active partition or master boot record.

Exam essentials

Identify the most common symptoms of hard drive issues.   These include but are not limited to read/write failures, slow performance, loud clicking noises, boot failures, unrecognizable drives, missing operating systems, and Blue Screens of Death.

List symptoms of RAID array issues.   These include missing arrays and RAID arrays that stop functioning.

5.4 Given a scenario, troubleshoot video, projector, and display issues

Video, projector, and display problems may not rate at the top of the priority list for technicians (unless the display is not functioning at all), but to a user, problems with their display may seem like a huge issue. This section discusses common video- and display-related symptoms and their possible sources.

Common symptoms

Display monitors and projectors can exhibit a wide range of symptoms when video-related problems arise. Some are as obvious as no signal whatsoever, whereas other symptoms can be so slight as to almost defy detection. This section discusses common symptoms and some approaches to dealing with these issues.

Incorrect data source

Sometimes the images you see in the display or being represented by the projector or video are not what you expect. You could be connected to the wrong data source. Check the input. You might have the incorrect input. Most projectors have multiple inputs for VGA or HDMI or HDMI1 and HDMI2 or Computer 1 and Computer 2, and so forth. Switch from input to input using the input button on the projector.

You also may need to hit the FN key and a function button with a monitor icon on your laptop to get the picture to project from your projector. It varies from laptop to laptop.

Physical cabling issues

When there is no image on the screen, the display is either dead or not receiving the signal from the computer. Check the cable from the back of the PC to the monitor, ensure it is tightly screwed in place, and reseat the cables if required. Also ensure that the monitor is plugged into a functional power outlet and that the brightness settings are high enough. Finally, for a laptop, you should use the appropriate Fn key to ensure that the signal isn't being sent to an external monitor.

To eliminate the video card as the problem, connect a known good display to the computer and see whether the same problem exists. If so, then the problem is not the display. If it works fine, the problem is the display. Displays do die and usually are not cost-effective to repair. The usual solution is to replace the display.

If the card is the problem, try reseating it. If that provides no relief, insert a known good card. Operating in the same fashion as you did with the display, you can determine whether the video card is the problem.

Burned-out bulb

When projectors have a dim image, it can be that the bulb is going bad. All bulbs have a stated lifetime that can be found in the documentation of the projector. The hours of lifetime that you find in the documentation have usually been stretched a bit, meaning that toward the end of the lifetime the bulb will start to fade in brightness.

Fuzzy image

A fuzzy image on a projector can be caused by several things:

- The lens is dirty or defective.
- The screen and the projector haven't been aligned properly.
- The lens cap is still on.
- The lens is out of focus.

With regard to computer display, adjusting the resolution may help. You might also try updating the graphics driver software. Finally, try downloading and installing the latest BIOS for your system.

Display burn-in

Burn-in is a condition that affected CRT monitors and still affects plasma and organic light-emitting diode (OLED) displays. LCDs are generally not affected. The condition occurs when images are left for extended periods of time on the screen. The early screen savers were designed to prevent this in unattended displays by displaying a constantly changing image.

Software and utilities can be used to remedy burn-in but will have little effect if the burn-in is severe. It is also useful to know that the display will be most susceptible to this when it is new, in the first few hours of operation. DVDs can be purchased that will "break in" a screen, and in some cases they can even eliminate existing burn-in if it is not severe.

Dead pixels

Pixels are the small dots on the screen that are filled with a color; as a group they present the image you see on the screen. Two conditions can occur with the pixels: stuck pixels and bad or dead pixels.

Stuck pixels have been filled with a color and are not changing as required to display changes in the image. Dead pixels are simply black with no color in them.

When there are few of these and they are not clustered in the same spot, you may not even be able to notice them. When they build to the point where they are noticeable, they cannot be fixed, and the monitor must be replaced. You may be able to get some satisfaction from the manufacturer depending on how old the monitor is and the policy of the vendor.

Flashing screen

When the image is flickering or flashing, check the cables and ensure they are seated properly. If that doesn't help, try different cables because it could be a problem with the cable itself.

Another possible reason is a mismatch between the resolution settings and the refresh rate. If this is the problem, it will occur only when using the higher resolutions. You should increase the refresh rate to support the higher resolutions.

While you won't see many CRT monitors, flickering on those can indicate a source of electromagnetic interference (EMI) or radio frequency interference (RFI) near the display, such as a radio. Degaussing CRT monitors can help.

Incorrect color display

When the image displayed uses incorrect color patterns or is garbled, the root of the problem could depend on when the condition presents itself. If the screen looks fine during the POST but then goes bad when Windows starts to load, it is probably because of an incorrect setting of the video card. For example, it may be set to do something the card is incapable of doing. Restart in safe mode (which will cause the system to use the VGA driver) and check all the settings of the card while ensuring that it is not set for a resolution level for which the card or the monitor is not capable. You may also try updating the driver if a new one is available.

If this problem occurs from the moment you turn the system on, the problem is hardware, and you should check the monitor, cable, and card, replacing each with a known good piece until you isolate the bad component.

Audio issues

In some cases you have no sound when playing a video that is using a data source such as the DisplayPort or High-Definition Media Interface (HDMI). While these interfaces are designed to also carry audio, in some cases the system may change the default audio playback device to the audio-supported cable assuming that another audio device is being used. The issue may occur when a laptop is coming out of sleep mode as the system is detecting the audio-capable cable first.

To change the default sound playback device in Windows 10:

1. Click Start, and then click Settings (gear icon).

2. Click System.

3. In the left menu, click Sound.

4. Under Choose Your Output Device, select the audio device that you want to use.

Dim image

If the image is fine but dim, first check the brightness setting, usually found in the front of the monitor. If this is a laptop, remember there are function keys that when hit inadvertently will dim the screen as well. Check that.

If the display is an LCD, the backlight may be going bad. You learned earlier that these are pencil-sized lights that go behind the screen. They can be replaced on a laptop by following the procedure for opening the laptop lid (where the display resides) and replacing the backlight. Keep in mind that opening the case voids the warranty, so if you still have warranty left, make use of that option.

If it is the backlight on a desktop LCD, the backlight can be replaced for about $20, so it makes a repair worth doing if you want to open the monitor. Use the documentation or the vendor website for details on opening the case.

Intermittent projector shutdown

When the video card is overheating, it can cause display problems and shutdowns. Overheating video cards usually exhibit symptoms like garbled output on the display or artifacts (covered later in this section). They also can result in flickers and flashes. In some cases, the display will cease functioning after being on a few seconds. After you restart the computer, the display again works for a few seconds and then fails.

When overheating is the problem, you must find the reason for the overheating. Clean all the dust out of the inside of the case and inspect all fans to ensure they are functioning—especially the fan on the video card if one is present. If the problem has been happening for some time, the card may have become damaged. Try using a different card and see whether the problem goes away. You may need to replace the video card.

Projectors

When projector bulbs are overheating, they may shut down to cool down. Simply waiting until the bulb has cooled and then restarting the projector will usually solve the problem. It may also be helpful to inform the users that many projectors will not allow the bulb to be restarted soon after you turn it off, so users may want to consider that if they intend to restart the projector soon after shutting it down.

Exam essentials

List the common symptoms of display problems and the appropriate troubleshooting technique for each. Symptoms include but are not limited to no image; overheating; dead pixels; incorrect color patterns; and dim, flickering, or distorted image. Resolution techniques include updating drivers, changing resolution settings, and replacing the monitor.

5.5 Given a scenario, troubleshoot common issues with mobile devices

Mobile devices have their own unique sets of issues that may not be encountered with desktop computers. This section discusses common issues and their solutions. Mobile devices require a different set of procedures for opening the case while protecting the integrity of the unit.

Common symptoms

Not all mobile device issues are unique to mobile devices. They suffer from many of the same issues as desktop machines. However, some problems are unique to laptops and mobile devices or at least are more prone to occur with laptops, as you will learn in this section.

Poor battery health

When battery life is not what it should be in a mobile device, there are a number of possible reasons. The following are some things that can drain a good battery:

- Leaving display brightness too high
- Constantly enabled wireless connections
- Constantly enabled location services
- Constantly enabled background data services

You may detect a trend in this list, and that is leaving things on! All of those services eat the battery. Setting the device to Airplane mode stops all of that battery sucking. Yes, you may have to manually turn it on to check email, but the convenience is eating the battery.

In other cases, the battery is nearing the end of its life. If using Airplane mode doesn't help, it's probably time for a new battery. All batteries have a limited number of recharges in them. Check the documentation of the device for guidance on this. If the battery does suddenly die shortly after a charge, it's a red flag.

Swollen battery

Just as swollen capacitors are a bad thing, so are swollen batteries. A swollen battery occurs when the battery's cells are overcharged because lithium-ion batteries react unfavorably to overcharging. When you encounter a swollen battery, the only solution is to replace it. But you should practice the following safe battery handling procedures when dealing with swollen batteries:

- Be careful not to puncture a swollen battery. The casing is under stress from the built-up gases within.
- If the swollen state makes the battery difficult to remove, take the device to an expert for removal.
- If you are able to safely remove the swollen battery, store it in a safe cool container and take it to an authorized acceptance center. Do not throw it in the trash!

To avoid a swollen battery altogether, follow the guidelines in the section "Poor battery health" to extend the life of batteries.

Broken screen

Tablets and smartphones use a touchscreen interface that eliminates the need for a keyboard. Touchscreen monitors use two technologies: touch flow and multitouch. Before we dive into solving a nonresponsive touchscreen, let's review these technologies.

TouchFlow

TouchFLO, is a user interface feature designed by HTC. It is used by dragging your finger up and down or left and right to access common tasks on the screen. This movement is akin to scrolling the screen up and down or scrolling the screen left and right.

Multitouch

Multitouch allows the screen to recognize multiple simultaneous screen touches. This allows for movements such as those used for expanding or enlarging pictures with two fingers and then reducing them back again with the reverse movement.

The first thing that all documentation will tell you to try is to restart the device, and in many cases the documentation is not blowing smoke at you; this does actually solve the issue. Unfortunately, if the screen is broken or the wires are cut, this will not help, but you should always try this first.

Devices with the Android operating system have a Device Diagnostics tool, which can test the touchscreen, among other things. To access this tool, use a special key sequence (see the documentation) on the same keypad where you enter phone numbers. When you hit the proper sequence, the menu for the tool will appear; Figure 5.4 shows the menu for the Device Diagnostic tool for the Samsung S4. There are two tests found here that apply to the touchscreen: TSP Dot Mode and TSP Grid Mode.

FIGURE 5.4   Samsung Device Diagnostics menu

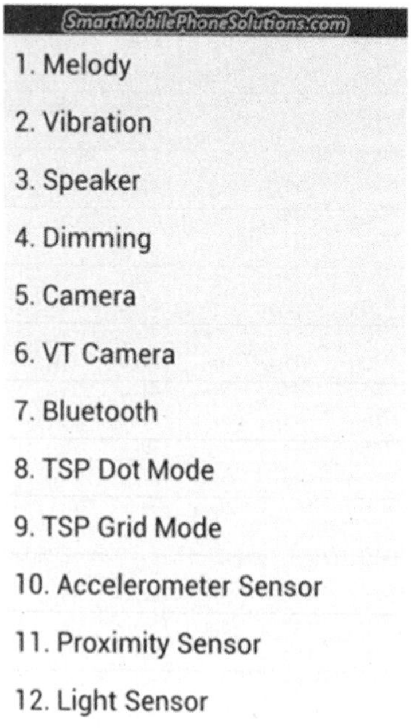

SmartMobilePhoneSolutions.com

1. Melody

2. Vibration

3. Speaker

4. Dimming

5. Camera

6. VT Camera

7. Bluetooth

8. TSP Dot Mode

9. TSP Grid Mode

10. Accelerometer Sensor

11. Proximity Sensor

12. Light Sensor

TSP Dot Mode allows you to verify that the screen is reading your touch. It will place a dot on the screen everywhere you touch it where it is reading the input. TSP Grid Mode allows you to test each section or grid of the screen. You can drag your finger across the screen and identify any dead spots that may be present.

If the device passes both of these tests, you have no problem with the screen; you have an issue with software, not hardware. Try removing the battery while the device is on (a soft reset). If the device doesn't allow this, it will typically have an operation you can execute called a *simulated battery pull*. If neither of these steps helps, the next step is to reboot the device to safe mode.

If booting to safe mode solves the issue, the issue lies in your application. It may be outdated or corrupted, so try reinstalling the latest version. But if none of the techniques so far works, you are ready to get more extreme and perform a hard reset, which returns the device to the factory settings. Don't do this until you have backed up all the data on the device. Also, do not do this if the device exhibited any hardware issues when you ran the diagnostics test. You will need it to work properly when you finish the reset so that you can set up the phone again.

If the device fails the diagnostic test, you have a hardware issue. If the damage is from liquids, submerge the phone in 99 percent isopropyl alcohol. Dry the phone completely and turn it on. This has actually fixed some phones with water damage. Unfortunately, in most cases, when the diagnostic test fails, you have to replace the screen.

These same options are also available with touchscreens on devices like the Microsoft Surface. The same general approach applies with some variation (clean screen, restart, recalibrate the screen, install the latest updates, restore from backup, refresh, reset). The terms *refresh* and *reset* mean the same here as when dealing with laptops and desktops.

Improper charging

Most NiCad batteries build up memory, and that memory can prevent a battery from offering a full charge. The biggest issue with DC power problems is a battery's inability to power the laptop as long as it should. If a feature is available to fully drain the battery, you should use it to eliminate the memory (letting the laptop run on battery on a regular basis greatly helps). If you can't drain the battery and eliminate the memory effect, you should replace the battery.

Poor/no connectivity

When there is no wireless connectivity, the cause is usually one of two things:

- The wireless capability is disabled (enabling and disabling this function is usually done with a key combination or a Fn key) because this is easy to disable inadvertently. This can also be a hardware switch on the side, front, or back of the case.
- The wireless antenna is bad or the cable needs to be reseated.

Bluetooth is also enabled and disabled with a key combination and can be disabled easily. The first thing to try is to reenable it. The second thing to try is to reseat the antenna cable. If all else fails, try a new antenna. Like the WLAN NIC, this can also be a hardware switch on the side, front, or back of the case.

Liquid damage

Exposure to even small amounts of liquid can cause batteries to function erratically, charger ports to charge intermittently, software to corrupt, or even total power failure. If this occurs:

- Turn off your device and remove the battery.

- Place the device in rice to reduce drying time.

If this doesn't work, completely disassemble your device and clean all remnants of the damage, including corrosion, contaminants, and rust. Replace components that were too badly damaged.

Overheating

When a mobile device is getting hot (and I'm talking very hot here, not just warm), the cause can be the battery. If you find that is the source of the heat, replace the battery. Beyond that, some issues that can cause or contribute to overheating are as follows:

- Excessive gaming

- Excessive browsing

- Using the device while charging the device

On a laptop, excessive heat can indicate that the vents are blocked. It also can be a case of running too many things at once. Clean vents often and ensure they are not blocked when the device is on. Laptops need a hard, even surface so that the vents can expel heat. This is why running a device on your lap produces so much heat.

Digitizer issues

In Chapter 1, "Mobile Devices," you learned that digitizers read pressure applied to the surface of the display and are what make touchscreens work. Symptoms of digitizer problems include:

- Erratic behavior of the touchscreen

- Poor response of the touchscreen

- Dead spots on the touchscreen

- Applications randomly opening

- No touch response

Replacing the digitizer is the solution. For some devices that means a field-replaceable unit (FRU). However, for other devices it may mean replacing the entire screen.

Physically damaged ports

There are not many physical ports on most smartphones, whereas laptops can have a wide range of interfaces. The port that usually gets the most use on a smartphone is the charging port. An easy fix is to use a toothpick to clean out the port. Replacement charging ports can be purchased directly from phone part suppliers like Repairs Universe, Injured Gadgets, and iFixit. Though it's possible to replace the stand-alone charging port with soldering, it's typically easier to replace the entire flex cable. Doing so will also ensure that the charging port is completely repaired in the event the issue is with the flex cable itself.

When physical interfaces break on a laptop, they are usually replaceable without buying a new motherboard. Replacing a bad DC jack, on the other hand, usually requires soldering. If this is not a skill you possess, just replace the motherboard. If you want to attempt it, remove all the parts to get to the motherboard. In some cases, the old DC jack can still be used; it just needs to have the old solder removed and replaced. If that is not the case, remove the old DC jack by unsoldering it from the connector. Then put the new jack in place and solder it to the connectors. Replace all the parts and pieces you removed to get to the board. In general, a bad DC jack usually means a new board.

Malware

When system performance drops, the first thing to check for is the presence of a virus. If the system seems to have an overabundance of disk activity, scan it for viruses, using a virus program that resides externally on a CD/DVD or memory stick.

Cursor drift/touch calibration

A second, or ghost, cursor can be caused when the laptop has a trackpad that is too sensitive. Some laptops and tablets also vent warm air through the keyboard, and when the lid is left down, it heats up the trackpad and causes this type of cursor behavior. Updating the driver for the touchpad has been known to help this problem. Another approach is to disable the touchpad completely and use an external mouse.

Pointer drift occurs when the mouse cursor slowly drifts across the screen with no assistance from the user. In some cases, it occurs only on a second or third monitor and not on the main monitor. If that is the case, there is a setting in the display properties that may solve the issue. In Windows 10, navigate to the display properties by right-clicking the display and selecting Preferences. Then in the menu at the bottom left of the resulting screen, choose Display. On the Display Settings page, select the Let Me Choose One Scaling Level For All My Displays check box.

In other cases, the problem is not related to multiple monitors at all. If you find that it is occurring only with certain applications, it may be neither a pointer nor a device problem at all but rather an application issue. Finally, on some laptops and other small devices that use trackpads, you or the user may be leaving your hand resting on a part of the device very close to the trackpad and it is picking that up and causing the pointer to move.

Touchscreens sometimes need calibration. Calibration is a process that varies by vendor but that usually requires touching the screen in certain places when it tells you to. See the documentation for the exact method.

Exam essentials

Identify common symptoms of mobile device issues.   Some of the symptoms include a dim, flickering, or blank display; sticking keys; intermittent or nonexistent wireless or Bluetooth connectivity; battery and power issues; and ghost cursors.

5.6 Given a scenario, troubleshoot and resolve printer issues

In the real world, you'll find that a large portion of all service calls relate to printing problems. This section will give you some general guidelines and common printing solutions to resolve printing problems.

Common symptoms

There is no single shared device in the network that more users come in contact with and use every day than the printer. You may have to troubleshoot the common symptoms in this section on a daily basis, depending on your environment. Your ability to get a down printer working will make you more valuable to your employer.

Lines down the printed pages

Vertical lines can appear in either of two forms.

Vertical black lines on the page

With laser printers, a groove or scratch in the electrophotographic (EP) drum can cause the problem of vertical black lines running down all or part of the page. Because a scratch is lower than the surface, it doesn't receive as much (if any) of a charge as the other areas. The result is that toner sticks to it as though it were discharged. Because the groove may go around the circumference of the drum, the line may go all the way down the page.

Another possible cause of vertical black lines is a dirty charge corona wire, which prevents a sufficient charge from being placed on the EP drum. Because the EP drum has almost zero charge, toner sticks to the areas that correspond to the dirty areas on the charge corona wire.

The solution to the first problem is, as always, to replace the toner cartridge (or EP drum, if your printer uses a separate EP drum and toner). You can also solve the second problem with a new toner cartridge, but in this case that would be an extreme solution. It's easier to clean the charge corona with the brush supplied with the cartridge.

When dealing with inkjet printers, vertical black lines on the page can mean the printhead needs cleaning or that the print cartridge needs to be replaced.

Vertical white lines on the page

With laser printers, vertical white lines running down all or part of the page are a relatively common problem on older printers, especially ones that see little maintenance. They're caused by foreign matter (more than likely toner) caught on the transfer corona wire. The dirty spots keep the toner from being transmitted to the paper at those locations, with the result that streaks form as the paper progresses past the transfer corona wire.

The solution is to clean the corona wires. Some printers come with a small corona-wire brush to help in this procedure. To use it, remove the toner cartridge and run the brush in the charge corona groove on top of the toner cartridge. Replace the cartridge and use the brush to brush away any foreign deposits on the transfer corona. Be sure to put it back in its holder when you're finished.

For inkjet printers, clean the printhead first (or run the built-in cleaning cycle) and then try replacing the cartridge. This behavior is usually caused by dust or debris.

Streaks

With laser printers, streaks usually indicate that the fuser is not fusing the toner properly on the paper. It could also be that the incorrect paper is being used. In laser printers, you can sometimes tell the printer that you are using a heavier paper. For dot-matrix, you can adjust the platen for thicker paper.

If you can pick up a sheet from a laser printer, run your thumb across it, and have the image come off on your thumb, you have a fuser problem. The fuser isn't heating the toner and fusing it onto the paper. This could be caused by a number of things—but all of them can be taken care of with a fuser replacement. For example, if the halogen light inside the heating roller has burned out, that will cause the problem. The solution is to replace the fuser. The fuser can be replaced with a rebuilt unit, if you prefer. Rebuilt fusers are almost as good as new fusers, and some even come with guarantees. Plus, they cost less.

 The whole fuser may not need to be replaced. You can order fuser components from parts suppliers and then rebuild them. For example, if the fuser has a bad lamp, you can order a lamp and replace it in the fuser.

Another, similar problem happens when small areas of smudging repeat themselves down the page. Dents or cold spots in the fuser heat roller cause this problem. The only solution is to replace either the fuser assembly or the heat roller.

If an ink cartridge becomes damaged or develops a hole, it can put too much ink on the page, and the letters will smear. In this case, the solution is to replace the ink cartridge. (However, a small amount of smearing is normal if the pages are laid on top of each other immediately after printing.) Because damage is possible in the process, you need to be careful when refilling cartridges, and many manufacturers do not suggest using refilled cartridges at all.

With inkjet or dot-matrix printers, streaks can mean the printhead needs cleaning. If cleaning doesn't help, try replacing the cartridge (inkjet) or the ribbon (dot-matrix).

Garbled print

Many problems with a printer that won't work with the operating system or that prints the wrong characters can be traced to problems with its software. Computers and printers can't talk to each other by themselves. They need interface software known as *drivers* to translate software commands into commands the printer can understand.

For a printer to work with a particular operating system, a driver must be installed for it. In Chapter 3, "Hardware," you learned about the page description languages (PDL) and drivers. Please review that section.

If the wrong printer driver is selected, the computer will send commands in the wrong language. If that occurs, the printer will print several pages of garbage (even if only one page of information was sent). This "garbage" isn't garbage at all, but the printer PDL commands printed literally as text instead of being interpreted as control commands.

Toner not fusing to paper

In laser printers, when the toner does not fuse properly to the paper, it will streak and smudge. See the section "Streaks" for more information.

Paper jams

Laser printers today run at copier speeds. As a result, their most common problem is paper jams. Paper can get jammed in a printer for several reasons. First, feed jams happen when the paper-feed rollers get worn. The solution to this problem is easy: replace the worn rollers.

If your paper-feed jams are caused by worn pickup rollers, there is something you can do to get your printer working while you're waiting for the replacement pickup rollers. Scuff the feed rollers with a pot scrubber pad (or something similar) to roughen up the surfaces. This trick works only once. After that, the rollers aren't thick enough to touch the paper.

Another cause of feed jams is related to the drive of the pickup roller. The drive gear (or clutch) may be broken or have teeth missing. Again, the solution is to replace it. To determine whether the problem is a broken gear or worn rollers, print a test page, but leave the paper tray out. Look into the paper-feed opening with a flashlight, and see whether the paper pickup rollers are turning evenly and don't skip. If they turn evenly, the problem is more than likely worn rollers.

Worn exit rollers can also cause paper jams. These rollers guide the paper out of the printer into the paper-receiving tray. If they're worn or damaged, the paper may catch on its way out of the printer. These types of jams are characterized by a paper jam that occurs just as the paper is getting to the exit rollers. If the paper jams, open the rear door and see where the paper is. If the paper is close to the exit roller, the exit rollers are probably the problem.

The solution is to replace all the exit rollers. You must replace all of them at the same time, because even one worn exit roller can cause the paper to jam. Besides, they're inexpensive. Don't be cheap and skimp on these parts if you need to have them replaced.

Paper jams can be the fault of the paper. If your printer consistently tries to feed multiple pages into the printer, the paper isn't dry enough. If you live in an area with high humidity, this could be a problem. Some solutions are pretty unconventional but may work (such as keeping the paper in a Tupperware-type airtight container or microwaving it to remove moisture). The best all-around solution, however, is humidity control and keeping the paper wrapped until it's needed. Keep the humidity around 50 percent or lower (but greater than 25 percent if you can in order to avoid problems with electrostatic discharge). Poor paper quality can also cause this problem.

Finally, a metal, grounded strip called the *static eliminator strip* inside the printer drains the corona charge away from the paper after it has been used to transfer toner from the EP cartridge. If that strip is missing, broken, or damaged, the charge will remain on the paper and may cause it to stick to the EP cartridge, causing a jam. If the paper jams after reaching the corona assembly, this may be the cause.

Faded print

In laser printers, faded output usually indicates that the toner cartridge is just about empty. You can usually remove it, shake it, and replace it and then get a bit more life out of it before it is completely empty, but this is a signal that you are near the end.

Another possibility is that the ink cartridge has dried out from lack of use. That's why the manufacturers include a small suction pump inside the printer that primes the ink cartridge before each print cycle. If this priming pump is broken or malfunctioning, this problem will manifest itself, and the pump will need to be replaced.

For dot-matrix printers, faded printing means you need to replace the ribbon, which is the source of ink in that printer type.

Incorrect paper size

When a print job is generated on an incorrect paper size, it means one of three things:

- The wrong paper is loaded into the tray.
- The user chose the wrong paper size or left it at its default, which resulted in an incorrect paper size.
- The printer has incorrect paper tray designations.

When setting up the printer, you need to specify what type paper is in each tray. If that is not done correctly, you can have this behavior. It can also occur when users load the wrong size or type of paper in a tray.

Paper not feeding

When the paper is not feeding into the printer, it means the pickup rollers have hardened and lost their ability to pick up the paper. Replacing these rollers usually fixes the problem.

In some cases, it's not the rollers but the paper-feed sensor. It is designed to tell the printer when it is out of paper. Always try cleaning the sensor first before replacing it. High humidity can also cause the paper to not feed properly.

Multipage misfeed

Another issue that is usually traced to the pickup rollers is when multiple pages are fed at a time rather than a single page. The problem could also be the paper. Paper-feed issues might result from dusty, torn, wrinkled, wet, or folded paper in the tray. Finally, the issue may also occur when the paper trays are overloaded.

Multiple prints pending in queue

Sometimes the printer will not print, and all attempts to delete print jobs or clear the print queue fail. It's almost as if the printer is just frozen. When this occurs, the best thing to do is restart the print spooler service on the computer that is acting as the print server. Unfortunately, all users will have to resend their print jobs after this, but at least the printer will be functional again.

Speckling on printed pages

A faulty ink or toner cartridge is one reason that ink specks may appear on documents; paper dust and ink particles on the printer's internal components can also cause this problem. If you are using a laser printer, inks specks can also be caused by a faulty photoconductor unit. A buildup of paper dust and ink particles inside your printer can also cause specks on your printed output as well as on blank paper.

If these are white specks, then the issue could be:

- Appropriate paper is not being used.
- Damp paper is being used.
- The drum in the toner cartridge is deteriorated.

Double/echo images on the print

A problem unique to laser printers, *ghosting*, occurs when you can see light images of previously printed pages on the current page. This is caused by one of two things: bad erasure lamps or a broken cleaning blade. If the erasure lamps are bad, the previous electrostatic discharges aren't completely wiped away. When the electrophotographic (EP) drum rotates toward the developing roller, some toner sticks to the slightly discharged areas. A broken cleaning blade, on the other hand, causes old toner to build up on the EP drum and consequently present itself in the next printed image.

Replacing the toner cartridge solves the second problem. Solving the first problem involves replacing the erasure lamps in the printer. Because the toner cartridge is the least expensive cure, you should try that first. Usually, replacing the toner cartridge will solve the problem. If it doesn't, you'll then have to replace the erasure lamps.

Incorrect chroma display

A chroma key is used in the green screen process that allows you to place a moving image taken on a green background and drop it into a second scene. When the chroma key display is incorrect, it means the process will not be as clean as you would like. Some of the issues can come from the following:

- Bad screen lighting
- Inconsistent green color
- Special effects that ruin the lighting
- Inconsistent lighting in multiple images being dropped

Correcting chroma display issues such as these is involved and beyond the scope of the exam. For more information, visit www.videomaker.com/article/c13/18075-green-screen-lighting-mistakes-and-how-to-fix-them

Grinding noise

When there is a grinding noise when you either start the printer or print a job, it means either a carriage stall or a paper jam. The carriage assembly, which holds the ink cartridges, may be stalled at the left side of the printer. A paper jam may have occurred previously. The cause of the problem may be that the printer's clutch actuator is disengaged.

Locate the metal gear assembly at the left side of the printer. Directly above the metal gear is the clutch actuator. The arrow on the clutch actuator should be in the space to the right of the metal gear and plastic half-gear just below the clutch actuator.

If the arrow on the clutch actuator is stuck between the metal gear and the plastic half-gear, lift the clutch actuator and move the arrow to the right of the plastic half-gear. Once the arrow on the clutch actuator is to the right of the gears, the clutch actuator should move freely.

Finishing issues

The finishing process is when pages are stapled and holes are punched if so configured. In this section you'll learn about finishing issues.

Staple jams

Printers that staple will hold the staples in what is sometimes called the *stapling mailbox*. When staples get jammed, follow this procedure:

1. Press the button to release the stapling mailbox, and slide it away from the printer.
2. Press the latch to release the stapler door.
3. Open the stapler door.
4. Lift the green tab on the staple cartridge upward, and then pull the staple cartridge straight out of its slot.
5. Lift up on the small lever at the back of the staple cartridge.
6. Remove the jammed staples from the staple cartridge.
7. Load new staples and reverse the steps to put the printer back together.

Hole punch

The hole-punch system can get jammed if the hole-punch waste container used to hold the small pieces punched out of each sheet is full. To empty it:

1. Open the finisher door.
2. Slide the hole-punch waste container out of the finisher.
3. Dispose of the waste.
4. Insert the emptied hole-punch waste container into the printer.

Incorrect page orientation

Page orientation specifies whether to print landscape or portrait. This is a choice you can make when sending the print job, so if incorrectly chosen it will result in this behavior. But it can also be the result of an incorrect or corrupted printer driver.

Exam essentials

Identify the most common symptoms of printing problems. These include streaks, faded prints, ghost images, incompletely fused toner, creased paper, paper jams and feeding issues, no connectivity, garbled characters, vertical lines, print queue issues, total print failure, and incorrect print colors.

5.7 Given a scenario, troubleshoot problems with wired and wireless networks

At one time, wireless networks were considered an extravagant and insecure addition to the enterprise network, but now users expect wireless access. No longer is it a business advantage; it is now a business requirement. This section discusses troubleshooting both wired and wireless networks.

Common symptoms

Network problems, usually manifesting themselves as an inability to connect to resources, can arise from many different sources. This section discusses some common symptoms of networking issues.

Intermittent wireless connectivity

When a connectivity issue comes and goes, it can be a hardware issue or a software issue. The following hardware components should be checked for functionality:

Network Cable   A damaged cable connecting the AP to the network can cause intermittent connectivity.

Network Interface Card (NIC)   In cases where the WLAN card is not integrated, if the WLAN NIC is not properly seated or has worked its way partially out of its slot, it can cause connections that come and go.

Interference   On a wireless network, cordless phones, microwave ovens, and other wireless networks can interfere with transmissions. Also, users who stray too far from the AP can experience a signal that comes and goes.

The following are software issues that can cause intermittent connectivity:

DHCP Issues   When the DHCP server is down or out of IP addresses, the problem will not manifest itself to those users who already have an IP address until their lease expires and they need a new address. In this case, some users will be fine and others will not, and then users who were fine earlier in the day may have problems later when their IP address lease expires.

DNS Problems   If the DNS server is down or malfunctioning, it will cause problems for DNS clients who need name resolution requests answered. For users who have already connected to resources in the last hour before the outage, connectivity to those resources will still be possible until the name-to–IP address mapping is removed from the client DNS resolver cache.

Slow network speeds

Slow transmission on the network can be caused by hardware and software issues. Some of the physical issues that can cause slow performance are:

Incorrect Cabling   The network can go only as fast as its weakest link. Using CAT 3 cabling, for example, will only allow the network to operate at 10 Mbps even if all the network cards are capable of 10 Gbps.

Malfunctioning NIC   NICs can malfunction and cause a broadcast storm. These broadcast packets fill the network with traffic that slows performance for all users. Use a protocol analyzer to determine the MAC address of the offending computer.

From a software standpoint, the following issues can result in less than ideal performance:

Router Misconfiguration   If the router is not configured correctly, it can cause slow performance because of less than optimal routing paths. Escalate the issue to the appropriate administrators.

Switch Misconfiguration   An improperly implemented redundant switch network can result in switching loops that cause slow performance. Escalate the issue to the appropriate administrators.

Limited connectivity

In some cases, the computer has connectivity to some but not all resources. When this is the case, issues that may reside on other layers of the OSI model should come under consideration. These include the following:

Authentication Issues   Does the user have the permission to access the resource?

DNS Issues   You may be able to ping the entire network using IP addresses, but most access is done by name, not IP address. If you can't ping resources by name, DNS is not functional, meaning either the DNS server is down or the local machine is not configured with the correct IP address of the DNS server. If recent changes have occurred in the DNS mappings or if your connection to the destination device has recently failed because of a temporary network issue that has been solved, you may need to clear the local DNS cache using the ipconfig /flushdns command.

Remote Problem   Don't forget that establishing a connection is a two-way street, and if the remote device has an issue, communication cannot occur. Always check the remote device as well. Any interconnecting device between the computer and resource, such as a switch or router, should also be checked for functionality.

Jitter

When there is a variation in the amount of packet delay, it is called *jitter*. This fluctuation in delay causes congestion in the network. It can also cause packets at the end of the queue to get dropped, requiring retransmissions that cause further delay. Possible solutions include:

- Upgrading the router
- Increasing the bandwidth
- Implementing a jitter buffer

Poor Voice over Internet Protocol (VoIP) quality

Although voice over the PSTN is circuit-switched, voice can also be encapsulated in packets and sent across packet-switching networks. When this is done over an IP network, it is called Voice over IP (VoIP). Where circuit-switching networks use the Signaling System 7 (SS7) protocol to set up, control, and disconnect a call, VoIP uses Session Initiation Protocol (SIP) to break up the call sessions. When VOIP quality is poor, it is usually a matter of network congestion. In VoIP implementations, QoS is implemented to ensure that certain traffic (especially voice) is given preferential treatment over the network.

SIP is an application layer protocol that can operate over either TCP or UDP with voice traffic using the same network used for regular data. Because latency is always possible on these networks, protocols have been implemented to reduce the impact as this type of traffic is much more affected by delay. Applications such as voice and video need to have protocols and devices that can provide an isochronous network. Isochronous networks guarantee continuous bandwidth without interruption. Isochronous networks don't use an internal clock source or start and stop bits. All bits are of equal importance and are anticipated to occur at regular intervals.

Port flapping

Port flapping is a situation in which a physical interface on the switch continually goes up and down, caused by bad, unsupported, or nonstandard cable or other link synchronization issues. Some network devices allow you to set Link Flap Prevention Settings on a switch that *err-disable* a flapping port. If you have a redundant network, this feature will help. Otherwise, it will make the situation even worse.

The root cause must be discovered, and while it can be a hardware issue, keep in mind that in cases where two ends of a link require compatible settings of some kind or require authentication, the settings are not compatible or the authentication is failing.

High latency

High latency simply means the network is slow. It is rare that the entire network is slow; it's usually one or two sections (subnets). Use `tracert` to determine where the slow subnet(s) reside(s) and then concentrate your troubleshooting effort there. You will learn more about using both `ping` and `tracert` in Chapter 6, "Operating Systems."

External interference

Both wireless and wired networks can be affected by electromagnetic interference (EMI) and radio frequency interference (RFI). EMI will degrade network performance. This can be identified by the poor operation you may experience. Be sure to run cables around (not over) ballasts and other items that can cause EMI. RFI is a similar issue introduced by radio waves. Wireless networks suffer even more from both of these issues.

Exam essentials

Identify common symptoms of network issues and their potential causes.   Examples include limited, intermittent, or no connectivity; slow transfer speeds; and low RF signal.

Review Questions

You can find the answers in the appendix.

1. Which of the following is the final step in the CompTIA troubleshooting method?
   A. Establish a plan of action to resolve the problem and implement the solution.
   B. Document findings, actions, and outcomes.
   C. Establish a theory of probable cause (question the obvious).
   D. Identify the problem.

2. Which of the following is the first step in the CompTIA troubleshooting method?
   A. Establish a plan of action to resolve the problem and implement the solution.
   B. Document findings, actions, and outcomes.
   C. Establish a theory of probable cause (question the obvious).
   D. Identify the problem.

3. What is the most common reason for an unexpected reboot?
   A. Overheating
   B. ESD damage
   C. RFI
   D. Memory leak

4. Which of the following is typically not a cause of system lockups?
   A. Memory issues
   B. Virus
   C. Video driver
   D. Bad NIC driver

5. What are proprietary screen crashes called in Windows?
   A. Pin wheel
   B. BSOD
   C. Bomb screen
   D. PSOID

6. Which operating system uses the Pinwheel of Death as a proprietary screen crash?
   A. Apple
   B. Linux
   C. Windows
   D. Unix

7. What are the small dots on the screen that are filled with a color?

  A. Pixels

  B. Hypervisors

  C. Cells

  D. Capacitors

8. What are visual anomalies that appear on the screen called?

  A. Pixels

  B. Artifacts

  C. Cells

  D. Dead spots

9. What is the light in the device that powers the LCD screen?

  A. Backlight

  B. Inverter

  C. Charger

  D. Reflector

10. Which of the following is a user interface feature designed by HTC?

  A. Type I

  B. TouchFLO

  C. Type II

  D. Container-based

11. Which of the following indicates that the fuser is not fusing the toner properly on the paper?

  A. Black spots

  B. Streaks

  C. Blank spots

  D. Garbled output

12. Which of the following indicates that the toner cartridge is just about empty?

  A. Black spots

  B. Streaks

  C. Faded prints

  D. Garbled output

13. If you can ping resources by IP address but not by name, which of the following is not functioning?

A. HTTP

B. DNS

C. DHCP

D. ARP

14. Which of the following should be set to the IP address of the router interface connecting to the local network?

A. IP address

B. Subnet mask

C. Default gateway

D. DHCP server

CompTIA
A+ Core 2
Exam 220-1102

Chapter

6

Operating Systems

COMPTIA A+ CERTIFICATION EXAM CORE 2 (220-1102) OBJECTIVES COVERED IN THIS CHAPTER:

✓ **1.1 Identify basic features of Microsoft Windows editions**

- **Windows 10 editions**
  - Home
  - Pro
  - Pro Workstations
  - Enterprise
- **Feature differences**
  - **Domain access vs. workgroup**
  - **Desktops styles/user interface**
  - **Availability of Remote Desktop Protocol (RDP)**
  - **Random-access memory (RAM) support limitations**
  - **BitLocker**
  - **gpedit.msc**
- **Upgrade paths**
  - In-place upgrade

✓ **1.2 Given a scenario, use the appropriate Microsoft command-line tool**

- **Navigation**
  - **cd**
  - **dir**
  - **md**
  - **rmdir**
  - **Drive navigation inputs:**
    - C:\ or D:\ or x:\

- **Command-line tools**
  - **ipconfig**
  - **ping**
  - **hostname**
  - **netstat**
  - **nslookup**
  - **chkdsk**
  - **net user**
  - **net use**
  - **tracert**
  - **format**
  - **xcopy**
  - **copy**
  - **robocopy**
  - **gpupdate**
  - **gpresult**
  - **shutdown**
  - **sfc**
  - **[command name] /?**
  - **diskpart**
  - **pathping**
  - **winver**

✓ **1.3 Given a scenario, use features and tools of the Microsoft Windows 10 operating system (OS)**

- **Task Manager**
  - **Services**
  - **Startup**
  - **Performance**
  - **Processes**
  - **Users**

- » **Microsoft Management Console (MMC) snap-in**
  - ▪ **Event Viewer (eventvwr.msc)**
  - ▪ **Disk Management (diskmgmt.msc)**
  - ▪ **Task Scheduler (taskschd.msc)**
  - ▪ **Device Manager (devmgmt.msc)**
  - ▪ **Certificate Manager (certmgr.msc)**
  - ▪ **Local Users and Groups (lusrmgr.msc)**
  - ▪ **Performance Monitor (perfmon.msc)**
  - ▪ **Group Policy Editor (gpedit.msc)**
- » **Additional tools**
  - ▪ **System Information (msinfo32. exe)**
  - ▪ **Resource Monitor (resmon.exe)**
  - ▪ **System Configuration (msconfig.exe)**
  - ▪ **Disk Cleanup (cleanmgr.exe)**
  - ▪ **Disk Defragment (dfrgui.exe)**
  - ▪ **Registry Editor (regedit.exe)**

✓ **1.4   Given a scenario, use the appropriate Microsoft Windows 10 Control Panel utility**

- ▪ Internet Options
- ▪ Devices and Printers
- ▪ Programs and Features
- ▪ Network and Sharing Center
- ▪ System
- ▪ Windows Defender Firewall
- ▪ Mail
- ▪ Sound
- ▪ User Accounts
- ▪ Device Manager

- Indexing Options
- Administrative Tools
- File Explorer Options
  - Show hidden files
  - Hide extensions
  - General options
  - View options
- Power Options
  - Hibernate
  - Power plans
  - Sleep/suspend
  - Standby
  - Choose what closing the lid does
  - Turn on fast startup
  - Universal Serial Bus (USB) selective suspend
- Ease of Access

✓ **1.5 Given a scenario, use the appropriate Windows settings**

- **Time and Language**
- **Update and Security**
- **Personalization**
- **Apps**
- **Privacy**
- **System**
- **Devices**
- **Network and Internet**
- **Gaming**
- **Accounts**

✓ **1.6 Given a scenario, configure Microsoft Windows networking features on a client/desktop**

- ◾ **Workgroup vs. domain setup**
  - ◾ **Shared resources**
  - ◾ **Printers**
  - ◾ **File servers**
  - ◾ **Mapped drives**
- ◾ Local OS firewall settings
  - ◾ Application restrictions and exceptions
  - ◾ Configuration
- ◾ **Client network configuration**
  - ◾ **Internet Protocol (IP) addressing scheme**
  - ◾ **Domain Name System (DNS) settings**
  - ◾ **Subnet mask**
  - ◾ **Gateway**
  - ◾ **Static vs. dynamic**
- ◾ **Establish network connections**
  - ◾ **Virtual private network (VPN)**
  - ◾ **Wireless**
  - ◾ **Wired**
  - ◾ **Wireless wide area network (WWAN)**
- ◾ **Proxy settings**
- ◾ **Public network vs. private network**
- ◾ **File Explorer navigation – network paths**
- ◾ **Metered connections and limitations**

✓ **1.7 Given a scenario, apply application installation and configuration concepts**

- ◾ System requirements for applications
  - ◾ 32-bit vs. 64-bit dependent application requirements

- Dedicated graphics card vs. integrated
- Video random-access memory (VRAM) requirements
- RAM requirements
- Central processing unit (CPU) requirements
- External hardware tokens
- Storage requirements
- OS requirements for applications
  - Application to OS compatibility
  - 32-bit vs. 64-bit OS
- Distribution methods
  - Physical media vs. downloadable
  - ISO mountable
- Other considerations for new applications
  - Impact to device
  - Impact to network
  - Impact to operation
  - Impact to business

✓ **1.8 Explain common OS types and their purposes**

- **Workstation OSs**
  - **Windows**
  - **Linux**
  - **macOS**
  - **Chrome OS**
- **Cell phone/tablet OSs**
  - **iPadOS**
  - **iOS**
  - **Android**

- Various filesystem types
  - New Technology File System (NTFS)
  - File Allocation Table 32 (FAT32)
  - Third extended filesystem (ext3)
  - Fourth extended filesystem (ext4)
  - Apple File System (APFS)
  - Extensible File Allocation Table (exFAT)
- Vendor life-cycle limitations
  - End-of-life (EOL)
  - Update limitations
- Compatibility concerns between OSs

✓ **1.9   Given a scenario, perform OS installations and upgrades in a diverse OS environment**

- Boot methods
  - USB
  - Optical media
  - Network
  - Solid-state/flash drives
  - Internet-based
  - External/hot-swappable drive
  - Internal hard drive (partition)
- Types of installations
  - Upgrade
  - Recovery partition
  - Clean install
  - Image deployment
  - Repair installation
  - Remote network installation
  - Other considerations
    - Third-party drivers

- apt-get
- yum
- ip
- df
- grep
- ps
- man
- top
- find
- dig
- cat
- nano
- Best practices
  - Backups
  - Antivirus
  - Updates/patches
- Tools
  - Shell/terminal
  - Samba

This chapter focuses on the exam topics related to operating systems. It follows the structure of the CompTIA A+ 220-1102 exam blueprint, objective 1, and it explores the 11 subobjectives that you need to master before taking the exam.

This book covers Windows 10 and Windows 11, but most of the examples use Windows 10. We will call out differences when necessary.

1.1 Identify basic features of Microsoft Windows editions

This section contains numerous tables because of the nature of the information that it covers. It is imperative that you be familiar with Windows 10. Make certain you understand the features in each of the editions of Windows 10 that are made available.

Windows 10 editions

As most previous versions of Windows, Windows 10 is available in multiple editions. These editions vary in the features that are available because they are designed for different scenarios. In this section you'll learn about these editions.

Home

Windows 10 Home edition is designed for use in a noncorporate setting and thus lacks many of the features that you might need in an enterprise setting. For example, it does not offer BitLocker as some other editions do. Following the coverage of the general use of each edition, Table 6.1 will compare the editions on the basis of Windows features, all of which will be discussed later in this chapter.

Pro

Windows Pro offers many of the features required to use the system in a domain-based corporate environment while lacking some of the advanced security features that you might require in a higher security environment. These features will be found in the Enterprise edition (covered later in this section).

Pro for Workstations

Some applications require significantly more power as compared to typical office applications. When editing video or using computer-aided design tools or performing extremely difficult mathematics, more power is needed. Windows Pro for Workstations is designed to operate in these type of environments.

Enterprise

As was mentioned earlier, when an organization wants all features required for a domain-based enterprise and they require high security functions, Windows Enterprise is the edition of choice. With the exception of workstations that run resource-hungry applications (which includes Windows Pro for Workstations), this system is appropriate for all Enterprise workstations.

Windows 11

Microsoft described Windows as an "operating system as a service" that would receive ongoing updates to its features and functionality. It was released in October 2021. There are two versions, Home and Pro. In this section we will mention differences between Windows 10 and Windows 11 only when discussing the features.

Feature differences

The features found in Table 6.1 are examined in this section. It is important that you not only understand these features and their purpose but that you know which editions offer which features. As an IT professional you may be involved in the selection of the proper edition for a scenario.

Domain access vs. workgroup

A workgroup is a collection of systems that each maintains its own security system. Local security means that to log into a system in a workgroup you need an account created on that machine as a local account. Therefore, each system is its own "castle" and in charge of its own security.

In a domain, the systems are all related in that domain-based accounts are used to log into these systems (although local accounts can still be created). These domain accounts are not tethered to the individual systems, meaning that a user with a domain account can log into any system that is a member of the domain. Later in this chapter you'll learn how to join a computer to a domain.

Microsoft provides the option to join a domain in three versions of Windows 10: Windows 10 Pro, Windows Enterprise, and Windows 10 Education.

Desktop styles/user interface

Windows offers a feature in some editions called Windows Virtual Desktop User Rights. It is meant to be used when providing virtual desktops (you learned about these in Chapter 4) from a cloud platform such as Windows Azure. This feature allows for exerting control of what users features are available to the recipients of the virtual desktops and what their experience may be.

A related feature is User Experience Virtualization (UE-V) for Windows 10, which captures user-customized Windows and application settings and store them on a centrally managed network file share. This is again tied to the use of virtual desktops and is only available in certain editions.

Availability of Remote Desktop Protocol (RDP)

In Chapter 2, "Networking," you learned about the Remote Desktop Protocol (RDP). It allows members of the Administrators group to gain access to the workstation. (You can specifically allow other users as well.) While any edition of Windows 10 can act as Remote Desktop Client, to host a remote session, you need to be running Windows 10 Pro or Enterprise.

Random-access memory (RAM) support limitations

Each of the editions of Windows 10 place a minimum requirement on the memory required to run the operating system. There will be a maximum amount of RAM each edition can make use of. This is valuable to know when selecting an OS for a system. Please refer to Table 6.1 for details. Windows 11 requires at least 4 GB of memory.

BitLocker

In Chapter 3, "Hardware," you learned about the concept of whole-drive encryption and TPM chips. The Windows feature that makes use of TPM chips and provides whole-drive encryption is BitLocker. BitLocker is the whole-drive encryption tool that can also seal a device such that it will not boot if any system files are altered. It can also lock the drive to a particular machine, preventing anyone from stealing the drive and connecting it to another device. You will learn more about implementing BitLocker in Chapter 8, "Software Troubleshooting." See Table 6.1 for availability in the various editions.

gpedit.msc

Group Policies can be used in certain editions to exert control over both security and desktop settings. This configuration is done with a tool called the Group Policy Editor. This tool can be added to an interface called the Microsoft Management Console (MMC). The underlying program you are invoking when you open this tool is called gpedit.msc and is only available in certain editions. You will learn more about the Group Policy Editor later in this chapter and again in Chapter 8. For availability across editions, see Table 6.1.

TABLE 6.1   Features across Windows 10 editions

	Domain access	Desktop styles/ user interface	RDP	RAM min	BitLocker	`gpedit.msc`
Home	no	no	no	64 bit 2 GB 32 bit 1 GB	no	no
Pro	yes	no	yes	64 bit 2 GB 32 bit 1 GB	yes	yes
Pro for Workstations	yes	no	yes	64 bit 2 GB 32 bit 1 GB	no	yes
Enterprise	yes	yes	yes	64 bit 2 GB 32 bit 1 GB	yes	yes

Upgrade paths

When installing or upgrading an operating system, it is important to know what is possible and what is not. Not all systems can be directly upgraded to the newest version. Some must be completely reinstalled. There are several things to be aware of regarding upgrade paths, including the differences between in-place upgrades, the available compatibility tools, and the Windows Upgrade Advisor. In this section, we'll look at some possible upgrade paths and other installation considerations.

In-place upgrade

One Windows operating system can often be upgraded to another, if compatible. When you are faced with a scenario in which you cannot upgrade, you can always do a clean installation. There's one more thing to consider when evaluating installation methods. Some methods work only if you're performing a clean installation and not an upgrade. Table 6.2

lists the minimum system requirements for Windows 10. If your existing Windows 10 PC is running the current version of Windows 10 and meets the minimum hardware specifications to run Windows 11, it will be able to upgrade.

TABLE 6.2 Minimum system requirements for Windows 10

Hardware	Minimum supported for all editions of Windows 10
Processor	1 GHz with support for PAE, NX, and SSE
Memory	1 GB for 32-bit; 2 GB for 64-bit
Free hard disk space	16 GB free for 32-bit; 20 GB free for 64-bit
CD-ROM or DVD	DVD-ROM
Video	DirectX 9 with WDDM 1.0 (or higher) driver

If there is one thing to be learned from Table 6.2 it's that Microsoft is nothing if not optimistic. For your own sanity, though, I strongly suggest you always take the minimum requirements with a grain of salt. They are minimums. Even the recommended requirements should be considered minimums. Bottom line: Make sure you have a good margin between your system's performance and the minimum requirements listed. Always run Windows on more hardware rather than less!

Upgrading to Windows 10

With Windows 10, the in-place upgrade is now a first-class deployment option and is the preferred approach for Windows 10 deployment—even in enterprises. It allows Windows 10 installations to be initiated from within an existing Windows OS. Upgrading to Windows 11 from Windows 10 is also allowed as long as the system supports the new hardware requirements.

Windows 11 Installation Assistant

The Windows 11 Installation Assistant can be useful in any upgrade process. It will check your system, verify that it can run the desired operating system, and give you a report of any identified compatibility issues.

Exam essentials

Identify the hardware requirements of various Windows 10 editions. These include all editions of Windows 10: Home, Pro, Pro for Workstations, and Enterprise.

1.2 Given a scenario, use the appropriate Microsoft command-line tool

Although the 220-1102 exam is on the Windows operating systems, it tests many concepts that carry over from the earlier Microsoft Disk Operating System (MS-DOS), which was never meant to be extremely friendly. Its roots are in CP/M, which was based on the command line, and so is MS-DOS. In other words, these systems use long strings of commands typed in at the computer keyboard to perform operations. Some people prefer this type of interaction with the computer, including many folks with technical backgrounds (such as yours truly). Although Windows has left the full command-line interface behind, it still contains a bit of DOS, and you get to it through the command prompt.

Although you can't tell from looking at it, the Windows command prompt is actually a Windows program that is intentionally designed to have the look and feel of a DOS command line. Because it is, despite its appearance, a Windows program, the command prompt provides all the stability and configurability you expect from Windows. You can access a command prompt by running CMD.EXE.

A number of diagnostic utilities are often run at the command prompt. Since knowledge of each is required for the exam, they are discussed next in this section.

Navigation

Some commands are used to navigate the filesystem. The three commands in this section are used for that purpose.

cd

The change directory (cd) command is used to move to another folder or directory. It is used in both Unix and Windows. Parameters are shown in Table 6.3.

TABLE 6.3   The change directory (cd) command

Unix	
cd or cd ~	Puts you in your home directory
cd .	Leaves you in the same directory you are currently in
cd ~username	Puts you in username's home directory
cd dir (without a /)	Puts you in a subdirectory

Unix	
cd —	Switches you to the previous directory
cd ..	Moves you up one directory
DOS and Windows	
no attributes	Prints the full path of the current directory
-p	Prints the final directory stack
-n	Entries are wrapped before they reach the edge of the screen
-v	Entries are printed one per line, preceded by their stack positions
cd\	Returns to the root directory
..	Moves you up one directory

dir

The dir command is used to view a listing of the files and folders that exist within a directory, subdirectory, or folder. Here is the syntax:

```
dir [Drive:][Path][FileName] [...] [/p] [/q] [/w] [/d]
[/a[[:]attributes]][/o[[:]SortOrder]] [/t[[:]TimeField]] [/s] [/b]
[/l] [/n] [/x] [/c] [/4]
```

The parameters are shown in Table 6.4.

TABLE 6.4   dir command parameters

[Drive:][Path]	Specifies the drive and directory for which you want to see a listing.
[FileName]	Specifies a particular file or group of files for which you want to see a listing.
/p	Displays one screen of the listing at a time. To see the next screen, press any key on the keyboard.
/q	Displays file ownership information.
/w	Displays the listing in wide format, with as many as five filenames or directory names on each line.
D	Same as /w but files are sorted by column.

(continues)

TABLE 6.4 dir command parameters *(continued)*

I	Displays only the names of those directories and files with the attributes you specify.
/o [[:]SortOrder]	Controls the order in which dir sorts and displays directory names and filenames.
/t [[:]TimeField]	Specifies which time field to display or use for sorting.
/s	Lists every occurrence in the specified directory, and all subdirectories, of the specified filename.
/b	Lists each directory name or filename, one per line, including the filename extension. /b does not display heading information or a summary. /b overrides /w.
/l	Displays unsorted directory names and filenames in lowercase. /l does not convert extended characters to lowercase.
/n	Displays a long list format with filenames on the far right of the screen.
/x	Displays the short names generated for files on NTFS and FAT volumes. The display is the same as the display for /n, but short names are displayed after the long name.
/c	Displays the thousand separator in file sizes.
/4	Displays four-digit year format.

md

The md command is the shorthand version of the mkdir command and is used to create a new folder. Its syntax is:

md [<drive>:]<path>

The parameters are shown in Table 6.5.

TABLE 6.5 md command parameters

<drive>:	Specifies the drive on which you want to create the new directory.
<path>	Specifies the name and location of the new directory. The maximum length of any single path is determined by the file system. This is a required parameter.
/?	Displays help at the command prompt.

rmdir

The remove directory (rmdir) command deletes an existing directory. This command is the same as the rd command. Its syntax is as follows:

rmdir [<drive>:]<path> [/s [/q]]

The parameters are shown in Table 6.6.

TABLE 6.6   The remove directory (rmdir) command

[<drive>:]<path>	Specifies the location and the name of the directory that you want to delete. Path is required. If you include a backslash (\) at the beginning of the specified path, then the path starts at the root directory (regardless of the current directory).
/s	Deletes a directory tree (the specified directory and all its subdirectories, including all files).
q	Specifies quiet mode. Does not prompt for confirmation when deleting a directory tree. The /q parameter works only if /s is also specified.
	CAUTION: When you run in quiet mode, the entire directory tree is deleted without confirmation. Make sure that important files are moved or backed up before using the /q command-line option.
/?	Displays help at the command prompt.

Drive navigation inputs

Before accessing a file or running an executable file, you must navigate to its location. This is explained in the next section.

C:\ or D:\ or x:\

To specify the location to which you would like to navigate, first you must specify the drive letter. For example, if you type **c:**, your prompt will change to C:\>. Then if you specify the subfolder as **c:\>sales** the prompt will change to c:\>sales, meaning you are located inside the Sales folder.

Command-line tools

There are many other commands that are not used for navigation but are used to perform special tasks. In this section you'll learn about these command-line tools.

ipconfig

The ipconfig command is used to view the IP configuration of a device and, when combined with certain switches or parameters, can be used to release and renew the lease of an IP address obtained from a DHCP server and to flush the DNS resolver cache. Its most common use is to view the current configuration. Figure 6.1 shows its execution with the /all switch, which results in a display of a wealth of information about the IP configuration.

FIGURE 6.1   Using ipconfig

```
C:\Users\tmcmillan>ipconfig/all

Windows IP Configuration

        Host Name . . . . . . . . . . . . : tmcmillan
        Primary Dns Suffix  . . . . . . . : alpha.kaplaninc.com
        Node Type . . . . . . . . . . . . : Hybrid
        IP Routing Enabled. . . . . . . . : No
        WINS Proxy Enabled. . . . . . . . : No
        DNS Suffix Search List. . . . . . : alpha.kaplaninc.com
                                            kaplaninc.com

Ethernet adapter Local Area Connection:

        Connection-specific DNS Suffix  . : alpha.kaplaninc.com
        Description . . . . . . . . . . . : Broadcom NetXtreme 57xx Gigabit Controlle
r
        Physical Address. . . . . . . . . : 00-1A-A0-E1-95-AB
        DHCP Enabled. . . . . . . . . . . : Yes
        Autoconfiguration Enabled . . . . : Yes
        Link-local IPv6 Address . . . . . : fe80::ada3:8b73:a66e:6bc0%10(Preferred)
        IPv4 Address. . . . . . . . . . . : 10.88.2.103(Preferred)
        Subnet Mask . . . . . . . . . . . : 255.255.254.0
        Lease Obtained. . . . . . . . . . : Monday, January 30, 2012 9:38:37 AM
        Lease Expires . . . . . . . . . . : Tuesday, January 31, 2012 9:38:37 AM
        Default Gateway . . . . . . . . . : 10.88.2.6
        DHCP Server . . . . . . . . . . . : 10.88.10.48
        DHCPv6 IAID . . . . . . . . . . . : 234887840
        DHCPv6 Client DUID. . . . . . . . : 00-01-00-01-14-EE-0F-98-00-1A-A0-E1-95-AB

        DNS Servers . . . . . . . . . . . : 10.88.10.48
                                            10.75.139.18
        NetBIOS over Tcpip. . . . . . . . : Enabled
```

A scenario in which this command would be valuable is when you are dealing with a device you have never touched before that is having communication issues. This command would show a wealth of information with its output.

You can use ipconfig to release and then renew a configuration obtained from a DHCP server by issuing the following commands:

```
ipconfig /release
ipconfig /renew
```

It is also helpful to know that when you have just corrected a configuration error (such as an IP address) on a destination device, you should ensure that the device registers its new IP address with the DNS server by executing the ipconfig /registerdns command.

It may also be necessary to clear incorrect IP addresses–to-hostname mappings that may still exist on the devices that were attempting to access the destination device. This can be done by executing the `ipconfig /flushdns` command.

If you are using a Linux or Unix system, the command is not `ipconfig` but `ifconfig`. Figure 6.2 shows an example of the command and its output. The `ifconfig` command with the `-a` option shows all network interface information, even if the network interface is down.

FIGURE 6.2   Using `ifconfig`

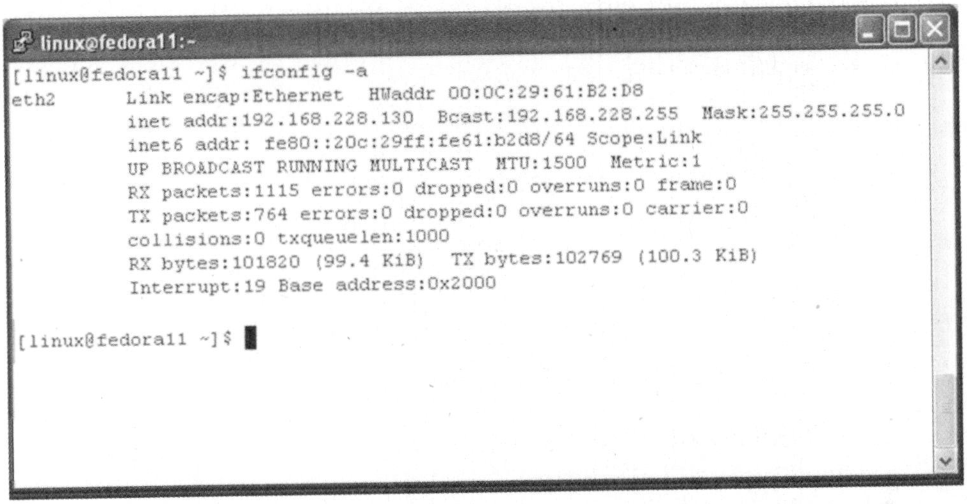

```
linux@fedora11:~
[linux@fedora11 ~]$ ifconfig -a
eth2      Link encap:Ethernet  HWaddr 00:0C:29:61:B2:D8
          inet addr:192.168.228.130  Bcast:192.168.228.255  Mask:255.255.255.0
          inet6 addr: fe80::20c:29ff:fe61:b2d8/64 Scope:Link
          UP BROADCAST RUNNING MULTICAST  MTU:1500  Metric:1
          RX packets:1115 errors:0 dropped:0 overruns:0 frame:0
          TX packets:764 errors:0 dropped:0 overruns:0 carrier:0
          collisions:0 txqueuelen:1000
          RX bytes:101820 (99.4 KiB)  TX bytes:102769 (100.3 KiB)
          Interrupt:19 Base address:0x2000

[linux@fedora11 ~]$
```

ping

The `ping` command makes use of the Internet Control Message Protocol (ICMP) to test connectivity between two devices. `ping` is one of the most useful commands in the TCP/IP suite. It sends a series of packets to another system, which in turn sends a response. The `ping` command can be extremely useful for troubleshooting problems with remote hosts.

The `ping` command indicates whether the host can be reached and how long it took for the host to send a return packet. On a LAN, the time is indicated as less than 10 milliseconds. Across WAN links, however, this value can be much greater. When the `-a` parameter is included, it will also attempt to resolve the hostname associated with the IP address. Figure 6.3 shows an example of a successful ping.

A common scenario for using `ping` is when you need to determine whether the network settings are correct. If you can ping another device that is correctly configured, the settings are correct. The syntax is as follows:

```
ping [-t] [-a] [-n count] [-l size] [-f] [-i TTL] [-v TOS] [-r count] [-s
count] [-w timeout] [-R] [-S srcaddr] [-p] [-4] [-6] target [/?]
```

FIGURE 6.3   The ping command

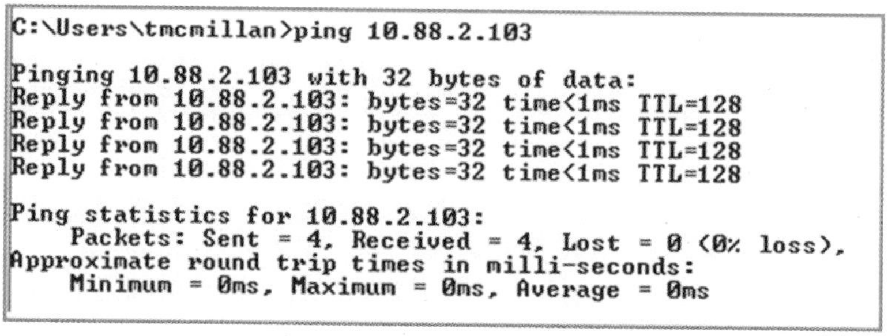

```
C:\Users\tmcmillan>ping 10.88.2.103

Pinging 10.88.2.103 with 32 bytes of data:
Reply from 10.88.2.103: bytes=32 time<1ms TTL=128
Reply from 10.88.2.103: bytes=32 time<1ms TTL=128
Reply from 10.88.2.103: bytes=32 time<1ms TTL=128
Reply from 10.88.2.103: bytes=32 time<1ms TTL=128

Ping statistics for 10.88.2.103:
    Packets: Sent = 4, Received = 4, Lost = 0 (0% loss),
Approximate round trip times in milli-seconds:
    Minimum = 0ms, Maximum = 0ms, Average = 0ms
```

Some switches used with ping are shown in Table 6.7.

TABLE 6.7   ping switches

Switch	Purpose
T	Pings the target until you force it to stop by pressing Ctrl+C
-a	Resolves, if possible, the hostname of an IP address target
-n count	Sets the number of ICMP echo requests to send (4 by default)
-l size	Sets the size, in bytes, of the echo request packet (32 by default)
-f	Prevents ICMP echo requests from being fragmented by routers between you and the target
-i TTL	Sets the Time to Live (TTL) value, the maximum of which is 255
-r count	Specifies the number of hops between your computer and the target computer
-s count	Reports the time, in Internet Timestamp format, that each echo request is received and when an echo reply is sent

hostname

You can use the hostname command to find out the name of the computer. This prints only the NetBios name of the PC. Here is an example of using the command. The hostname of the system is DESKTOP-QSRHMTD. After displaying the name, it returns to the previous prompt.

```
C:\>hostname
DESKTOP-QSRHMTD


C:\>
```

netstat

The netstat (network status) command is used to see what ports are listening on the TCP/IP-based system. The –a option is used to show all ports, and /? is used to show what other options are available (the options differ based on the operating system you are using). When executed with no switches, the command displays the current connections, as shown in Figure 6.4.

FIGURE 6.4   Using netstat

```
C:\Users\tmcmillan>netstat

Active Connections

   Proto  Local Address          Foreign Address          State
   TCP    10.88.2.103:51273      64.94.18.154:https       ESTABLISHED
   TCP    10.88.2.103:51525      srat1060:microsoft-ds    ESTABLISHED
   TCP    10.88.2.103:51529      gmonsalvatge:microsoft-ds  ESTABLISHED
   TCP    10.88.2.103:51573      sjc-not18:http           ESTABLISHED
   TCP    10.88.2.103:51716      schexv02:2785            ESTABLISHED
   TCP    10.88.2.103:51720      schvoip01:epmap          ESTABLISHED
   TCP    10.88.2.103:51721      schvoip01:1297           ESTABLISHED
   TCP    10.88.2.103:51722      schvoip01:1299           ESTABLISHED
   TCP    10.88.2.103:51824      69.31.116.27:http        CLOSE_WAIT
   TCP    10.88.2.103:51965      dcalpsch2:1026           ESTABLISHED
   TCP    10.88.2.103:53865      cs219p3:5050             ESTABLISHED
   TCP    10.88.2.103:53871      sip109:http              ESTABLISHED
   TCP    10.88.2.103:62522      ord08s08-in-f22:https    ESTABLISHED
   TCP    10.88.2.103:62567      ord08s08-in-f22:https    CLOSE_WAIT
   TCP    10.88.2.103:62682      by2msg3010613:http       ESTABLISHED
   TCP    10.88.2.103:63554      baymsg1020213:msnp       ESTABLISHED
   TCP    10.88.2.103:63770      v-client-2b:https        CLOSE_WAIT
   TCP    10.88.2.103:63771      ec2-174-129-205-197:https  CLOSE_WAIT
   TCP    10.88.2.103:63772      v-client-2b:https        CLOSE_WAIT
   TCP    10.88.2.103:63773      65.55.121.231:http       ESTABLISHED
   TCP    10.88.2.103:63774      168.75.207.20:http       ESTABLISHED
   TCP    10.88.2.103:63777      65.55.17.30:http         ESTABLISHED
   TCP    10.88.2.103:63779      70.37.131.11:http        ESTABLISHED
   TCP    10.88.2.103:63781      65.124.174.56:http       ESTABLISHED
   TCP    10.88.2.103:63788      69.31.76.41:http         ESTABLISHED
   TCP    10.88.2.103:63791      207.46.140.46:http       ESTABLISHED
   TCP    10.88.2.103:63792      64.4.21.39:http          ESTABLISHED
   TCP    127.0.0.1:2002         tmcmillan:51543          ESTABLISHED
   TCP    127.0.0.1:19872        tmcmillan:51571          ESTABLISHED
   TCP    127.0.0.1:51543        tmcmillan:2002           ESTABLISHED
   TCP    127.0.0.1:51549        tmcmillan:51550          ESTABLISHED
   TCP    127.0.0.1:51550        tmcmillan:51549          ESTABLISHED
   TCP    127.0.0.1:51571        tmcmillan:19872          ESTABLISHED
   TCP    127.0.0.1:53869        tmcmillan:53870          ESTABLISHED
   TCP    127.0.0.1:53870        tmcmillan:53869          ESTABLISHED
   TCP    127.0.0.1:63557        tmcmillan:63574          ESTABLISHED
   TCP    127.0.0.1:63574        tmcmillan:63557          ESTABLISHED

C:\Users\tmcmillan>
```

A common scenario for using netstat is when you suspect that a host is "calling home" to a malicious server. If so, the connection would appear in the output.

The syntax is as follows:

```
ping [-t] [-a] [-n count] [-l size] [-f] [-i TTL] [-v TOS] [-r count] [-s
count] [-w timeout] [-R] [-S srcaddr] [-p proto] [-4] [-6] target [/?]
```

Table 6.8 shows some switches used with netstat.

TABLE 6.8   netstat switches

Switch	Purpose
-a	Displays all connections and listening ports
-b	Displays the executable involved in creating each connection or listening port
-e	Displays Ethernet statistics
-n	Displays addresses and port numbers in numerical form
-o	Displays the owning process ID associated with each connection
-p proto	Shows connections for the protocol specified by proto
-r	Displays the routing table

nslookup

The nslookup command is a command-line administrative tool for testing and troubleshooting DNS servers. It can be run in two modes: interactive and noninteractive. While noninteractive mode is useful when only a single piece of data needs to be returned, interactive allows you to query for either an IP address for a name or a name for an IP address without leaving nslookup mode.

A common scenario for using nslookup is when a system cannot resolve names and you need to see what DNS server it is using.

The command syntax is as follows:

```
nslookup [-option] [hostname] [server]
```

Table 6.9 shows selected switches used with nslookup.

TABLE 6.9   nslookup switches

Switch	Purpose
All	Prints all options, current server, and host information
[no]debug	Provides debugging info
[no]d2	Provides exhaustive debugging information
[no]defname	Appends a domain name to each query
[no]recurse	Asks for a recursive answer to the query
[no]search	Uses the domain to search the list
[no]vc	Always uses a virtual circuit
domain=*name*	Sets the default domain name to *name*

To enter interactive mode, simply enter nslookup as shown here:

```
C:\> nslookup
Default Server: nameserver1.domain.com
Address: 10.0.0.1
```

When you do this, by default it will identify the IP address and name of the DNS server that the local machine is configured to use, if any, and then will go to the > prompt. At this prompt you can enter either an IP address or a name, and the system will attempt to resolve the IP address to a name or the name to an IP address.

```
>
```

The following are other queries that can be run that may prove helpful when troubleshooting name resolution issues:

- Looking up different data types in the database (such as Microsoft records). For example, the following command will filter for mail server records:

  ```
  C: Nslookup
  Set Type=mx
  ```

- Querying directly from another name server (different from the one the local device is configured to use). The command for the DNS server named some.dns.server in the somewhere.com domain is as follows:

  ```
  nslookup somewhere.com some.dns.server
  ```

- Performing a zone transfer. This example is from wayne.net to dns.wayne.net:

```
C: nslookup
set Type=any
> ls -d wayne.net > dns.wayne.net
> exit
```

chkdsk

You can use the Windows CHKDSK utility to create and display status reports for the hard disk. CHKDSK can also correct filesystem problems (such as cross-linked files) and scan for and attempt to repair disk errors. CHKDSK can be run from the command line, or you can use a version in Windows Explorer.

To use the Windows Explorer version, right-click the problem disk and select Properties. This will bring up the Properties dialog box for that disk, which shows the current status of the selected disk drive. By clicking the Tools tab at the top of the dialog box and then clicking the Check button in the Error Checking section, you can start CHKDSK.

net user

The net user command is used to add, remove, and make changes to the user accounts on a computer, all from the command prompt. It has the following command syntax:

```
netuser [username [password | *] [/add] [options]] [/domain]] [username [/
delete] [/domain]] [/help] [/?]
```

Parameters are shown in Table 6.10

TABLE 6.10 netuser parameters

netuser	Displays a simple list of every user account, active or not, on the computer you're currently using
Username	The name of the user account
Password	Modifies an existing password or assigns one when creating a new username
*	Used in place of a password to force the entering of a password in the Command Prompt window after executing the net user command
/add	Adds a new username on the system
/domain	Forces net user to execute on the current domain controller instead of the local computer
/delete	Removes the specified username from the system
/help	Displays detailed information

net use

Network shares can be mapped to drives to appear as if the resources are local. The net use command is used to establish network connections via a command prompt. For example, to connect to a shared network drive and make it your M drive, you would use the syntax net use m: \\server\share. Figure 6.5 shows an example of mapped drives. This can also be done in File Explorer, as shown in Figure 6.6.

FIGURE 6.5   Mapped network drives

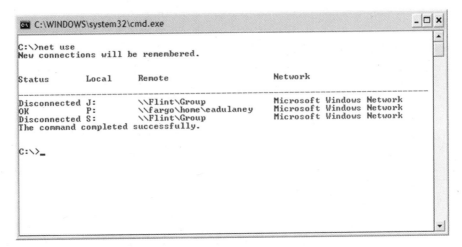

FIGURE 6.6   Mapping a drive

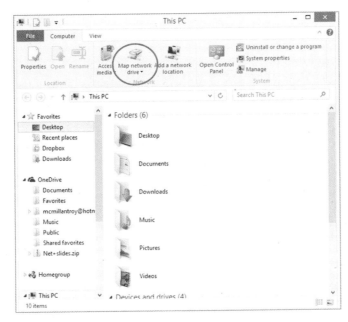

net use can also be used to connect to a shared printer: net use lpt1: \\
printername.

tracert

The tracert command (called traceroute in Linux and Unix) is used to trace the path of
a packet through the network. Its best use is in determining exactly where in the network the
packet is being dropped. It will show each hop (router) the packet crosses and how long it
takes to do so. Figure 6.7 shows a partial display of a traced route to www.msn.com.

FIGURE 6.7   Using tracert

```
C:\Users\tmcmillan>tracert www.msn.com

Tracing route to us.co1.cb3.glbdns.microsoft.com [70.37.131.153]
over a maximum of 30 hops:

  1    11 ms     1 ms     1 ms  10.88.2.6
  2     2 ms     2 ms     1 ms  208-47-7-130.dia.static.qwest.net [208.47.7.130]

  3     7 ms     7 ms     7 ms  frp-edge-04.inet.qwest.net [205.168.14.213]
  4     7 ms     7 ms     7 ms  frp-core-02.inet.qwest.net [205.171.22.49]
  5    22 ms    22 ms    22 ms  chx-edge-03.inet.qwest.net [67.14.38.1]
  6    22 ms    22 ms    23 ms  63-234-10-14.dia.static.qwest.net [63.234.10.14]

  7    23 ms    23 ms    23 ms  xe-0-1-2-0.ch1-16c-1b.ntwk.msn.net [207.46.43.20
4]
  8    24 ms    24 ms    24 ms  xe-0-1-0-0.ch1-96c-1a.ntwk.msn.net [207.46.46.13
3]
  9    34 ms    34 ms    34 ms  ge-2-1-0-0.ash-64cb-1b.ntwk.msn.net [207.46.45.1
4]
 10    38 ms    38 ms    38 ms  ge-4-0-0-0.nyc-64cb-1b.ntwk.msn.net [207.46.46.5
7]
 11    39 ms    38 ms    38 ms  xe-3-1-0-0.ewr-96cbe-1b.ntwk.msn.net [207.46.47.
2]
 12    39 ms       *     39 ms  xe-3-0-0-0.ewr-96cbe-1a.ntwk.msn.net [207.46.43.
250]
 13
```

A common scenario for using tracert is when there is a slow remote connection and
you would like to find out which part of the path is problematic.

The syntax used is as follows:

tracert [-d] [-h MaxHops] [-w TimeOut] [-4] [-6] target [/?]

Table 6.11 shows some selected switches used with tracert.

TABLE 6.11   tracert switches

Switch	Purpose
-d	Prevents tracert from resolving IP addresses to hostnames
-h MaxHops	Specifies the maximum number of hops in the search for the target (30 by default)

Switch	Purpose
-w *TimeOut*	Specifies the time, in milliseconds, to allow each reply before timeout using this tracert option
-4	Forces tracert to use IPv4 only
-6	Forces tracert to use IPv6 only
Target	Destination, either an IP address or a hostname
/?	Shows detailed help about the command

format

The format command is used to wipe data off disks and prepare them for new use. Before a hard disk can be formatted, it must have partitions created on it. (Partitioning is done in Windows using diskpart, discussed later.) The syntax for format is as follows:

```
FORMAT [volume] [switches]
```

The volume parameter describes the drive letter (for example, D:), mount point, or volume name. Table 6.12 lists some common format switches.

TABLE 6.12   format switches

Switch	Purpose
/FS:[filesystem]	Specifies the type of filesystem to use (FAT, FAT32, or NTFS)
/V:[label]	Specifies the new volume label
/Q	Executes a quick format

There are other options as well to specify allocation sizes, the number of sectors per track, and the number of tracks per disk size. However, I don't recommend you use these unless you have a specific need. The defaults are just fine.

So, if you wanted to format your D: drive as NTFS with a name of HDD2, you would enter the following:

```
FORMAT D: /FS:NTFS /V:HDD2
```

Before you format anything, be sure you have it backed up or be prepared to lose whatever is on that drive!

xcopy

If you are comfortable with the copy command, learning xcopy shouldn't pose too many problems. It's basically an extension of copy with one notable exception—it's designed to copy directories as well as files. The syntax is as follows:

XCOPY [source] [destination][switches]

There are 26 xcopy switches; Table 6.13 lists some of the commonly used ones.

TABLE 6.13   xcopy switches

Switch	Purpose
/A	Copies only files that have the Archive attribute set and does not clear the attribute. This is useful for making a quick backup of files while not disrupting a normal backup routine.
/E	Copies directories and subdirectories, including empty directories.
/F	Displays full source and destination filenames when copying.
/G	Allows copying of encrypted files to a destination that does not support encryption.
/H	Copies hidden and system files as well.
/K	Copies attributes. (By default, xcopy resets the Read-Only attribute.)
/O	Copies file ownership and ACL information (NTFS permissions).
/R	Overwrites read-only files.
/S	Copies directories and subdirectories but not empty directories.
/U	Copies only files that already exist in the destination.
/V	Verifies each new file.

Perhaps the most important switch is /O. If you use xcopy to copy files from one location to another, the filesystem creates a new version of the file in the new location without changing the old file. In NTFS, when a new file is created, it inherits permissions from its new parent directory. This could cause problems if you copy files. (Users who didn't have access to the file before might have access now.) If you want to retain the original permissions, use XCOPY /O.

copy

The copy command does what it says: it makes a copy of a file in a second location. (To copy a file and remove it from its original location, use the move command.) Here's the syntax for copy:

```
COPY [filename] [destination]
```

It's pretty straightforward. There are several switches for copy, but in practice they are rarely used. The three most used ones are /A, which indicates an ASCII text file; /V, which verifies that the files are written correctly after the copy; and /Y, which suppresses the prompt asking whether you're sure you want to overwrite files if they exist in the destination directory.

When any sort of copy operation is performed, the file will take on the permissions of the folder in which you place it.

The copy command cannot be used to copy directories. Use xcopy for that function.

One useful tip is to use wildcards. For example, in DOS (or at the command prompt), the asterisk (*) is a wildcard that means *everything*. So, you could enter COPY *.EXE to copy all files that have an .exe extension, or you could enter COPY *.* to copy all files in your current directory.

robocopy

The robocopy command (Robust File Copy for Windows) is included with Windows 10 and 11 and has the big advantage of being able to accept a plethora of specifications and keep NTFS permissions intact in its operations. The /MIR switch, for example, can be used to mirror a complete directory tree.

You can find an excellent TechNet article on how to use Robocopy at http://technet .microsoft.com/en-us/magazine/ec85e01678.aspx.

The syntax is as follows:

```
robocopy <Source> <Destination> [<File>[ ...]] [<Options>]
```

Some common switches when using the robocopy option appear in Table 6.14.

TABLE 6.14 robocopy switches

Switch	Purpose
/s	Copies subdirectories. Note that this option excludes empty directories.
/e	Copies subdirectories. Note that this option includes empty directories.
/lev:<N>	Copies only the top N levels of the source directory tree.
/z	Copies files in restartable mode.
/b	Copies files in Backup mode.
/efsraw	Copies all encrypted files in EFS RAW mode.
/copy:<copyflags>	Specifies the file properties to be copied. The following are the valid values for this option:

	/copy:<copyflags>	Specifies which file properties to copy. The valid values for this option are:
		▪ D - Data
		▪ A - Attributes
		▪ T - Time stamps
		▪ S - NTFS access control list (ACL)
		▪ O - Owner information
		▪ U - Auditing information
		The default vaule for this option is DAT (data, attributes, and time stamps).

D	Data.
A	Attributes.
T	Time stamps.
S	NTFS access control list (ACL).
O	Owner information.
U	Auditing information.
/dcopy:<copyflags>	Defines what to copy for directories. Default is DA. Options are D = data, A = attributes, and T = timestamps.

gpupdate

Configuration settings on Windows devices can be controlled through the use of policies. These policies can be applied on a local basis or on a domain and organizational unit basis when a device is a member of an Active Directory domain. When changes are made by an administrator to these policies, some types of changes will not take effect until the next schedule refresh time.

An administrator can force a device to update its policies after a change by executing the gpupdate command on the device. This is the syntax of the command:

```
gpupdate [/target:{computer|user}] [/force] [/wait:value] [/logoff] [/boot]
```

The parameters are shown in Table 6.15.

TABLE 6.15 gpupdate parameters

/target: { computer | user }	Processes only the *computer* settings or the current *user* settings. By default, both the computer settings and the user settings are processed.
/force	Ignores all processing optimizations and reapplies all settings.
/wait: *value*	Number of seconds that policy processing waits to finish. The default is 600 seconds. 0 means "no wait," and –1 means "wait indefinitely."
/logoff	Logs off after the refresh has completed. This is required for those Group Policy client-side extensions that do not process on a background refresh cycle but that do process when the user logs on, such as user software installation and folder redirection. This option has no effect if there are no extensions called that require the user to log off.
/boot	Restarts the computer after the refresh has completed. This is required for those Group Policy client-side extensions that do not process on a background refresh cycle but do process when the computer starts up, such as computer software installation. This option has no effect if there are no extensions called that require the computer to be restarted.

gpresult

Group policies can be applied to Windows devices at the local, organizational unit (OU), and domain levels, and when the policies are applied to the device, the results can be somewhat confusing because of variables that can affect how the policies interact with one another. If you need to determine the policies that are in effect for a particular device, you can execute the gpresult command on the device, and it will list the currently applied and defective policies. This is the command syntax:

```
gpresult [/s <COMPUTER> [/u <USERNAME> [/p [<PASSWORD>]]]] [/user
[<TARGETDOMAIN>\]<TARGETUSER>] [/scope {user | computer}]
{/r | /v | /z | [/x | /h] <c06f0xx.png> [/f] | /?}
```

The parameters are shown in Table 6.16.

TABLE 6.16   gpresult parameters

/s <COMPUTER>	Specifies the name or IP address of a remote computer. Do not use backslashes. The default is the local computer.
/u <USERNAME>	Uses the credentials of the specified user to run the command. The default user is the user who is logged on to the computer that issues the command.
/p [<Password>]	Specifies the password of the user account that is provided in the /u parameter. If /p is omitted, gpresult prompts for the password. /p cannot be used with /x or /h.
/user [<TARGETDOMAIN>\]<TARGETUSER>	Specifies the remote user whose data is to be displayed.
/scope {user	computer}	Displays data for either the user or the computer. If /scope is omitted, gpresult displays data for both the user and the computer.
[/x	/h] <c06f0xx.png>	Saves the report in either XML (/x) or HTML (/h) format at the location and with the filename that is specified by the c06f0xx.png parameter. This cannot be used with /u, /p, /r, /v, or /z.
/f	Forces gpresult to overwrite the filename that is specified in the /x or /h option.
/r	Displays summary data.
/v	Displays verbose policy information. This includes detailed settings that were applied with a precedence of 1.
/z:	Displays all available information about Group Policy. This includes detailed settings that were applied with a precedence of 1 and higher.

shutdown

The SHUTDOWN.EXE utility can be used to schedule a shutdown (complete or a restart) locally or remotely. A variety of reasons can be specified and announced to users for the shutdown. Three parameters to be aware of are /S (turns the computer off), /R (restarts the computer), and /M (lets you specify a computer other than this one).

sfc

The System File Checker (SFC) is a command line–based utility that checks and verifies the versions of system files on your computer. If system files are corrupted, the SFC will replace the corrupted files with correct versions.

The syntax for the sfc command is as follows:

SFC [switch]

While the switches vary a bit between different versions of Windows, Table 6.17 lists the most common ones available for sfc.

TABLE 6.17   sfc switches

Switch	Purpose
/CACHESIZE=X	Sets the Windows File Protection cache size, in megabytes
/PURGECACHE	Purges the Windows File Protection cache and scans all protected system files immediately
/REVERT	Reverts SFC to its default operation
/SCANFILE (Windows 7 and Vista only)	Scans a file that you specify and fixes problems if they are found
/SCANNOW	Immediately scans all protected system files
/SCANONCE	Scans all protected system files once
/SCANBOOT	Scans all protected system files every time the computer is rebooted
/VERIFYONLY	Scans protected system files and does not make any repairs or changes
/VERIFYFILE	Identifies the integrity of the file specified and makes any repairs or changes
/OFFBOOTDIR	Does a repair of an offline boot directory
/OFFFWINDIR	Does a repair of an offline Windows directory

To run the SFC, you must be logged in as an administrator or have administrative privileges. If the System File Checker discovers a corrupted system file, it will automatically overwrite the file by using a copy held in the %systemroot%\system32\dllcache directory. If you believe that the dllcache directory is corrupted, you can use SFC /SCANNOW, SFC /SCANONCE, SFC /SCANBOOT, or SFC /PURGECACHE, depending on your needs, as described in Table 6.17, to repair its contents.

The C:\Windows\System32 directory is where many of the Windows system files reside.

If you attempt to run SFC, or many other utilities, from a standard command prompt, you will be told that you must be an administrator running a console session in order to continue. Rather than opening a standard command prompt, choose Start ➤ All Programs ➤ Accessories and then right-click Command Prompt and choose Run As Administrator. The User Account Control (UAC) will prompt you to continue, and then you can run the SFC without a problem.

[command name] /?

You can also get help information by typing /? after a command.

The /? switch is slightly faster and provides more information than the help command. help provides information only for system commands (it does not include network commands). For example, if you enter **help ipconfig** at a command prompt, you get no useful information (except to try /?); however, typing **ipconfig /?** provides the help file for the ipconfig command.

diskpart

The diskpart command shows the partitions and lets you manage them on the computer's hard drives. A universal tool for working with hard drives from the command line, it allows you to convert between disk types, extend/shrink volumes, and format partitions and volumes, as well as list them, create them, and so on. The diskpart command sets the command prompt at the diskpart prompt as follows:

Diskpart>

Then subcommands like those in Table 6.18 are used.

TABLE 6.18 diskpart parameters

Parameter	Purpose
ACTIVE	Marks the selected partition as active
ADD	Adds a mirror to a simple volume
ATTRIBUTES	Manipulates volume or disk attributes
ASSIGN	Assigns a drive letter or mount point to the selected volume
ATTACH	Attaches a virtual disk file
AUTOMOUNT	Enables and disables automatic mounting of basic volumes
BREAK	Breaks a mirror set
CLEAN	Clears the configuration information, or all information

And that's only the beginning. You can find a list of all the available commands at
http://technet.microsoft.com/en-us/library/bb490893.aspx.

pathping

This command displays information about network latency and network loss at intermediate
hops between a source and destination. That means it works in a similar fashion to tracert. An example of output is shown in Figure 6.8, which shows the latency in the path to
www.nascar.com.

FIGURE 6.8 Using pathping

```
C:\>hostname
DESKTOP-QSRHMTD

C:\>pathping www.nascar.com

Tracing route to e7436.g.akamaiedge.net [104.127.157.226]
over a maximum of 30 hops:
  0  DESKTOP-QSRHMTD.home [192.168.1.23]
  1  192.168.1.1
  2    *        *        *
Computing statistics for 25 seconds...
            Source to Here   This Node/Link
Hop  RTT    Lost/Sent = Pct  Lost/Sent = Pct  Address
  0                                            DESKTOP-QSRHMTD.home [192.168.1.23]
                             0/ 100 =  0%   |
  1   4ms    0/ 100 =  0%    0/ 100 =  0%  192.168.1.1

Trace complete.
```

winver

The winver command shows details on the version of operating system running. Figure 6.9 shows an example. When the command is executed, the system will open a GUI dialog box that tells all about the version of Windows running.

FIGURE 6.9   Using winver

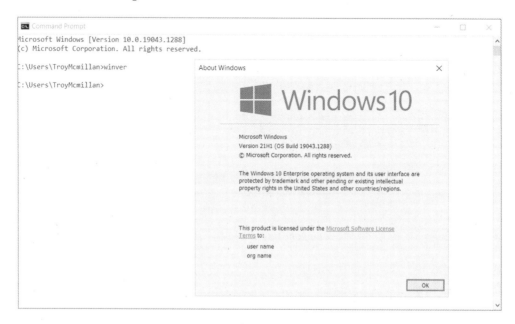

Exam essentials

Use command-line tools and their switches.   These tools include ipconfig, ping, tracert, netstat, shutdown, sfc, chkdsk, diskpart, gpupdate, gpresult, format, copy, xcopy, robocopy, net use, and net user.

1.3 Given a scenario, use features and tools of the Microsoft Windows 10 operating system (OS)

This objective requires you to know how to work at the command line and run common command-line utilities available with the Windows-based operating systems, as well as use administrative tools. Some of the material here overlaps with other objectives, but you'll want to make certain you know each utility discussed.

Although most of the information presented about Windows utilities and administration should seem like second nature to you (on-the-job experience is expected for A+ certification), you should read these sections thoroughly to make certain you can answer any questions that may appear about them.

Task Manager

This tool lets you shut down nonresponsive applications selectively in all Windows versions. In current versions of Windows, it can do much more. Task Manager allows you to see which processes and applications are using the most system resources, view network usage, see connected users, and so on. To display Task Manager, press Ctrl+Alt+Del and click the Task Manager button. You can also right-click an empty spot in the taskbar and choose Task Manager from the pop-up menu that appears.

To get to the Task Manager directly in any of the Windows versions, you can press Ctrl+Shift+Esc.

In Windows 10 and 11, Task Manager has seven tabs: Processes, Performance, App History, Startup, Users, Details, and Services. The Networking tab is shown only if your system has a network card installed (it is rare to find one that doesn't). The Users tab is displayed only if the computer you are working on is a member of a workgroup or is a stand-alone computer. The Users tab is unavailable on computers that are members of a network domain. Let's look at some of these tabs, as shown in Figure 6.10.

Services

The Services tab (shown in Figure 6.11) lists the name of each running service, as well as the process ID associated with it, its description, its status, and its group. A button labeled Services appears on this tab, and clicking it will open the MMC console for Services, where you can configure each service. Within Task Manager, right-clicking a service will open a context menu listing three choices: Start Service, Stop Service, and Go To Process (which takes you to the Processes tab).

Startup

The Startup tab displays the programs that will start automatically when the computer is booted up. It will also indicate the impact on performance if that function is enabled. As you can see in Figure 6.12, this function is not enabled and thus is not measuring impact.

FIGURE 6.10   Task Manager

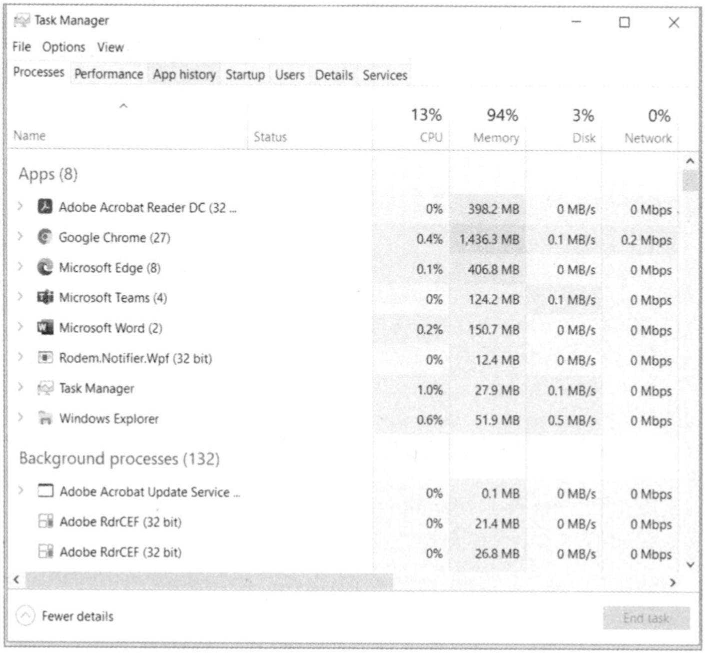

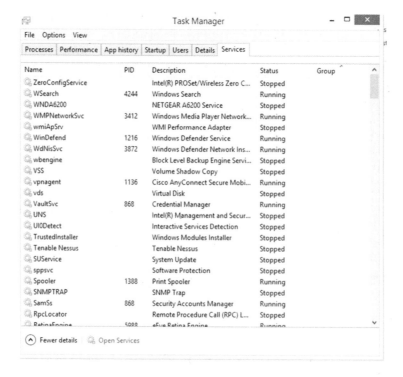

FIGURE 6.11   The Services tab

FIGURE 6.12   The Startup tab

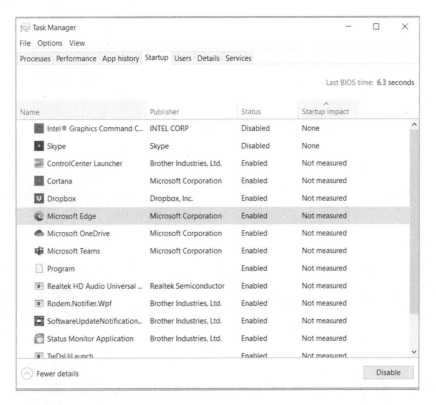

Performance

The Performance tab (shown in Figure 6.13) contains a variety of information, including overall CPU usage percentage, a graphical display of CPU usage history, page-file usage in megabytes, and a graphical display of page-file usage. Figure 6.14 shows the Performance tab in Windows 11.

This tab also provides you with additional memory-related information such as physical and kernel memory usage, as well as the total number of handles, threads, and processes. Total, limit, and peak commit-charge information also displays. Some of the items are beyond the scope of this book, but it's good to know that you can use the Performance tab to keep track of system performance. Note that the number of processes, CPU usage percentage, and commit charge always display at the bottom of the Task Manager window, regardless of which tab you have currently selected.

FIGURE 6.13   The Performance tab: Windows 10

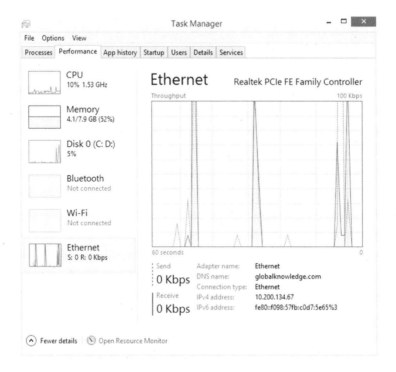

FIGURE 6.14   The Performance tab: Windows 11

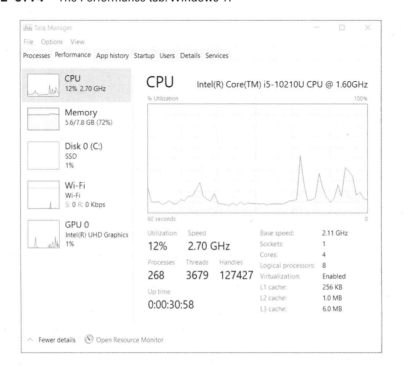

Processes

The Processes tab (shown in Figure 6.15) lets you see the names of all the processes running on the machine. You also see the user account that's running the process, as well as how much CPU and RAM resources each process is using. To end a process, select it in the list and click End Process. Be careful with this choice, since ending some processes can cause Windows to shut down. If you don't know what a particular process does, you can look for it in any search engine and find a number of sites that will explain it.

FIGURE 6.15   The Processes tab

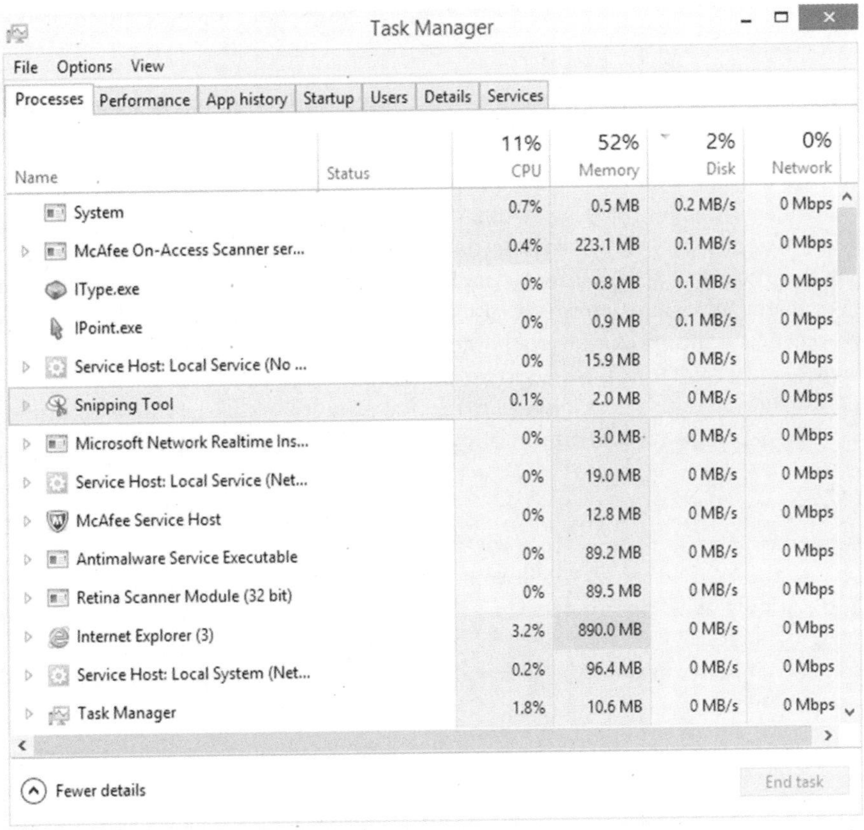

You can also change the priority of a process on the Details tab.

The six priorities, from lowest to highest, are as follows:

Low   For applications that need to complete at some time but that you don't want interfering with other applications. On a numerical scale from 0 to 31, this equates to a base priority of 4.

Below Normal   For applications that don't need to drop all the way down to Low. This equates to a base priority of 6.

Normal   The default priority for most applications. This equates to a base priority of 8.

Above Normal   For applications that don't need to boost all the way to High. This equates to a base priority of 10.

High   For applications that must complete soon, when you don't want other applications to interfere with the application's performance. This equates to a base priority of 13.

Realtime   For applications that must have the processor's attention to handle time-critical tasks. Applications can be run at this priority only by a member of the Administrators group. This equates to a base priority of 24.

If you decide to change the priority of an application, you'll be warned that changing the priority of an application may make it unstable. You can generally ignore this warning when changing the priority to Low, Below Normal, Above Normal, or High, but you should heed it when changing applications to the Realtime priority. Realtime means that the processor gives precedence to this process over all others—over security processes, over spooling, over everything—and is sure to make the system unstable.

Task Manager changes the priority only for that instance of the running application. The next time the process is started, priorities revert to that of the base (typically Normal).

Users

The Users tab (shown in Figure 6.16) provides you with information about the users connected to the local machine. You'll see the username, ID, status, client name, and session type. You can right-click any connected user to perform a variety of functions, including disconnecting the user.

Use Task Manager whenever the system seems bogged down by an unresponsive application.

Microsoft Management Console (MMC) snap-in

Microsoft Management Consoles (MMC) are preconfigured dashboards for various functions that can be combined into a single console or invoked in a dedicated console. An MMC with no tools added is shown in Figure 6.17. As you see, you can add a tool (called snap-ins) by using the menu.

In this section you'll learn about key utilities and tools you can add to an MMC.

FIGURE 6.16 Users tab

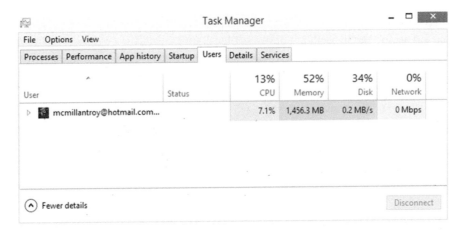

FIGURE 6.17 MMC

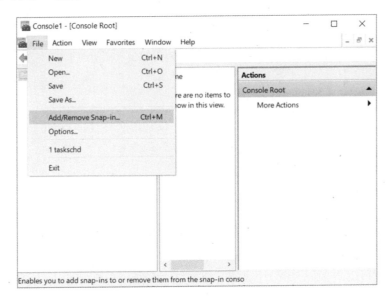

Event Viewer (*eventvwr.msc*)

Windows employs comprehensive error and informational logging routines. Every program and process theoretically could have its own logging utility, but Microsoft has come up with a rather slick utility, Event Viewer, which, through log files, tracks all events on a particular

Windows computer. Normally, though, you must be an administrator or a member of the Administrators group to have access to Event Viewer.

The process for starting Event Viewer differs based on the operating system you are running, but always log in as an administrator (or equivalent). Choose Start ➤ Programs ➤ Administrative Tools ➤ Event Viewer (or you can always right-click the Computer desktop icon and choose Manage Event Viewer). In the resulting window (shown in Figure 6.18), you can view the System, Application, Security, Setup, and Forwarded Events log files.

- The System log file displays alerts that pertain to the general operation of Windows.

- The Application log file logs application errors.

- The Security log file logs security events such as login successes and failures.

- The Setup log appears on domain controllers and contains events specific to them.

- The Forwarded Events log contains events that have been forwarded to this log by other computers.

FIGURE 6.18   The opening interface of Event Viewer

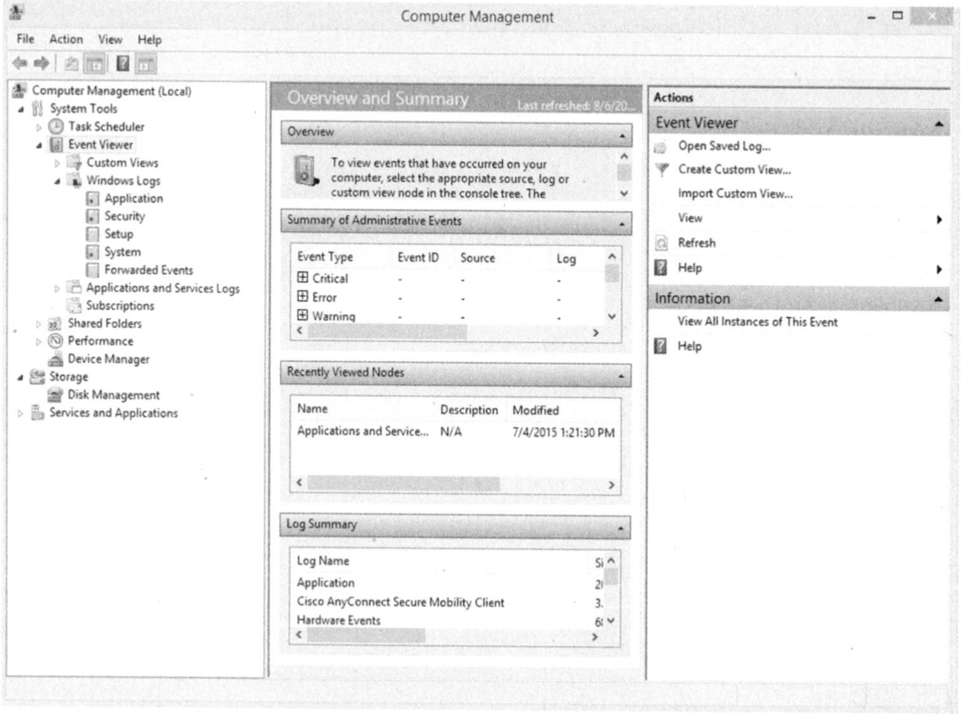

These log files can give a general indication of a Windows computer's health.

One situation that does occur with Event Viewer is that the log files get full. Although this isn't really a problem, it can make viewing log files confusing because there are so many entries. Even though each event is time- and date-stamped, you should clear Event Viewer every so often. To do this, open Event Viewer, right-click the log, choose Properties, and click the Clear Log button. Doing so erases all events in the current log file, allowing you to see new events more easily when they occur. You can set maximum log size by right-clicking the log and choosing Properties. By default, when a log fills to its maximum size, old entries are deleted in first in, first out (FIFO) order. Clearing the log, setting maximum log size, and setting how the log is handled when full are done in the Log Properties dialog box, as shown in Figure 6.19.

FIGURE 6.19   The Log Properties dialog box

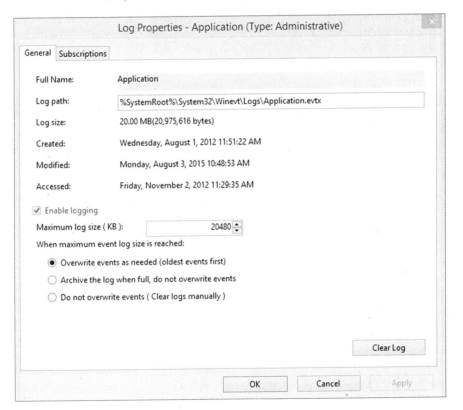

You can save the log files before erasing them. The saved files can be burned to a CD or DVD for future reference. Often, you are required to save the files to CD or DVD if you are working in a company that adheres to strict regulatory standards.

In addition to just erasing logs, you can configure three different settings for what you want to occur when the file does reach its maximum size. The first option is Overwrite Events As Needed (Oldest Events First), which replaces the older events with the new entries. The second option is Archive The Log When Full, Do Not Overwrite Events, which will create another log file as soon as the current one runs out of space. The third option, Do Not Overwrite Events (Clear Logs Manually), will not record any additional events once the file is full.

A scenario for using Event Viewer would be in the case of an attempted improper login. You could use the log to identify the time, machine, and other information concerning the attempt.

Disk Management (*diskmgmt.msc*)

In Windows, you can manage your hard drives using the Disk Management tool. To access Disk Management, access the Control Panel and double-click Administrative Tools. Then double-click Computer Management. Finally, double-click Disk Management.

The Disk Management screen lets you view a host of information regarding all the drives installed in your system, including CD-ROM and DVD drives. The list of devices in the top portion of the screen shows you additional information for each partition on each drive, such as the filesystem used, status, free space, and so on. If you right-click a partition in either area, you can perform a variety of functions, such as formatting the partition and changing the name and drive letter assignment. For additional options and information, you can also access the properties of a partition by right-clicking it and selecting Properties.

The basic unit of storage is the disk. Disks are partitioned (primary, logical, extended) and then formatted for use. With the Windows operating systems this exam focuses on, you can choose to use either FAT32 or NTFS; the advantage of the latter is that it offers security and many other features that FAT32 can't handle.

If you're using FAT32 and want to change to NTFS, the convert utility will allow you to do so. For example, to change the E: drive to NTFS, the command is convert e: /FS:NTFS.

Once the disk is formatted, the next building block is the directory structure, in which you divide the partition into logical locations for storing data. Whether these storage units are called directories or folders is a matter of semantics—they tend to be called *folders* when viewed in the graphical user interface (GUI) and *directories* when viewed from the command line.

Drive status

The status of a drive can have a number of variables associated with it (System, Boot, and so on), but what really matters is whether it falls into the category of *healthy* or *unhealthy*. As the title implies, if it is healthy, it is properly working, and if it is unhealthy, you need to attend to it and correct problems. In Figure 6.20 you can see in the Status column of Disk Management that all drives are healthy.

FIGURE 6.20   Status in Disk Management

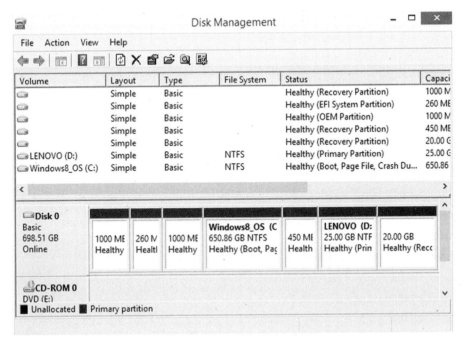

Mounting

Drives must be mounted before they can be used. Within Windows, most removable media (flash drives, CDs, and so forth) are recognized when attached and mounted. Volumes on basic disks, however, are not automatically mounted and assigned drive letters by default. To mount them, you must manually assign them drive letters or create mount points in Disk Management.

> You can also mount from the command line using either the Diskpart or Mountvol utility.

Initializing

Initializing a disk makes it available to the disk management system, and in most cases the drive will not show up until you do this. Once the drive has been connected or installed, it should be initialized. Initializing the drive can be done at the command line using diskpart or in the Disk Management tool. You need to know that initialization will wipe out any drive contents! To use diskpart to perform the initialization on 2 TB drives and smaller, follow these steps:

1. Open the Start menu and enter **diskpart**.

2. Enter **list disk**.

3. Enter **select disk** *X* (where *X* is the number your drive shows up as).

4. Enter **clean**.

5. Enter **create partition primary**.

6. Enter **format quick fs=ntfs**.

7. Enter **assign**.

8. Enter **exit**.

To use diskpart to perform the initialization on drives that are 2.5 TB or larger, follow these steps:

1. Open the Start menu and enter **diskpart**.

2. Enter **list disk**.

3. Enter **select disk** *X* (where *X* is the number your drive shows up as).

4. Enter **clean**.

5. Enter **convert gpt**.

6. Enter **create partition primary**.

7. Enter **format quick fs=ntfs**.

8. Enter **assign**.

9. Enter **exit**.

To use Disk Management, follow this procedure:

1. Install the drive and reboot the device.

2. In the search line, enter **Disk Management**. With the drive connected, you will get the pop-up box shown in Figure 6.21.

3. If you got the pop-up, choose either MBR or GPT and click OK.

FIGURE 6.21 The Initialize Disk pop-up

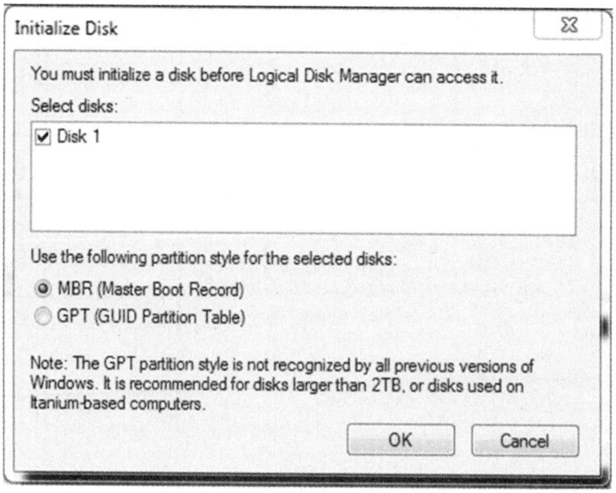

If you didn't get the pop-up, right-click and select to initialize the newly added drive under where it says Disk 1, as shown in Figure 6.22.

FIGURE 6.22   The Initialize Disk option

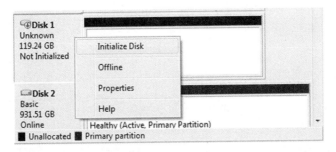

Extending partitions

It is possible to add more space to partitions (and logical drives) by extending them into unallocated space. This is done in Disk Management by right-clicking and choosing Extend or by using the Diskpart utility.

Splitting partitions

Just as you can extend a partition, you can also reduce the size of it. While this operation is generically known as *splitting* the partition, the menu option in Disk Management is Shrink. By shrinking an existing partition, you are creating another with unallocated space that can then be used for other purposes. You can shrink only basic volumes that use the NTFS filesystem (and space exists) or that do not have a filesystem.

Shrinking partitions

It is also possible to shrink a volume from its size at creation. To do so in Disk Management, access the volume in question, right-click the volume, and select Shrink Volume, as shown in Figure 6.23.

This will open another box that will allow you to control how much you want to shrink the volume, as shown in Figure 6.24.

Assigning/changing drive letters

Mounting drives and assigning drive letters are two tasks that go hand-in-hand. When you mount a drive, you typically assign it a drive letter to be able to access it. Right-clicking a volume in Disk Management gives the option Change Drive Letter And Paths, as shown in Figure 6.25.

FIGURE 6.23 The Shrink Volume option

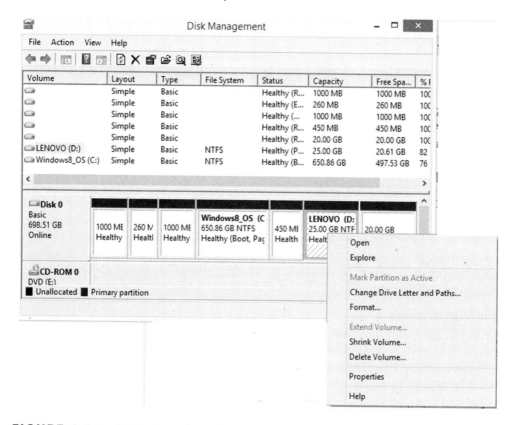

FIGURE 6.24 Setting the volume size

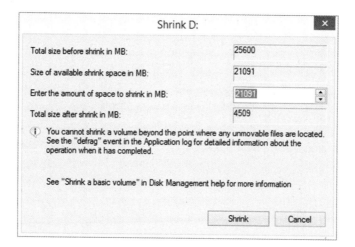

FIGURE 6.25   Changing the drive letter

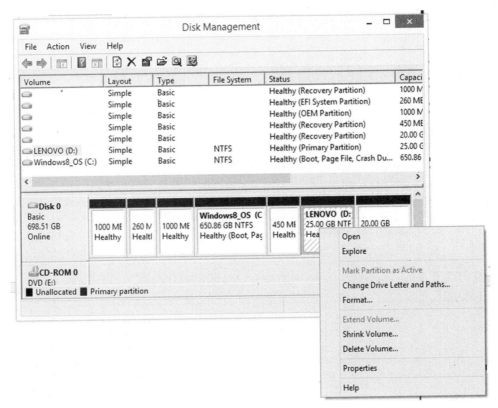

Adding drives

When removable drives are added, the Windows operating system is configured, by default, to identify them and assign a drive letter. When nonremovable drives are added, you must mount them and assign a drive letter, as mentioned earlier.

Adding arrays

Arrays are added to increase fault tolerance (using RAID) or performance (striping). Disk Management allows you to create and modify arrays as needed.

Storage spaces

Configuring storage spaces is a fault tolerance and capacity expansion technique that can be used as an alternative to the techniques described earlier when discussing dynamic volume types. It enables you to virtualize storage by grouping industry-standard disks into storage pools and then creating virtual disks called *storage spaces* from the available capacity in the storage pools. This means that, at a high level, you have to do three tasks to use storage spaces:

1. Create a storage pool, which is a collection of physical disks.

2. From the storage pool, create a storage space, which can also be thought of as a virtual disk.

3. Create one or more volumes on the storage space.

First let's look at creating the pool from several physical disks. Each of the disks must be at least 4 GB in size and should not have any volumes in it. The number of disks required depends on the type of resiliency you want to provide to the resulting storage space. Resiliency refers to the type of fault tolerance desired. Use the following guidelines:

- For simple resiliency (no fault tolerance), only a single disk is required for the pool.

- For mirror resiliency, two drives are required.

- For parity resiliency (RAID 5), three drives are required.

To create the pool, access the Control Panel using any of the methods discussed so far and click the applet Storage Spaces. On the resulting page, select the option Create A New Pool And Storage Space. On the Select Drives To Create Storage Pools page, the drives that are available and supported for storage pools will appear, as shown in Figure 6.26.

FIGURE 6.26   The Select Drives To Create A Storage Pool page

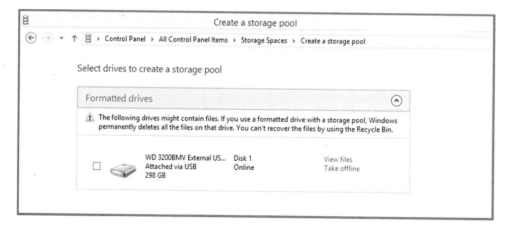

In this case, only one drive is eligible, so you can create only a simple type pool. Check the drive and click the Create Pool button at the bottom of the page. On the next page, give the space a name, select a drive letter, and choose the filesystem (NTFS or REFS), the resiliency type (in this case you can select only Simple), and the size of the pool. Figure 6.27 shows the pool as Myspace, with a drive letter of F, an NTFS filesystem, simple resiliency, and a maximum size of 100 GB. When you click Create Storage Space, the space will be created. Be aware that any data on the physical drive will be erased in this process!

FIGURE 6.27   Creating a storage space

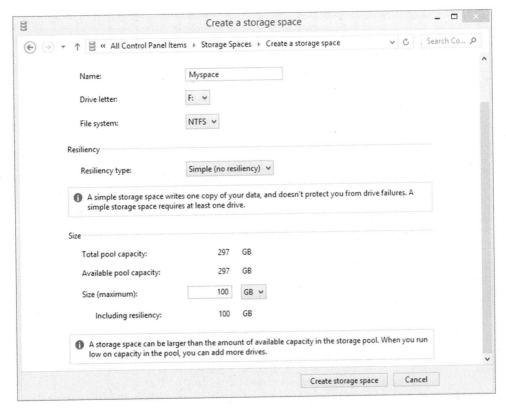

When the process is finished, the new space will appear on the Manage Storage Spaces page. Now you have a pool and a space derived from the pool. The last step is to create a volume in the storage space. If you now access Disk Management, you will see a new virtual disk called Myspace. It will be a basic disk, but you can convert it to dynamic by right-clicking it and selecting Convert To Dynamic Disk. This will allow to you shrink or delete the existing volume if you desire.

A scenario for using diskpart is to extend a partition that is getting full:

1. In the command prompt, enter **diskpart**.
2. At the Diskpart prompt, enter **list disk**.
3. Then enter **select disk** *n* where *n* is the partition you want to extend.
4. Enter **list partition**.
5. Select the partition which you want to extend. Enter **partition** *n*, where *n* is the partition you want to extend.
6. Enter **extend size=** *n*, where *n* is the size in megabytes you want to add to the partition.

Task Scheduler (*taskschd.msc*)

Task Scheduler allows you to configure jobs to automatically run unattended. For the run frequency, you can choose any of the following options: Daily, Weekly, Monthly, One Time Only, When The Computer Starts, or When You Log On. You can access a job's advanced properties any time after the job has been created. To do so, double-click the icon for the job in the Scheduled Tasks screen. In the resulting dialog box, you can configure such things as the username and password associated with the job, the actual command line used to start the job (in case you need to add parameters to it), and the working directory. At any time, you can delete a scheduled job by deleting its icon, or you can simply disable a job by removing the check mark from the Enabled box on the Task tab of the task's properties dialog box. For jobs that are scheduled to run, a picture of a clock appears in the bottom-left corner of the icon; jobs not scheduled to run do not have that clock. This tool is shown in Figure 6.28.

FIGURE 6.28   Task Scheduler

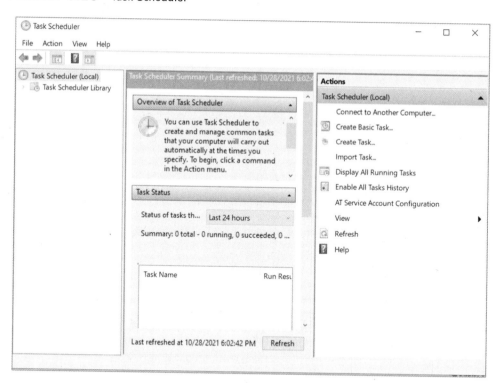

Device Manager (*devmgmt.msc*)

Device Manager shows a list of all installed hardware and lets you add items, remove items, update drivers, and more. This tool is shown in Figure 6.29.

FIGURE 6.29   Device Manager

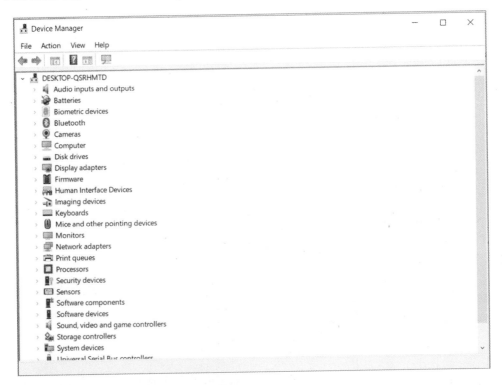

Certificate Manager (*certmgr.msc*)

Certificate Manager is a tool for managing all certificate issues. You can view currently held certificates and their details, and can request, export, and import certificates. A common scenario is when a user is presented with a certificate and the system rejects it because the certificate of the root server that issued the certification being rejected is not found in the local certificate store. Importing the root certificate into the proper location will solve the issue. The tool is shown in Figure 6.30. In Windows 11, to open the tool execute the command certmgr.msc at the command line.

Local Users and Groups (*lusrmgr.msc*)

If Local Users And Groups is not visible in the left pane of MMC, choose File Add/Remove Snap-in and select Local Users And Groups from the list of possible snap-ins. You can choose to manage the local computer or another computer (requiring you to provide its address). The built-in groups for a domain are a superset of local groups. You must manage user accounts using the User Accounts applet in Control Panel, and you cannot create or manage groups. The default users created are Administrator, Guest, and the administrative account created during the installation. This tool is shown in Figure 6.31.

FIGURE 6.30 Certificate Manager

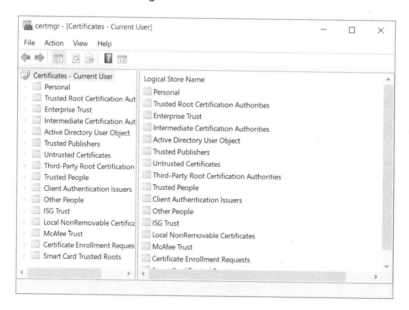

FIGURE 6.31 Local Users and Groups

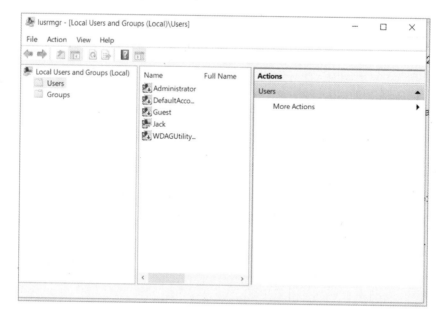

Performance Monitor (*perfmon.msc*)

Performance Monitor, invoked by executing `perfmon.msc` in the Run box or by adding its snap-in, contains monitoring tools. Among them is Resource Monitor, which can help you see how your system resources are being used; System Reliability Monitor, which allows you to view the performance impact of software updates and installations, Performance Monitor, or real-time statistics, and the ability to create datasets of values you would like to monitor over time. This tool is shown in Figure 6.32, where it is focused on the Performance Monitor tool, which is currently monitoring the realtime use of the processor.

FIGURE 6.32   Performance Monitor

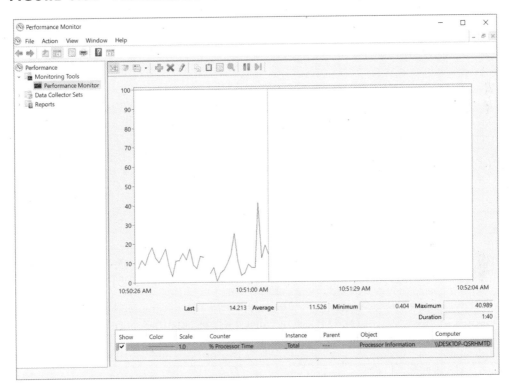

Group Policy Editor (*gpedit.msc*)

As you learned earlier in this chapter, Group Policies can be used in certain editions to exert control over both security and desktop settings. This configuration is done with a tool called the Group Policy Editor, invoked by executing **gpedit.msc** in the Run box or by adding its snap-in. Please review the earlier section on `gpedit.msc`. The tool is shown in Figure 6.33.

FIGURE 6.33   Group Policy Editor

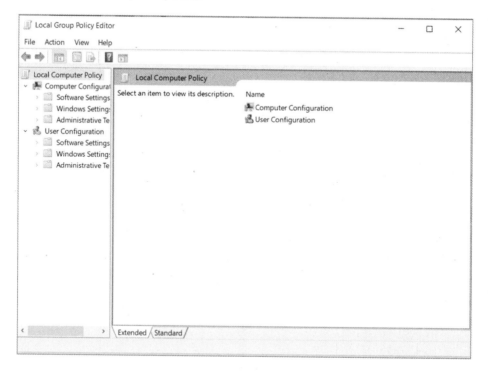

Group Policy can be used to control the behavior of both users and computers and has a section for each type of policy. Policies that impact users will be effective on any machine they log into that is a member of the domain. Likewise, policies that impact computers will be effective regardless of who logs into the machine. In cases where these policies don't agree, administrators have the ability to configure the superior policy.

Policies are not applied to security groups but are applied to containers in Active Directory (domain, OU, or child OU, etc.). Policies also leverage the concept of inheritance, which means a policy applied to a domain will be inherited by all OUs in the domain. This inheritance is also under the control of the administrators, meaning it can be enabled and disabled as needed.

Additional tools

If there's one thing Windows 10 has plenty of it's tools to make management easier. In this section you'll learn about additional tools at your disposal.

System Information (*msinfo32.exe*)

The System Information dialog box displays a thorough list of settings on the machine. You cannot change any values from here, but you can search, export, save, and run a number of utilities. It is primarily used during diagnostics because it is an easy way to display settings such as IRQs and DMAs. This dialog box is shown in Figure 6.34, where it is currently displaying general information about the system, including operating system version.

FIGURE 6.34   System Information

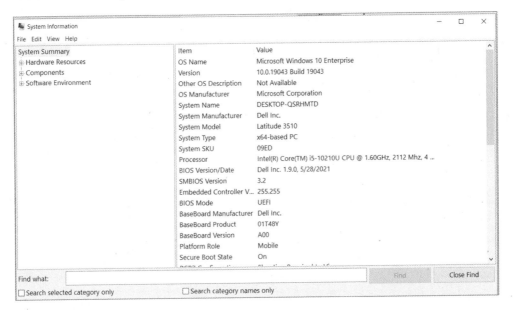

Resource Monitor (*resmon.exe*)

This tool displays information about the use of hardware (CPU, memory, disk, and network) and software (file handles and modules) resources in real time. While this can also be done with Performance Monitor, this tool organizes the information to focus on the use of these four hardware resources in real time. It is shown in Figure 6.35, where it's focused on the Overview tab, where a graph for each resource appears at the right. By selecting the tabs for a resource, you can focus just on this resource.

System Configuration (*msconfig.exe*)

MSConfig, also known as the System Configuration utility, helps you troubleshoot startup problems by allowing you to selectively disable individual items that normally are executed at startup. The MSConfig system configuration tool features five tabs: General, Boot, Services, Startup, and Tools.

FIGURE 6.35   Resource Monitor

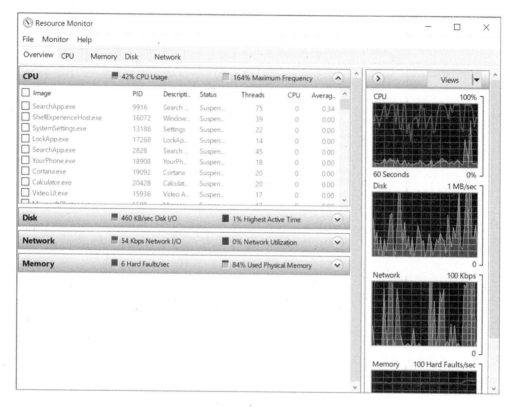

General

On the General tab, you can choose the startup type. There are three sets of options: Normal, Diagnostic, and Selective. A normal startup loads all drivers and services, whereas a diagnostic startup loads only the basic drivers and services. Between the two extremes is the selective startup, which gives you limited options on what to load. Figure 6.36 shows the General tab.

Boot

The Boot tab shows the boot menu and allows you to configure parameters such as the number of seconds the menu should appear before the default option is chosen and whether you want to safe boot. You can toggle on/off the display of drivers as they load during startup and choose to log the boot, go with basic video settings, and similar options. Figure 6.37 shows the Boot tab.

FIGURE 6.36   The General tab

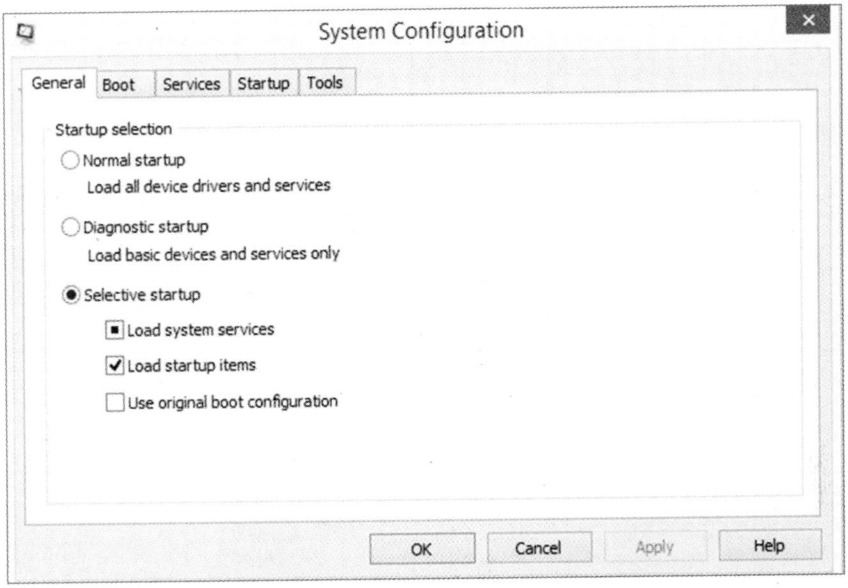

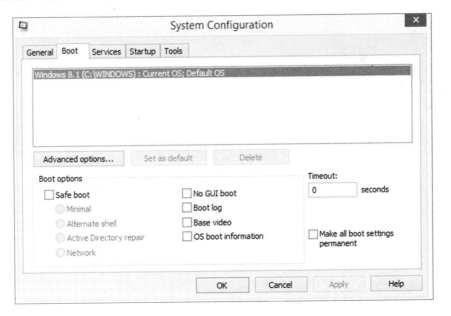

FIGURE 6.37   The Boot tab

Services

The Services tab shows the services configured and their current status. From here, you can enable or disable all and hide Microsoft services from the display (which greatly reduces the display in most cases). Figure 6.38 shows the Services tab.

FIGURE 6.38 The Services tab

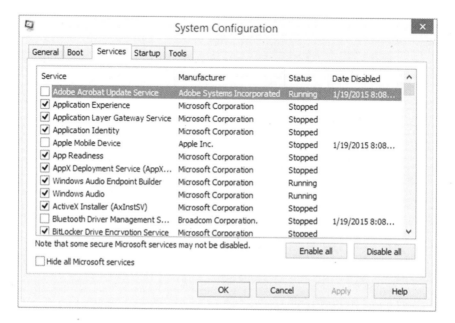

Startup

The Startup tab shows the items scheduled to begin at startup, the command associated with them, and the location where the configuration is done (usually, but not always, in the Registry). From here, you can enable or disable all. Figure 6.39 shows the Startup tab.

Tools

The Tools tab contains quick access to some of the most useful diagnostic tools in Windows. You can launch such items as the Registry Editor as well as many Control Panel applets, and you can enable or disable User Account Control (UAC). Figure 6.40 shows the Tools tab.

A scenario for using MSConfig would be when a device is performing slowly; you can check to see what applications and services are starting at boot, and you may find spyware and other software loading that is causing the performance hit.

FIGURE 6.39   The Startup tab

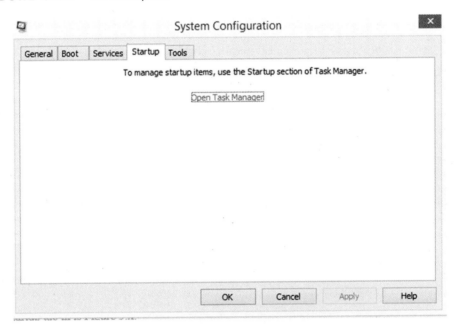

FIGURE 6.40   The Tools tab

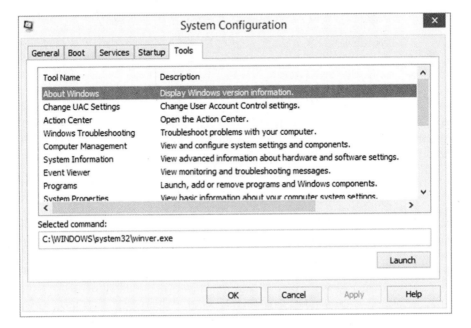

Disk Cleanup (*cleanmgr.exe*)

Disk Cleanup, invoked at the Run box by executing **cleanmgr.exe**, provides a utility for removing the data clutter that is hindering performance while not providing any benefits. It will suggest data locations where data is typically safe to delete, such as the Recycle Bin and Temp folders. The tool is shown in Figure 6.41.

FIGURE 6.41   Disk Cleanup

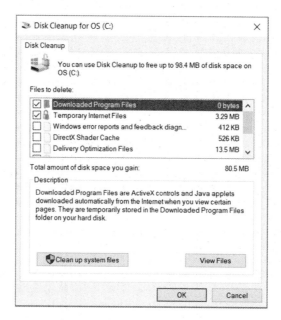

Disk Defragment (*dfrgui.exe*)

Microsoft Drive Optimizer (formerly Disk Defragmenter) is a utility used to eliminate the fragmentation of data on a drive that makes it more difficult for data to be located when requested and thus slowing performance. It rearranges the data such that there is no fragmentation. Running this from time to time will improve performance. The tool is shown in Figure 6.42.

Registry Editor (*regedit.exe*)

Registry Editor is used to open and edit the Registry. Regedit does not have save or undo features (though you can import and export); once you make a change, you've made the change for better or worse, and this is not a place to play around in if you're not sure what you're doing. The Registry is divided into five "hives" that hold all settings. The two main hives are HKEY_USERS (which contains settings for all users) and HKEY_LOCAL_MACHINE (which contains settings for the machine itself). HKEY_CURRENT_USER is a subset of HKEY_USERS, holding information only on the current user. HKEY_CURRENT_CONFIG and HKEY_CLASSES_ROOT are both subsets of HKEY_LOCAL_MACHINE for the current configuration. The tool is shown in Figure 6.43.

FIGURE 6.42   Disk Defragmenter

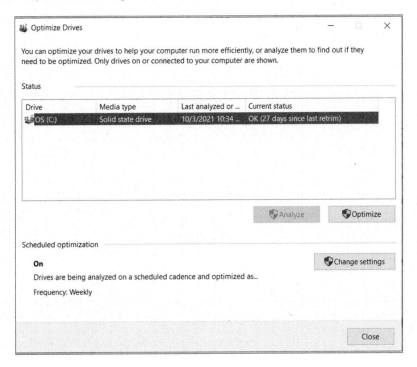

FIGURE 6.43   Registry Editor

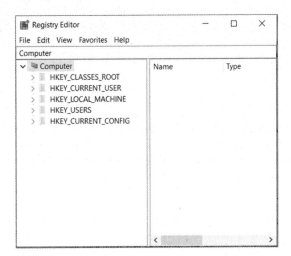

Exam essentials

Describe the administrative tools in Windows.   These tools include Computer Management, Device Manager, Users and Groups, Local Security Policy, Performance Monitor, Services, System Configuration, and Task Scheduler.

1.4 Given a scenario, use the appropriate Microsoft Windows 10 Control Panel utility

Control Panel is often the first place to turn for configuration settings. The applets contained within it allow you to customize the system and personalize it for each user.

Among the applets that every version of Windows has in common, CompTIA specifically singles out a number of them for you to know. In this section you'll learn about these applets.

Internet Options

The configuration settings for Internet Options provide a number of Internet connectivity possibilities. The tabs here include Connections, Security, General, Privacy, Content, Programs, and Advanced.

Connections

As the name implies, from this tab you can configure connections for an Internet connection, a dial-up or VPN connection, and LAN settings, as shown in Figure 6.44.

A scenario for using this tool would be when a user needs you to configure their laptop with a VPN connection to the office.

Security

On the Security tab, as shown in Figure 6.45, you can choose both a zone and a security level for the zone. The zones include Internet, Local Intranet, Trusted Sites, and Restricted Sites. The default security level for most of the zones is between High and Medium-High, but you can also select lower levels.

FIGURE 6.44   The Connections tab

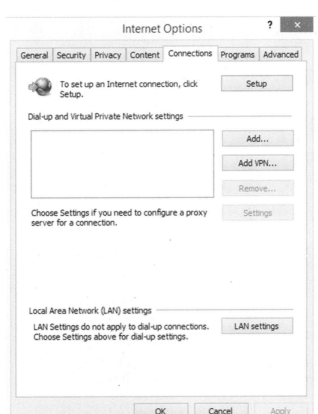

A scenario in which you would use this tool is when a user wants more secure settings on their Internet connection while loosening the settings somewhat for their home network.

General

On the General tab, as shown in Figure 6.46, you can configure the home page that appears when the browser starts or a new tab is opened. You can also configure the history settings, search defaults, what happens by default when new tabs are opened, and the appearance of the browser (colors, languages, fonts, and accessibility). The General tab in Windows 11 is shown in Figure 6.47.

FIGURE 6.45 The Security tab

A scenario for using this tool is when a user would like to change their home page to the company intranet site.

Privacy

Privacy settings, as shown in Figure 6.48, allow you to configure the privacy level, choose whether you want to provide location information, use Pop-up Blocker, and disable toolbars (and extensions) when InPrivate Browsing starts. The Privacy tab in Windows 11 is shown in Figure 6.49.

FIGURE 6.46   The General tab: Windows 10

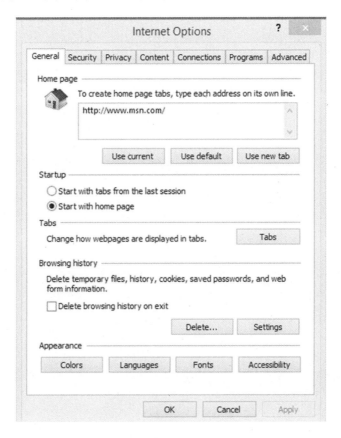

A scenario for using this tool would be when a user needs to disable pop-ups for a site that requires them to function properly.

Programs

On the Programs tab, as shown in Figure 6.50, you specify which browser you want to be the default browser, what editor to use if HTML needs editing, and what programs to associate with various file types. You can also manage add-ons from here. The Programs tab in Windows 11 is shown in Figure 6.51.

FIGURE 6.47   The General tab: Windows 11

A scenario for using this tool is when a user has an unusual file type that their system doesn't recognize. You could use this tool to associate the file type with the application that opens it.

FIGURE 6.48　　The Privacy tab Windows 10

Advanced

On the Advanced tab, as shown in Figure 6.52, you can reset settings to their default options. You can also toggle configuration settings for granular settings not found on other tabs.

FIGURE 6.49 The Privacy tab Windows 11

A scenario for using this tab would be when a user has played with the settings and would like to get them back to the default; this tool will do it.

FIGURE 6.50   The Programs tab Windows 10

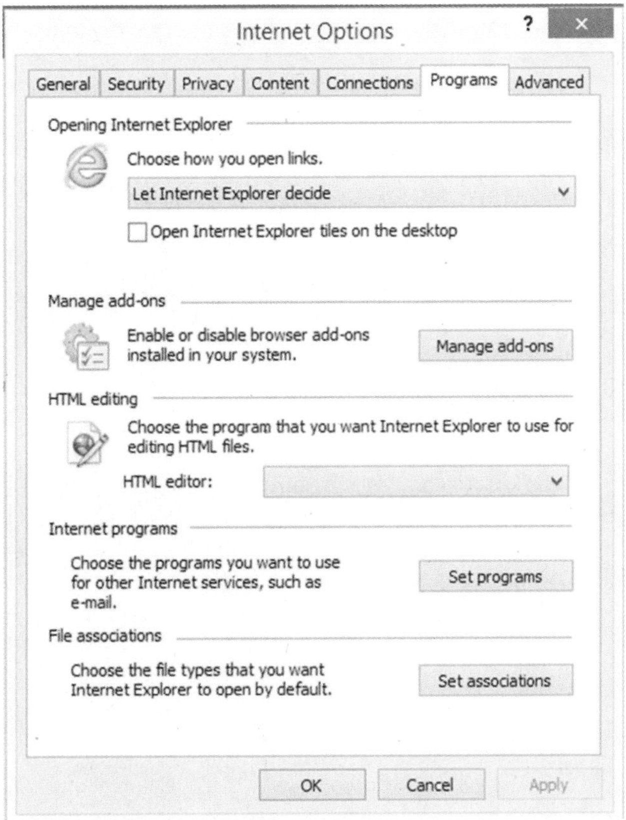

Devices and Printers

The Devices And Printers applet is the place where printers and other devices are managed. This tool is divided into three sections with printers in one, multimedia devices in another, and other devices in a third, as shown in Figure 6.53. To manage any device, you right-click the device and select its properties. The printers also can be double-clicked, and you can see what's printing, manage the print queue, and adjust additional settings. The Devices and Printers applet in Windows 11 is shown in Figure 6.54.

FIGURE 6.51   The Programs tab Windows 11

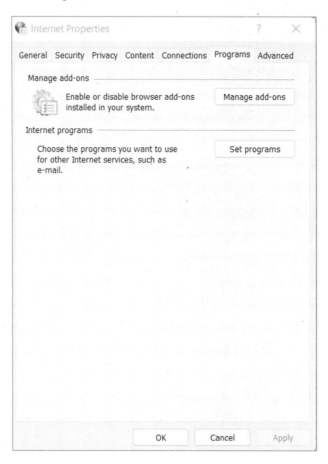

FIGURE 6.52 The Advanced tab

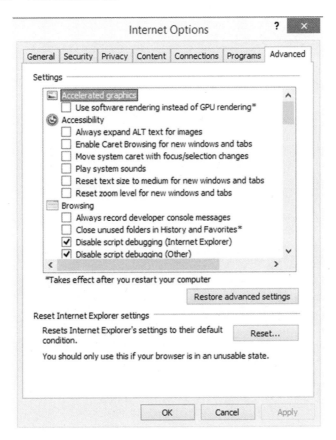

Programs and Features

Formerly known as Add/Remove Programs, this tool allows you to manage the programs running on the machine and the Windows features as well. Windows Features are tools and utilities that come with the operating system that may or may not be installed and running. You can uninstall any program you have installed here. When you select Turn Windows Features On Or Off from the menu on the left, you get a box that allows you to enable and disable Windows features, as shown in Figure 6.55.

FIGURE 6.53   The Devices And Printers applet: Windows 10

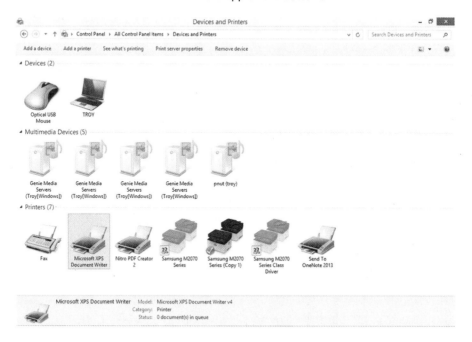

FIGURE 6.54   The Devices And Printers applet: Windows 11

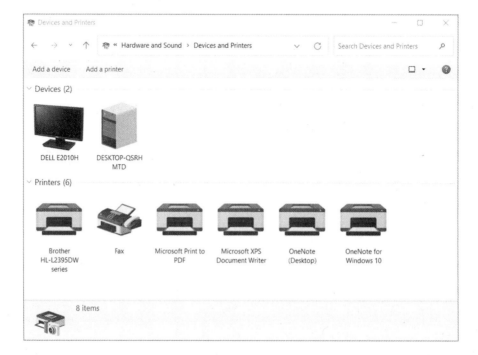

FIGURE 6.55   Programs and Features

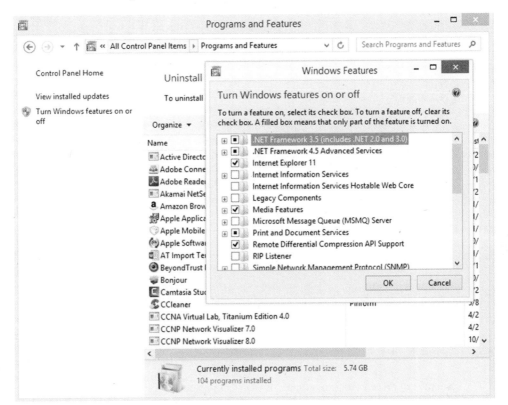

Network and Sharing Center

All network settings have been combined in an applet called Network And Sharing Center, where many sharing functions have also been relocated. While most of the tools are dedicated to creating and managing both wireless and wired network connections, some Advanced sharing functions are available in this applet. Figure 6.56 shows this applet.

System

This utility allows you to view and configure various system elements. From within this one relatively innocuous panel, you can make a large number of configuration changes to a Windows machine. The different versions of Windows have different options available in this panel, but they will include some of the following: General, Network Identification, Device Manager, Hardware, Hardware Profiles, User Profiles, Environment, Startup/Shutdown, Performance, System Restore, Automatic Updates, Remote, Computer Name, and Advanced. System are found in Control Panel.

FIGURE 6.56   The Network And Sharing Center applet

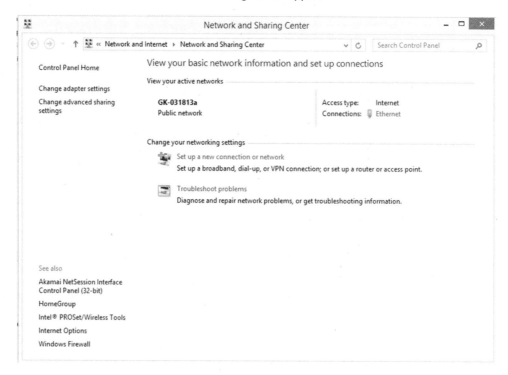

The General tab gives you an overview of the system, such as OS version, registration information, basic hardware levels (Processor and RAM), and the service pack level that's installed, if any.

 To access System Properties in Windows 11, enter **SystemProperties-Hardware.exe** in the search bar.

Performance (virtual memory)

Performance settings are configured on the Advanced tab, as shown in Figure 6.57. Clicking the Settings button allows you to change the visual effects used on the system and configure Data Execution Prevention (DEP). Data Execution Prevention is a security feature that prevents the execution of certain processes in key files. You can also configure virtual memory on the Advanced tab. Virtual memory is the paging file used by Windows as RAM.

FIGURE 6.57   Advanced tab

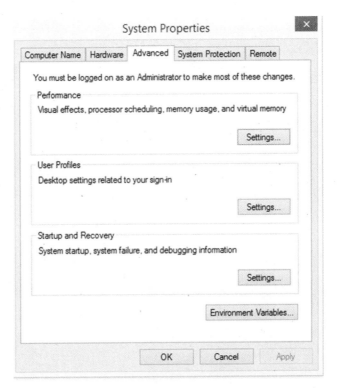

In most cases you should never change the virtual memory section, but when performance is lagging, you can try to dedicate more disk space for this function.

Remote settings

On the Remote tab, as shown in Figure 6.58, you can choose whether to allow Remote Assistance to be enabled. The Remote tab in Windows 11 is shown in Figure 6.59.

System protection

On the System Protection tab, as shown in Figure 6.60, you can choose to do a system restore as well as create a manual restore point and see the date and time associated with the most recent automatic restore point.

FIGURE 6.58 Remote tab: Windows 10

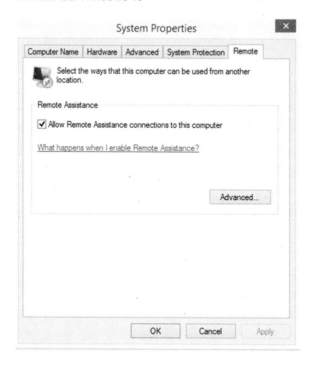

FIGURE 6.59 Remote tab: Windows 11

FIGURE 6.60   The System Protection tab

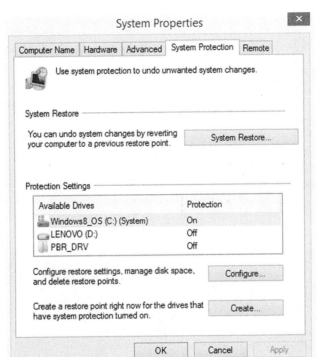

Windows Defender Firewall

As the name implies, the Windows Firewall applet can be used to manage the firewall included with the operating system. Figure 6.61 shows an example. In this case, the computer's firewall settings are being managed by the domain administrator. When the computer is outside of that network, the firewall settings are available to the user of the computer.

Mail

Mail, formerly known as Windows Mail, is the email client built into Windows 10 and 11. It contains preset server configurations for Outlook.com, Office 365, Gmail, iCloud, Yahoo! Mail, AOL Mail, as well as other Exchange Server and IMAP accounts. Figure 6.62 shows the interface.

FIGURE 6.61   The Windows Firewall

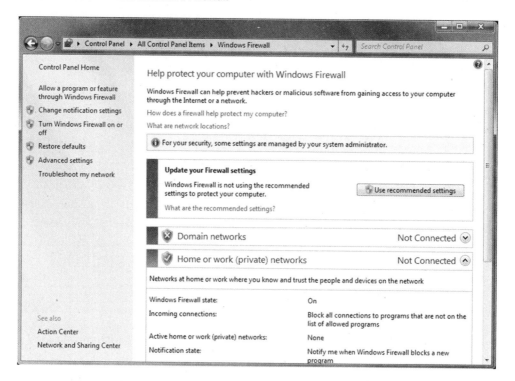

Sound

Windows 10 and 11 has a Control Panel item called Sound that is used to manage all sound settings. You can manage the input devices (microphones, lines in) and the output devices (speakers, headphones) in one place. Moreover, you can enable and disable the various Windows sounds that you hear when certain events occur. Figure 6.63 shows the Sound applet.

To open the classic Sounds applet in Windows 11, first enter **sound** in the search bar and select Sound Settings. Then go to the bottom of the next page and select More Sound Settings.

FIGURE 6.62   Mail

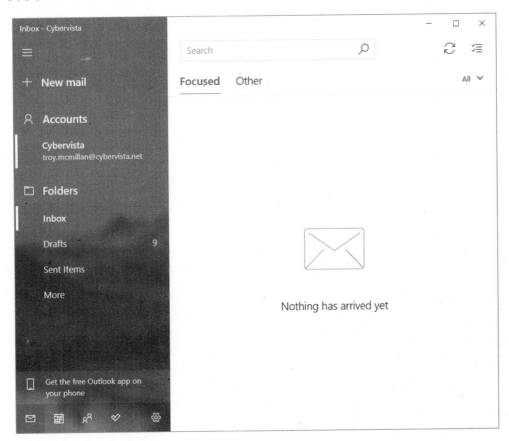

User Accounts

This dialog box, shown in Figure 6.64, lets you create and manage user accounts, parental controls, and related settings. The default users created are Administrator, Guest, and the administrative account created during the installation. This applet has the same functions but looks different in Windows 11, as shown in Figure 6.65.

FIGURE 6.63   Sound applet

FIGURE 6.64   User Accounts: Windows 10

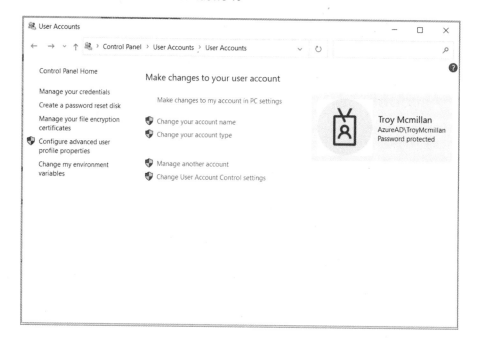

FIGURE 6.65   User Accounts: Windows 11

Device Manager

You learned about using Device Manager to troubleshoot device issues earlier in this chapter. The interface is shown in Figure 6.66.

FIGURE 6.66   Device Manager

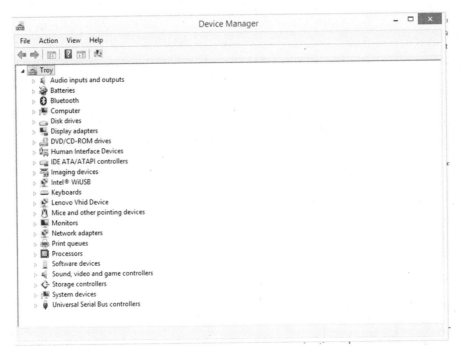

Indexing Options

The Indexing Options applet allows you to index data, resulting in faster searches. While it will automatically index certain common locations on your drive, such as the Offline files, Start menu, User profile, and Internet Explorer browsing history, you can have it index other datasets as well. In some cases, rebuilding the index may be required when you are failing to find certain items that you know are there. The Indexing Options applet is shown in Figure 6.67.

FIGURE 6.67   Indexing Options

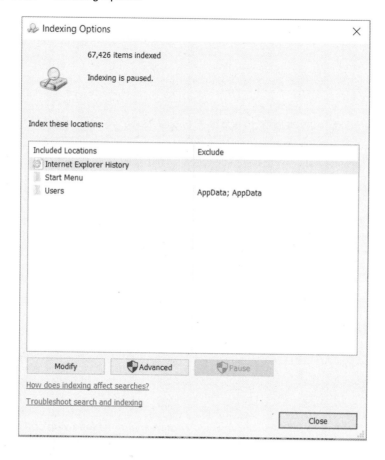

Administrative Tools

Table 6.19 lists the administrative tools, and the purpose for each, that you need to know for this objective. The majority of these run in the Microsoft Management Console (MMC).

TABLE 6.19   Windows administrative tools

Tool	Purpose
Computer Management	The Computer Management Console includes the following system tools: Device Manager, Event Viewer, Shared Folders, and Performance/ Performance Logs And Alerts (based on the OS you are running, you may also see Local Users And Groups or Task Scheduler). Computer Management also has the Storage area, which lets you manage removable media, defragment your hard drives, and manage partitions through the Disk Management utility. Finally, you can manage system services and applications through Computer Management as well. It also has a Storage section, which includes Disk Management and a Services and Applications section, which includes Services and WMI Control.
Device Manager	Device Manager shows a list of all installed hardware and lets you add items, remove items, update drivers, and more.
Local Users And Groups	If Local Users And Groups is not visible in the left pane of MMC, choose File Add/Remove Snap-in and select Local Users And Groups from the list of possible snap-ins. You can choose to manage the local computer or another computer (requiring you to provide its address). The built-in groups for a domain are a superset of local groups. The default users created are Administrator, Guest, and the administrative account created during the installation.
Performance Monitor	Performance Monitor displays performance counters. Two tools are available—System Monitor and Performance Logs And Alerts. System Monitor will show the performance counters in graphical format. The Performance Logs And Alerts utility collects the counter information and then sends it to a console (such as the one in front of the admin so they can be aware of the problem) or event log.
Services	The Services tab is illustrated and discussed later in this section.
System Configuration	MSConfig, known as the System Configuration utility, helps you troubleshoot startup problems by allowing you to selectively disable individual items that normally are executed at startup. It works in all versions of Windows, although the interface window is slightly different among versions.
Task Scheduler	Task Scheduler allows you to configure jobs to automatically run unattended. For the run frequency, you can choose any of the following options: Daily, Weekly, Monthly, One Time Only, When The Computer Starts, or When You Log On. You can access a job's advanced properties any time after the job has been created. To do so, double-click the icon for the job in the Scheduled Tasks screen. In the resulting dialog box, you can configure such things as the username and password associated with the job, the actual command line used to start the job (in case you need to add parameters to it), and the working directory. At any time, you can delete a scheduled job by deleting its icon, or you can simply disable a job by removing the check mark from the Enabled box on the Task tab of the task's properties dialog box. For jobs that are scheduled to run, a picture of a clock appears in the bottom-left corner of the icon; jobs not scheduled to run do not have that clock.

(continues)

TABLE 6.19   Windows administrative tools *(continued)*

Tool	Purpose
Component Services	Component Services is an MMC snap-in that allows you to administer, as well as deploy, component services and to configure behavior such as security (Component Services is located beneath Administrative Tools).
Data Sources	ODBC Data Source Administrator (located beneath Administrative Tools) allows you to interact with database management systems.
Windows Memory Diagnostics	The Windows Memory Diagnostic Tool (located beneath Administrative Tools) can be used to check a system for memory problems. For the tool to work, the system must be restarted. The two options that it offers are to restart the computer now and check for problems or wait and check for problems on the next restart. Upon reboot, the test will take several minutes, and the display screen will show which pass number is being run and the overall status of the test (percentage complete). When the memory test concludes, the system will restart again, and nothing related to it is apparent until you log in. If the test is without error, you'll see a message that no errors were found. If anything else is found, the results will be displayed.
Windows Firewall	Windows Firewall (Start ➢ Control Panel ➢ Windows Firewall) is used to block access from the network. While host-based firewalls are not as secure as other types of firewalls, this provides much better protection than previously and is turned on by default. It is also included in the Security component of the Action Center and can be tweaked significantly using the Advanced Settings.
Advanced Security	Continuing the discussion of Windows Firewall, once you click Advanced Settings, Windows Firewall with Advanced Security opens. Here, you can configure inbound and outbound rules as well as import and export policies and monitoring. Monitoring is not confined only to the firewall; you can also monitor security associations and connection security rules. Not only can this MMC snap-in do simple configuration, but it can also configure remote computers and work with Group Policy.
User Account Management	Used to create, delete, and configure properties of user accounts.

File Explorer Options

This dialog box lets you configure how folders are displayed in Windows Explorer.

Show hidden files

On the View tab, shown in Figure 6.68, beneath Advanced Settings, you can choose the option Show Hidden Files, Folders, And Drives, and this will allow you to see those items. The opposite of this—the default setting—is Don't Show Hidden Files, Folders, Or Drives. Radio buttons allow you to choose only one of these options.

FIGURE 6.68   View tab

A related check box that you should also clear in order to see all files is Hide Protected Operating System Files (Recommended) (not shown in Figure 6.68.) When this check box is cleared, those files will also appear in the view you are seeing.

Hiding these files is recommended so that users do not inadvertently delete or change these critical files. Hiding them is the default setting.

Hide extensions

On the View tab, shown in Figure 6.68, you must clear the check box Hide Extensions For Known File Types in order for the extensions to be shown with the files.

General options

You can configure the layout on the General tab of Folder Options (shown in Figure 6.69). Browsing options allow you to choose whether each folder will open in its own folder or the same folder. The Navigation Pane setting allows you to control what items are included in the tree structure that appears to the left when using File Explorer.

FIGURE 6.69   The General tab

View options

Along with the setting that allows you to hide or show file extensions and to show hidden files are a number of other settings that affect what you see when you use File Explorer (as shown in Figure 6.68 earlier).

Always Show Icons, Never Thumbnails   Always show icons, rather than thumbnail previews of files. Use this setting if thumbnail previews are slowing down your computer.

Always Show Menus   Always show menus above the toolbar. Use this setting if you want access to the classic menus, which are hidden by default.

Display File Icon On Thumbnails   Always shows the icon for a file in addition to the thumbnail (for easier access to the related program).

Display File Size Information In Folder Tips   See the size of a folder in a tip when you point to the folder.

Hide Protected Operating System Files   See all system files that are usually hidden from view.

Hide Empty Drives In The Computer Folder   Show removable media drives (such as card readers) in the `Computer` folder even if they currently don't have media inserted.

Launch Folder Windows In A Separate Process   Increase the stability of Windows by opening every folder in a separate part of memory.

Restore Previous Folder Windows At Logon   Automatically open the folders that you were using when you last shut down Windows whenever you start your computer.

Show Drive Letters   Hide or show the drive letter of each drive or device in the `Computer` folder.

Show Encrypted Or Compressed NTFS Files In Color   Display encrypted or compressed NTFS files with unique color coding to identify them.

Show Pop-Up Description For Folder And Desktop Items   Turn off the tips that display file information when you point to files.

Show Preview Handlers In Preview Pane   Never show or always show the contents of files in the preview pane. Use this setting to improve the performance of your computer or if you don't want to use the preview pane.

Use Check Boxes To Select Items   Add check boxes to file views for easier selection of several files at once. This can be useful if it's difficult for you to hold down the Ctrl key while clicking to select multiple files.

When typing in list view, there are two radio buttons.

Automatically Type Into The Search Box   Automatically puts the cursor in the search box when you start typing.

Select The Typed Item In The View   Does not automatically put the cursor in the search box when you start typing.

Power Options

Here you can configure different power schemes to adjust power consumption, dictating when devices—the display and the computer—will turn off or be put to sleep. Through the Advanced Settings, you can configure the need to enter a password to revive the devices, as well as configure wireless adapter settings, Internet options (namely, JavaScript), and the system sleep policy. Common choices are covered in the following sections.

Hibernate

Hibernate saves your workspace (all your open windows) and then turns the computer off.

Power plans

Power plans are collections of power settings that determine when various components in the device are shut down. There are some built-in plans available, or you can create your own. The three default plans are Balanced, which strikes a balance between performance and saving power; Power Saver, which errs on the side of saving power at the expense of performance; and High Performance, which errs on the side of performance over power saving. These options appear on the opening page when you open Power Options, as shown in Figure 6.70. To create a power plan, select Create A Power Plan from the tree menu on the left. To open this box in Windows11, enter **power** in the search box and select Edit Power Plan.

FIGURE 6.70 Power Options: Windows 10

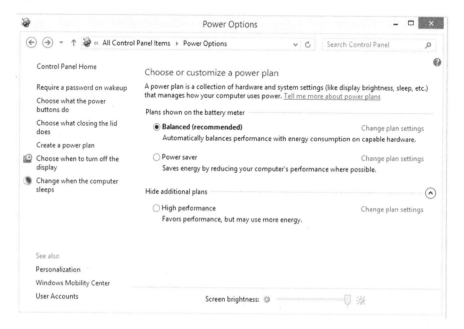

Sleep/suspend

Sleep/suspend puts your computer into an even deeper energy-saving mode than Standby, where it uses even less power.

Standby

Standby puts your computer into energy-saving mode, where it uses little power.

Choose what closing the lid does

This setting, which can contain different options for when the system is plugged in and when on battery, allows for configuring the behavior when closed. The choices are shown in Figure 6.71.

FIGURE 6.71   Choosing what closing the lid does

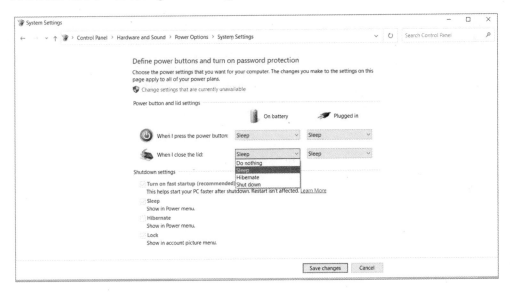

Turn on fast startup

This setting—which Microsoft recommends you enable—saves some data to the hard drive, which makes startup much faster. Be aware that this setting can cause issues in the following scenarios and may need to be disabled:

- Computer cannot perform a regular shutdown: Since you are required to shut down a PC when applying new system updates. new system updates will be affected because of Fast Startup.

- Windows hard disk will be locked so if configured to dual-boot and you boot to another operating system and then access or modify items on the disk or partition of the hibernating Windows PC, it can result in corruption.

- When you shut down a computer with Fast Startup enabled, you will fail to access the BIOS/UEFI settings on some systems.

Universal Serial Bus (USB) selective suspend

The USB 3.0 specification allows a device to enter suspended state when not in use. This mechanism is known as USB Selective Suspend and requires the software to cancel all transfers to the device and then sends the device to the suspended state.

Ease of Access

Ease of Access is a collection of settings intended to make using the system easier for those with disabilities. These include settings to add additional brightness, narrate screen readings, and make the cursor bigger. Selected settings are shown in Figure 6.72.

FIGURE 6.72   Ease of Access

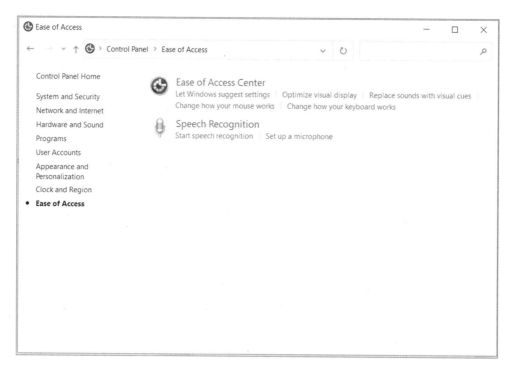

Exam essentials

Identify the purpose of Control Panel utilities.   These tools include Internet Options, User Accounts, File Explorer Options, Windows Defender Firewall, Power Options, Devices And Printers, Sound, and Device Manager.

1.5 Given a scenario, use the appropriate Windows settings

While we've already covered many settings found in Windows 10, there are some additional ones you need to know. In this section you'll learn about some others found in various locations in Windows 10. These settings are all included in the applet called, appropriately, Settings, shown in Figure 6.73. This screen looks a bit different in Windows 11, as shown in Figure 6.74.

FIGURE 6.73   Settings: Windows 10

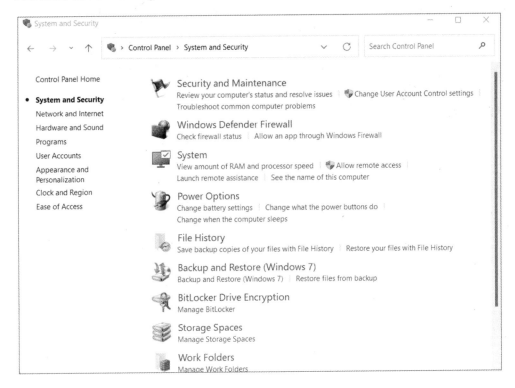

FIGURE 6.74   Settings: Windows 11

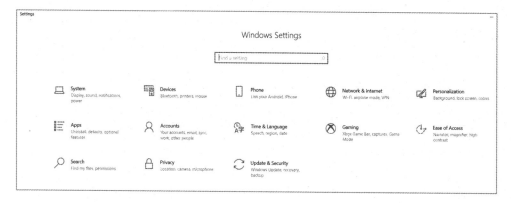

Time and Language

When you click on the Time & Language tile in the Settings applet, you will be presented with the screen shown in Figure 6.75. This window looks different in Windows 11, as shown in Figure 6.76, but offers the same functions.

FIGURE 6.75   Time & Language: Windows 10

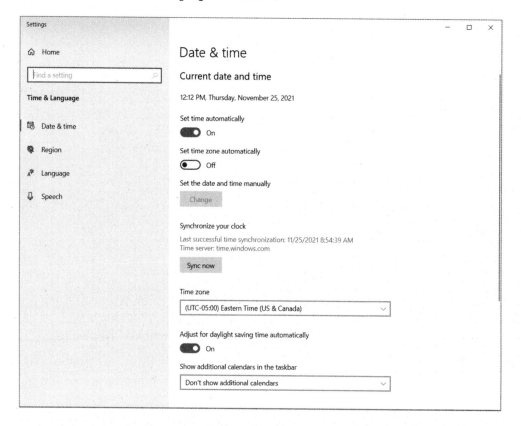

FIGURE 6.76   Time & Language: Windows 11

Here you can make settings for the date time and time zone. While not the focus of this section, notice you can also set the region in which you are located and the languages(s) you need to support. Finally there is a section for setting up the microphone and the voice that is used if the system is reading or talking to you.

Update and Security

This section, shown in Figure 6.77, is called Update and Security but it does much more.

FIGURE 6.77   Update and Security

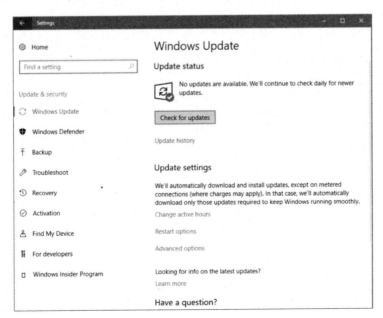

Table 6.20 shows what can be done in each section.

TABLE 6.20 Update and Security settings

Update	Sets the behavior of Windows Updates.
Deliver Optimization	Settings for allowing updates from other computers.
Windows Security	A wide range of settings, including setting up virus protection, account security, application and browser security, and more.
Backup	Sets up an external drive for backup.
Troubleshoot	Offers automated troubleshooting scripts.
Recovery	Contains settings to reset the PC and to boot to advanced options when there are boot issues.
Activation	Displays activation status and offers the ability to attempt activation.
Find My Device	If enabled, this tracks the location of your device. If the device is on a work network or school network this setting is disabled.
For developers	Contains certain settings that are typically used by software developers, including settings for Remote Desktop and PowerShell settings.
Windows Insiders Program	You can join this group and receive preview builds that you can review and provide input for.
Device Encryption	Where device encryption can be enabled, helps to protect the data if the device is stolen.

In Windows 11, these settings are contained in two different applets in Control Panel. Privacy & Security is shown in Figure 6.78, and Windows Update is shown in Figure 6.79.

Personalization

The settings in this section mostly apply to the display. As you can see in Figure 6.80, you can set the background of the desktop, the colors used in various boxes, a screen lock that can appear when you step away, theme settings (which are a collection of display settings that follow a theme, size, and font style), the layout of the Start Menu, and the location and layout of the taskbar. The Windows 11 version is shown in Figure 6.81.

FIGURE 6.78   Privacy & Security: Windows 11

FIGURE 6.79   Windows Update: Windows 11

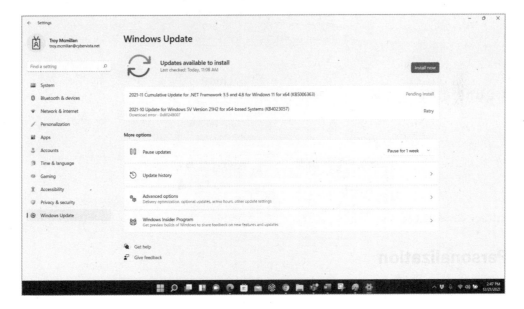

FIGURE 6.80 Personalization: Windows 10

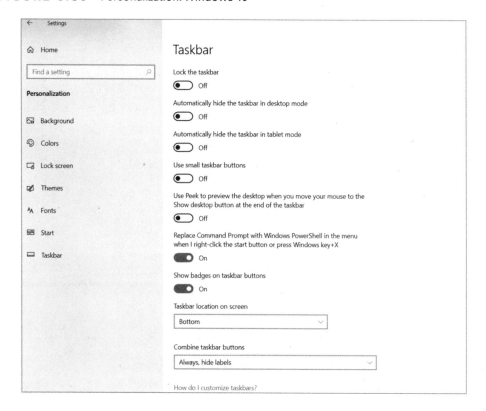

FIGURE 6.81 Personalization: Windows 11

Apps

This section is concerned with the download and installation of applications. It displays the apps currently available, offers a section to set the default application used for various file types, a section to download maps to use when the Internet is not available, a section to associate a website with a particular browser or application, a section for the behavior of videos when played on the system, and finally one more location where you can specify applications that start when you start the system. Apps is shown in Figure 6.82. The Windows 11 version is shown in Figure 6.83.

FIGURE 6.82   Apps: Windows 10

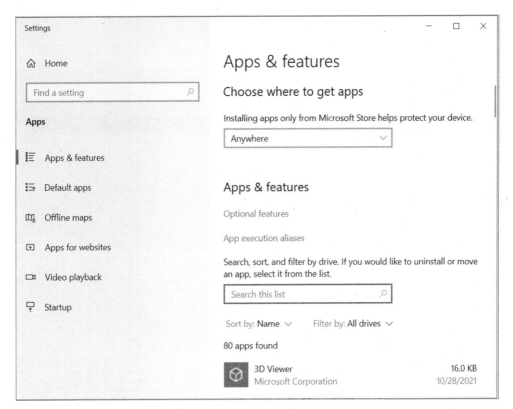

FIGURE 6.83 Apps: Windows 11

Privacy

As you might suspect, this tool contains settings that are used to maintain the privacy of your data. It also contains many other settings as well, including but not limited to:

- Enable speech recognition
- Enable typing and handwriting history so the system can make suggestions
- Allow or disallow sending diagnostic information to Microsoft
- Enable storing activity history on the device
- Enable app location tracking
- Allow app access to the camera
- Allow app access to the mic
- Allow apps to use voice activation

Privacy is shown in Figure 6.84. In Windows 11, these functions are in the Privacy & Security applet shown earlier.

FIGURE 6.84   Privacy

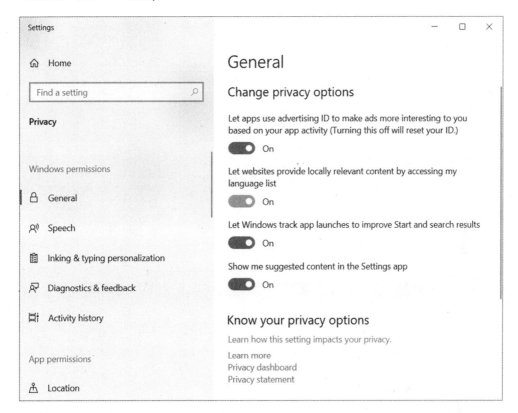

System

This section contains a wide array of settings, many of which are also found in other locations as well. Most of the System settings are shown in Figure 6.85. The Windows 11 version is shown in Figure 6.86.

Devices

This section contains settings for the external devices and peripherals that are connected to the system. Devices is shown in Figure 6.87. In Windows 11, devices are managed in Printers & Scanners covered later.

FIGURE 6.85 System: Windows 10

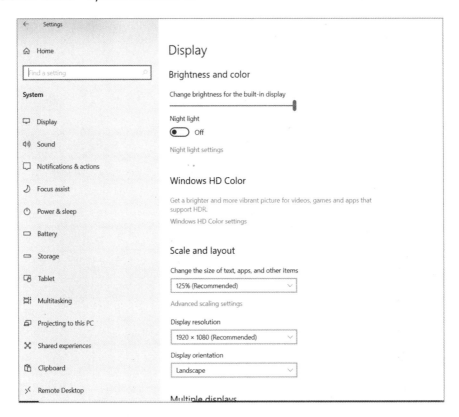

FIGURE 6.86 System: Windows 11

FIGURE 6.87 Devices

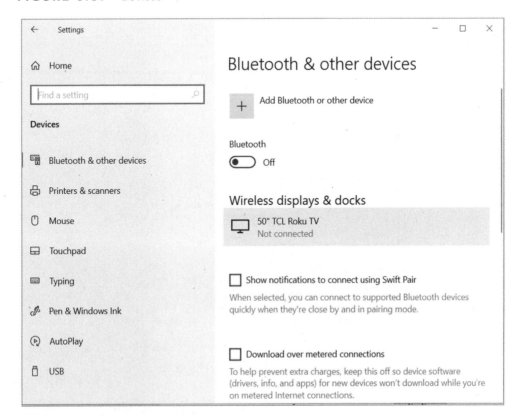

Network and Internet

This section is for setting and configuring network connection of all types, including:

- Ethernet
- WLAN
- Dial-up
- VPN

It also is where you can set your WLAN interface for Airplane mode, set up a mobile hotspot, and configure a proxy server. Network & Internet is shown in Figure 6.88. The Windows 11 version is shown in Figure 6.89.

FIGURE 6.88   Network & Internet: Windows 10

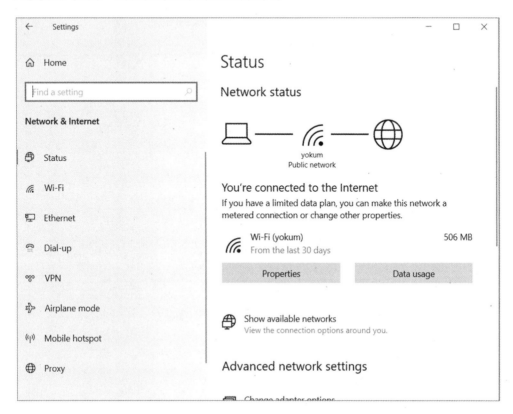

FIGURE 6.89   Network & Internet: Windows 11

Gaming

If you are into gaming, then you will visit this section often. Here you can adjust settings that affect the gaming experience. You can control the Xbox Game bar, set the system to record screenshots of games, enable game mode (to optimize performance), and view the amount of packet loss and latency. Gaming is shown in Figure 6.90. The Windows 11 version is shown in Figure 6.91.

FIGURE 6.90   Gaming: Windows 10

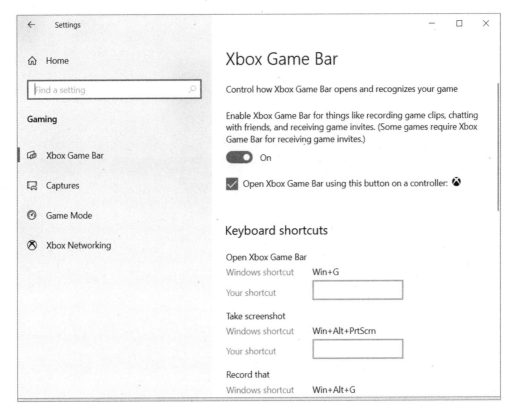

FIGURE 6.91   Gaming: Windows 11

Accounts

This section displays the information of the currently logged-on user and also has sections to do the following:

- Manage the sign-on process
- Set default email
- A section to access a school or work network
- Add a work or school user account and grant access
- Settings to sync data across devices

Accounts is shown in Figure 6.92. The Windows 11 version is shown in Figure 6.93.

Exam essentials

Identify Settings tiles.   These commands include Time & Language, Update & Security, Personalization, Apps, Privacy, System, Devices, Network & Internet, Gaming, and Accounts.

FIGURE 6.92   Accounts: Windows 10

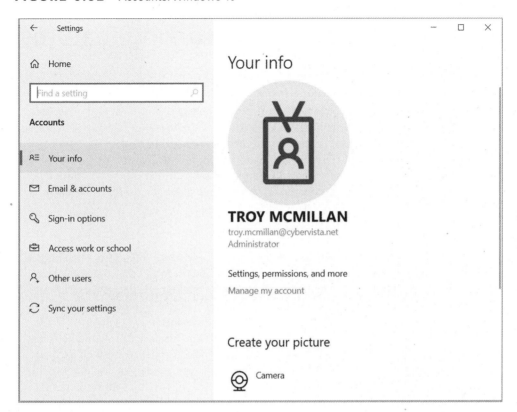

FIGURE 6.93   Accounts: Windows 11

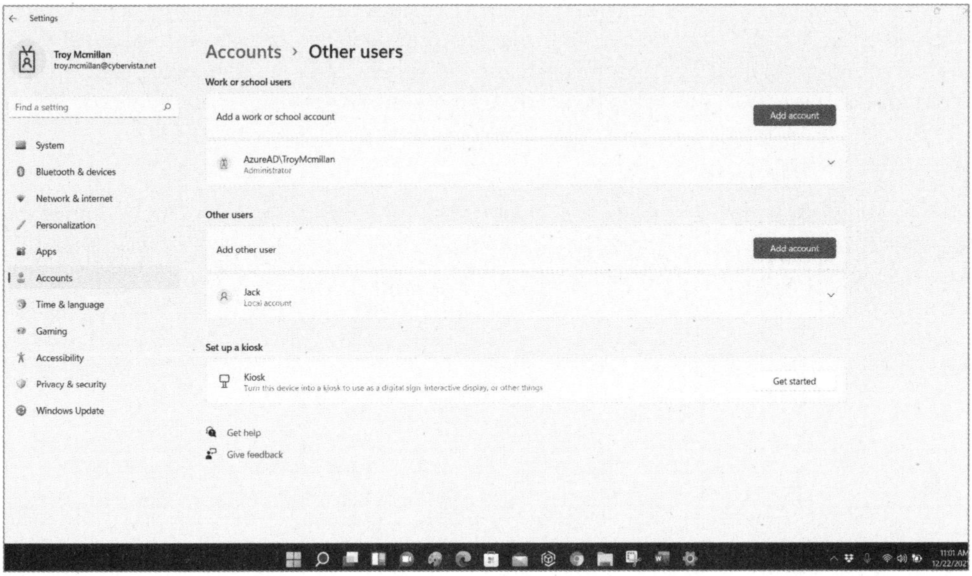

1.6 Given a scenario, configure Microsoft Windows networking features on a client/desktop

CompTIA offers a number of exams and certifications on networking (Network+, Server+, and so on), but to become A+ certified, you must have good knowledge of basic networking skills as they relate to the Windows operating system.

It's important to know how network addressing works and the features offered in the Windows operating systems to simplify configuration. CompTIA expects you to have a broad range of knowledge in this category, including some obscure features (such as QoS).

Workgroup vs. domain setup

A peer-to-peer network, one of two network types you can create in Windows (also known as a *workgroup*), consists of a number of workstations (two or more) that share resources among themselves. The resources shared are traditionally file and print access, and every computer has the capacity to act as a workstation (by accessing resources from another machine) and as a server (by offering resources to other machines).

The other network type is client-server (or a domain). The primary distinction between workgroups and client-server networks is where security is controlled: locally on each workstation or centrally on a server. A domain is a centrally managed group of computers, and physical proximity does not matter; the computers within a domain may all be on the same LAN or spread across a WAN.

The advantage of a peer-to-peer network is that the cost is lower; you need only add cards and cables to the computers you already have if you're running an operating system that allows such modifications. With a server-based network, you must buy a server—a dedicated machine—and thus the costs are higher. It's never recommended that a peer-to-peer network be used for more than 10 workstations because the administration and management become so significant that a server-based network makes far greater sense.

Domain setup

In a domain (also known as a *client-server network*), users log on to the server by supplying a username and password. They're then authenticated for the duration of their session. Rather than requiring users to give a password for every resource they want to access (which would be share-level), security is based on how they authenticated themselves at the beginning of their session. This is known as *user-level* security, and it's much more powerful than share-level security.

Enterprise networks join servers, workstations, and other devices into security associations called *domains* or *realms*. These associations are made possible through the use of directory services such as Active Directory. These associations are what make the concept of single sign-on possible. This means that any user can log into the network using any device that is a domain member and receive all their assigned rights and privileges by using a single logon.

Joining a computer to the domain can be done during the installation in some cases, but many administrators do this after the successful installation of the operating system. An example of how this is done in Windows 10 is shown in Figure 6.94. This is done on the Computer Name tab of System Properties by clicking the Change button. To navigate to System Properties, open Control Panel and select the System icon (using icon view). Then select Advanced System Settings from the menu on the left side of the page. This opens the System Properties dialog box shown in Figure 6.94.

FIGURE 6.94 Joining the server to the domain

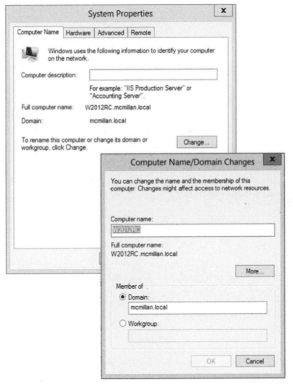

Shared resources

An administrative share is one that is hidden to those file browsing. To connect to these drives, you must reference the name of the drive. While you can create a hidden drive at any time simply by adding a dollar sign at the end of its name, there are some default administrative drives.

Table 6.21 gives information on the default administrative drives.

TABLE 6.21 Default administrative drives

Share name	Location	Purpose
ADMIN$	%SystemRoot%	Remote administration
IPC$	N/A	Remote interprocess communication
print$	%SystemRoot%\System32\spool\drivers	Access to printer drivers
C$, D$, E$, and so on	The root of any drive	Remote administration

Printers

In Chapter 3, in the section "Public/shared devices," you learned how to share a printer that is connected locally to a computer. It is also possible to connect to a network printer that is not tied to a computer but that has its own IP address and probably built-in print server. To connect or map a user's device to one of these devices, follow the procedure to add a shared printer, and on the page you normally enter the UNC path to the shared printer, select the option Add A Printer Using A TCP/IP Address Or Hostname, as shown in Figure 6.95, and click Next.

FIGURE 6.95 Adding a printer using a TCP/IP address

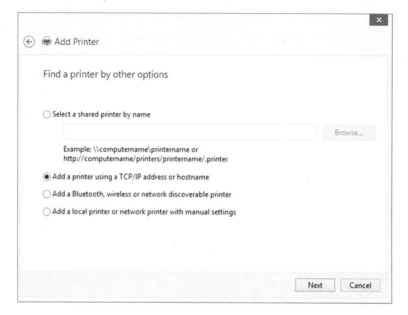

Enter the IP address or the hostname of the printer, as shown in Figure 6.96, and click Next.

FIGURE 6.96   Adding the printer IP address

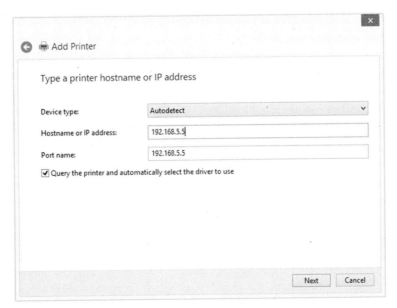

If the IP address is correct and can be reached, the printer driver will download, and the printer will be added to the printer's area of Control Panel.

File servers

In Chapter 2, "Networking," you learned about the role of file servers in the network. Shares are typically created on these devices that make resources such as files and folders available to users, while controlling their specific access with permissions. Review this section in Chapter 2.

Mapped drives

Network shares can be mapped to drives to appear as if the resources are local. The net use command is used to establish network connections via a command prompt. For example, to connect to a shared network drive and make it your M drive, you would use the syntax **net use m: \\server\share**. This can also be done in File Explorer.

Local OS firewall settings

Windows Firewall (Start ➢ Control Panel ➢ Windows Firewall) is used to block access from the network. It is divided into separate settings for private networks and public networks.

Application restrictions and exceptions

Exceptions are configured as variations from the rules. Windows Firewall will block incoming network connections except for the programs and services that you choose to allow through. For example, you can make an exception for Remote Assistance to allow communication from other computers when you need help (the scope of the exception can be set to allow any computer, only those on the network, or a custom list of allowed addresses you create). Exceptions can include programs as well as individual ports.

A scenario for using exceptions would be when you want to block all traffic with the exception of *only* required traffic. You define each allowed traffic type as an exception and disallow all others by default.

Restrictions prevent an application from sending traffic though the interfaces of the firewall. A scenario for using this would be when you need to prevent malicious traffic of a particular type.

Configuration

Most of the configuration is done as network connection settings. You can configure both ICMP and Services settings. Examples of ICMP settings include allowing incoming echo requests, allowing incoming router requests, and allowing redirects. Examples of services often configured include an FTP server, Post Office Protocol Version 3 (POP3), and web server (HTTP).

A scenario for using this setting is to disallow ICMP traffic to prevent ping sweeps. This type of network probing is used to discover the devices in your network.

Enabling/disabling Windows Firewall

On the General tab of Windows Firewall, it is possible to choose the radio button Off (Not Recommended). As the name implies, this turns Windows Firewall completely off. The other radio button option, On (Recommended), enables the firewall. You can also toggle the check box Don't Allow Exceptions. This option should be enabled when you're connecting to a public network in an unsecure location (such as an airport or library), and it will then ignore any exceptions that were configured.

A scenario where you might choose to turn the firewall off is when you are using another firewall product instead. You want to use only one firewall. The option used in Window 11 is shown in Figure 6.97.

FIGURE 6.97   Enabling Defender Firewall

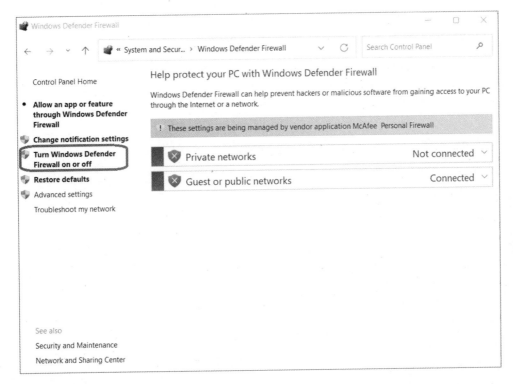

Client network configuration

In Chapter 2 you learned about the concepts covered in this section of the A+ objectives. These include coverage of the following:

- Internet Protocol (IP) addressing scheme
- Domain Name System (DNS) settings
- Subnet mask
- Gateway
- Static vs. dynamic

Please review that chapter because these are critical objectives for the A+ exam.

Establish network connections

When configuring the connection method for accessing the Internet, the three choices Windows offers are This Computer Connects Directly To The Internet, This Computer Connects Through A Residential Gateway Or Another Computer, and Other. If you choose the first option, you can turn on Internet Connection Sharing (ICS) and allow this machine to serve as a proxy. The network connection you configure can be wireless or wired, dial-up, or a virtual private network (VPN). In Windows 11 the choices are all there but the boxes look as shown in Figure 6.98.

FIGURE 6.98   Network connections in Windows 11

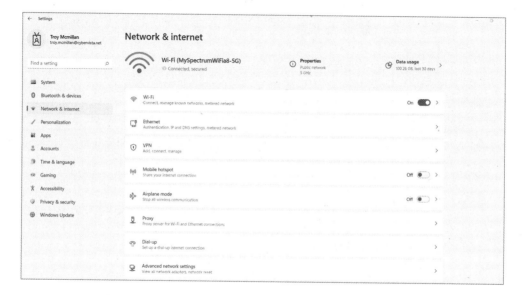

Virtual private network (VPN)

A VPN is used when you want to connect from a remote location (such as home) to the company's network (authenticating the user and encrypting the data).

Wireless

A wireless connection uses one of the 802.11 technologies along with encryption to connect to the network.

Wired

A wired connection uses a wire to connect the computer to the network. Typically, this is an Ethernet cable, such as 100BaseT, which connects to a hub or switch and offers network access to the host.

Wireless wide area network (WWAN)

A wireless wide area network (WWAN) connection is one that uses cellular to connect the host to the network. A wireless service provider (such as AT&T, Sprint, or T-Mobile) will provide a card that is plugged into the host to make the cellular connection possible.

Options available are shown in Table 6.22.

TABLE 6.22   Network connection options

Option	Purpose
Connect To The Internet	Use for connection to a proxy server or other device intended to provide Internet access. This includes wireless, broadband, and dial-up.
Set Up A New Network	Use to set a new WLAN router or access point.
Manually Connect To A Wireless Network	If you have a wireless network already in place and the device (such as the router) is not directly connected to this machine, use this option.
Connect To A Workplace	If you need to dial into a VPN from a remote location, this is the option to use.

Regardless of which option you choose, you will need to fill out the appropriate fields for the device to be able to communicate on the network. With TCP/IP, required values are an IP address for the host, subnet mask, address for the gateway, and DNS information.

Proxy settings

Proxy settings identify the proxy server to be used to gain Internet access. The proxy server is responsible for making the Internet access possible and may utilize network address translation (NAT) to translate between the public network (Internet) and the private network (on which the host sits). These settings are configured by using the LAN Settings button in the Connections tab to open the dialog box shown in Figure 6.99. Proxy settings for Windows 11 are shown in Figure 6.98 earlier (network connections).

Public network vs. private network

In Windows 10 when you make a new connection, you are asked to identify whether it is a private or a public network. If you choose one of the first two, *network discovery* is on by default, allowing you to see other computers and other computers to see you. If you choose Public, network discovery is turned off.

Network discovery, when enabled, is a security issue, and this function should *not* be used on untrusted networks.

FIGURE 6.99   LAN settings

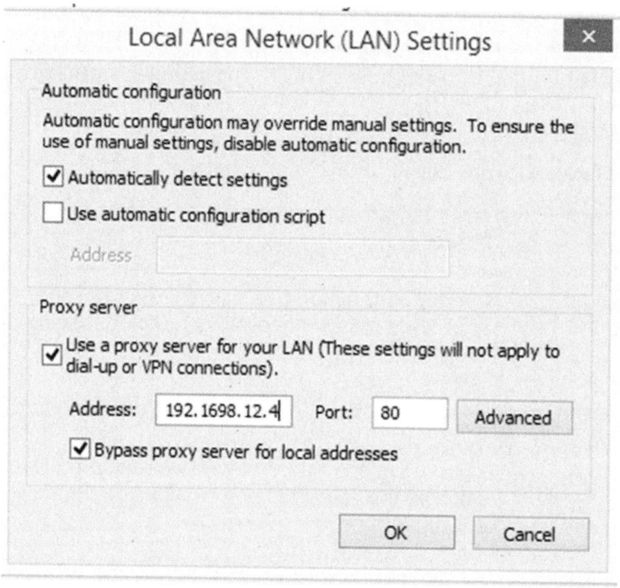

Local Area Network (LAN) Settings   ☒

Automatic configuration

Automatic configuration may override manual settings. To ensure the use of manual settings, disable automatic configuration.

☑ Automatically detect settings

☐ Use automatic configuration script

Address

Proxy server

☑ Use a proxy server for your LAN (These settings will not apply to dial-up or VPN connections).

Address: 192.1698.12.4   Port: 80   Advanced

☑ Bypass proxy server for local addresses

OK   Cancel

In Figure 6.100, you can see that the device is connected to a public network. The Windows 11 version is shown in Figure 6.101.

FIGURE 6.100   Public network: Windows 10

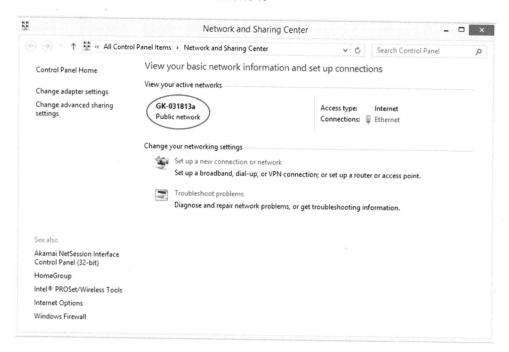

FIGURE 6.101   Public network: Windows 11

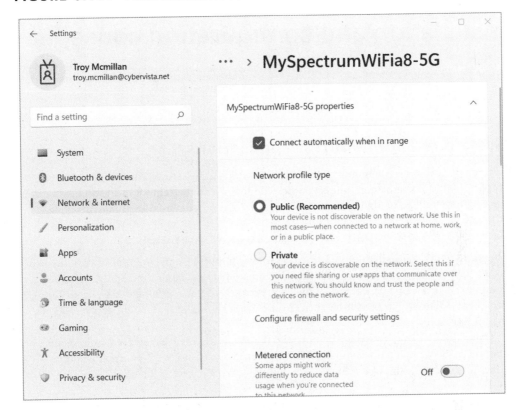

File Explorer navigation – network paths

Earlier in this chapter you learned about network paths, mapped drives, and the use of File Explorer in creating and accessing them. Please review that section.

Metered connections and limitations

In Chapter 4, "Virtualization and Cloud Computing," you learned about metered connections and metered services. Please review that chapter.

Exam essentials

Join a computer to a domain.   Describe the steps involved in placing a computer in a domain using a directory service such as Active Directory.

1.7 Given a scenario, apply application installation and configuration concepts

When you're installing applications, there are a number of considerations. Unless the proper computing environment and resources are available, there will be issues. In this section you'll learn about considerations when installing applications.

System requirements for applications

Every application has minimum system requirements with regard to computing resources. Applications also cannot run unless you provide them with the required CPU architecture. In this section you'll learn about these considerations and other system requirements issues.

32-bit vs. 64-bit dependent application requirements

The primary difference between 32-bit and 64-bit computing is the amount of data the processor (CPU) is able to process effectively. To run a 64-bit version of the operating system, you must have a 64-bit processor. To find out whether you are running the 32-bit or 64-bit version of Windows, you can look at the information shown in the System applet in Control Panel.

Other differences between 64-bit and 32-bit systems are their hardware requirements and the types of applications you can run on them. You can run a 32-bit application on either a 64-bit or 32-bit operating system, but you can only run 64-bit applications on a 64-bit system.

Dedicated graphics card vs. integrated

In Chapter 3 you learned that many applications such as CAD, video-editing software, and gaming software require high-end graphics cards not typically installed in systems. Systems today come with integrated cards, which means they are built into the motherboard.

A graphics processing unit (GPU) is a specialized circuit designed to rapidly manipulate and alter memory to accelerate the building of images in a frame buffer intended for output to a display. It improves the graphic abilities of the PC when this feature is present in the CPU.

Some visual features provided by operating systems such as Windows 10 are unavailable unless the CPU has dedicated graphics memory or a GPU. For example, the Aero view in Windows 10 requires a card capable of DirectX, which is a technology that requires the `DirectCompute` API, which in turn requires a GPU.

Video random-access memory (VRAM) requirements

As you can imagine, the video demands of graphics such as 3D are much higher than those of common office applications. For example, AutoCAD 2012 requires a 1360×768 true-color video display adapter. Note that the graphics card should have a minimum of 128 MB of VRAM for its operations.

RAM requirements

The minimum of RAM required should be viewed as just that: a minimum. Make sure you have more than required for satisfactory performance.

Central processing unit (CPU) requirements

In Chapter 3 you learned about processors and their characteristics. You learned that as all operating systems have minimum CPU requitements, so do applications. For example, installing the Office 2021 suite requires a 1.1 GHz or faster 2-core processor. If this minimum is not met, the application will not install.

External hardware tokens

Physical tokens are anything that a user must have on them to access network resources and are often associated with devices that enable the user to generate a one-time password authenticating their identity. SecurID, from RSA, is one of the best-known examples of a physical token; learn more at `www.rsa.com/node.aspx?id=1156`.

Storage requirements

Every application or software package has a set of requirements just as do operating systems. One of these requirements will be the amount of storage required to hold the application. While ensuring this has been taken care will be easy (because if the space is not there the installation will not proceed), determining the amount of space to hold the output of the application (documents etc) may be more difficult. Consult the documentation for recommendations and guidelines. You might also look for support articles and posts by other users that may yield information.

OS requirements for applications

For applications to run properly or even install in most cases, there must be compatibility between the operating system and the application. While many of these issues have already been covered, let's review.

Application to OS compatibility

The first requirement that must be met is the proper version of the operating system. For example, if the documentation for the application says it requires Windows 10, it may not install or run on Windows 8.1. Also make sure it's made to run on Windows and not Apple or Linux.

32-bit vs. 64-bit OS

As you now know, the primary difference between 32-bit and 64-bit computing is the amount of data the processor (CPU) is able to process effectively. As was stated earlier, you can run a 32-bit application on either a 64-bit or a 32-bit operating system, but you can only run 64-bit applications on a 64-bit system.

Distribution methods

There are several ways the installation files may be introduced to your system. Let's look at three of the most common.

Physical media vs. downloadable

The first two ways you will learn about may already be familiar to you.

Local (CD/USB)

Outside of the enterprise, most installations are done by using the CD that came with the software or by placing these same files on a USB stick and accessing them from the USB drive.

Network-based

In most enterprises, installations are done by placing the installation files in a network location and accessing and running them from the network location. This saves administrative effort involved in visiting each machine manually with the installation CD.

ISO mountable

You can also install a software program from an ISO file. To do so, first you obtain the application as an ISO file or image. Use the following steps:

1. Download the ISO file, then open File Explorer and right-click on the file. From the context menu, select the Mount command. See Figure 6.102.

FIGURE 6.102 Mounting an ISO file

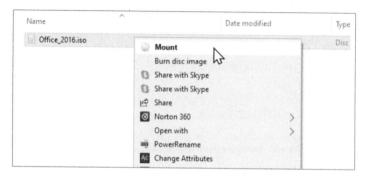

2. This opens a virtual drive from which you can install the software. On that virtual drive, you should find a `setup.exe` file or a similar file for installing the program. Double-click that file to install it, as shown in Figure 6.103.

FIGURE 6.103   Running the setup

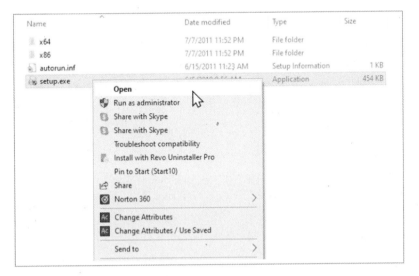

3. Open the This PC folder in File Explorer. Right-click on the new virtual drive and click the Eject command. This removes the virtual drive, though your ISO file is still alive and well.

Other considerations for new applications

Applications can serve as a security opening to hackers. Always research and consider the relative security of an application. Also consider how the application may impact issues unrelated to security.

Impact to device

Some software can be compromised in such a way as to potentially allow compromise of the entire device. Consider the application's reputation in the industry with regard to such weaknesses. Also consider the impact of the application on the performance of the device and take into account what other applications may be running as well.

Impact to network

While it's bad enough that a software compromise can lead to device compromise, it can also lead to a compromise of multiple devices on the network. Moreover, give consideration to the level of network traffic this application may create in its operation.

Impact to operation

While focusing on hardware minimums, security issues, and network traffic, it may be easy to overlook the application's impact on operations. How will this new application fit into current workflows? Will it cause disruption and, if so, for how long? Will the learning curve be steep for users? Consider all these factors when choosing applications.

Impact to business

Always keep in mind that the organization may have many missions but the most critical one for survival is to make money. If an organization is dependent on an application as a revenue source, such as an e-commerce system, the stakes are even higher. These applications should undergo a robust review process and lots of testing!

Exam essentials

Identify methods of installation and deployment.   These methods include local (CD/USB), network-based, and ISO mountable.

Understand critical system requirements.   Identify the system resources that must be fulfilled during each installation, including RAM, CPU, and disk space.

1.8 Explain common OS types and their purposes

While the overwhelming percentage of devices you will come into contact with will be Windows devices, you will also encounter other operating systems. The Linux operating system and macOS are increasingly found in enterprise networks in situations where their strengths can be leveraged. There are also many other technologies that you may not be directly managing, but you should still be familiar with them and understand their purpose. This section will focus on these areas, as well as other operating systems such as those found on smartphones.

Workstation OSs

Workstations are the most common types of devices in our networks. These are the user machines, both laptops and desktops. There are four main operating systems used on workstations: Windows, Linux, macOS, and Chrome OS.

Windows

While there are many Windows operating systems available, the exam asks that you know the intricacies of only Windows 10 and Windows 11. You learned about Windows 10 earlier in this chapter. We called out where major differences exist.

Linux

Linux is probably used more often than macOS in enterprise networks, in part because many proprietary operating systems that reside on devices such as access points, switches, routers, and firewalls are Linux-based. Linux systems also predominate in the software development area.

macOS

In your career, you are almost certain to come in contact with the macOS operating systems (originally called Mac OS X until 2012 and then OS X until 2016, so you may consider those terms interchangeable). Even though these systems constitute only a small percentage of the total number of devices found in enterprise environments, there are certain environments where they dominate and excel, such as music and graphics.

Chrome OS

Chrome is an operating system by Google that runs on its Chrome laptop. Based on the Linux kernel, it uses the Chrome browser as an interface. Originally it ran Chrome apps, but now Android apps have been made to run on it.

Cell phone/tablet OSs

Computer operating systems are not the only type of operating system with which you will come into contact. Many tablets, smartphones, and other small devices will have operating systems that are designed to run on devices that have different resource capabilities and therefore require different systems. This section will look at operating systems for such mobile devices.

iPadOS

The iPadOS is a rebranded variant of iOS, the operating system used by Apple's iPhones. It differs by supporting multitasking capabilities and keyboard use. The current version is iPadOS 15.1, released on October 25, 2021.

iOS

Apple iOS is a vendor-specific system made by Apple for mobile devices. Developers must use the software development kit (SDK) from Apple and register as Apple developers.

Android

The Android operating system from Google is built on a Linux kernel with a core set of libraries that are written in Java. It is an open source operating system, which means that developers have full access to the same framework application programming interfaces (APIs) used by the core applications.

Various filesystem types

While New Technology File System (NTFS) is available with Windows, Windows also recognizes and supports FAT32. Linux and macOS use different systems. This section lists the major filesystems and the differences among them.

New Technology File System (NTFS)

Introduced along with Windows NT, NT File System (NTFS) is a much more advanced filesystem in almost every way than all versions of the FAT filesystem. It includes such features as individual file security and compression, RAID support, and support for extremely large file and partition sizes and disk transaction monitoring. It is the filesystem of choice for high-performance computing. Finally, it supports both file compression and file encryption.

File Allocation Table 32 (FAT32)

FAT, which stands for File Allocation Table, is an acronym for the file on a filesystem used to keep track of where files are. It's also the name given to this type of filesystem, introduced in 1981. The largest FAT disk partition that could be created was approximately 2 GB. FAT32 was introduced along with Windows 95 OEM Service Release 2. As disk sizes grew, so did the need to be able to format a partition larger than 2 GB. FAT32 was based more on VFAT than on FAT16. It allowed for 32-bit cluster addressing, which in turn provided for a maximum partition size of 2 TB (2048 GB). It also included smaller cluster sizes to avoid wasted space. FAT32 support is included in current Windows versions.

Third extended filesystem (ext3), Fourth extended filesystem (ext4)

ext3 and ext4 are Linux filesystems. While ext4 has the following advantages, it should be noted that it is not compatible with Windows but that ext3 is. Here are the strengths of ext4:

- It supports individual file sizes up to 16 TB (16 GB for ext3).

- The overall maximum ext4 file system size is 1 EB (exabyte); 1 EB = 1,024 PB (petabytes), and 1 PB = 1,024 TB (terabytes) (32 TB limit for ext3).

- The directory can contain 64,000 subdirectories as compared to 32,000 in ext3.

- You can mount an existing ext3 fs as ext4 fs (without having to upgrade it).

- It improves the performance and reliability of the filesystem when compared to ext3.

- In ext4, you also have the option of turning off the journaling feature. A journaling filesystem keeps track of changes not yet committed to the filesystem.

Apple File System (APFS)

APFS is the successor to the Hierarchical File System (HFS) developed by Apple for use in computer systems running macOS. Designed for floppy and hard disks, it can also be found on read-only media such as CD-ROMs. With the introduction of Mac OS X 10.6, Apple dropped support for formatting or writing HFS disks and images, which remain supported as read-only volumes.

APFS was developed and deployed for macOS Sierra (10.12.4) and later, iOS 10.3. APFS is optimized for solid-state drive storage and supports encryption, snapshots, and increased data integrity, among other capabilities.

Extensible File Allocation Table (exFAT)

Extended File Allocation Table (exFAT) is a Microsoft filesystem optimized for flash drives. It is proprietary and has also been adopted by the SD Card Association as the default filesystem for SDXC cards larger than 32 GB. The proprietary nature and licensing requirements make this filesystem difficult to use in any open source or commercial software. This filesystem is supported in Windows 10 and 11.

Vendor life-cycle limitations

Vendors of operating systems impose certain restrictions and limitations on the support provided to their systems. Two of the most important of these are covered in this section.

End-of-life (EOL)

Whenever a vendor sets an end-of-life date, it means that after that date they will no longer offer help and support for that product. After that you are on your own regarding errors and troubleshooting. Even worse, there will be no more security patches and updates.

Update limitations

When Microsoft and possibly other vendors release operating system updates, they sometimes make the update package available only to those who purchased a full copy of the previous version. In cases like this, the update package will be cheaper than the full operating system, the idea being to give the customer credit for the purchase of the previous system. Those without the previous system must pay full price for a new installation of the updated operating system.

Compatibility concerns between OSs

While using a mix of desktop operating systems in an organization is not recommended, you may find yourself in that scenario. If that is the case, you may also find yourself supporting many more applications, as they are specific to the OS, and sometimes even to an OS version such as Windows 10. Be aware that you may encounter compatibility issues between the systems and between the documents produced by the applications. Always research online about these issues, as someone has probably already solved the issue!

Exam essentials

Describe the major differences between the Android and iOS operating systems.   Android is an open source operating system, and iOS is a vendor-specific system made by Apple. Apps for Android systems can be obtained from Google Play or many other sites, whereas iOS apps are available only on the App Store site.

1.9 Given a scenario, perform OS installations and upgrades in a diverse OS environment

While most administrators will agree that there are benefits to operating in an environment where all systems are the same version and make, you may be installing and supporting multiple types of operating systems in a diverse environment. In this section you'll learn about installation considerations.

Boot methods

You can begin the installation or upgrade process by booting from a number of sources. In this section you'll learn methods of booting up the destination system and getting the installation files to the devices.

USB

Most systems will allow you to boot from a USB device, but you must often change the BIOS settings to look for USB first. Using a large USB drive, you can store all the necessary installation files on one device and save the time needed to swap media.

Optical media

Inserting optical media in the destination device and booting to the optical media is very common but requires a lot of administrative effort. The option most commonly used for an attended installation is the CD-ROM/DVD boot (they are identical). Today's systems are too large to fit on a CD and are usually on a DVD.

Network

It is also possible to boot a system to the network and then perform the installation over the network. This is a much more efficient way to do this as you can do multiple systems at once. Let's look at two methods.

PXE

Booting the computer from the network without using a local device creates a *Preboot Execution Environment* (PXE). Once it is up, it is common to load the Windows Preinstallation Environment (WinPE) into RAM as a stub operating system and install the operating system image to the hard drive.

WinPE can be installed onto a bootable CD, USB, or network drive using the `copype.cmd` command. This environment can be used in conjunction with a Windows deployment from a server for unattended installations.

Netboot

NetBoot is a method developed by Apple that allows an Apple device to boot from a network location rather than from the hard drive. The device uses Dynamic Host Configuration Protocol (DHCP) to receive a network configuration and to receive the IP address of a Trivial File Transport protocol (TFTP) server from which the device will download an operating system image from a server. This entire process is similar to the way an IP phone learns through DHCP the IP address of the server from which it downloads its configuration file.

Solid-state/flash drives

If boot files and installation files are located on a solid-state drive or flash drive and the device is set to look on those drives for boot files, you can boot from these devices and install the operating system in the same way that you boot from a CD or DVD drive.

Internet-based

It is also possible to download and install the OS from an Internet location, such as a vendor site where you purchase an operating system. Moreover, a tool called Windows Installer accepts a Uniform Resource Locator (URL) as a valid source for an installation. Windows Installer can install packages, patches, and transforms from a URL location.

While purchasing and then downloading and installing to a single system at a time is inefficient and probably *not* the way you will be doing this, using a tool such as Windows Installer to provision multiple systems at a time is more likely. For more information on Windows Installer, visit `https://docs.microsoft.com/en-us/windows/win32/msi/windows-installer-portal`.

External/hot-swappable drive

Just as boot files can be located on a USB drive, CD, DVD, and flash drive, they can also be located on an external hard drive. Most of these drives are also hot-swappable (you can connect and remove them with the devices on). As always, you will probably have to alter the boot order of the device so that it looks on the external drive before the other drives if boot files are also located in these locations.

Internal hard drive (partition)

Finally, the most common location of boot files is on the internal hard drive. These files are placed there during the installation and will be executed as long as the device is set to look for them there. By default most systems are set to look on the internal hard drive first, and even if the device is not set to look there first, it will eventually boot to those files if there are no boot files located on any of the other drives or boot sources.

Types of installations

Operating system installations can be lumped into two generic methods: attended or unattended. During an attended installation, you walk through the installation and answer the questions as prompted. Questions typically ask for the product key, the directory in which you want to install the OS, and relevant network settings.

As simple as attended installations may be, they're time-consuming and administrator-intensive in that they require someone to fill in a fair number of fields to move through the process. Unattended installations allow you to configure the OS with little or no human intervention. Table 6.23 shows you four common unattended installation methods and when they can be used.

TABLE 6.23   Windows unattended installation methods

Method	Clean installation	Upgrade
Unattended install	Yes	Yes
Bootable media	Yes	No
Sysprep	Yes	No
Remote install	Yes	No

Another decision you must make is which method you are going to use to access the Windows installation files. It is possible to boot to the installation DVD and begin the installation process. However, your system must have a system BIOS that is capable of supporting bootable media.

If you don't have a bootable DVD, you must first boot the computer using some other bootable media, which then loads the disk driver so that you can access the installation program on the DVD. Boot methods were covered earlier in this chapter.

Unattended installation

Answering the myriad of questions posed by Windows Setup doesn't qualify as exciting work for most people. Fortunately, there is a way to answer the questions automatically: through an unattended installation. In this type of installation, an *answer file* is supplied with all the correct parameters (time zone, regional settings, administrator username, and so on), so no one needs to be there to tell the computer what to choose or to hit Next 500 times.

Unattended installations are great because they can be used to upgrade operating systems. The first step is to create an answer file. This XML file, which must be named `unattend.xml`, contains configuration settings specific to the computer on which you are installing the OS, which means that for every installation the answer file will be unique. See the following for details on these settings:

`https://docs.microsoft.com/en-us/windows-hardware/manufacture/desktop/update-windows-settings-and-scripts-create-your-own-answer-file-sxs`

Generally speaking, you'll want to run a test installation using that answer file first before deploying it on a large scale because you'll probably need to make some tweaks to it. After you create your answer file, place it on a network share that will be accessible from the target computer. (Most people put it in the same place as the Windows installation files for convenience.)

Boot the computer that you want to install on using a boot disk or CD, and establish the network connection. Once you start the setup process, everything should run automatically.

Upgrade

An upgrade involves moving from one operating system to another and keeping as many of the settings as possible. An example of an upgrade would be changing the operating system on a laptop computer from Windows 8.1 to Windows 10 and keeping the user accounts that existed.

It is also possible to upgrade from one edition of an operating system to another—for example, from Windows 10 Professional to Windows 10 Enterprise.

To begin the upgrade, insert the DVD, and the Setup program should automatically begin (if it doesn't, run `setup.exe` from the root folder). From the menu that appears, choose Install Now and then select Upgrade when the Which Type Of Installation Do You Want? screen appears. Answer the prompts to walk through the upgrade.

Booting from the DVD is also possible but recommended only if the method just described does not work. When you boot, you will get a message upon startup that says Press Any Key To Boot From CD, and at this point you simply press a key. (Don't worry that it is a DVD and not a CD.)

Recovery partition

In the past, many devices that were purchased with the operating system installed by the OEM came with recovery media that could be used to boot the device and recover or replace the operating system if needed. Now many come with an additional partition on the drive called a *recovery partition*. The users could use a specific key sequence during bootup that would cause the device to boot to the recovery partition and make available tools to either recover the installation or replace it. The downside of this approach is that if the hard drive fails or if the partition is overwritten, the recovery partition is useless. In an effort to address this concern, many OEMs now make available recovery media if requested by the user.

Clean install

With a clean installation, you delete the volume where the old operating system existed and place a new one there. An example of a clean installation would be changing the operating system on a laptop from Windows 10 to Windows 11. The user accounts and other settings that existed with Windows 10 would be removed in the process and would need to be re-created under Windows 11.

Image deployment

Systems can also be deployed as images. In this section you'll learn about creating an image and installing it.

Creating an image

Creating an image isn't actually an objective, but it is something important that you'll need to know how to do in the real world. Creating an image involves taking a snapshot of a model system (often called a *reference computer*) and then applying it to other systems (see the section "Image deployment" later). A number of third-party vendors offer packages that can be used to create images, and you can use the system preparation tool, *Sysprep*. The Sysprep utility works by making an exact image or replica of the reference computer (sometimes also called the *master computer*) to be installed on other computers. Sysprep removes the master computer's security ID (a process sometimes called *generalization*) and will generate new IDs for each computer where the image is used to install.

    All Sysprep does is create the system image. You still need a cloning utility to copy the image to other computers.

Perhaps the biggest caveat to using Sysprep is that because you are making an exact image of an installed computer (including drivers and settings), all the computers that you will be installing the image on need to be identical (or close) to the configuration of the primary computer. Otherwise, you would have to go through and fix driver problems on every installed computer. Sysprep images can be installed across a network or copied to a CD or DVD for local installation. Sysprep cannot be used to upgrade a system; plan on all data on the system (if there is any) being lost after a format.

Several third-party vendors provide similar services, and you'll often hear the process referred to as *disk imaging* or *drive imaging*. The third-party utility makes the image, and then the image file is transferred to the computer without an OS. You boot the new system with the imaging software and start the image download. The new system's disk drive is made into an exact sector-by-sector copy of the original system.

Imaging has major upsides. The biggest one is speed. In larger networks with multiple new computers, you can configure tens to hundreds of computers by using imaging in just hours, rather than the days it would take to individually install the OS, applications, and drivers.

Image deployment

System images created with Sysprep and other tools can be deployed for installation on hosts across the network. The Windows Automated Installation Kit (AIK) can be useful for this purpose.

Repair installation

A repair installation overwrites system files with a copy of new ones from the same operating system version and edition. For example, a laptop running Windows 10 is hanging on boot, and the cause is traced to a corrupted system file. A repair installation can replace that corrupted file with a new one (from the DVD or other source) without changing the operating system or settings (for configuration, accounts, and so on).

Remote network installation

Older Windows Server operating systems have a feature called Remote Installation Service (RIS), which allows you to perform several network installations at one time. Beginning with Windows Server 2003 SP2, RIS was replaced by Windows Deployment Services (WDS). This utility offers the same functionality as RIS.

A *network installation* is handy when you have many installations to do and installing by CD is too much work. In a network installation, the installation CD is copied to a shared location on the network. Then individual workstations boot and access the network share. The workstations can boot either through a boot disk or through a built-in network boot device known as a PXE ROM. Boot ROMs essentially download a small file that contains an OS and network drivers and has enough information to boot the computer in a limited fashion. At the least, it can boot the computer so that it can access the network share and begin the installation.

Other considerations

There are some other scenarios you may encounter during installation that require your consideration, which you'll learn about in this section.

Third-party drivers

During the installation, it may be necessary to load a third-party driver that you update later. The goal during installation is to get the operating system up and running and in a state where you can interact with it. To add a mass storage driver (which is what you need to access the drive), you hit the F7 key when you are prompted during the installation.

Also you will be presented with the option to download any required updates and new driver packages that may have become available since the time the installation DVD was created. If the device will have an active Internet connection, you may want to take advantage of this because it will download the required files and make them part of the installation. If this is not an option, you can always perform this step by visiting Windows Update after the installation.

Partitioning

For a hard disk to be able to hold files and programs, it has to be partitioned and formatted. Partitioning is the process of creating logical divisions on a hard drive. A hard drive can have one or more partitions. Formatting is the process of creating and configuring a file allocation table (FAT) and creating the root directory. Several filesystem types are supported by the various versions of Windows, such as FAT32 and NTFS.

The partition that the operating system boots from must be designated as *active*. Only one partition on a disk may be marked active. Each hard disk can be divided into a total of four partitions, either four primary partitions or three primary and one extended partition.

Dynamic

Partitions can be made dynamic, which—as the name implies—means they can be configured and reconfigured on the fly. The big benefits they offer are that they can increase in size (without reformatting) and can span multiple physical disks. Dynamic partitions can be simple, spanned, or striped.

Dynamic partitions that are simple are similar to primary partitions and logical drives (which exist on basic partitions, discussed next). This is often the route you choose when you have only one dynamic disk and want the ability to change allocated space as needed.

Choosing spanned partitions means that you want space from a number of disks (up to 32) to appear as a single logical volume to users. A minimum of two disks must be used, and no fault tolerance is provided by this option.

Striped partitions are similar to spanned in that multiple disks are used, but the big difference is that data is written (in fixed-size stripes) across the disk set in order to increase I/O performance. Although read operations are faster, a concern is that if one disk fails, none of the data is retrievable (like Spanned, the Striped option provides no fault tolerance).

Basic

With basic storage, Windows drives can be partitioned with *primary* or *logical* partitions. Basic partitions are a fixed size and are always on a single physical disk. This is the simplest storage solution and has been the traditional method of storing data for many years.

You can change the size of primary and logical drives by *extending* them into additional space on the same disk. You can create up to four partitions on a basic disk, either four primary or three primary and one extended.

Primary

A primary partition contains the boot files for an operating system. In older days, the operating system had to also be on that partition, but with the Windows versions you need to know for this exam, the OS files can be elsewhere as long as the boot files are in that primary partition.

Primary partitions cannot be further subdivided.

Extended

Extended partitions differ from primary in that they can be divided into one or more logical drives, each of which can be assigned a drive letter.

Logical

In reality, all partitions are logical in the sense that they don't necessarily correspond to one physical disk. One disk can have several logical divisions (partitions). A logical partition is any partition that has a drive letter.

 Sometimes, you will also hear of a logical partition as one that spans multiple physical disks. For example, a network drive that you know as drive H might actually be located on several physical disks on a server. To the user, all that is seen is one drive, or H.

GUID [globally unique identifier] Partition Table (GPT)

Devices that use the Unified Extensible Firmware Interface (UEFI) specification) instead of a BIOS also use a partitioning standard called GUID Partition Table (GPT). Since 2010, most operating systems support this and use a master boot record (MBR), which is the alternative method of booting to a legacy BIOS firmware interface. Today, almost all operating systems support it, and many *only* support booting from a GPT rather than from an MBR.

Moreover, GPT is also used on some BIOS systems because of the limitations of MBR partition tables, which was the original driver for the development of UEFI and GPT. MBR works with disks up to 2 TB in size, but it can't handle larger disks. MBR also supports only up to four primary partitions, so to have more than four, you had to make one of your primary partitions an "extended partition" and create logical partitions inside it. GPT removes both of these limitations. It allows up to 128 partitions on a GPT drive.

Master boot record (MBR)

Master boot record was discussed in the previous section. Please review that section.

Drive format

Filesystems available when formatting the drive were covered earlier in this chapter in the section Various filesystem types. Please review that section.

Upgrade considerations

When you're upgrading a system from one edition to another or from one version to another, there are things you need to think about before you jump in. In this section you'll learn about upgrade considerations.

Backup files and user preferences

In Chapter 5, "Hardware and Network Troubleshooting," you learned the importance of backing up files prior to making changes to a system that has an issue. This is also advisable before performing an upgrade just in case something goes wrong.

When doing so, you want to back up not only all the user files but also the user preferences. This will save the user aggravation from having to modify all the settings again. You will learn much more about backups of all types in Chapter 9, "Operational Procedures."

Application and driver support/backward compatibility

This is another area where some prior research can be invaluable. Applications are made to work on specific operating systems. While you'll have fewer problems with an upgrade, a new installation, especially when going from one vendor to another (say, Microsoft to Apple) may result in application incompatibility.

OS compatibility/upgrade path

Keep in mind that some upgrades are not possible and require new installations. See the tables earlier in this chapter on allowable upgrade paths.

Hardware compatibility

Before installing or upgrading an OS, you should ensure that the system supports all the hardware prerequisites (these were provided earlier in this chapter). It also is a good idea to check whether any additional hardware is compatible with the system. The upgrade advisors provided with many upgrade programs (for example Windows Upgrade Advisor) can assist with this as well. If you don't check ahead of time, the installation or upgrade may fail when you attempt it.

Feature updates

Features are Windows tools and utilities that are provided to make certain operations easier. Often when updating a system, features may update, which may result in users needing to be trained on the new feature. When Windows updates occur, you can choose *not* to download feature updates. These will be listed as optional updates.

Product life cycle

All products have a life cycle policy. An example is the Microsoft Fixed Lifecycle Policy. This is only a policy and does not apply to all products. The policy describes when the product is end of life and when it is end of support. End of support means no more help with trouble-shooting, and end of life means no more security updates.

Exam essentials

Identify methods of installation and deployment.   These methods include local (CD/USB), network-based, using flash drives, over the Internet, and using an internal hard drive.

1.10 Identify common features and tools of the macOS/desktop OS

While the overwhelming percentage of devices you will come into contact with will be Windows devices, you may also encounter other operating systems. The Linux operating system and macOS are increasingly found in enterprise networks in situations where their strengths can be leveraged. There are also many other technologies that you may not be directly managing, but you should still be familiar with them and understand their purpose. This section will focus on these areas.

Installation and uninstallation of applications

When you are new to macOS, it may seem that installing applications is confusing. There are various file types and sources of applications. In this section you'll learn about the file types involved in installation, where to get applications, and the process for uninstalling.

File types

When installing applications on macOS, you may encounter several different types of files. In this section you'll learn about three file types you may come across.

.dmg

Files with a .dmg extension are Apple Disk Image files. These are digital reconstructions of a physical disk. Only versions of the Mac newer than OS X 9 support these files. Older systems use the .img file type, a mountable image used to distribute software to macOS.

To open a DMG file, simply double-click it. macOS will use the DiskImageMounter utility to open the file. Then it will mount a virtual disk and open an Apple Finder window as if it was a CD or a USB flash drive that was just inserted into the computer.

Windows can open a DMG file with any compression/decompression program that supports the format. You can open these files in Linux if your machine or version supports the Hierarchical File System (HFS) as a disk filesystem format. To enable HFS and HFS+ support on your Linux machine, you will need to install HFS tools and kernel modules.

.pkg

Package, or PKG, files are very similar to the MSI files used to install software in Windows. On a Mac you install this type of file by double-clicking the file or by choosing Open With installer.app from the context menu. If you simply want to see what's inside the package without installing, choose Show Package Content from the context menu.

- In Windows, if you know which application uses the PKG file, use it to open PKG file.
- If the PKG file is in macOS installation file format, you should use a Mac machine to open it.

In Linux you will have to convert the PKG file to another format that is supported by Linux.

.app

APP files are executable application program files and are similar to the Windows EXE file format. To open these, you will need a program compatible with the specific file. Since these files are made for macOS you can interact with them in a similar way to how you treat DMG files. You can right-click the package and select Show Package Contents to view the files contained in the package and open it by double-clicking it.

App Store

The App Store is the recommended and safest location to discover and download apps. It's not just for apps, however. All Apple products, including laptops, smartphones, and accessories, are available for purchase there as well. Downloading apps from other locations is discouraged because you don't know the actual source and contents of the app.

Uninstallation process

Surprisingly there is no uninstall function built into Mac as there is in Windows. To uninstall you can simply drag the icon of the app to the Trash. Be aware that some apps store files in multiple locations rather than all in one place (called bundled files). This means that some files will be left behind. You may try seeing if the app has its own uninstall program that will do a better job of cleaning up. Many software programs can clean up for you. Popular examples include AppTrap, AppCleaner, and AppZapper.

Apple ID and corporate restrictions

Apple ID is an authentication method used to access iPhone, iPad, Mac, and other Apple devices. It's more than just a username; it also contains all your settings and preferences, which are applied when you log in.

A company can create Managed Apple IDs for employees to use for business purposes. These IDs don't allow the user to make purchases, and unlike personal Apple IDs, IT administrators can manage the services that your Managed Apple ID can access.

Best practices

Like any operating system, macOS will function better and with more reliability when given the proper care. This section will discuss some of the best practices that have been developed over the years for using these operating systems.

Backups

In macOS, you can use the rsync utility from the command line. The basic syntax is as follows, where the -a switch tells rsync to work in "archive" mode:

```
rsync -a [source dir] [destination dir]
```

As with any command-line utility, you can create batch files and schedule the backups.

Another tool, Time Machine, lets you back up your entire Mac, including system files, apps, music, photos, emails, and documents. When Time Machine is enabled, it automatically backs up your Mac and performs hourly, daily, and weekly backups of your files. You will learn more about Time Machine later in this chapter.

Antivirus

All the major antivirus and antimalware vendors create products for both Mac and commercial versions of Linux. Updates to the engines and definitions for these applications are done in a similar fashion to Windows. Checks for updates can be scheduled just as is done in Windows.

Updates/patches

In macOS, updates can come either directly from Apple or from the App Store. To make updates automatic, access Software Update preferences, where you can specify daily, monthly, or weekly, as shown in Figure 6.104.

FIGURE 6.104   Software Update preferences

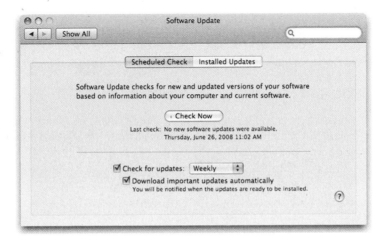

System Preferences

System Preferences is a central location where you can make configuration settings, somewhat like Control Panel in Windows. An example is shown in Figure 6.105.

FIGURE 6.105 System Preferences

While the exact icons found in this window can differ, in this section you'll learn about the utility of some common icons or tools.

Displays

The Displays preference pane, shown in Figure 6.106, is used to adjust the setting of the display. The window has three tabs: Display, Arrangement, and Color. Display is where you set the resolution, Arrangement is used to manage multiple displays, and Color is for choosing and creating a color profile.

Networks

The Network preference pane lets you manage your network connections of all types. As you can see in Figure 6.107, on the left all network connections appear, and by choosing one, you can manage its TCP/IP settings on the right.

FIGURE 6.106   Display options

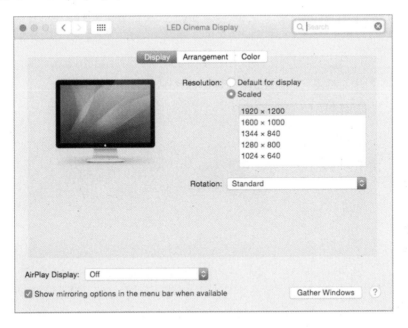

FIGURE 6.107   Network preference

Printers/Scanners

Printers and scanners are managed in the same preference pane; Figure 6.108 shows the options. Printers and scanners appear on the left side, and after selecting one, you can manage it on the right side.

FIGURE 6.108   Printers & Scanners preference pane

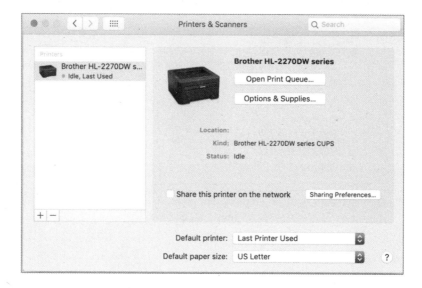

Privacy

You will find privacy settings in the Security & Privacy pane in System Preferences. You can decide for each application or service how much and what type of information you would like to share with the application or service. As shown in Figure 6.109, you choose the application or service on the left and then you are offered options with respect to how that application handles your data.

Accessibility

Some users face challenges with using a computer. They may have poor eyesight, be hard of hearing, or have tremors in their hands. The Accessibility preference pane, shown in Figure 6.110, offers options to make using the system easier to navigate by reading things aloud, making the screen font larger, or offering a keyboard on the screen that be managed with the mouse.

FIGURE 6.109   Security & Privacy preference pane

FIGURE 6.110   Accessibility preference pane

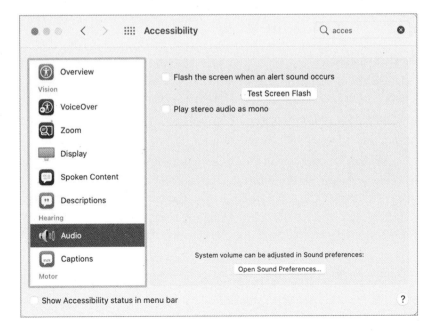

Time Machine

On macOS you can use Time Machine, discussed earlier in the section "Backups." Figure 6.111 shows this tool and some of its options.

FIGURE 6.111   Time Machine

Features

Now that you have looked at maintenance on these systems, let's examine some of the key features you will find in macOS. You can find many of these features in Windows with different names and different combinations of functions.

Multiple desktops

In Apple, Mission Control provides a quick way to see everything that's currently open on your Mac. To use Mission Control, do one of the following:

- Swipe up with three or four fingers on your trackpad.
- Double-tap the surface of your Magic Mouse with two fingers.
- Click the Mission Control icon in the Dock or Launchpad.
- On an Apple keyboard, press the Mission Control key.

Regardless of how you invoke Mission Control, all your open windows and spaces are visible, grouped by app. You can also use the tool to create desktops that are called *spaces* and place certain apps in certain spaces. Moreover, you can switch between the spaces in the same session.

When you enter Mission Control, all your spaces appear along the top of your screen. The desktop you're currently using is shown below the row of spaces. To move an app window to another space, drag it from your current desktop to the space at the top of the screen.

To switch between spaces, do one of the following:

- Enter Mission Control and click the space you want at the top of the Mission Control window.
- Swipe three or four fingers left or right across your trackpad to move to the previous or next space.
- Press Control+Right Arrow or Control+Left Arrow on your keyboard to move through your current spaces. Then click a window to bring it to the front of your view.

Mission Control

Mission Control was covered in the previous section.

Keychain

Keychain is the password management system in macOS. It can contain private keys, certificates, and secure notes. Keychain files are stored in /Library/Keychains/ and /Network/Library/Keychains/. The Keychain Access app allows a user to access the keychain and configure its contents.

Spotlight

Spotlight is a search tool built into Mac systems. To open Spotlight, click the magnifying glass icon in the upper-right corner of the menu bar, or press Command+spacebar in any app. Spotlight results can include dictionary definitions, currency conversions, and quick calculations. It will search the web as well, but you can limit its scope to just the local computer.

iCloud

iCloud is Apple's cloud storage solution, much like OneDrive in Windows. iCloud allows for the automatic synchronization of information across all a user's devices. In addition, it can be used to locate an iPhone and can serve as a location in which a backup can be stored. All Mac users are provided with 5 GB of free storage and then can purchase additional storage for a monthly fee.

Gestures

Gestures are used in Mac to interact with a touchscreen. The system is based on using multi-touch, which allows you to touch the screen in more than one place and initiate specific sub-routines called *gestures*, such as when expanding or reducing a photo.

Finder

While the Finder can also be used on a Mac to search for files, its main function is a file-system navigation tool, much like Windows Explorer. To open a new Finder window, click the Finder icon in the Dock and then select File ➤ New Window. Figure 6.112 shows a Finder window.

FIGURE 6.112   Finder

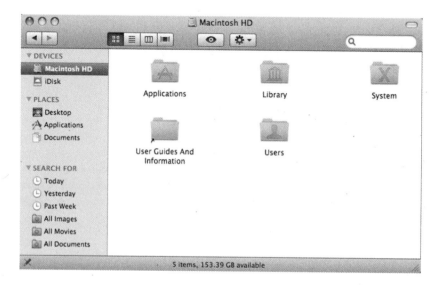

Remote Disc

The Remote Disc icon appears under Devices as well as under Computer. Remote Disc allows you to see which computers on the same network have drives available to share with your Mac. When computers on the same network have disk sharing enabled and are online, you can highlight that icon to see a list of them. To share optical discs from a Mac that has a built-in or external optical drive, use these steps:

1. On the Mac that has an optical drive, choose System Preferences from the Apple menu.

2. Click the Sharing icon in the System Preferences window.

3. Enter a name in the Computer Name field.

4. Enable the check box DVD Or CD Sharing.

5. You can also restrict who has access to your optical drive by selecting Ask Me Before Allowing Others To Use My DVD Drive.

Dock

The Dock is the series of icons that usually appear on the bottom of the screen on a Mac. It provides quick access to applications that come with the Mac, and you can add your own items to the Dock as well. In many ways, it is like the taskbar in Windows. It keeps apps on its left side; folders, documents, and minimized windows are kept on the right side of the Dock. Figure 6.113 shows the Dock.

FIGURE 6.113   The Dock

Disk Utility

Disk Utility is used for a variety of disk-related functions. Let's look at some.

macOS needs defragmentation in only a small number of cases. If the user creates large numbers of multimedia files and the drive has been filling for quite some time, the system may benefit from defragmentation. However, in most cases, this is not required.

One task that is beneficial to execute from time to time is to check the health of the disk using Disk Utility's Verify Disk functionality. While many disk operations (including the use of Time Machine) require booting to a different drive to perform the operation on the drive in question, Disk Utility can perform a live verification without doing that.

Recovering an entire image in either system is not different from restoring a single file. On the Mac you use Disk Utility in conjunction with a backup of the system and the OS media. To do this, follow these steps:

1. Connect the external hard drive that contains the backup to the Mac to which you are restoring.

2. Insert the macOS CD and restart it.

3. Hold down the C key while booting to the macOS CD and select your language.

4. From the Utilities menu, select Disk Utility.

5. Select the drive the backup is stored on.

6. Select the Restore tab. Select that disk and drag it to the Source window. If you created a DMG image, you'll need to click the drive you saved the image to (do not drag it), click Image, and select the disk image from the drive you stored it on.

7. In the left pane of Disk Utility, click your hard drive and drag it to the Destination window.

8. Select the Erase Destination check box to erase your old hard drive and replace it with the disk image you've selected as the source.

9. Click Restore. Click OK to verify.

Disk maintenance utilities

While I covered the disk maintenance utilities in the various sections earlier, Table 6.24 summarizes the tools discussed.

TABLE 6.24 Disk maintenance utilities

Tool	Function
rsync	Backs up and restores files
Time Machine	Backs up and restores files and images
fsck	File system checker
Disk utility	Verifies disk health and restores images
tar	Backs up files

FileVault

FileVault is Apple's form of encryption. Its first implementation was only for files in the user's home directory, and there it would perform encryption on the fly to everything located there. Now it can also be enabled in the startup disk, a behavior similar to BitLocker in Windows. Mac OS X Lion (10.7) and newer offer FileVault 2, which is a significant redesign. This encrypts the entire startup volume and typically includes the home directory, abandoning the disk image approach. For this approach to disk encryption, authorized users' information is loaded from a separate nonencrypted boot volume.

Terminal

Shells and terminals both accept commands, but they are two separate programs. The following are some differences:

▪ A terminal window can run different shells depending on what you have configured.

- Certain interactive applications can be run in the terminal emulator, and they will run in the same window.
- Remote logins, using a program like SSH, can be run from inside a terminal window.

macOS calls the shell Terminal, and you can find it under Applications ➤ Utilities ➤ Terminal, as shown in Figure 6.114.

FIGURE 6.114   The Mac terminal

Force Quit

Force Quit can be used on a Mac to stop an unresponsive application. To use this function, follow these steps:

1. Choose Force Quit from the Apple menu or press Command+Option+Esc.
2. Select the unresponsive app in the Force Quit Applications window, as shown in Figure 6.115, and then click Force Quit.

FIGURE 6.115   Force Quit Applications window

Exam essentials

Identify basic macOS tools.   These tools, part of System Preferences, include Displays, Networks, Printers, Scanners, Privacy, Accessibility, and Time Machine.

Identify macOS features.   These features include Mission Control, KeyChain, Spotlight, iCloud and Finder

1.11 Identify common features and tools of the Linux client/desktop OS

In your career, you are almost certain to come in contact with the Linux operating system. Linux is probably used more often than Mac, in part because many proprietary operating systems that reside on devices such as access points, switches, routers, and firewalls are Linux-based. In this section you will be introduced to some common features and functions of this operating system.

Common commands

While you may not be expected to be an expert in Linux, you will be responsible for knowing some basic Linux commands. This section will go over the main ones you need to know.

ls

The `ls` command lists information about the files in the current directory. Its syntax is as follows:

```
ls [OPTION]... [FILE]...
```

While the file options are too numerous to mention here, they mostly specify the format of the output. For a complete listing and their use, see `www.tutorialspoint.com/unix_commands/ls.htm`.

pwd vs. *passwd*

While the `passwd` command changes passwords for user accounts, the `pwd` command prints the full path name of the current working directory. The syntax for the `passwd` command is as follows:

```
passwd [options] [LOGIN]
```

For information on the numerous options that can be used, see `www.computerhope.com/unix/upasswor.htm`.

The syntax for the pwd command is as follows:

```
pwd [OPTION]...
```

The options that can be used are shown in Table 6.25.

TABLE 6.25   passwd command

`-L, --logical`	If the contents of the environment variable PWD provide an absolute name of the current directory with no . or .. components, then output those contents, even if they contain symbolic links. Otherwise, fall back to the default −P handling.
`-P, --physical`	This prints a fully resolved name for the current directory in which all components of the name are actual directory names and not symbolic links.
`--help`	This displays a help message and exits.
`--version`	This displays version information and exits.

mv

While the mv command can be used to move or rename a file in Linux, it's usually used to move a file. In that scenario, the syntax is as follows:

```
mv [OPTION]... [-T] SOURCE DEST
```

For information on the parameters that can be used, see `www.computerhope.com/unix/umv.htm`.

cp

The `cp` command is used to copy files and directories. Its syntax is as follows:

`cp [OPTION]... SOURCE... DIRECTORY`

For information on the parameters that can be used, see `www.computerhope.com/unix/ucp.htm`.

rm

The `rm` command removes (deletes) files or directories when it is combined with the `-r` option. The syntax is as follows:

`rm [OPTION]... FILE...`

For information on using parameters, see `www.computerhope.com/unix/urm.htm`.

chmod

The `chmod` command is used to change the permissions of files or directories. Its syntax is as follows:

`chmod options permissions filename`

For information on using parameters, see `www.computerhope.com/unix/uchmod.htm`.

chown

The `chown` command is used to change the ownership of a file. The syntax is as follows, where *new_owner* is the username or the numeric user ID (UID) of the new owner and *object* is the name of the target file, directory, or link:

`chown [options] new_owner object(s)`

The ownership of any number of objects can be changed simultaneously. The options are as follows:

- `-R` operates on filesystem objects recursively.
- `-v` (verbose) provides information about every object processed.
- `-c` reports only when a change is made.

su/sudo

The sudo command can be added at the front of a command to execute the command using root privileges. For example, to remove a package with root privileges, the command is as follows:

```
sudo apt-get remove {package-name}
```

The su command is used to change from one user account to another. When the command is executed, you will be prompted for the password of the account to which you are switching, as shown here:

```
$ su mact
password:
mact@sandy:&#xF07E;$
```

apt-get

apt-get is the command-line tool for working with Advanced Packaging Tool (APT) software packages. These tools install packages on your system. The syntax of the command is as follows:

```
apt-get [-asqdyfmubV] [-o=config_string] [-c=config_file]
[-t=target_release][-=architecture] {update | upgrade |
dselect-upgrade | dist-upgrade |install pkg
[{=pkg_version_number |
/target_release}]... | remove pkg... | purge pkg... | source
pkg
[{=pkg_version_number | /target_release}]... | build-dep pkg
[{=pkg_version_number | /target_release}]... | download pkg
[{=pkg_version_number | /target_release}]... | check | clean |
autoclean | autoremove | {-v | -version} | {-h | -help}}
```

For additional information on its use and the options, see www.computerhope.com/unix/apt-get.htm.

yum

This is also a package management command. Yellowdog Updater Modified (yum) is the traditional package manager for Red Hat–based systems.

The general syntax of yum command is as follows:

```
yum [options] <command> [<args>...]
```

Available commands include install, search, query, among others. Arguments can be a package name, a group name, or subcommand(s) specific to the command.

For more on this command, visit www.computerhope.com/unix/yum.htm.

ip

The ip command is used to configure and manage network interfaces. Here is the syntax:

```
ip [ OPTIONS ] OBJECT { COMMAND | help }
```

where *OBJECT* may be:

```
{ link | addr | addrlabel | route | rule | neigh | ntable | tunnel |
tuntap maddr | mroute | mrule | monitor | xfrm | netns | 12tp |
tcp_metrics }
```

and *OPTIONS* may be:

```
{ -V[ersion] | -s[tatistics] | -r[esolve] | -f[amily]
{ inet | inet6 | ipx | dnet | link } | -o[neline] }
```

For more on this command, visit www.computerhope.com/unix/ip.htm.

df

This command is used to assess the disk space used by a filesystem. The syntax is as follows:

```
df [OPTION]... [FILE]...
```

Common Options are in Table 6.26

TABLE 6.26   df options

-a, --all	Includes dummy filesystems.
-B,--block-size=SIZE	Scales sizes by SIZE before printing.
--total	Displays a grand total.
-h, --human-readable	Prints sizes in human-readable format.
-H, --si	Same as -h, but uses powers of 1000 instead of 1024.
-i, --inodes	Lists inode information instead of block usage.
-k	Like --block-size=1K.
-l, --local	Limits listing to local filesystems.
--no-sync	Does not invoke a sync before getting usage information.
-P, --portability	Uses the POSIX output format.
--sync	Invokes a sync before getting usage information.

-t, --type=*TYPE*	Limits listing to filesystems of type *TYPE*.
-T, --print-type	Prints filesystem type.
-x,--exclude-type=*TYPE*	Limits listing to filesystems not of type *TYPE*.
-v	Ignored; included for compatibility reasons.
--help	Displays a help message and exits.
--version	Outputs version information and exits.

For more on this command, visit www.computerhope.com/unix/udf.htm.

grep

The grep command is used to search text or to search a file for lines containing a match to the given strings or words. Its syntax is as follows, where *PATTERN* is the pattern you are trying to match:

grep [*OPTIONS*] *PATTERN* [*FILE*...]

It has options that govern the matching process as well as options that specify the output. For more information on the options and their use, visit www.computerhope.com/unix/ugrep.htm.

ps

The ps command displays information about a selection of the active processes. Its syntax is as follows:

ps [*options*]

For information on the use of the options, visit www.computerhope.com/unix/ups.htm.

man

This command is used to view the system's reference manuals. The syntax is as follows:

man [-C file] [-d] [-D] [--warnings[=warnings]] [-R encoding] [-L locale] [-m system[,...]] [-M path] [-S list] [-e extension] [-i|-I][--regex|--wildcard] [--names-only] [-a] [-u] [--no-subpages] [-P pager] [-r prompt] [-7] [-E encoding] [--no-hyphenation] [--no-justification][-p string] [-t] [-T[device]] [-H[browser]] [-X[dpi]] [-Z] [[section] page ...] ...

For more information on the arguments, visit www.computerhope.com/unix/uman.htm.

top

top provides a dynamic real-time view of a running system. The syntax is as follows:

```
top -hv | -bcHisS -d delay -n limit -u|U user | -p pid -w [cols]
```

For more information on the arguments, visit www.computerhope.com/unix/top.htm.

find

As you might suspect, the find command searches for files and directories in a filesystem. The syntax is as follows:

```
find [-H] [-L] [-P] [-D debugopts] [-Olevel] [path...] [expression]
```

For more information on the arguments, visit www.tutorialspoint.com/unix_commands/find.htm.

dig

The dig command performs network DNS lookups. It can be used to troubleshoot DNS by interrogating DNS name servers.

The syntax is as follows:

```
dig [@server] [-b address] [-c class] [-f filename] [-k filename]   [-m] [-p
port#] [-q name] [-t type] [-x addr] [-y [hmac:]name:key]   [-4] [-6] [name]
[type] [class] [queryopt...]
```

For more information on the arguments, visit www.computerhope.com/unix/dig.htm.

cat

The simplest way to display the contents of a file at the command line is with the cat command. It can be used to do the following:

- Display text files
- Copy text files into a new document
- Append the contents of a text file to the end of another text file, combining them

Its syntax is as follows:

```
cat [OPTION]… [FILE]...
```

The options are in table 6.27

Table 6.27 cat options
:

-A, --show-all	Equivalent to -vET.
-b, --number-nonblank	Number of non-empty output lines. This option overrides -n.

`-e`	Equivalent to `-vE`.
`-E, --show-ends`	Displays "$" at end of each line.
`-n, --number`	Numbers all output lines.
`-s, --squeeze-blank`	Suppresses repeated empty output lines.
`-t`	Equivalent to `-vT`.
`-T, --show-tabs`	Displays Tab characters as `^I`.
`--help`	Displays a help message, and exits.
`--version`	Outputs version information, and exits.

nano

nano is a terminal-based text editor for Linux. It is functionally the same as another command called `pico`. Its syntax is as follows:

`nano [ options ] [ file ]`

For more information on its numerous options, visit `www.tutorialspoint.com/unix_commands/nano.htm`.

Best practices

Like any operating system, Linux will function better and with more reliability when given the proper care. This section will discuss some of the best practices that have been developed over the years for using this operating system.

Backups

For all Linux versions, backup tools are available for free and for a fee. You can also use the `tar` and `cpio` command-line utilities to construct full or partial backups of the system. Each utility constructs a large file that contains, or *archives*, other files. In addition to file contents, an archive includes header information for each file it holds. Table 6.28 lists the parameters of the `tar` command.

TABLE 6.28   tar parameters

Option	Effect
`--append (-r)`	Appends files to an archive
`--catenate (-A)`	Adds one or more archives to the end of an existing archive
`--create (-c)`	Creates a new archive

(continues)

TABLE 6.28 tar parameters *(continued)*

Option	Effect
--delete	Deletes files in an archive, not on tapes
--diff (-d)	Compares files in an archive with disk files
--extract (-x)	Extracts files from an archive
--help	Displays a help list of tar options
--list (-t)	Lists the files in an archive
--update (-u)	Like the −r option, but the file is not appended if a newer version is already in the archive

In Linux, backups of data can also be scheduled using the rsync utility from the command line. While there is another utility, cp, that can be used, rsync prevents unnecessary copying when the destination file has not been changed. It also can operate both locally and remotely. It also encrypts the transfer. The basic syntax is as follows, where the −a switch tells rsync to work in "archive" mode:

rsync -a [*source dir*] [*destination dir*]

As with any command-line utility, you can create batch files and schedule these backups. Because Linux systems manage the disk differently than Windows, they need no defragmentation. There is a maintenance task you may want to schedule in Linux. From time to time you should run a file system checker called fsck. This is a logical filesystem checker.

Antivirus

All the major antivirus and antimalware vendors create products for commercial versions of Linux. Develop and administer a system to ensure that all systems have an antivirus program installed and that virus definitions are updated on a regular basis.

Updates/patches

While in the past patch management in Linux presented more of a challenge than with Windows, today the same tool used to manage patches with Windows (System Center Configuration Manager) can now be used to patch additional systems such as Linux.

Many of the versions of Linux now make updates much easier than in the past. Both Ubuntu and Fedora offer a GUI tool for this. In Ubuntu, for example, choosing System ➤ Administration and then selecting Update Manager will open Update Manager. When it opens, click the Check button to see whether any updates are available. Figure 6.116 shows a list of available updates.

FIGURE 6.116   Ubuntu Update Manager

Of course, you can still do this from the command line. Follow these steps:

1. Open a terminal window.
2. Issue the command **sudo apt-get upgrade**.
3. Enter your user's password.
4. Look over the list of available updates and decide whether you want to go through with the entire upgrade.
5. When the desired updates have been selected, click the Install Updates button.
6. Watch as the update happens.

Driver/firmware updates

Updating drivers and firmware in Linux can be done either during the installation or afterward. Some versions, such as Red Hat, recommend installing first and then performing the upgrade. While the upgrade process varies from version to version, in Ubuntu either you can wait until a new version of the OS is released (which is once every six months) and get the update from the Software Update Center, or you can access what is called a *personal package archive* (PPA). PPAs are repositories containing drivers that can be easily made available to the Ubuntu Update Manager by adding the PPA to the local system. Once added, the drivers will appear as available when you access the local Ubuntu Update Manager, as shown in Figure 6.117.

FIGURE 6.117   Update Manager with PPA

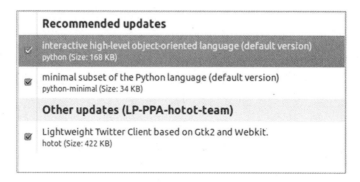

In Red Hat, for driver and firmware updates, download the driver update RPM package from the location specified by Red Hat or your hardware vendor. Then locate and double-click the file that you downloaded. The system might prompt you for the root password, after which it will present Installing Packages, as shown in Figure 6.118. Then click Apply.

FIGURE 6.118   Installing packages

Tools

Tools exist to perform maintenance, some of which I have already mentioned. This section will cover some of these utilities and functions.

Shell/terminal

In Linux, a shell is a command-line interface, of which there are several types. A terminal is a window that appears when you press Ctrl+Alt+T. They both accept commands, but they are two separate programs. The following are some differences:

- A terminal window can run different shells depending on what you have configured.
- Certain interactive applications can be run in the terminal emulator, and they will run in the same window.
- Remote logins, using a program like SSH, can be run from inside a terminal window.

Samba

Samba is a free implementation of the SMB protocol. Samba runs on most Unix-like systems and is standard on nearly all distributions of Linux. Samba allows file and print sharing between computers running Microsoft Windows and computers running Unix/Linux.

Exam essentials

Identify basic Linux commands.   These commands include `ls`, `grep`, `cd`, `pwd`, `passwd`, `mv`, `cp`, `rm`, `chmod`, `chown`, `ps`, `su`, `sudo`, and `apt-get`.

Describe the use of Samba.   Samba allows file and print sharing between computers running Microsoft Windows and computers running Unix/Linux

Review Questions

You can find the answers in the appendix.

1. Which of the following cannot be a member of a domain?
   - **A.** Windows 10 Pro
   - **B.** Windows 10 Enterprise
   - **C.** Windows 10 Pro for Workstations
   - **D.** Windows 10 Home

2. Which command in Windows is used to create a new folder?
   - **A.** md
   - **B.** dir
   - **C.** cd
   - **D.** rd

3. Which tool lets you shut down unresponsive applications selectively in all Windows versions?
   - **A.** Action Center
   - **B.** Task Manager
   - **C.** Windows Firewall
   - **D.** Defender

4. From which tab in Internet Options do you configure a VPN?
   - **A.** Security
   - **B.** General
   - **C.** Connections
   - **D.** Start

5. Where can you reset Windows 10 to improve performance?
   - **A.** Personalization
   - **B.** Privacy
   - **C.** System
   - **D.** Update & Security

6. In the Windows 10 Firewall, if you set the network as Public, which service is turned off?
   - **A.** Network Discovery
   - **B.** ICMP
   - **C.** IPv6
   - **D.** SMB

7. Which Windows command is used to view a listing of the files and folders that exist within a directory, subdirectory, or folder?

   A. net use

   B. dir

   C. cd

   D. ipconfig

8. Which Windows command is used to move to another folder or directory?

   A. net use

   B. dir

   C. cd

   D. ipconfig

9. Which Windows tool shows a list of all installed hardware and lets you add items, remove items, update drivers, and more?

   A. Device Manager

   B. Event Viewer

   C. Users And Groups

   D. Sync Center

10. Which Windows tool tracks all events on a particular Windows computer?

   A. Device Manager

   B. Event Viewer

   C. Users And Groups

   D. Sync Center

11. Which of the following can be used on a Mac to stop an unresponsive application?

   A. Task Manager

   B. File Vault

   C. Finder

   D. Force Quit

12. Which of the following is true?

   A. You can only run a 32-bit application on a 64-bit operating system.

   B. You can run a 32-bit application on either a 64-bit or a 32-bit operating system, but you can only run 64-bit applications on a 64-bit system.

   C. You can only run a 32-bit application on a 32-bit operating system.

   D. You can run a 64-bit application on either a 64-bit or a 32-bit operating system.

13. Which of the following should you exceed for good performance?

   A. Minimum RAM

   B. Resolution

   C. Disk space

   D. Pixel count

14. Which type of installation is most likely to take place in a SOHO?

   A. Network

   B. RIS

   C. CD

   D. Unattended

15. Many proprietary operating systems that reside on devices such as access points, switches, routers, and firewalls are based on which operating system?

   A. Windows

   B. Mac

   C. Linux

   D. Android

16. Which of the following can be used to connect to a shared printer?

   A. net use

   B. net user

   C. robocopy

   D. xcopy

17. Which of the following is a command-line interface in Linux?

   A. shell

   B. domain

   C. cmd

   D. DOS

18. Which of the following provides a quick way to see everything that's currently open on your Mac?

   A. Shell

   B. Mission Control

   C. Sandbox

   D. Beeker

Chapter

7

Security

COMPTIA A+ CERTIFICATION EXAM CORE 2 (220-1102) OBJECTIVES COVERED IN THIS CHAPTER:

✓ **2.1 Summarize various security measures and their purposes**

- Physical security
    - Access control vestibule
    - Badge reader
    - Video surveillance
    - Alarm systems
    - Motion sensors
    - Door locks
    - Equipment locks
    - Guards
    - Bollards
    - Fences
- Physical security for staff
    - Key fobs
    - Smart cards
    - Keys
    - Biometrics
    - Retina scanner
    - Fingerprint scanner
    - Palmprint scanner
    - Lighting
    - Magnetometers

- Logical security
    - Principle of least privilege
    - Access control lists (ACLs)
    - Multifactor authentication (MFA)
    - Email
    - Hard token
    - Soft token
    - Short message service (SMS)
    - Voice call
    - Authenticator application
- Mobile device management (MDM)
- Active Directory
    - Login script
    - Domain
    - Group Policy/updates
    - Organizational units
    - Home folder
    - Folder redirection
    - Security groups

✓ **2.2 Compare and contrast wireless security protocols and authentication methods**

- Protocols and encryption
    - WiFi Protected Access 2 (WPA2)
    - WPA3
    - Temporal Key Integrity Protocol (TKIP)
    - Advanced Encryption Standard (AES)
- Authentication
    - Remote Authentication Dial-In
    - User Service (RADIUS)
    - Terminal Access Controller Access-Control System (TACACS+)

- Kerberos
- Multifactor

✓ 2.3 Given a scenario, detect, remove, and prevent malware using the appropriate tools and methods

- Malware
  - Trojan
  - Rootkit
  - Virus
  - Spyware
  - Ransomware
  - Keylogger
  - Boot sector virus
  - Cryptominers
- Tools and methods
  - Recovery console
  - Antivirus
  - Anti-malware
  - Software firewalls
  - Anti-phishing training
  - User education regarding common threats
  - OS Reinstallation

✓ 2.4 Explain common social-engineering attacks, threats, and vulnerabilities

- Social engineering
  - Phishing
  - Vishing
  - Shoulder surfing
  - Whaling
  - Tailgating

- Impersonation
- Dumpster diving
- Evil twin
- Threats
  - Distributed denial of service (DDoS)
  - Denial of service (DoS)
  - Zero-day attack
  - Spoofing
  - On-path attack
  - Brute-force attack
  - Dictionary attack
  - Insider threat
  - Structured Query Language (SQL) injection
  - Cross-site scripting (XSS)
- Vulnerabilities
  - Non-compliant systems
  - Unpatched systems
  - Unprotected systems (missing antivirus/ missing firewall)
  - EOL OSs
  - Bring your own device (BYOD)

✓ **2.5 Given a scenario, manage and configure basic security settings in the Microsoft Windows OS**

- Defender Antivirus
  - Activate/deactivate
  - Updated definitions
- Firewall
  - Activate/deactivate
  - Port security
  - Application security

- Users and groups
    - Local vs. Microsoft account
    - Standard account
    - Administrator
    - Guest user
    - Power user
- Login OS options
    - Username and password
    - Personal identification number (PIN)
    - Fingerprint
    - Facial recognition
    - Single sign-on (SSO)
- NTFS vs. share permissions
    - File and folder attributes
    - Inheritance
- Run as administrator vs. standard user
    - User Account Control (UAC)
- BitLocker
- BitLocker To Go
- Encrypting File System (EFS)

✓ **2.6 Given a scenario, configure a workstation to meet best practices for security**

- Data-at-rest encryption
- Password best practices
    - Complexity requirements
    - Length
    - Character types
    - Expiration requirements
    - Basic input/output system (BIOS)/Unified Extensible Firmware Interface (UEFI) passwords

- End-user best practices
  - Use screensaver locks
  - Log off when not in use
  - Secure/protect critical hardware (e.g., laptops)
  - Secure personally identifiable information (PII) and passwords
- Account management
  - Restrict user permissions
  - Restrict login times
  - Disable guest account
  - Use failed attempts lockout
  - Use timeout/screen lock
- Change default administrator's user account/password
- Disable AutoRun
- Disable Autoplay

✓ 2.7 Explain common methods for securing mobile and embedded devices

- Screen locks
  - Facial recognition
  - PIN codes
  - Fingerprint
  - Pattern
  - Swipe
- Remote wipes
- Locator applications
- OS updates
- Device encryption
- Remote backup applications
- Failed login attempts restrictions
- Antivirus/anti-malware

- Firewalls
- Policies and procedures
    - BYOD vs. corporate owned
    - Profile security requirements
- Internet of Things (IoT)

✓ 2.8 Given a scenario, use common data destruction and disposal methods

- Physical destruction
    - Drilling
    - Shredding
    - Degaussing
    - Incinerating
- Recycling or repurposing best practices
    - Erasing/wiping
    - Low-level formatting
    - Standard formatting
- Outsourcing concepts
    - Third-party vendor
    - Certification of destruction/recycling

✓ 2.9 Given a scenario, configure appropriate security settings on small office/home office (SOHO) wireless and wired networks

- Home router settings
    - Change default passwords
    - IP filtering
    - Firmware updates
    - Content filtering
    - Physical placement/secure locations
    - Dynamic Host Configuration Protocol (DHCP) reservations

- Static wide-area network (WAN) IP
- Universal Plug and Play (UPnP)
- Screened subnet
- Wireless specific
  - Changing the service set identifier (SSID)
  - Disabling SSID broadcast
  - Encryption settings
  - Disabling guest access
  - Changing channels
- Firewall settings
  - Disabling unused ports
  - Port forwarding/mapping

✓ **2.10 Given a scenario, install and configure browsers and relevant security settings**

- Browser download/installation
  - Trusted sources
    - Hashing
  - Untrusted sources
- Extensions and plug-ins
  - Trusted sources
  - Untrusted sources
- Password managers
- Secure connections/sites – valid certificates
- Settings
  - Pop-up blocker
  - Clearing browsing data
  - Clearing cache
  - Private-browsing mode
  - Sign-in/browser data synchronization
  - Ad blockers

This chapter focuses on the exam topics related to security. It follows the structure of the CompTIA A+ 220-1102 exam blueprint, objective 2, and it explores the 10 subobjectives that you need to master before taking the exam.

2.1 Summarize various security measures and their purposes

To properly secure a network environment you must understand the available security mechanisms, their purpose, and their operation. It is also important to be able to match the technique with the vulnerability it is meant to address. In this section you'll learn about security measures and when to implement them.

Physical security

Physical security is a grab bag of elements that can be added to an environment to aid in securing it. It ranges from key fobs to retinal scanners. In this section you will examine the physical security components as listed by CompTIA.

Access control vestibule

An access control vestibule, sometimes also called a mantrap, is a series of two doors with a small room between them. The user is authenticated at the first door and then allowed into the room. At that point, additional verification will occur (such as a guard visually identifying the person), and then they are allowed through the second door. These doors are normally used only in high-security situations. Access control vestibules also typically require that the first door is closed prior to enabling the second door to open. Figure 7.1 shows an access control vestibule design.

Badge reader

Radio frequency identification (RFID) is a wireless, no-contact technology used with badges or cards and their accompanying reader. The reader is connected to the workstation and validates against the security system. This increases the security of the authentication process because the user must be in physical possession of the smartcard to use the resources. Of course, if the card is lost or stolen, the person who finds the card can access the resources it allows. Badge readers are used not only to provide access to devices but to provide access to doors as well.

FIGURE 7.1 Aerial view of an access control vestibule

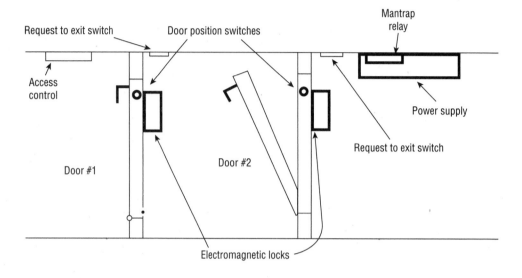

Video surveillance

IP video systems provide a good example of the benefits of networking applications. These systems can be used for both surveillance of a facility and facilitating collaboration. An example of the layout of an IP surveillance system is shown in Figure 7.2.

IP video has also ushered in a new age of remote collaboration. It has saved a great deal of money on travel expenses while at the same time making more efficient use of time.

Issues to consider and plan for when implementing IP video systems include the following:

- Expect a large increase in the need for bandwidth.
- QoS needs to be configured to ensure performance.
- Storage needs to be provisioned for the camera recordings. This could entail cloud storage, if desired.
- The initial cost may be high.

FIGURE 7.2   IP surveillance

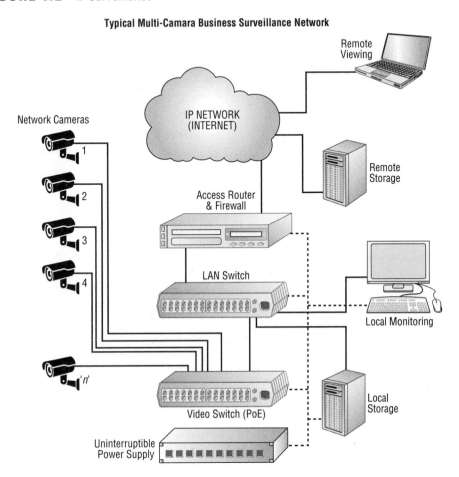

Alarm systems/motion sensors

Alarm systems can alert you when a physical intrusion has occurred. There are various technologies you can deploy, including these:

- Passive infrared systems (PIR) operate by identifying changes in heat waves in an area. Because the presence of an intruder would raise the temperature of the surrounding air particles, this system alerts or sounds an alarm when this occurs.

- Electromechanical systems operate by detecting a break in an electrical circuit. For example, the circuit might cross a window or door and when the window or door is opened, the circuit is broken, setting off an alarm of some sort. Another example might be a pressure pad placed under the carpet to detect the presence of individuals.

- Photoelectric systems operate by detecting changes in the light and thus are used in windowless areas. They send a beam of light across the area and if the beam is interrupted (by a person, for example), the alarm is triggered.

- Acoustical detection systems use strategically placed microphones to detect any sound made during a forced entry. These systems only work well in areas where there is not a lot of surrounding noise. They are typically very sensitive, which would cause many false alarms in a loud area, such as a door next to a busy street.

- Wave motion detectors generate a wave pattern in the area and detect any motion that disturbs the wave pattern. When the pattern is disturbed, an alarm sounds.

- Capacitance detectors emit a magnetic field and monitor that field. If the field is disrupted, which will occur when a person enters the area, the alarm will sound.

Door locks

One of the easiest ways to prevent people intent on creating problems by physically entering your environment is to lock your doors and keep them out.

Door locks are the most universal form of *physical barriers*, which are a key aspect of access control. The objective of a physical barrier is to prevent access to computers and network systems. The most effective physical barrier implementations require that more than one physical barrier be crossed to gain access. This type of approach is called a *multiple-barrier system*.

Ideally, your systems should have a minimum of three physical barriers. The first barrier is the external entrance to the building, referred to as a *perimeter*, which is protected by burglar alarms, external walls, *fencing*, surveillance, and so on. An *access list* should exist to specifically identify who can enter and be verified by a guard or someone in authority. The second barrier is the entrance into the building and could rely on such items as *ID badges* to gain access. The third barrier is the entrance to the computer room itself (and could require fobs, or keys). Each of these entrances can be individually secured, monitored, and protected with alarm systems.

Think of the three barriers this way: outer (the fence), middle (guards, locks, and access control vestibules), and inner (key fobs).

Although these three barriers won't always stop intruders, they will potentially slow them down enough that law enforcement can respond before an intrusion is fully developed. Once inside, a truly secure site should be dependent on a physical token for access to the actual network resources.

Equipment locks

While not all devices support this, larger mobile devices such as laptops come with a notch where you can attach a cable lock and lock the device to something solid, as you would lock a bicycle to a rack. This may even be advisable on some desktop systems if those systems are vulnerable to theft and contain sensitive data. Users who carry company devices that support cable locks should be instructed to never leave the device unattended and, if necessary, lock the device to an immovable object.

Server locks

Both rack and nonrack server systems can come with physical locks that prevent tampering with the server if physical access becomes possible. Having said that, all servers should be locked in a room, but the inclusion of physical server locks as well is an example of defense in depth.

Guards

Although many other less manual methods of monitoring are available, nothing takes the place of a human being. Security guards can exercise judgment and common sense (sometimes an automated system seems to lack that) as they encounter issues.

Bollards

Barriers called bollards have become quite common around the perimeter of new office and government buildings. These are short vertical posts placed at the building's entrance way and lining sidewalks that help to provide protection from vehicles that might either intentionally or unintentionally crash into or enter the building or injure pedestrians. They can be made of many types of materials. Three types of bollards are shown in Figure 7.3.

FIGURE 7.3   Bollards

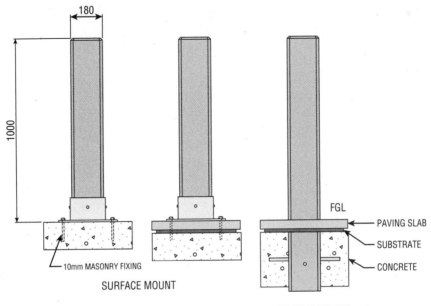

Fences

Fencing is the first line of defense in the concentric circle paradigm. When selecting the type of fencing to install, consider the determination of the individual you are trying to discourage. Use the following guidelines with respect to height:

- Three to four feet tall fences deter only casual intruders.

- Six to seven feet tall fences are too tall to climb easily.

- Eight feet and taller fences deter more determined intruders, especially when augmented with razor wire.

Physical security for staff

Some mitigations or techniques are designed to address access to resources and devices by staff. In this section you'll learn about measures designed to allow them to do their job but in a secure fashion.

Key fobs

Key fobs are named after the chains used to hold pocket watches to clothes. They are security devices that you carry with you that display a randomly generated code that you can then use for authentication. This code usually changes quickly (every 60 seconds is probably the average), and you combine the code with your PIN for authentication.

Smart cards

A smartcard is a type of badge or card that gives you access to resources, including buildings, parking lots, and computers. It contains information about your identity and access privileges. Each area or computer has a card scanner or a reader in which you insert your card.

Smartcards are difficult to counterfeit, but they're easy to steal. Once a thief has a smartcard, that person has all the access the card allows. To prevent this, many organizations don't put any identifying marks on their smartcards, making it harder for someone to utilize them. Many modern smartcards require a password or PIN to activate the card, and they employ encryption to protect the card's contents.

Keys

As you learned in the section on door locks, some doors have physical keys that fit into the lock. These keys must be accounted for at all times. It might be advantageous to create a chain of custody document that tracks the location of each key at all times. Chain of custody documents are used to account for evidence gathered in an investigation. They can also be used in this scenario.

Biometrics

Biometric devices use physical characteristics to identify the user. Such devices are becoming more common in the business environment. Biometric systems include hand scanners, retinal scanners, and, possibly soon, DNA scanners. To gain access to resources, you must pass a physical screening process. In the case of a hand scanner, this may include identifying fingerprints, scars, and markings on your hand. Retinal scanners compare your eye's retinal pattern to a stored retinal pattern to verify your identity. DNA scanners will examine a unique portion of your DNA structure to verify that you are who you say you are.

With the passing of time, the definition of *biometric* is expanding from simply identifying physical attributes about a person to being able to describe patterns in their behavior. Recent advances have been made in the ability to authenticate someone based on the key pattern they use when entering their password (how long they pause between each key, the amount of time each key is held down, and so forth). A company adopting biometric technologies needs to consider the controversy they may face (some authentication methods are considered more intrusive than others). It also needs to take into account the error rate and that errors can include both false positives and false negatives.

Biometric systems, like most security tools, make mistakes. When the system improperly allows an individual in who should not be, it is called a *false acceptance* and the rate at which this occurs is called the *false acceptance rate* (FAR). When the system improperly rejects a legitimate user, it is called a *false rejection*, and the rate at which these occur is called the *false rejection rate* (FRR).

In the following sections you'll learn about several biometric systems.

Retina scanner

A retina scan scans the retina's blood vessel pattern. A retina scan is considered by some to be intrusive as it can disclose medical conditions.

Fingerprint scanner

A fingerprint scan usually scans the ridges of a finger for matching. A special type of fingerprint scan called minutiae matching is more microscopic in that it records the bifurcations and other detailed characteristics. Minutiae matching requires more authentication server space and more processing time than ridge fingerprint scans. Fingerprint scanning systems have a lower user acceptance rate than many systems because users are concerned with how the fingerprint information will be used and shared.

Palmprint scanner

A palm or hand scan combines fingerprint and hand geometry technologies. It records fingerprint information from every finger as well as hand geometry information.

Lighting

One of the best ways to deter crime and mischief is to shine a light on the areas of concern. In this section, we look at some types of lighting and some lighting systems that have proven to be effective. Lighting is considered a physical control for physical security.

Types of Systems

There are several types of lighting systems:

- Continuous lighting: An array of lights that provides an even amount of illumination across an area

- Standby lighting: A type of system that illuminates only at certain times or on a schedule

- Movable lighting: Lighting that can be repositioned as needed

- Emergency lighting: Lighting systems with their own power source to use when power is out

Types of Lighting

The following are the most common choices when choosing the illumination source or type of light:

- Fluorescent: Very low pressure mercury-vapor gas-discharge lamp that uses fluorescence to produce visible light

- Mercury vapor: Gas-discharge lamp that uses an electric arc through vaporized mercury to produce light

- Sodium vapor: Gas-discharge lamp that uses sodium in an excited state to produce light

- Quartz lamps: A lamp consisting of an ultraviolet light source, such as mercury vapor, contained in a fused-silica bulb that transmits ultraviolet light with little absorption

Regardless of the light source, it will be rated by its feet of illumination. When positioning the lights, you must take this rating into consideration. For example, if a controlled light fixture mounted on a 5-meter pole can illuminate an area 30 meters in diameter, for security lighting purposes, the distance between the fixtures should be 30 feet. Moreover, there should be extensive exterior perimeter lighting of entrances or parking areas to discourage prowlers or casual intruders.

Magnetometers

Magnetometers allow you to measure the strength and, depending on the instrument, the direction of a magnetic field at a point in space. So what does this have to do with security? While they can be used to measure the earth's magnetic field, in geographical surveys, used by the military to detect submarines, our interest is in their ability to detect weapons. Sadly with the workplace shootings that have occurred in recent years this can be a concern and might be a good addition to perimeter security. They come in both handheld models and as walk-through devices.

Logical security

Whereas physical security focused on keeping individuals out, digital security focuses mostly on keeping harmful data/malware out. In this section you'll learn both principles and techniques.

Principle of least privilege

The concept of least privilege is a simple one: when assigning permissions, give each user only the permissions they need to do their work and no more. This is especially true with administrators. Users who need administrative-level permissions should be assigned two accounts: one for performing nonadministrative, day-to-day tasks and the other to be used only when performing administrative tasks that specifically require an administrative-level user account. Those users should be educated on how each of the accounts should be used.

The biggest benefit to following this policy is the reduction of risk. The biggest headache is trying to deal with users who may not understand it. A manager, for example, may assert that he should have more permission than those who report to him, but giving those permissions to him also opens up all the possibilities for inadvertently deleting files, crippling accounts, and so forth.

A least-privilege policy should exist, and be enforced, throughout the enterprise. Users should have only the permissions and privileges needed to do their jobs and no more. ISO standard 27002 (which updates 17799) sums it up well: "Privileges should be allocated to individuals on a need-to-use basis and on an event-by-event basis, i.e., the minimum requirement for their functional role when needed." Adopting this as the policy for your organization is highly recommended.

Access control lists (ACLs)

Access control lists (ACLs) are sets of rules that either control access to a resource or are configured on a router or firewall to control the type of traffic allowed to enter or leave an interface. These lists are what make packet filtering firewalls work. Using these lists, an administrator can at a granular level define who can send specific types of traffic to specific locations. For example, you could prevent a user from using Telnet to connect to the sales server, without preventing him from using Telnet to connect to any other devices and without impacting any of his other activities

Multifactor authentication (MFA)

You learned about multifactor authentication in Chapter 1, "Mobile Devices." Please review that section.

Email

While email filtering is typically discussed in the context of preventing spam, the organization must also be concerned about the contents and types of email sent by its users. Because the users are representing the organization in everything they do, you want them to follow certain guidelines. Email filtering allows for the recognition and the blocking of messages that contain content that is not compliant with these guidelines. Configuring the filtering solution in such a way that it recognizes and blocks noncompliant emails while also leaving compliant emails unaffected can be a tremendous challenge.

Hard token

You learned about hardware tokens in Chapter 6, "Operating Systems." Please review that chapter.

Soft token

Software tokens are stored in software and can be duplicated. They are typically used in multifactor authentication mechanisms. Their purpose and use is the same as a hardware or physical token (see Chapter 6). Software tokens are cheaper than hardware tokens and do not have a battery that can run down as hardware tokens do.

Short message service (SMS)

Short Message Service (SMS) is a text messaging service component of most telephone, World Wide Web, and mobile telephony systems. Multimedia Messaging Service (MMS) handles messages that include graphics or videos. Both technologies present security challenges. Because messages are sent in clear text, both are susceptible to spoofing and spamming.

Voice call

When you combine phishing with Voice over IP (VoIP), it becomes known as vishing and is just an elevated form of social engineering. While crank calls have been in existence since the invention of the telephone, the rise in VoIP now makes it possible for someone to call you from almost anywhere in the world, without the worry of tracing, caller ID, and other features of the landline, and pretend to be someone they are not in order to get data from you.

Authenticator application

You learned about authenticator applications in Chapter 1, "Mobile Devices." Please review that chapter.

Mobile device management (MDM)

In recent years, mobile device management (MDM) and mobile application management (MAM) systems have become popular in enterprises. They are implemented to ensure that an organization can control mobile device settings, applications, and other parameters when those devices are attached to the enterprise network. In Chapter 1 you learned how MDM policies can be implemented through Active Directory or in the MDM software. Please review that chapter.

Active Directory

Active Directory (AD) is the directory service used in Windows since Windows 2000. It is used to locate resources and is also the point of configuration for all things security in a Windows domain (a concept to be explained shortly). It has a hierarchical structure that can be leveraged when using one of the more powerful tools of AD, Group Policy. Let's survey some of the concepts of AD.

Login script

While not required, login scripts run as soon as a user completes successful authentication. These scripts can automate a wide variety of operations, like mapping drives for users and checking for updates.

Domain

When a new AD structure is created, a new forest containing one domain is created. By default, all objects residing in a domain share the same security policies. Domains can be subdivided into organizational units (OUs), which can be used as targets for additional policies that you would like to confine to the OU.

Group Policy/updates

When Group Policies are created, they can be applied to both computers and users and can be applied at either the domain or the OU level in the hierarchy.

When policies are added or updated, these changes are refreshed at certain intervals on the computers. Outside of these intervals, devices also check when rebooting and starting up. Finally, administrators can force an update at any time using the gpudate command.

Organizational units

As noted, domains can be subdivided into OUs, and OUs can also have child OUs. You can build whatever structure suits the efficient application of policies. While policy inheritance can be prevented, doing so complicates things, and a well thought-out structure will result in allowing inheritance to operate.

Home folder

Home folders make it easier for an administrator to back up user files and manage user accounts by collecting the user's files in one location. If you assign a home folder to a user, you can store the user's data in a central location on a server and make backup and recovery of data easier and more reliable. If no home folder is assigned, the computer assigns the default local home folder to the user account. The home folder can use the same location as the My Documents folder.

Folder redirection

Along with creating a Home folder, folder redirection is an alternative method of automatically rerouting I/O to/from standard folders (directories) to use storage elsewhere on a network.

Security groups

There are a number of groups created on the operating system by default. The following sections look at the main ones of these.

Administrator

The Administrator account is the most powerful of all: it has the power to do everything from the smallest task all the way up to removing the operating system. Because of the great power it holds and the fact that it is always created, many who try to do harm will target this account as the one they try to break into. To increase security, during the installation of the Windows operating systems in question, you are prompted for a name of a user who will be designated as the Administrator. The power then comes not from being truly called Administrator (in my case it might now be tmcmillan, mcmillant, or something similar) but from being a member of the Administrators group (notice the plural for the group and singular for the user).

Because members of the Administrators group have such power, they can inadvertently do harm (such as accidentally deleting a file that a regular user could not). To protect against this, the practice of logging in with an Administrators account for daily interaction is strongly discouraged. Instead, system administrators should log in with a user account (lesser privileges) and change to the Administrators group account (elevated privileges) only when necessary for specific tasks.

Power user

The Power Users group is not as powerful as the Administrators group. Membership in this group gives read/write permission to the system, allowing members to install most software but keeping them from changing key operating system files. This is a good group for those who need to test software (such as programmers) and junior administrators.

Guest

The Guest account is created by default (and should be disabled) and is a member of the Guests group. For the most part, members of Guests have the same rights as Users except they can't get to log files. The best reason to make users members of the Guests group is if they are accessing the system only for a limited time.

 As part of operating system security, you should rename the default Administrator and Guest accounts that are created at installation.

Standard user

This group is the default that regular users belong to. Members of this group have read/write permission to their own profile. They cannot modify systemwide Registry settings or do much harm outside of their own account. Under the principle of least privilege, users should be made a member of the Users group only unless qualifying circumstances force them to have higher privileges.

Exam essentials

Describe the purpose of an access control vestibule.   An access control vestibule is a series of two doors with a small room between them. The user is authenticated at the first door and then allowed into the room. At that point, additional verification will occur (such as a guard visually identifying the person), and then they are allowed through the second door.

2.2 Compare and contrast wireless security protocols and authentication methods

CompTIA wants administrators of SOHO networks to be able to secure those networks in ways that protect the data stored on them. This objective looks at the security protection that can be added to a wireless or wired SOHO network.

Protocols and encryption

More and more, networks are using wireless as the medium of choice. It is much easier to implement, reconfigure, upgrade, and use than wired networks. Unfortunately, there can be downsides, and security is one of the largest.

The 802.11 standard applies to wireless networking, and there have been many versions of it released; the main ones are a, b, g, n, and ac. Encryption has gone from very weak (WEP) to much stronger with increments along the way, including WPA, WPA2, and implementations of TKIP and AES.

Wireless protocols are covered in detail in Chapter 2, "Networking."

WiFi Protected Access 2 (WPA2)

The Wi-Fi Protected Access (WPA) and Wi-Fi Protected Access 2 (WPA2) technologies were designed to address the core problems with WEP. These technologies implement the 802.11i standard. WPA implements most—but not all—of 802.11i to communicate with older wireless cards (which might still need an update through their firmware to be compliant), whereas WPA2 implements the full 802.11i standard for security and is not compatible with older wireless cards.

While WPA and WPA2 are primarily covered in Chapter 2, we need to say a few words more about these protocols. There are four variants, as described in Table 7.1.

TABLE 7.1   WPA and WPA2

Protocol	Authentication	Encryption
WPA Personal	Passwords	TKIP
WPA Enterprise	RADIUS	TKIP
WPA2 Personal	Passwords	AES
WPA2 Enterprise	RADIUS	AES

WARNING   Never assume that a wireless connection is secure. The emissions from a wireless portal may be detectable through walls and for several blocks from the portal. Interception is easy to accomplish, given that RF is the medium used for communication. Newer wireless devices offer data security, and you should use it. You can set newer WAPs and wireless routers to nonbroadcast. This is also sometimes called *disabling the broadcast* of the SSID. Given the choice, you should choose to use WPA2, WPA, or WEP at its highest encryption level, in that order.

WPA3

WPA 3 was announced in 2018 and makes the following enhancements to the protocol:

- Uses an equivalent 192-bit cryptographic strength in WPA3-Enterprise mode (AES-256 in GCM mode with SHA-384 as HMAC)

- Mandates the use of CCMP-128 (AES-128 in CCM mode) as the minimum encryption algorithm in WPA3-Personal mode

- Replaces the preshared key (PSK) exchange with Simultaneous Authentication of Equals (SAE) exchange, resulting in a more secure initial key exchange in personal mode and forward secrecy

- Mitigates security issues posed by weak passwords and simplifies the process of setting up devices with no display interface
- Protects management frames as specified in the IEEE 802.11w amendment, which is also enforced by the WPA3 specifications

Temporal Key Integrity Protocol (TKIP)

WPA was able to increase security by using a *Temporal Key Integrity Protocol* (TKIP) to scramble encryption keys using a hashing algorithm. The keys are issued an integrity check to verify they have not been modified or tampered with during transit. Though a good solution, it was far from perfect. Corporate security today favors WPA2 since it replaces TKIP with Counter Mode with Cipher Block Chaining Message Authentication Code Protocol (CCMP).

Advanced Encryption Standard (AES)

CCMP uses 128-bit Advanced Encryption Security (AES) with a 48-bit initialization vector, making it much more difficult to crack and minimizing the risk of a replay attack. AES was also covered in Chapter 2.

Authentication

Authentication occurs when a user provides a username (identification) and then proper credentials (the authentication). In this section we'll look at authentication, accounting, and authorization (AAA) services and then the types of authentication.

Remote Authentication Dial-In User Service (RADIUS)/Terminal Access Controller Access-Control System (TACACS+)

When users are making connections to the network through a variety of mechanisms, they should be authenticated first. These users could be accessing the network through any of the following:

- Dial-up remote access servers
- VPN access servers
- Wireless access points
- Security-enabled switches

At one time, each of these access devices would perform the authentication process locally on the device. The administrators would need to ensure that all remote access policies and settings were consistent across them all. When a password required changing, it had to be done on all devices.

To streamline this process, the Remote Authentication Dial-In User Service (RADIUS) and Terminal Access Controller Access-Control System Plus (TACACS+) networking protocols were developed to provide centralized authentication and authorization. These services can be run at a central location, and all the access devices, such as the access point (AP), remote access, virtual private network (VPN), and so on, can be made clients of the server. Whenever authentication occurs, the TACACS+ or RADIUS server performs the authentication and authorization. This provides one location to manage the remote access policies and passwords for the network.

Another advantage of using these systems is that the audit and access information (logs) are not kept on the access server.

TACACS and TACACS+ are Cisco proprietary services that operate in Cisco devices, whereas RADIUS is a standard defined in RFC 2138. Cisco has implemented several versions of TACACS over time. It went from TACACS to XTACACS to the latest version, TACACS+. The latest version provides authentication, accounting, and authorization, which is why it is sometimes referred to as an AAA service. TACACS+ employs tokens for two-factor, dynamic password authentication. It also allows users to change their passwords.

RADIUS is designed to provide a framework that includes three components. The *supplicant* is the device seeking authentication. The *authenticator* is the device to which they are attempting to connect (AP, switch, remote access server), and the *RADIUS server* is the authentication server. Note that the device seeking entry is not the RADIUS client. The authenticating server is the RADIUS server, and the authenticator (AP, switch, remote access server) is the RADIUS client.

In some cases, a RADIUS server can be the client of another RADIUS server. In that case, the RADIUS server acts as a proxy client for its RADIUS clients.

Kerberos

Kerberos is an authentication protocol that uses a client-server model developed by MIT's Project Athena. It is the default authentication model in the recent editions of Windows Server and is also used in Apple, Oracle, and Linux operating systems.

Kerberos is an SSO system that uses symmetric key cryptography. Kerberos provides confidentiality and integrity. Kerberos assumes that messaging, cabling, and client computers are not secure and are easily accessible. In a Kerberos exchange involving a message with an authenticator, the authenticator contains the client ID and a timestamp. Because a Kerberos ticket is valid for a certain time, the timestamp ensures the validity of the request.

Multifactor

Multifactor authentication was covered in Chapter 1. Please review that chapter.

Exam essentials

Understand wireless connectivity.   Networks work in the same way whether there is a physical wire between the hosts or that wire has been replaced by a wireless signal. The same order of operations and steps are carried out regardless of the medium employed.

2.3 Given a scenario, detect, remove, and prevent malware using the appropriate tools and methods

Over time, best practices have been developed through trial and error that help minimize the chances of getting viruses and reduce the effort involved in getting rid of malware. Some of these practices are discussed in this section.

Malware

Malware is a category of software that performs malicious activities on a device. It might wipe the hard drive or create a back door. In this section we'll look at types of malware and attacks.

Trojan

Trojan horses are programs that enter a system or network under the guise of another program. A Trojan horse may be included as an attachment or as part of an installation program. The Trojan horse can create a back door or replace a valid program during installation. It then accomplishes its mission under the guise of another program. Trojan horses can be used to compromise the security of your system, and they can exist on a system for years before they're detected.

The best preventive measure for Trojan horses is not to allow them entry into your system. Immediately before and after you install a new software program or operating system, back it up! If you suspect a Trojan horse, you can reinstall the original programs, which should delete the Trojan horse. A port scan may also reveal a Trojan horse on your system. If an application opens a TCP or IP port that isn't supported in your network, you can track it down and determine which port is being used.

Rootkit

Rootkits have become the software exploitation program du jour. They are software programs that have the ability to hide certain things from the operating system. With a rootkit, there may be a number of processes running on a system that don't show up in Task Manager, or connections may be established/available that don't appear in a netstat display—the rootkit masks the presence of these items. The rootkit does this by manipulating function calls to the operating system and filtering out information that would normally appear.

Unfortunately, many rootkits are written to get around antivirus and antispyware programs that aren't kept up-to-date. The best defense you have is to monitor what your system is doing and catch the rootkit in the process of installation.

Virus

Viruses can be classified as polymorphic, stealth, retroviruses, multipartite, armored, companion, phage, and macro viruses. Each type of virus has a different attack strategy and different consequences.

 Estimates for losses due to viruses are in the billions of dollars. These losses include financial loss as well as lost productivity.

The following sections will introduce the symptoms of a virus infection, explain how a virus works, and describe the types of viruses you can expect to encounter and how they generally behave. I'll also discuss how a virus is transmitted through a network.

Symptoms of a virus/malware infection

Many viruses will announce that you're infected as soon as they gain access to your system. They may take control of your system and flash annoying messages on your screen or destroy your hard disk. When this occurs, you'll know that you're a victim. Other viruses will cause your system to slow down, cause files to disappear from your computer, or take over your disk space.

You should look for some of the following symptoms when determining whether a virus infection has occurred:

- The programs on your system start to load more slowly. This happens because the virus is spreading to other files in your system or is taking over system resources.

- Unusual files appear on your hard drive, or files start to disappear from your system. Many viruses delete key files in your system to render it inoperable.

- Program sizes change from the installed versions. This occurs because the virus is attaching itself to these programs on your disk.

- Your browser, word processing application, or other software begins to exhibit unusual operating characteristics. Screens or menus may change.

- The system mysteriously shuts itself down or starts itself up and does a great deal of unanticipated disk activity.

- You mysteriously lose access to a disk drive or other system resources. The virus has changed the settings on a device to make it unusable.

- Your system suddenly doesn't reboot or gives unexpected error messages during startup.

This list is by no means comprehensive. What is an absolute, however, is that you should immediately quarantine the infected system. It is imperative that you do all you can to contain the virus and keep it from spreading to other systems within your network or beyond.

How viruses work

A virus, in most cases, tries to accomplish one of two things: render your system inoperable or spread itself to other systems. Many viruses will spread to other systems given the chance and then render your system unusable. This is common with many of the newer viruses.

If your system is infected, the virus may try to attach itself to every file in your system and spread each time you send a file or document to other users. When you give removable media to another user or put it into another system, you then infect that system with the virus.

Most viruses today are spread using email. The infected system attaches a file to any email that you send to another user. The recipient opens this file, thinking it's something you legitimately sent them. When they open the file, the virus infects the target system. The virus might then attach itself to all the emails the newly infected system sends, which in turn infects the recipients of the emails. Figure 7.4 shows how a virus can spread from a single user to thousands of users in a short time using email.

FIGURE 7.4   An email virus spreading geometrically to other users

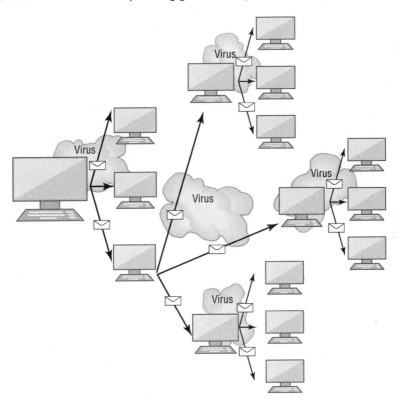

Types of viruses

Viruses take many different forms. The following sections briefly introduce these forms and explain how they work. These are the most common types, but this isn't a comprehensive list.

The best defense against a virus attack is to install and run antivirus software. The software should be on all workstations as well as the server.

Armored Virus   An *armored virus* is designed to make itself difficult to detect or analyze. Armored viruses cover themselves with protective code that stops debuggers or disassemblers from examining critical elements of the virus. The virus may be written in such a way that some aspects of the programming act as a decoy to distract analysis while the actual code hides in other areas in the program.

From the perspective of the creator, the more time it takes to deconstruct the virus, the longer it can live. The longer it can live, the more time it has to replicate and spread to as many machines as possible. The key to stopping most viruses is to identify them quickly and educate administrators about them—the very things that the armor intensifies the difficulty of accomplishing.

Companion Virus   A *companion virus* attaches itself to legitimate programs and then creates a program with a different extension. This file may reside in your system's temporary directory. When a user types the name of the legitimate program, the companion virus executes instead of the real program. This effectively hides the virus from the user. Many of the viruses that are used to attack Windows systems make changes to program pointers in the Registry so that they point to the infected program. The infected program may perform its dirty deed and then start the real program.

Macro Virus   A *macro virus* exploits the enhancements made to many application programs. Programmers can expand the capability of applications such as Microsoft Word and Excel. Word, for example, supports a mini-BASIC programming language that allows files to be manipulated automatically. These programs in the document are called *macros*. For example, a macro can tell your word processor to spell-check your document automatically when it opens. Macro viruses can infect all the documents on your system and spread to other systems via email or other methods.

Multipartite Virus   A *multipartite virus* attacks your system in multiple ways. It may attempt to infect your boot sector, infect all your executable files, and destroy your application files. The hope here is that you won't be able to correct all the problems and will allow the infestation to continue. The multipartite virus in Figure 7.5 attacks your boot sector, infects application files, and attacks your Word documents.

Phage Virus   A *phage virus* alters other programs and databases. The virus infects all these files. The only way to remove this virus is to reinstall the programs that are infected. If you miss even a single instance of this virus on the victim system, the process will start again and infect the system once more.

Polymorphic Virus   *Polymorphic viruses* change form in order to avoid detection. The virus will attempt to hide from your antivirus software. Frequently, the virus will encrypt parts of itself to avoid detection. When the virus does this, it's referred to as *mutation*. The mutation process makes it hard for antivirus software to detect common characteristics of the virus. Figure 7.6 shows a polymorphic virus changing its characteristics to avoid detection. In this example, the virus changes a signature to fool antivirus software.

FIGURE 7.5   A multipartite virus commencing an attack on a system

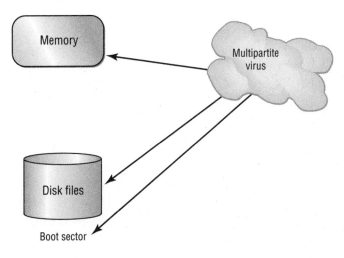

FIGURE 7.6   The polymorphic virus changing its characteristics

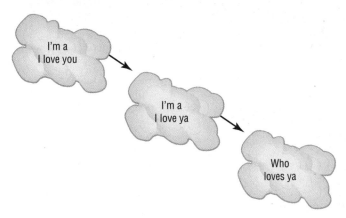

A *signature* is an algorithm or other element of a virus that uniquely identifies it. Because some viruses have the ability to alter their signature, it is crucial that you keep signature files current, whether you choose to manually download them or configure the antivirus engine to do so automatically.

Retrovirus   A *retrovirus* attacks or bypasses the antivirus software installed on a computer. You can consider a retrovirus to be an anti-antivirus. Retroviruses can directly attack your antivirus software and potentially destroy the virus definition database file. Destroying this information without your knowledge would leave you with a false sense of security. The virus may also directly attack an antivirus program to create bypasses for itself.

Stealth Virus   A *stealth virus* attempts to avoid detection by masking itself from applications. It may attach itself to the boot sector of the hard drive. When a system utility or program runs, the stealth virus redirects commands around itself to avoid detection. An infected file may report a file size different from what is actually present to avoid detection. Figure 7.7 shows a stealth virus attaching itself to the boot sector to avoid detection. Stealth viruses may also move themselves from file A to file B during a virus scan for the same reason.

FIGURE 7.7   A stealth virus hiding in a disk boot sector

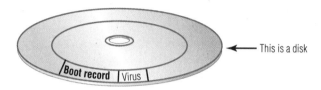

This is a disk

Boot record   Virus

Present Virus Activity

New viruses and threats are released on a regular basis to join the cadre of those already in existence. From an exam perspective, you need to be familiar with the world only as it existed at the time the questions were written. From an administrative standpoint, however, you need to know what is happening today.

To find this information, visit the CERT/CC Current Activity web page. Here you'll find a detailed description of the most current viruses as well as links to pages on older threats.

`www.cisa.gov/uscert/ncas/current-activity`

Spyware

Spyware differs from other malware in that it works—often actively—on behalf of a third party. Rather than self-replicating, like viruses and worms, spyware is spread to machines by users who inadvertently ask for it. The users often don't know they have asked for the spyware but have done so by downloading other programs, visiting infected sites, and so on.

The spyware program monitors the user's activity and responds by offering unsolicited pop-up advertisements (sometimes known as *adware*), gathers information about the user to pass on to marketers, or intercepts personal data such as credit card numbers.

Ransomware

Ransomware is a type of malware that usually encrypts the entire system or an entire drive with an encryption key that only the hacker possesses. Once they encrypt the machine, the hacker will hold the data residing on the device hostage until a ransom is paid.

The latest version of this attack arrives as an attachment that appears to be a résumé. However, when the attachment is opened, the malware uses software called Cryptowall to encrypt the device. What usually follows is a demand for $500 to decrypt the device.

Keylogger

A keylogger records everything typed and sends a record of this to the attacker. It can be implemented as a malicious software package, maybe even as part of a rootkit, or it may be a hardware device inserted between the keyboard and the USB port.

Boot sector virus

Earlier in this section you learned that many viruses can infect the boot sector of floppy disks or the Master Boot Record (MBR) of hard disks (some infect the boot sector of the hard disk instead of the MBR). The infected code runs when the system is booted. If the virus cannot be removed due to encryption or excessive damage to existing code, the hard drive may need reformatting to eliminate the infection.

Cryptominers

Cryptominers are tools that generate new units of a cryptocurrency like Bitcoin. Cryptomining isn't itself malicious in nature. But bad actors are illegally accessing important business assets such as servers to use their processing power to solve the mathematical puzzles required to mine. This consumes CPU cycles and increases the power usage in the datacenter. The result will be slower performance such as you might get from malware.

Tools and methods

Whereas physical security focused on keeping individuals out, digital security focuses mostly on keeping harmful data/malware out. The areas of focus are antivirus software, antimalware, Recovery Console, backup/restore, end-user education, software firewalls, and DNS configuration. Each of these is addressed in the sections that follow.

Recovery console

The Recovery Console isn't installed on a Windows system by default. To install it, follow these steps:

1. Place the Windows disc in the system.

2. From a command prompt, change to the i386 directory of the CD.

3. Type **winnt32 /cmdcons**.

4. A prompt appears, alerting you to the fact that 7 MB of hard drive space is required and asking whether you want to continue. Click Yes.

Upon successful completion of the installation, the Recovery Console is added as a menu choice at the bottom of the startup menu. To access it, you must choose it from the list at startup. If more than one installation of Windows exists on the system, another boot menu will appear, asking which you want to boot into, and you must make a selection to continue.

To perform this task, you must give the administrator password. You'll then arrive at a command prompt. You can give a number of commands from this prompt, two of which are worth special attention: exit restarts the computer, and help lists the commands you can give. Table 7.2 explains some options.

TABLE 7.2   Recovery Console options

Option	Explanation
Startup Repair	Fixes missing or damaged system files, which might prevent Windows from starting correctly
System Restore	Restores your computer's system files to an earlier point in time without affecting your files, such as email, documents, or photos
System Image Recovery	Requires a system image, a personalized backup of the partition that contains Windows, and includes programs and user data, like documents, pictures, and music
Windows Memory Diagnostic Tool	Scans your computer's memory for errors

Antivirus/Anti-malware

In Chapter 6 you learned the importance of keeping antivirus software installed and updated. The primary method of preventing the propagation of malicious code involves the use of *antivirus software*, a type of application that is installed on a system to protect it and to scan for viruses as well as worms and Trojan horses. Most viruses have characteristics that are common to families of a virus or viruses. Antivirus software looks for these characteristics, or fingerprints, to identify and neutralize viruses before they impact you.

More than 200,000 known viruses, worms, bombs, and other malware have been defined. New ones are added all the time. Your antivirus software manufacturer will usually work hard to keep the definition database files current. The definition database file contains all the known viruses and countermeasures for a particular antivirus software product. If you keep the virus definition database files in your software up-to-date, you probably won't be overly vulnerable to attacks.

The best method of protection is to use a layered approach. Antivirus software should be at the gateways, at the servers, and at the desktop. If you want to go one step further, you can use software at each location from different vendors to make sure you're covered from all angles.

Software firewalls

You can add a second layer of defense by utilizing personal or software firewalls on devices. This can be in addition to your network firewall and help prevent attacks locally on machines. The Windows Firewall is a good example of such a software firewall.

Anti-phishing training

In the section following this one you will learn about social engineering attacks. *Phishing* is a form of social engineering in which you simply ask someone for a piece of information that you are missing by making it look as if it is a legitimate request. An email might look as if it is from a bank and contain some basic information, such as the user's name. In the email, it will often state that there is a problem with the person's account or access privileges. They will be told to click a link to correct the problem. After they click the link—which goes to a site other than the bank's—they are asked for their username, password, account information, and so on. The person instigating the phishing can then use the values entered there to access the legitimate account.

 One of the best counters to phishing is to simply mouse over the Click Here link and read the URL. Almost every time it is pointing to an adaptation of the legitimate URL as opposed to a link to the real thing.

The only preventive measure in dealing with social engineering attacks is to educate your users and staff to never give out passwords and user IDs over the phone or via email or to anyone who isn't positively verified as being who they say they are.

User education regarding common threats

In many cases, users are partly responsible for a virus infection. After an infection occurs is a great time to impress on users the principles of secure computing. They should be reminded that antivirus software and firewalls can go only so far in protecting them and that they should exercise safe browsing habits and refrain from opening any attachments in email from unknown sources, regardless of how tempting.

OS reinstallation

In many cases, especially with some of the advanced malware, the only way to be assured that all of the infection and vulnerability created by the infection are removed is to format the hard drive and reinstall the operating system.

Exam essentials

Describe the options available in Windows system recovery.   These include Startup Repair, System Restore, System Image Recovery, and Windows Memory Diagnostic Tool.

2.4 Explain common social-engineering attacks, threats, and vulnerabilities

This objective explores security threats and vulnerabilities. A number of important topics are discussed in this section that fall into the realm of two broad categories: social engineering and malware. You'll look at malware and then several different types of attacks, as well as some of the reasons your network is vulnerable.

Social engineering

Social engineering is a process in which an attacker attempts to acquire information about your network and system by social means, such as by talking to people in the organization. A social engineering attack may occur over the phone, by email, or by a visit. The intent is to acquire access information, such as user IDs and passwords. When the attempt is made through email or instant messaging, it is known as *phishing* (discussed later) and often is made to look as if it is coming from sites where users are likely to have accounts (eBay and PayPal are popular).

These types of attacks are relatively low-tech and are more akin to con jobs. Take the following example. Your help desk gets a call at 4 a.m. from someone purporting to be the vice president of your company. They tell the help-desk personnel that they are out of town to attend a meeting, their computer just failed, and they are sitting in a hotel trying to get a file from their desktop computer back at the office. They can't seem to remember their password and user ID. They tell the help-desk representative that they need access to the information right away or the company could lose millions of dollars. Your help-desk rep knows how important this meeting is and gives the vice president their user ID and password over the phone.

Another common approach is initiated by a phone call or email from your software vendor, telling you that they have a critical fix that must be installed on your computer system. If this patch isn't installed right away, your system will crash, and you'll lose all your data. For some reason, you've changed your maintenance account password and they can't log on. Your system operator gives the password to the person. You've been hit again.

Phishing

You were introduced to phishing and the importance of training to prevent these attacks in the previous section of this chapter. You also learned about one variant, vishing. In this section you'll learn about some other variants.

Vishing

You learned about vishing in the previous section of this chapter. Please review that section.

Shoulder surfing

Shoulder surfing involves nothing more than watching someone when they enter their sensitive data. They can see you entering a password, typing in a credit card number, or entering any other pertinent information. The best defense against this type of attack is simply to survey your environment before entering personal data. Privacy filters can be used that make the screen difficult to read unless you are directly in front of it.

Spear phishing/Whaling

Two other forms of phishing to be aware of are *spear phishing* and *whaling*, and they are similar in nature. With spear phishing, the person conducting it uses information that the target would be less likely to question because it appears to be coming from a trusted source. As an example, instead of Wells Fargo sending you a message telling you to click here to fix a problem with your account, the message that comes in appears to be from your spouse and it says to click here to see a video of your children from last Christmas. Because it appears far more likely to be a legitimate message, it cuts through the user's standard defenses like a spear and has a higher likelihood of being clicked. Generating the attack requires much more work on the part of the miscreant and often involves using information from contact lists, friend lists from social media sites, and so on.

Whaling is nothing more than phishing, or spear phishing, for big users. Instead of sending out a To Whom It May Concern message to thousands of users, the whaler identifies one person from whom they can gain all the data they want—usually a manager or owner—and targets the phishing campaign at them.

Tailgating

Tailgating is the term used for someone being so close to you when you enter a building that they are able to come in right behind you without needing to use a key, a card, or any other security device. Many social engineering intruders who need physical access to a site will use this method of gaining entry. Educate users to beware of this and other social engineering ploys and prevent them from happening.

Access control vestibules are a great way to stop tailgating. Access control vestibules are a series of two doors with a small room between them that helps prevent unauthorized people from entering a building. For more information, see the earlier section "Access control vestibule."

Impersonation

Impersonation occurs when an individual pretends to be an IT technician, heating and air repairperson, or other personnel to get in the facility or to convince someone to disclose sensitive information.

Dumpster diving

It is amazing the information that can be gleaned from physical documents even in the age when there is such a push to go paperless. *Dumpster diving* is a common physical access method. Companies normally generate a huge amount of paper, most of which eventually winds up in dumpsters or recycle bins. Dumpsters may contain information that is highly sensitive in nature (such as passwords after a change and before the user has the new one memorized). In high-security and government environments, sensitive papers should be either shredded or burned. Most businesses don't do this. In addition, the advent of "green" companies has created an increase in the amount of recycled paper, which can often contain all kinds of juicy information about a company and its individual employees.

Evil twin

Rogue access points are APs that you do not control and manage. There are two types: those that are connected to wired infrastructure and those that are not. The ones that are connected to a wired network present a danger to your wired and wireless network. They may have been placed there by your own users without your knowledge, or they may have been purposefully put there by a hacker to gain access to the wired network.

In either case, they allow access to your wired network. Wireless intrusion prevention system (WIPS) devices are usually used to locate rogue access points and alert administrators of their presence.

A special type of rogue AP, an evil twin is one that has the same SSID as your legitimate AP while residing on a different channel. The hacker jams the frequency (channel) where the legitimate AP is located, disconnecting all systems from that AP. At that point all of the stations will associate and connect to the evil twin since this is done by SSID and not channel number. When the stations are connected to the evil twin, they are susceptible to peer-to-peer attacks from the hacker. This process is shown in Figure 7.8.

FIGURE 7.8   Evil twin

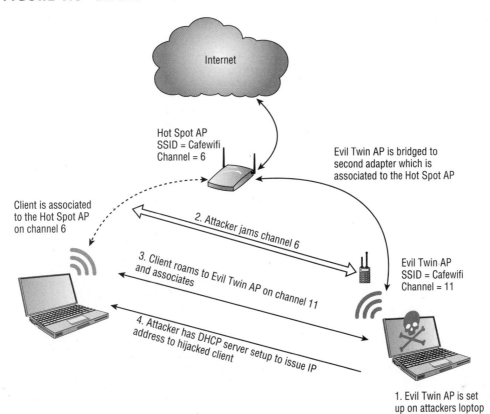

Threats

Social engineering attacks are not the only type with which we are confronted. There are many others. In this section you'll learn about the major vulnerabilities and attacks you will face.

Denial of service (DoS)

A denial-of-service (DoS) attack is one in which the attacker's goal is to make the device unavailable to do its job. It consumes all the resources of the device, leaving none for its regular work.

Distributed denial of service (DDoS)

A distributed denial-of-service (DDoS) attack is one in which the attacker recruits additional devices (called *zombies*) to assist in the attack. This greatly magnifies the effect of the denial of service.

Zero-day attack

Vulnerabilities are often discovered in live environments before a fix or patch exists. Such vulnerabilities are referred to as *zero-day* vulnerabilities. A zero-day attack is one that occurs when a security vulnerability in an application is discovered on the same day the application is released. Monitoring known hacking community websites can often provide an early alert because hackers often share zero-day exploit information.

New zero-day attacks are announced on a regular basis against a broad range of technology systems. You should create an inventory of applications and maintain a list of critical systems to manage the risks of these attack vectors.

Spoofing

Spoofing is the process of masquerading as another user or device. It is usually done for the purpose of accessing a resource to which the hacker should not have access or to get through a security device such as a firewall that may be filtering traffic based on a source IP address.

Spoofing can take various forms. The hacker may change their IP address to one that belongs to a trusted user or device to get through a firewall filtering at the IP layer. In other cases, they might spoof the MAC address of a trusted device to defeat layer 2 security applied on a switch or wireless access point (AP). It could also be the spoofing of a username and password to access a resource. Finally, it might be the spoofing of an email address to launch one of the email-based attacks.

On-path attack

An on-path attack, also called a man-in-the-middle (MITM) attack, is one in which the hacker uses one of several techniques to position themselves in the middle of a current communication session between two devices. One way they might do this is by polluting the ARP cache (mappings of IP addresses to MAC addresses) such that the users on either end of the session think they are sending data to one another when in reality they are sending it to the hacker. This allows the hacker to monitor the entire conversation.

Brute-force attack

A brute-force attack is a password, encryption key, or hash value attack that operates by attempting every possible combination of characters that could be in a password. These can be performed online or offline. Given enough time and processing power, any password can be cracked, so most enterprises use some sort of password policy that locks an account after a certain number of incorrect attempts. For this reason, online attacks are largely unsuccessful.

In contrast, the offline mode of the attack requires the attacker to steal the password file first but enables an unconstrained guessing of passwords, free of any application- or network-related rate limitations.

Dictionary attack

Dictionary attacks rely on the use of large files that contain words from the dictionary. These attacks are most often attempts to crack an encrypted password by encrypting each word in the dictionary file using the same algorithm used to encrypt the users' passwords and then comparing this value to the encrypted password for a match. These attacks are performed offline to eliminate the disabling of the account through password policies.

Insider threat

Insider threats should be one of the biggest concerns for security personnel. Insiders have knowledge of and access to systems that outsiders do not have, giving insiders a much easier avenue for carrying out or participating in an attack. An organization should implement the appropriate event collection and log review policies to provide the means to detect insider threats as they occur. These threats fall into two categories: intentional and unintentional.

Intentional

Intentional insider threats are insiders who have ill intent. These folks typically either are disgruntled over some perceived slight or are working for another organization to perform corporate espionage. They may share sensitive documents with others or they may impart knowledge used to breach a network. This is one of the reasons that users' permissions and rights must not exceed those necessary to perform their jobs. This helps to limit the damage an insider might inflict.

Unintentional

Sometimes internal users unknowingly increase the likelihood that security breaches will occur. Such unintentional insider threats do not have malicious intent; they simply do not understand how system changes can affect security.

Security awareness and training should include coverage of examples of misconfigurations that can result in security breaches occurring and/or not being detected. For example, a user may temporarily disable antivirus software to perform an administrative task. If the user fails to reenable the antivirus software, they unknowingly leave the system open to viruses. In such a case, an organization should consider implementing Group Policies or some other mechanism to periodically ensure that antivirus software is enabled and running. Another solution could be to configure antivirus software to automatically restart after a certain amount of time.

Recording and reviewing user actions via system, audit, and security logs can help security professionals identify misconfigurations so that the appropriate policies and controls can be implemented.

Structured Query Language (SQL) injection

A Structured Query Language (SQL) injection attack inserts, or "injects," a SQL query as the input data from the client to the application. This type of attack can result in the attacker being able to read sensitive data from the database, modify database data, execute administrative operations on the database, recover the content of a given file, and even issue commands to the operating system.

Cross-site scripting (XSS)

Cross-site scripting (XSS) occurs when an attacker locates a website vulnerability and injects malicious code into the web application. Many websites allow and even incorporate user input into a web page to customize the web page. If a web application does not properly validate this input, one of two things could happen: the text may be rendered on the page, or a script may be executed when others visit the web page.

Vulnerabilities

Many attacks are made possible because our systems are not secured as well as they could be. When this is the situation, we say a vulnerability exists. In this section you'll learn about some major vulnerabilities.

Non-compliant systems

Upon infection, some viruses destroy the target system immediately. The saving grace is that the infection can be detected and corrected. Some viruses won't destroy or otherwise tamper with a system; they use the victim system as a carrier. The victim system then infects servers, file shares, and other resources with the virus. The carrier then infects the target system again. Until the carrier is identified and cleaned, the virus continues to harass systems in this network and spread.

You should use some type of enterprise-grade malware management system that scans the network for noncompliant devices. Most of these systems can automate the entire process of locating, isolating, and remediating noncompliant devices.

Unpatched systems

When systems do not receive updates and patches, they will be susceptible to the issue the patch was intended to resolve. When these are security updates, the situation becomes more serious. As you learned in the previous section, some types of enterprise-grade malware management system that scans the network for noncompliant devices will at least alert you to missing updates.

Unprotected systems (missing antivirus/missing firewall)

All systems should have antivirus software fully updated and a functional host-based firewall. This is in addition to the network firewalls you may have. When either of these are not present, the system is a sitting duck for all sorts of attacks.

EOL OSs

In Chapter 6 you learned that systems that have reached end-of-life designation from the vendor need to be replaced. Please review that chapter.

Bring your own device (BYOD)

One of the decisions that must be made is whether to allow only company-owned mobile devices on the network or to allow personal devices as well. Many organizations have launched bring-your-own-device (BYOD) initiatives. While this certainly makes the users happy, it brings with it new challenges in securing a wide range of user devices running on all sorts of platforms.

One of the ways enterprises have successfully implemented these initiatives without sacrificing the security of the network is by turning to enterprise mobility management systems. These systems can be used to control a wide variety of mobile devices and to manage the installation of updates, the tracking of devices, and the deployment of remote wipes and GPS location services when needed. Without one of these utilities, deploying BYOD can be a security nightmare.

Exam essentials

Know the various types of social engineering.   Social engineering variants include shoulder surfing (watching someone work) and phishing (tricking someone into believing they are communicating with a party other than the one they are communicating with). Variations on phishing include vishing and whaling as well as spear phishing.

2.5 Given a scenario, manage and configure basic security settings in the Microsoft Windows OS

There is an entire domain dedicated to security for A+. In addition, CompTIA provides security certifications with Security+ and CompTIA Advanced Security Practitioner+ (CASP+), so you can see how important this topic is to those creating the exam. Because of that, make sure you have a good understanding of the topics covered here.

You want to make certain that your Windows systems, and the data within them, are kept as secure as possible. The security prevents others from changing the data, destroying it, or inadvertently harming it. This can be done by assigning users the least privileges possible and hardening as much of the environment as possible.

Defender Antivirus

Since the release of these exam objectives, the name of Windows Defender Antivirus has been changed to Windows Security. Despite the name change, this is still an antivirus tool that comes free with the system. There is a version that works on macOS as well. In this section you will learn how to activate or deactivate Windows Security and update definitions.

Activate/Deactivate

While you can use only Windows Security for protection, you can still use another product at the same time. To activate Security, follow these steps:

1. Click the Windows logo in the bottom-left corner of the screen to open the Start menu.

2. Scroll down and click Windows Security to open the application.

3. On the Windows Security screen, if no antivirus program has been installed and running in your computer, the Virus & Protection icon will be unchecked.

4. Click the Virus & Threat Protection icon.

5. Select Virus & Threat Protection Settings.

6. Select Real-Time Protection.

 If you have another antimalware product installed, you will see the screen in Figure 7.9 instead, which will offer you the option to scan with Windows Security as well.

FIGURE 7.9 Defender and another product

Updated definitions

If you are using Windows Security, you will want to keep the definitions updated. To do so, follow this procedure:

1. Open Windows Security, and click/tap the Virus & Threat Protection icon.

2. Click/tap the Check For Updates link under Virus & Threat Protection Updates.

3. Click/tap the Check For Updates button.

   If a new security intelligence definition update is available, it will automatically download and install.

Firewall

You learned about Windows Firewall in Chapter 6. Please review that chapter.

Activate/deactivate

If your antivirus has a firewall, you can use that, but you can also use the Windows Firewall. Go to Control Panel ➤ System and Security ➤ Security And Maintenance. Select the drop-down arrow next to Security to expand that section. Under Network Firewall, ensure that Windows Firewall is set to On.

Port security

One of the basic principles of security is to reduce the attack surface of all devices. This means shutting off all services and applications that are not required and closing all ports not being used. With respect to switches and hubs, it means disabling any ports that do not have devices connected to them. If this is not done, anyone could walk up to any unused wall outlet, plug in a device, get an IP address through DHCP, and be on your network.

But sometimes you want to prevent someone from unplugging a legitimate device and plugging in one that is not legitimate. That's where port security comes in. By configuring port security on the port, you can prevent the transmission of data by any device other than the legitimate one. You can even shut the port down if this occurs.

Port security can also refer to the limitation of access that allows only well-known TCP and UDP port numbers. Limiting access to allow only required ports reduces the attack surface.

Application security

You can control which applications can send data through the firewall. Filtering can be done on either a port number or by simply identifying the application. When you are creating inbound and outbound rules, one of the steps is to identify the service or application. For example, to block Skype follow these steps:

1. Go to Windows Defender Firewall with Advanced Security and select Outbound Rules on the left side of the screen. Click New Rule in the column on the right.

2. In the New Outbound Rule Wizard, select the program you want to block.

3. In the Program Path box, enter the path to the skype.exe file (or browse to its location) and click Next.

4. Select the action to take. In this case choose Block The Connection.

5. Select the network(s) where the rule applies (options are the domain network, public networks, and trusted private networks).

Users and Groups

You learned about the Users and Groups tool and types of accounts earlier in this chapter and in Chapter 6 as well. Please review that section and that chapter.

Local vs. Microsoft account

When you install Windows 10 or 11, you can choose to use either a local account or a Microsoft account. A local account will only be good for accessing the device. A Microsoft account will give access also to Microsoft services (like Outlook), devices running on one of Microsoft's current operating systems, and Microsoft application software (including Visual Studio). You can choose either during installation, but Microsoft doesn't make it easy to find the option for a local account, so I'll show you the steps here (they would prefer to keep you in their ecosystem).

1. Disconnect the computer from the network.
2. In the Sign In With Microsoft section, click Next without specifying an account name.
3. Click Create Account.
4. Click Skip.
5. Specify a name for your local account.
6. Click Next.
7. Create a password for the local account.
8. Click Next.
9. Confirm the password.
10. Click Next.
11. Select your first security question using the drop-down menu.
12. Confirm your first answer.
13. Click Next.
14. Repeat steps 11, 12, and 13 two more times to complete setting up the local account security.
15. Continue with the on-screen directions.

Standard account/Administrator

One of the security recommendations from Microsoft is to have administrative users log on with a standard user account and, when necessary, elevate the privileges of the account temporarily to perform a task and then remove that permission when the task is complete.

This is done by running the task, tool, or utility as an administrator. This can be done by right-clicking the tool and selecting Run As Administrator. Once the tool is closed, that security session ends, and the permissions are returned to those of a standard user. Having these highly privileged accounts logged in as infrequently as possible helps prevent hackers from gaining control of the accounts when they are live.

Guest user

You learned about the Guest account in Chapter 6 and also earlier in this chapter. In Windows, the Guest account is automatically created with the intent that it is to be used when someone must access a system but lacks a user account on that system. Because it is so widely known to exist, I recommend that you not use this default account and instead create another one for the same purpose if you truly need one. The Guest account leaves a security risk at the workstation and should be disabled to prevent it from being accessed by those attempting to gain unauthorized access.

Power user

You also learned about the Power users group earlier in this chapter. Please review that section.

Login OS Options

When users log into the system, they can authenticate in many ways besides using passwords. In this section you'll learn more about authentication.

Username and password

While usernames and passwords are the most common authentication mechanism, they are probably the least secure because they are so easily stolen. If you are using the password/username option, follow the best practices you will learn later in this chapter.

Personal identification number (PIN)

A simpler option to the password/username option is a numeric PIN. While not as hard to remember, PINs may be easier to view and record from a distance, and since they are all numbers, there are fewer possible combinations and thus they are easier to crack.

Fingerprint

You learned about fingerprint locks for mobile devices in Chapter 1. This is a very secure option because fingerprints (like all biometrics options) are difficult to copy. Review this technology in Chapter 1.

Facial recognition

You learned about facial recognition in Chapter 1. Please review that chapter.

Single sign-on (SSO)

One of the big problems that larger systems must deal with is the need for users to access multiple systems or applications. This may require a user to remember multiple accounts and passwords. The purpose of single sign-on (SSO) is to give users access to all the applications and systems they need when they log on. This is becoming a reality in many environments, including Kerberos, Microsoft Active Directory, Novell eDirectory, and some certificate model implementations.

> Single sign-on is both a blessing and a curse. It's a blessing in that once users are authenticated, they can access all the resources on the network and browse multiple directories. It's a curse in that it removes the doors that otherwise exist between the user and various resources.

NTFS vs. share permissions

The New Technology File System (NTFS) was introduced with Windows NT to address security problems. Before Windows NT was released, it had become apparent to Microsoft that a new filesystem was needed to handle growing disk sizes, security concerns, and the need for more stability than FAT32 provided. NTFS was created to address those issues.

Although FAT was relatively stable, if the systems that were controlling it kept running, it didn't do well when the power went out or the system crashed unexpectedly. One of the benefits of NTFS was a transaction tracking system, which made it possible for Windows NT to back out of any disk operations that were in progress when Windows NT crashed or lost power.

With NTFS, files, directories, and volumes can each have their own security. NTFS's security is flexible and built in. Not only does NTFS track security in ACLs, which can hold permissions for local users and groups, but each entry in the ACL can specify what type of access is given—such as Read, Write, Modify, or Full Control. This allows a great deal of flexibility in setting up a network. In addition, special file-encryption programs were developed to encrypt data while it was stored on the hard disk.

Microsoft strongly recommends that all network shares be established using NTFS. Several current operating systems from Microsoft support both FAT32 and NTFS. It's possible to convert from FAT32 to NTFS without losing data, but you can't do the operation in reverse (you would need to reformat the drive and install the data again from a backup tape).

> If you're using FAT32 and want to change to NTFS, the convert command will allow you to do so. For example, to change the E drive to NTFS, the command is convert e: /FS:NTFS.

Share permissions apply only when a user is accessing a file or folder through the network. Local permissions and attributes are used to protect the file when the user is local. With FAT and FAT32, you do not have the ability to assign "extended" or "extensible" permissions, and the user sitting at the console effectively is the owner of all resources on the system. As such, they can add, change, and delete any data or file that they want.

With NTFS as the filesystem, however, you are allowed to assign more comprehensive security to your computer system. NTFS permissions are able to protect you at the file level. Share permissions can be applied to the directory level only. NTFS permissions can affect users logged on locally or across the network to the system where the NTFS permissions are applied. Share permissions are in effect only when the user connects to the resource via the network.

Share and NTFS permissions are not cumulative. Permission must be granted at both levels to allow access. Moreover, the effective permission that the user has will be the most restrictive of the combined NTFS permission and the combined share permissions.

Allow vs. deny

Within NTFS, permissions for objects fall into one of three categories: allow, not allow, and deny. When viewing the permissions for a file or folder, you can select Allow, which effectively allows that group that action. You can also deselect Allow, which does not allow that group that action. Alternatively, you can select Deny, which prevents that group from using that action. There is a difference between not allowing (a cleared check box) and Deny (which specifically prohibits), and you tend not to see Deny used often. Deny, when used, trumps other permissions.

Permissions set at a folder are inherited down through subfolders, unless otherwise changed. Permissions are also cumulative: if a user is a member of a group that has read permission and a member of a group that has write permission, they effectively have both read and write permission.

Moving vs. copying folders and files

When you copy a file, you create a new entity. When you move a file, you simply relocate it and still have but one entity. This distinction is important for understanding permissions. A copy of a file will generally have the permissions assigned to it that are placed on newly created files in that folder—regardless of what permissions were on the original file.

A moved file, on the other hand, will attempt to keep the same permissions it had in the original location. Differences will occur if the same permissions cannot exist in the new location—for example, if you are moving a file from an NTFS volume to FAT32, the NTFS permissions will be lost. If, on the other hand, you are moving from a FAT32 volume to an NTFS volume, new permissions will be added that match those for newly created entities.

Folder copy and move operations follow similar guidelines to those with files.

File and folder attributes

Permissions can be allowed or denied individually on a per-folder basis. You can assign any combination of the values shown in Table 7.3.

TABLE 7.3 NTFS directory permissions

NTFS Permission	Meaning
Full Control	This gives the user all the other choices and the ability to change permission. The user can also take ownership of the directory or any of its contents.
Modify	This combines the Read & Execute permission with the Write permission and further allows the user to delete everything, including the folder.
Read & Execute	This combines the permissions of Read with those of List Folder Contents and adds the ability to run executables.
List Folder Contents	The List Folder Contents permission (known simply as List in previous versions) allows the user to view the contents of a directory and to navigate to its subdirectories. It does not grant the user access to the files in these directories unless that is specified in file permissions.
Read	This allows the user to navigate the entire directory structure, view the contents of the directory, view the contents of any files in the directory, and see ownership and attributes.
Write	This allows the user to create new entities within the folder, as well as to change attributes.

Clicking the Advanced button allows you to configure auditing and ownership properties. You can also apply NTFS permissions to individual files. This is done from the Security tab for the file. Table 7.4 lists the NTFS file permissions.

TABLE 7.4 NTFS file permissions

NTFS permission	Meaning
Full Control	This gives the user all the other permissions as well as permission to take ownership and change permission.
Modify	This combines the Read & Execute permission with the Write permission and further allows the user to delete the file.
Read	This allows the user to view the contents of the file and to see ownership and attributes.
Read & Execute	This combines the Read permission with the ability to execute.
Write	This allows the user to overwrite the file, as well as to change attributes and see ownership and permissions.

By default, the determination of NTFS permissions is based on the *cumulative* NTFS permissions for a user. Rights can be assigned to users based on group membership and individually; the only time permissions do not accumulate is when the Deny permission is invoked.

Shared files and folders

You can share folders, and the files within them, by right-clicking them and choosing Properties. Then on the Sharing tab, select Share and then select the users you want to share with, as shown in Figure 7.10.

FIGURE 7.10 Sharing a folder

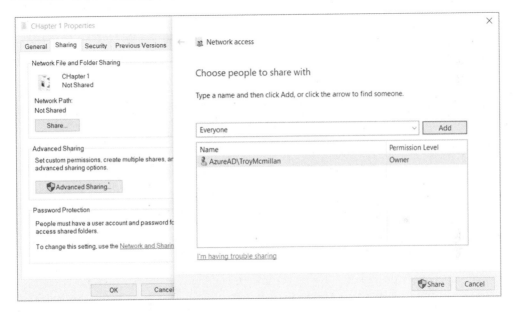

Selecting Advanced Sharing opens the dialog box shown in Figure 7.11.

Administrative shares vs. local shares

Administrative shares are created on servers running Windows on the network for administrative purposes. These shares can differ slightly based on which OS is running but always end with a dollar sign ($) to make them hidden. There is one for each volume on a hard drive (c$, d$, and so on) as well as admin$ (the root folder, usually c:\windows), and print$ (where the print drivers are located). These are created for use by administrators and usually require administrator privileges to access.

Local shares, as the name implies, are those created locally and are visible with the icon of a group of two individuals.

FIGURE 7.11   Advanced Sharing dialog box

Permission propagation

As mentioned earlier, permissions are cumulative. A user who is a member of two groups will effectively have the permissions of both groups combined. In cases where a user has a Deny permission from a group they are in, that overrules all other permissions they may have from other groups.

Inheritance

Inheritance is the default throughout the permission structure unless a specific setting is created to override this. A user who has read and write permissions in one folder will have that in all the subfolders unless a change has been made specifically to one of the subfolders.

Run as administrator vs. standard user

You learned about using the Run As Administrator command earlier in in the section "Standard account/Administrator." Please review that section.

User Account Control (UAC)

As you learned in Chapter 6, if you attempt to run System File Checker (SFC) or many other utilities from a standard command prompt, you will be told that you must be an administrator running a console session in order to continue. Rather than opening a standard command prompt, choose Start ➢ All Programs ➢ Accessories and then right-click Command Prompt and choose Run As Administrator.

The User Account Control (UAC) will prompt you to continue, and then you can run SFC without a problem. When this function is enabled (and it is by default). you will always be challenged for the administrator password if you attempt any operation that requires that permission.

As you also learned in Chapter 6, on the Tool tab of System Configuration, you can enable and disable this UAC as well as many others. Once you select it and click Launch, you will see the dialog box shown in Figure 7.12.

FIGURE 7.12   UAC settings

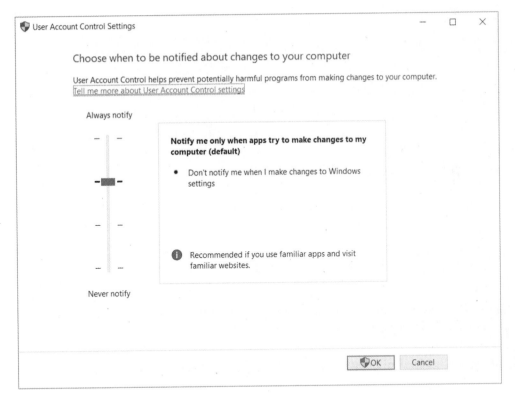

BitLocker

You were first introduced to BitLocker in Chapter 3, "Hardware," when you learned how it can operate with a TPM chip. You also learned more about it in Chapter 6, where you learned its value in encrypting both startup files and data files.

The BitLocker Drive Encryption Control Panel applet is used to turn on, suspend, or turn off BitLocker whole-drive encryption on your hard drives and flash drives and is shown in Figure 7.13.

FIGURE 7.13   BitLocker Drive Encryption

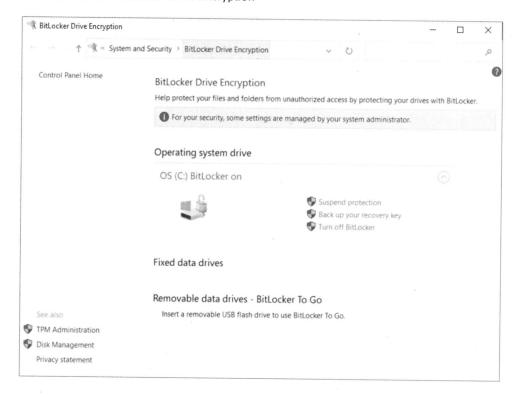

BitLocker To Go

You learned about BitLocker To Go to go in Chapter 7. Please review that chapter.

Encrypting File System (EFS)

The Encrypting File System (EFS) is an encryption tool built into Windows. It allows a user to encrypt files that can be decrypted only by the user who encrypted the files. It can be used only on NTFS volumes, but it is simple to use.

To encrypt a file, right-click the file, access the file properties, and on the General tab click the Advanced button. That will open the Advanced Attributes dialog box, shown in Figure 7.14. On this page, select the Encrypt Contents To Secure Data check box.

FIGURE 7.14   Advanced Attributes

Exam essentials

Know the difference between single sign-on and multifactor authentication.   Single sign-on is the concept of having the user be authenticated on all services they access after logging in once. Multifactor authentication is not the opposite of single sign-on but merely requires more than one entity to be authenticated for security purposes.

Know the NTFS permissions.   Permissions can be allowed or denied individually on a per-folder and per-file basis.

2.6 Given a scenario, configure a workstation to meet best practices for security

In the previous objectives, the importance of user education has been stressed. The user represents the weakest link in the security chain, whether the harm comes to them in the form of malware, social engineering, or simply avoidable mistakes. The workstation represents the digital arm of the user and must be properly and adequately secured to keep the user—and the network—protected.

A number of best practices are involved with securing a workstation. While a checklist could take many pages, depending on your environment, CompTIA has identified some that should appear on any roster.

Data-at-rest encryption

Earlier in this chapter you learned about encryption protocols and algorithms. When we talk about data-at-rest, we are talking about data that is stored somewhere and that's opposed to data that is in transit across a network. While data encryption is possible both on a drive level (BitLocker) and on an individual file level (EFS), always keep in mind the cost of encryption and save this tool for instances where you really need it. By cost I mean that any encrypted file must be decrypted to be opened and encrypted again to be saved. This requires CPU cycles on the device. If you attempt to encrypt everything, the performance of the device may make it practically unusable. You must strike a balance between security and usability.

Password best practices

One of the strongest ways to keep a system safe is to employ strong passwords and educate your users in the best security practices. In this section you'll explore various techniques that can enhance the security of your user passwords.

Complexity requirements (Length, Character types)

Passwords should be as long as possible. Most security experts believe a password of 10 characters is the minimum that should be used if security is a real concern. If you use only the lowercase letters of the alphabet, you have 26 characters with which to work. If you add the numeric values 0 through 9, you'll get another 10 characters. If you go one step further and add the uppercase letters, you'll then have an additional 26 characters, giving you a total of 62 characters with which to construct a password.

Most vendors recommend that you use nonalphabetical characters such as #, $, and % in your password, and some go so far as to require it.

If you used a 4-character password, this would be $62 \times 62 \times 62 \times 62$, or approximately 14 million password possibilities. If you used 5 characters in your password, this would give you 62 to the fifth power, or approximately 920 million password possibilities. If you used a 10-character password, this would give you 62 to the tenth power, or 8.4×10^{17} (a very big number) possibilities. As you can see, these numbers increase exponentially with each character added to the password. The 4-digit password could probably be broken in a fraction of a day, whereas the 10-digit password would take considerably longer and consume much more processing power.

If your password used only the 26 lowercase letters from the alphabet, the 4-digit password would have 26 to the fourth power, or 456,000 password combinations. A 5-character password would have 26 to the fifth power, or more than 11 million, and a 10-character password would have 26 to the tenth power, or 1.4×10^{14}. This is still a big number, but it would take considerably less time to break it. NIST now considers password length more important than complexity.

Expiration requirements

The longer that a password is used, the more likely the possibility that it will be compromised in some way. It is for this reason that requiring users to change their passwords at certain intervals increases the security of their passwords. You should require users to set a new password every 30 days (more frequently for higher-security networks), and you must also prevent them from reusing old passwords. Most password management systems have the ability to track previously used passwords and to disallow users from recycling old passwords.

Basic input/output system (BIOS)/Unified Extensible Firmware Interface (UEFI) passwords

Passwords should be configured and required to access either the BIOS or UEFI settings on all devices. If this is not the case, it would be possible for someone to reboot a device, enter the settings, change the boot order, boot to an operating system residing on a USB or optical drive, and use that OS as a platform to access data located on the other drives. While this is a worst-case scenario, there is also less significant mayhem a malicious person could cause in the BIOS and UEFI.

End-user best practices

While we do what we can as security professionals, ultimately we can't stand by and advise users on the safety of every action they take. In this section you'll learn about some best practices to convey to your users in the hope they will follow them.

Use screensaver locks

A screensaver should automatically start after a short period of idle time, and that screensaver should require a password before the user can begin the session again. This method of locking the workstation adds one more level of security.

Log off when not in use

Users should be taught to log off when not using the account. This prevents access to rights and permissions attached to that account if someone compromises or steals the device.

Secure/protect critical hardware (e.g., laptops)

Users should be taught to treat company devices as their own and protect them at all times. While you may not choose to have them bear the cost of replacing a damaged, stolen, or lost piece of hardware, you should impress upon users that they do bear responsibility for the safety of the hardware.

Secure personally identifiable information (PII) and passwords

While it may be obvious that passwords need to be protected, there are other types of information that if disclosed can cause severe damage and cost to the organization.

Personally identifiable information (PII) is any piece of information about a user that can be used alone or in combination with other pieces of information to identify an individual user. It is the responsibility of all organizations to protect PII that they may possess, and it is especially important in certain regulated industries such as healthcare and finance.

The danger of leaking PII is that much of this information, such as address, Social Security number, and place of employment, can be used to perform identity theft, a growing concern worldwide.

Account management

While I touched on one account management technique previously (preventing the reuse of passwords), there are a number of additional account management best practices that you should know and implement.

Restrict user permissions

When assigning user permissions, follow the principle of least privilege (discussed earlier) by giving users only the bare minimum they need to do their job. Assign permissions to groups, rather than users, and make users members of groups (or remove them from them) as they change roles or positions.

Restrict login times

Many users have a set work schedule, and it is only during these works hours that the user should access the network and its resources. Since an active account is an account vulnerable to misuse, any time in which you can disable an account while still allowing users to do their jobs enhances security, since a disabled account cannot be used for malicious purposes.

For this reason, many administrators allow users to log in only during certain hours. Typically, access is allowed from about an hour before their workday until about an hour after the day ends (to allow some flexibility). For certain users who tend to work throughout the day and night, this system may not work.

Disable guest account

To secure the system, disable all accounts that are not needed (especially the Guest account). Next, rename the accounts if you can (Microsoft won't allow you to rename an account to Administrator). Finally, change the passwords from the defaults and add them to the cycle of passwords that routinely get changed.

Use failed attempts lockout

Earlier you learned that a brute-force attack is a password attack that attempts all character combinations until the password is discovered. You also learned that the attacks are typically performed offline and not in a live environment. Why is that? It's because almost all password systems are set up to allow only a set number of failed password attempts before the account is locked. Although this policy may generate more password reset calls than you would like, that effect can be mitigated by implementing a complementary policy that allows the account to be automatically reenabled after a set amount of time (say five minutes). When this policy is communicated to the users, they know just to wait for five minutes and try again.

Use timeout/screen lock

While the relative sensitivity of the data appearing on the screen of a user's computer can vary from time to time and from user to user, it is a good practice to protect that information when someone steps away from the device. Moreover, when the device is in an out-of-the-way location, it may even afford someone the chance to browse the device. For this reason, you should require on all devices a password-protected screensaver that kicks in after a short period of inactivity.

Change default administrator's user account/password

All Windows devices and all infrastructure devices such as routers, firewalls, switches, and wireless access points and controllers come with default administrator accounts and default passwords. The names of these accounts and the default passwords are well known to malicious individuals. They can be looked up in five minutes on the Internet. Always change the default names and passwords for these accounts; otherwise, you may find someone else "owning" the device at some point in time.

Disable AutoRun

It is never a good idea to put any media in a workstation if you do not know where it came from or what it is. The reason is that the media (CD, DVD, USB) could contain malware. Compounding matters, that malware could be referenced in the `Autorun.inf` file, causing it to be summoned when the media is inserted in the machine and requiring no other action. `Autorun.inf` can be used to start an executable, access a website, or do any of a large number of different tasks. The best way to prevent a user from falling victim to such a ploy is to disable the AutoRun feature on the workstation.

Microsoft has changed (by default, disabled) the AutoRun function on Windows 10 and 11. The reason Microsoft changed the default action can be summed up in a single word: security. That text-based `Autorun.inf` file not only can take your browser to a web page but can also call any executable file, pass along variable information about the user, or do just about anything else imaginable. Simply put, it is *never* a good idea to take any media whose source or contents you have no idea of and plug it into your system. Such an action opens up the user—and their network—to any number of possible tribulations. An entire business's data could be jeopardized by such a minuscule act if a harmful CD were placed in a computer at work by someone with elevated privileges.

Disable Autoplay

AutoPlay examines newly discovered removable media and devices and, based on content such as pictures, music or video files, launches an appropriate application to play or display the content. It is closely related to AutoRun. To disable this function:

1. Press the Windows key or click the Windows icon in the lower-left corner of your desktop.

2. Type **autoplay** and click the AutoPlay Settings option.

3. On the resulting screen, toggle AutoPlay For All Media And Devices to Off. Also switch AutoPlay defaults for removable drives and memory cards to Take No Action.

Exam essentials

Understand the need for good passwords.   Passwords are the first line of defense for protecting an account. A password should be required for every account, and strong passwords should be enforced. Users need to understand the basics of password security and work to keep their accounts protected by following company policies regarding passwords.

List some techniques that enhance account management.   These techniques include but are not limited to disabling unused accounts, requiring frequent password changes, preventing the reuse of passwords, requiring complex passwords, and defining login hours for users.

2.7 Explain common methods for securing mobile and embedded devices

If laptops are easy to steal, smaller mobile devices are even more so. Because mobile devices are increasingly used to store valuable data and to perform functions once the domain of laptops and desktops, the need to secure these devices has grown. In this section methods of securing mobile devices will be discussed.

Screen locks

One of the most basic (but not necessarily the most utilized) security measures you can take is to implement a screen lock on the device. This is akin to implementing the password you use to log on to your desktop or laptop, but it's amazing how few people use this basic security measure. A screen lock can prevent someone from using the mobile device if it is stolen. There are several ways screen locks can be implemented, and in the following sections you'll examine each method.

Facial recognition

A face lock is one that uses a facial scan of the user to authenticate the user and, when successful authentication completes, unlocks the screen. It also is more secure than a passcode or swipe process.

PIN codes

Setting the password on an Android phone is done by navigating to Settings Location & Security ➢ Change Screen Lock. On the Change Screen Lock page, you can set the length of time the device remains idle until the screen locks as well as choose a method from None, Pattern, PIN, or Password. Select Password and then enter the desired password.

On an iOS-based device, navigate to Settings ➢ Settings ➢ Passcode Lock to set the password and Settings ➢ General ➢ Auto-Lock to set the amount of time before the iPhone locks.

Fingerprint

You learned about fingerprint locks in Chapter 1. Please review that chapter.

Pattern

Pattern locks eliminate the time taken while typing other passwords or numbers. You need to join the dots, and the phone is unlocked. An example of a pattern used to unlock a device is shown in Figure 7.15.

FIGURE 7.15   Pattern code

Pattern Code: 4 > 3 > 5 > 7 > 2 > 9 > 1 > 6

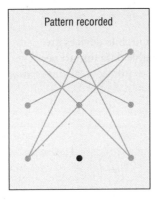

Swipe

Swipe locks use a gesture or series of gestures, sometimes involving the movement of an icon to open the screen. In some cases, they require only knowledge of the mobile platform in use; they offer no security to the process because no authentication of the user is occurring. In other cases like Android, they require a pattern between nine dots to be swiped to unlock the device.

Remote wipes

Remote wipes are instructions sent remotely to a mobile device that erase all the data when the device is stolen. In the case of the iPhone, this feature is closely connected to the locator application (discussed in the next section). To perform a remote wipe on an iPhone (which requires iOS 5), navigate to Settings ➤ iCloud. On this tab, ensure that Find My iPhone is enabled (set to On). Next, use the browser to go to iCloud.com and log in using the Apple ID you use on your phone.

Next, select Find My iPhone. The location of the phone will appear on a map. Click the *i* icon next to the location. In the dialog box that opens, select Remote Wipe. You will be prompted again to verify that is what you want to do. Select Wipe Phone.

The Android phones do not come with an official remote wipe. You can, however, install an Android app that will do this. Once the app, Lost Android, is installed, it works in the same way the iPhone remote wipe does. In this case, you log into the Lost Android website using your Google login. From the site, you can locate and wipe the device.

Android Device Manager, which is loaded on newer versions of Android, is available for download to any version of Android from 2.3 onward and provides nearly identical functionality to that of the iPhone.

Locator applications

Locator applications like the Lost Android app for Android are available where apps are sold for Androids. These apps allow you to locate the device, to lock the device, and even to send a message to the device offering a reward for its return. Finally, you can remotely wipe the device. The iOS devices and the newer Android devices have this feature built in, and it performs all the same functions.

OS updates

Security patches and operating system updates are available on an ongoing basis for both the iOS and the Android. For the iPhone, both operating system updates and security patches are available at the Apple support site. Automatic updates can be enabled for the device in iTunes. Use the Check For Updates button located in the middle of iTunes.

An auto-update feature is built into Android, and you can also manually check for patches and updates by navigating to Settings ➤ About Phone ➤ System Updates. Selecting these options will cause the phone to check for, download, and install patches or updates.

Device encryption

Full-device encryption is available for smartphones and other mobile devices. Most companies choose to implement this through the use of an enterprise mobility management system, since it can also manage the installation of updates, the tracking of devices, and the deployment of remote wipes and GPS location services when needed. There are also third-party applications that can provide full-device encryption.

Remote backup applications

Backing up your data with the iPhone can be done by connecting the device to a Mac and using iTunes to manage the content. (The data can also be backed up to a PC that has iTunes.) As users start to use the mobile device as their main tool, this may not be an optimal way to manage backups. New apps like Mozy are available that perform an online backup, which is attractive because the laptop or desktop where you backed up your data is not always close at hand but the Internet usually is.

Android has always taken a cloud approach to backups. There are many Android apps now that can be used to back up data to locations such as Dropbox or Box.net.

Failed login attempts restrictions

Most of us have become accustomed to the lockout feature on a laptop or desktop that locks out an account after a certain number of failed login attempts. This feature is available on a mobile device and can even be set to perform a remote wipe of the device after repeated failed login attempts.

On the iOS, the Erase Data function can be set to perform a remote wipe after 10 failed passcode attempts. After six failed attempts, the iPhone locks out users for a minute before another passcode can be entered. The device increases the lockout time following each additional failed attempt.

The Android does not have this feature built in but does provide APIs that allow enterprise developers to create applications that will do this.

Antivirus/anti-malware

Mobile devices can suffer from viruses and malware just like laptops and desktops. Major antivirus vendors such as McAfee and Kaspersky make antivirus and antimalware products for mobile devices that provide the same real-time protection that the products do for desktops. The same guidelines apply for these mobile devices: keep them up-to-date by setting the device to check for updates whenever connected to the Internet.

Firewalls

Because today's mobile devices function more like laptops and desktop systems, they need the same protection. Mobile device firewall products are those that install on the device and protect the device in the same way a personal firewall on a desktop system, such as Windows Firewall, does.

The disadvantage to this approach is that the software runs continuously, thus placing an ongoing load on the battery. Likewise, intrusion prevention and intrusion detection software can be placed on mobile devices, again with the same effect on battery lifetime.

If you need another reason to invest in an enterprise mobility management system, this is it. Most solutions include a firewall product of some sort in the suite. One consideration when choosing a solution is to balance the features you need against the memory footprint of the solution, because memory is a scarce resource in mobile devices.

Policies and procedures

With the introduction of mobile devices to the network, changes and additions may be called for in the organizational security policy. As procedures are derived from broader policies, these changes will also impact the procedures that users are required to follow. In this section you'll look at two issues that need to be considered with respect to policies and procedures.

BYOD vs. corporate owned

You learned the advantages and disadvantages to these two deployment options in Chapter 2. Please review that chapter.

Profile security requirements

The baseline or minimum security settings required on all mobile devices must be determined and standardized. This may require the creation of multiple security *profiles* based on different mobile device models and types, but the theory is the same. By defining a collection of security settings, implementing them on all devices, and constantly monitoring the settings for changes, you can ensure that these settings are maintained.

Internet of Things (IoT)

You learned about the Internet of Things (IoT) in Chapter 2. Please review that chapter.

Exam essentials

Describe the options available to secure the data on a mobile device.   These options include passcode locks, remote wipes, locator applications, failed login attempt restrictions, and remote backup applications.

List other security guidelines for mobile devices.   Always keep antivirus definitions up-to-date and set the mobile device to automatically check for OS updates and patches.

2.8 Given a scenario, use common data destruction and disposal methods

Think of all the sensitive data written to a hard drive. The drive can contain information about students, clients, users—anyone and anything. That hard drive can be in a desktop PC, a laptop, or even a printer (many laser printers above consumer grade offer the ability to add a hard drive to store print jobs). If it falls into the wrong hands, you can lose valuable data and also risk a lawsuit for not properly protecting privacy. An appropriate data destruction/disposal plan should be in place to avoid any potential problems.

Since data on media holds great value and liability, that media should never be simply tossed away for prying eyes to stumble upon. For the purposes of this objective, I'll talk about hard drives, and there are three key concepts to understand in regard to them: formatting, sanitation, and destruction. Formatting prepares the drive to hold new information (which can include copying over data already there). Sanitation involves wiping the data on the drive, whereas destruction renders the drive no longer usable.

While this objective is focused on hard drives, data can also be stored on portable flash drives, backup tapes, CDs, or DVDs. In the interest of security, I recommend that you destroy any of them before disposing of them as well.

Physical destruction

Physically destroying the drive involves rendering the component no longer usable. You can also physically destroy other forms of media, such as flash drives and CD/DVDs.

Drilling

If you don't have the budget for a hard drive shredder, you can accomplish similar results in a much more time-consuming way with a power drill. The goal is to physically destroy the platters in the drive. Start the process by removing the cover from the drive—this is normally done with a Torx driver (while #8 does not work with all, it is a good one to try first). You can remove the arm with a slotted screwdriver and then the cover over the platters using a Torx driver. Don't worry about damaging or scratching anything because nothing is intended to be saved. Everything but the platters can be tossed away.

As an optional step, you can completely remove the tracks using a belt sander, grinder, or palm sander. The goal is to turn the shiny surface into fine powder. This adds one more layer of assurance that nothing usable remains. Always be careful to wear eye protection and not breathe in any fine particles that you generate during the grinding/destruction process.

Following this, use the power drill to create the smallest particles possible. A drill press works much better for this task than trying to hold the drive and drill it with a handheld model. Finally you can use a hammer to destroy the platters as well; it provides a certain level of satisfaction if the drive died and you had to restore it from backup.

 Even with practice, you will find that manually destroying a hard drive is time-consuming. There are companies that specialize in this and can do it efficiently. One such company is Shred-it, which will pick it up from you and provide a chain-of-custody assurance and a certificate of destruction upon completion.

Shredding

Many commercial paper shredders include the ability to destroy DVDs and CDs. Paper shredders, however, are not able to handle hard drives; you need a shredder created for just such a purpose. Jackhammer makes a low-volume model that will destroy eight drives per minute and carries a suggested list price of just under $30,000.

Degaussing

Degaussing involves applying a strong magnetic field to initialize the media (this is also referred to as *disk wiping*). This process helps ensure that information doesn't fall into the wrong hands.

Since degaussing uses a specifically designed electromagnet to eliminate all data on the drive, that destruction also includes the factory prerecorded servo tracks. You can find wand model degaussers priced at just over $500 or desktop units that sell for up to $30,000.

Incinerating

A final option that exists for some forms of storage is to burn the media. Regardless of whether the media is a hard drive, CD, DVD, solid-state drive, or floppy disk, the media must be reduced to ash, or in the case of hard drive platters, the internal platters must be physically deformed using heat.

Recycling or repurposing best practices

Multiple levels of reformatting can be done to remove the contents of a drive. A standard format—accomplished using the operating system's format utility (or similar)—can mark space occupied by files as available for new files without truly deleting what was there. Such erasing—if you want to call it that—doesn't guarantee that the information isn't still on the disk and recoverable.

Erasing/wiping

Overwriting the drive entails copying over the data with new data. A common practice is to replace the data with 0s. A number of applications allow you to recover what was there prior to the last write operation, and for that reason, most overwrite software will write the same sequence and save it multiple times.

Drive wipe

If it's possible to verify beyond a reasonable doubt that a piece of hardware that's no longer being used doesn't contain any data of a sensitive or proprietary nature, that hardware can be recycled (sold to employees, sold to a third party, donated to a school, and so on). That level of assurance can come from wiping a hard drive or using specialized utilities.

   Degaussing hard drives is difficult and may render the drive unusable.

If you can't be assured that the hardware in question doesn't contain important data, the hardware should be destroyed. You cannot, and should not, take a risk that the data your company depends on could fall into the wrong hands.

Low-level formatting vs. standard formatting

A low-level format (typically accomplished only in the factory) can be performed on the system, or a utility can be used to completely wipe the disk clean. This process helps ensure that information doesn't fall into the wrong hands.

IDE hard drives are low-level formatted by the manufacturer. Low-level formatting must be performed even before a drive can be partitioned. In low-level formatting, the drive controller chip and the drive meet for the first time and learn to work together. Because IDE drives have their controllers integrated into the drive, low-level formatting is a factory process with these drives and does not depend on the operating system.

   Never low-level format IDE or SCSI drives! They're low-level formatted from the factory, and you may cause problems by using low-level utilities on these types of drives.

The main thing to remember for the exams is that most forms of formatting included with the operating system do not actually completely erase the data. Formatting the drive and then disposing of it has caused many companies problems when the data has been retrieved by individuals who never should have seen it using applications that are commercially available.

Outsourcing concepts

Driven mainly by cost, many companies outsource some functions to a third party—for example, outsourcing to cloud providers computing jobs that require a large number of processor cycles for a short duration. This situation allows a company to avoid a large investment in computing resources that will be used for only a short time. Assuming that the provisioned resources are dedicated to a single company, the main vulnerability associated with on-demand provisioning is traces of proprietary data that can remain on the virtual machine and may be exploited.

Third-party vendor

As part of prevention of privacy policy violations, any contracted third parties that have access to PII should be assessed to ensure that the appropriate controls are in place. In addition, third-party personnel should be familiarized with organizational policies and should sign nondisclosure agreements (NDAs).

Certification of destruction/recycling

Certificates of destruction are documents that attest to either the physical destruction of the media on which sensitive data was located or a scientifically approved method of removing the data from a drive.

These certificates are typically issued to the organization by a storage vendor or cloud provider to prove either that the data has been removed or that the media has been destroyed.

Exam essentials

Understand the difference between standard and low-level formatting.   Standard formatting uses operating system tools and makes the drive available for holding data without truly removing what was on the drive (thus the data can be recovered). A low-level format is operating system independent and destroys any data that was on the drive.

Understand how to physically destroy a drive.   A hard drive can be destroyed by tossing it into a shredder designed for such a purpose, or it can be destroyed with an electromagnet in a process known as degaussing. You can also disassemble the drive and destroy the platters with a drill or other tool that renders the data irretrievable.

2.9 Given a scenario, configure appropriate security settings on small office/home office (SOHO) wireless and wired networks

CompTIA wants administrators of SOHO networks to be able to secure those networks in ways that protect the data stored on them. This objective looks at the security protection that can be added to a wireless or wired SOHO network. First you'll look at issues specific to a WLAN, and then you'll explore security considerations for wired and wireless networks.

Home router settings

Today's SOHO networks will almost always contain a WLAN router to provide access to the local WLAN and beyond to the Internet. In this section you'll learn some of the key issues in setting up a home or SOHO WLAN router.

IP filtering

You learned about IP address filtering in Chapter 6. This technique is available on most WLAN routers and should be utilized to screen out unwanted IP addresses. Please review Chapter 6 coverage of Windows Defender and IP filtering.

Firmware updates

In the past, updating firmware on devices such as APs, routers, and switches was considered to be desirable but optional. More and more security attacks are based on attacking the firmware, and for this reason firmware updates should be part of whatever automated update system you may be using (not to mention the additional functionality and bug elimination you may experience). You may be able to get on a mailing list for each vendor so that you can be notified when firmware updates are available. In any case, some systematic method must be developed to ensure these updates are maintained.

Change default passwords

Default accounts include not only those created with the installation of the operating systems but often also accounts associated with hardware. Wireless APs, routers, and similar devices often include accounts for interacting with, and administering, those devices. You should always change the passwords associated with those devices and, where possible, change the usernames.

If there are accounts that are not needed, disable them or delete them. Make certain you use strong password policies and protect the passwords with the same security you do for any users or administrators (in other words, don't write the router's password on an address label and stick it to the bottom of the router).

Content filtering

Content filtering software examines all web connections, and in some cases emails, for objectionable content or sites that have been identified as off-limits by the administrator. While this can be helpful in preventing the introduction of malware or in screening objectionable content, you should be aware that these filters are making educated guesses about what to deny and what to allow.

A filter will invariably deny content that should be allowed and allow content that should be denied. Try to be as specific as possible when defining keywords that are used to identify sites and content, and set the expectation among users that the software is not perfect.

Physical placement/secure locations

Just as you would not park your car in a public garage and leave its doors wide open with the key in the ignition, you should educate users not to leave a workstation that they are logged into when they attend meetings, go to lunch, and so forth. They should log out of the workstation or lock it. "Lock when you leave" should be a mantra they become familiar with. Locking the workstation should require a password (usually the same as their user password) to resume working at the workstation.

Moreover, don't overlook the obvious need for physical security. Adding a cable to lock a laptop to a desk prevents someone from picking it up and walking away with a copy of your customer database. Laptop cases generally include a built-in security slot in which a cable lock can be added to prevent it from being carried away easily, like the one shown in Figure 7.16.

FIGURE 7.16 A cable in the security slot keeps the laptop from being carried away easily.

When it comes to desktop models, adding a lock to the back cover can prevent an intruder with physical access from grabbing the hard drive or damaging the internal components. You should also physically secure network devices—routers, APs, and the like. Place them in locked cabinets, if possible. If they are not physically secured, the opportunity exists for them to be stolen or manipulated in such a way as to allow someone unauthorized to connect to the network.

Antenna and access point placement

Antenna placement can be crucial in allowing clients to reach the AP. There isn't any one universal solution to this issue, and it depends on the environment in which the AP is placed. As a general rule, the greater the distance the signal must travel, the more it will attenuate, but you can lose a signal quickly in a short space as well if the building materials reflect or absorb the signal. You should try to avoid placing APs near metal (including appliances) or near the ground. Placing them in the center of the area to be served, and high enough to get around most obstacles, is recommended.

On the other end of the spectrum, you have to contend with the problem of the signal traveling outside your intended network (known as *signal leakage*) and being picked up in public areas by outsiders. To mitigate this problem, use RF-absorbent materials on external walls, essentially shielding the surroundings.

Radio power levels

On the chance that the signal is actually traveling too far, some APs include *power-level controls* that allow you to reduce the amount of output provided.

 You can find a great source for information on RF power values and antennas on the Cisco site at www.cisco.com/c/en/us/support/docs/wireless-mobility/wireless-lan-wlan/23231-powervalues-23231.html.

WPS

Wi-Fi Protected Setup (WPS) was a concept designed to make it easier for less knowledgeable users to add a new client to the WLAN without manually entering the security information on the client. One method involves pushing a button on the AP at the same time a client is attempting to join the network so that the settings are sent to the client. Other methods involve placing the client close to the AP, and near-field communication is used for the process.

Regardless of the details, as often happens when we try to make security simpler, we make it fail. It has been discovered that a hacker can identify the PIN used in a short period of time, and with it the network's WPA/WPA2 preshared key. For this reason, the Wi-Fi Alliance has recommended against using this feature.

Dynamic Host Configuration Protocol (DHCP) reservations

You learned about DHCP reservations in Chapter 2. By limiting the assignment of IP addresses to only those devices with reservation, you can limit WLAN access to only those devices with reservations.

Static wide-area network (WAN) IP

While many WAN connections receive an IP address from the ISP DHCP server, in some cases you may want to make that address static so that it does not change. One scenario in which this is required is when implementing port forwarding (covered later in this chapter). Another is when it is required due to an IP address filter in their firewall that allows the static IP address.

Universal Plug and Play (UPnP)

Universal Plug and Play (UPnP) is a protocol that lets computers, printers, and other devices make themselves easily discoverable to a network router. Promoted by the UPnP Forum, a computer industry initiative, it is available on many wireless APs and routers. While it makes it easier to connect devices, it does have security issues.

In one study more than 6,900 network-aware products from 1,500 companies at 81 million IP addresses responded to their discovery requests on the Internet. Depending on the security posture of the device, many of those devices can be accessed or manipulated. For this reason, many have called for disabling this feature on wireless routers or APs.

Screened subnet

Although the firewalls discussed thus far typically connect directly to an untrusted network (at least one interface does), a screened host is a firewall that is between the final router and the internal network. When traffic comes into the router and is forwarded to the firewall, it is inspected before going into the internal network.

A screened subnet takes this concept a step further. In this case, two firewalls are used, and traffic must be inspected at both firewalls to enter the internal network. It is called a screen subnet because there is a subnet between the two firewalls that can act as a DMZ for resources from the outside world. A screened subnet is shown in Figure 7.17.

Wireless specific

Wireless networks present a unique set of challenges that wired networks do not. The communication methods are somewhat different, as are the attack methods. In this section security issues that are relevant only to a WLAN are discussed.

FIGURE 7.17   Screened subnet

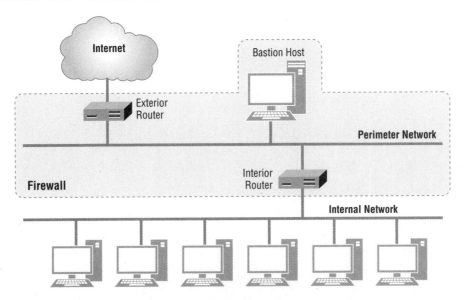

Changing the service set identifier (SSID)

Every wireless AP or wireless router on the market comes with a default SSID. Cisco models use the name *tsunami*, for example. You should change these defaults and create a new SSID to represent your WLAN. Typically, when hackers see a default SSID, they make the reasonable assumption that if the SSID was left at the default, the administrator password was as well. So if you also failed to change that, hackers can now log in, take over your AP, and lock you out.

Disabling SSID broadcast

One method of "protecting" the network that is often recommended is to turn off the SSID broadcast. The AP is still there and can be accessed by those who know about it, but it prevents those who are just scanning from finding it. This should be considered a weak form of security because there are still other ways, albeit a bit more complicated, to discover the presence of the AP besides the SSID broadcast.

Encryption settings

Earlier in this chapter you learned about WLAN encryption and its value. Please review that section.

Disabling guest access

Many wireless routers allow you to create two networks, one network for your personal devices and a guest network for folks who are just visiting. While this may be beneficial, to increase security it is possible to disable the guest network and guest access. As an example the setting on a Motorola is shown in Figure 7.18.

FIGURE 7.18   Disabling guest access

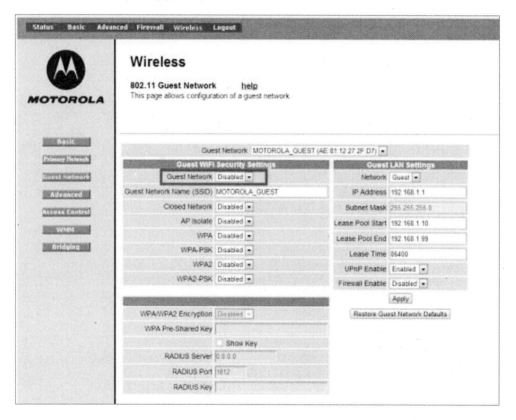

Changing channels

In Chapter 2, you learned about WLAN channels, which represent different frequencies. By performing a site survey prior to deployment, you can assess the load on various channels in the area and select one that is not busy, which will yield better performance.

Firewall settings

All devices both wired and wireless should have personal firewalls enabled and configured to protect each system. In Windows, you can leverage the personal firewall that comes on all Windows computers. For operating systems that don't come with a personal firewall, third-party software should be implemented for this purpose. These firewalls help to prevent other devices from connecting to each station without the approval of the users.

The presence of personal firewalls on all the devices does *not* mean you don't need a network firewall at the edge of the network and between sections of the network that may have varying security levels.

Disabling unused ports

Disable all unneeded protocols/ports. If you don't need them, remove them or prevent them from loading. Ports not in use present an open door for an attacker to enter.

Many of the newer SOHO router solutions (and some of the personal firewall solutions on end-user workstations) close down the ICMP ports by default. Keep this in mind; it can drive you nuts when you are trying to see whether a new station, server, or router is up and running by using the ping command. This command depends on the use of ICMP.

Port forwarding/mapping

Another option to harden the entrance to the network is to deploy port forwarding or mapping. Port forwarding is a function typically performed on the same device that may be performing network address translation (NAT). One port number is set aside on the gateway for the exclusive use of communicating with a service in the private network, located on a specific host. External hosts must know this port number and the address of the gateway to communicate with the network-internal service. The purpose of this is to hide the real IP address of the destination device or server to protect it from connections outside the LAN.

Exam essentials

Identify steps to harden a WLAN router.   These steps include changing default passwords, IP filtering, firmware updates, and content filtering.

Describe mitigations specific to WLAN.   These include changing the service set identifier (SSID), disabling SSID broadcast, encryption setting, disabling guest access, and changing channels.

2.10 Given a scenario, install and configure browsers and relevant security settings

In Chapter 6 you learned about settings involving the browser when we discussed Windows settings. In this final section of Chapter 7 we'll review some of those settings and dig deeper into some others.

Browser download/installation

In most cases users will simply use the browser that comes with the operating system. But in other cases users will want to download and install a different browser. For example, a user may prefer the Google Chrome browser. Not all sources of these browser downloads are safe. In this section you'll review some concepts we touched on earlier way back in Chapter 1.

Trusted sources/Untrusted sources

We spent some time in Chapter 1 discussing the difference between trusted and untrusted sources of any download. That applies to browsers as well. The best place to obtain browser downloads is the vendor website and not some third-party site that may be more interested in stealing your identity.

Hashing

Even when using a trusted site you still can't be sure there isn't malware in the download. Hash functions are used to ensure integrity. Most providers also will provide what is called a message digest of the file you can also download.

Hash values, also referred to as message digests, are calculated using the original message. A hash function takes a message of variable length and produces a fixed-length hash value. If the receiver calculates a hash value that is the same, then the original message is intact. If the receiver calculates a hash value that is different, then the original message has been altered.

Extensions and plug-ins

Extensions and plugs-ins are extra components that you can install in the browser that may add features or enable the browser to interact more closely with a site. The problem is, not all of these extensions are safe.

Trusted sources/Untrusted sources

While it might be easy to tell you to only download extensions from vendors, many users, especially developers, will want to use plug-ins that were created by individual developers. If you plan to allow this, ensure that users do the following:

- Investigate the developer's reputation.
- Read the explanation of the plug-in completely.
- Pay attention to the required permissions to operate. Are they too broad?
- Look for reviews.
- If it's open source, dig into the source code and verify its security.

Password managers

Password managers are applications that make managing multiple passwords easier and safer, storing such passwords in an encrypted database. They typically require a user to generate and remember one "master" password to unlock and access the password file.

Secure connections/sites – valid certificates

Users must also be instilled with lot of skepticism connecting to external sites, especially as it relates to secure sites (HTTPS). Later in Chapter 8, "Software Troubleshooting," you'll learn more about certain types of certificate warning dialog boxes. Users should be instructed to regard all of these messages seriously and not to dismiss them and carry on connecting to the site.

Settings

In Chapter 6 you learned about Internet settings that impact the browser. In this section I'll refer you back to some security-related settings to review and discuss some other ones as well.

Pop-up blocker

Pop-up blockers were discussed in Chapter 6. Please review that section. The setting is shown in Figure 7.19.

Clearing browsing data/Clearing cache

These two items are set in the same place. The clearing of browser data or history was also discussed in Chapter 6. Please review that section. The setting for taking care of the browser data and the cache is shown in Figure 7.20.

FIGURE 7.19 Pop-up blocker

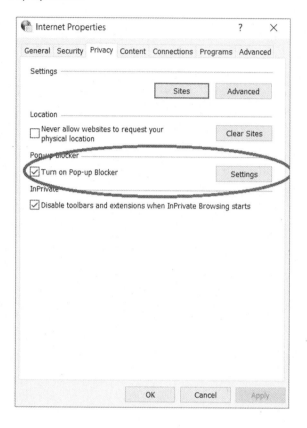

FIGURE 7.20 Clear browsing data and cache

Private-browsing mode

Most browsers today offer a private browsing mode. So what does this mean? Private browsers allow you to keep your Internet activity hidden from others who use the same computer or devices. This does not include:

- Your organization
- Your ISP

Cookies used during private browsing sessions can provide information about your browsing behavior to third parties. This means your web activity can still be tracked.

The setting for opening an InPrivate window is shown in Figure 7.21.

FIGURE 7.21 InPrivate browsing

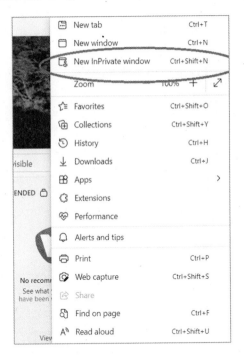

Sign-in/browser data synchronization

In Chapter 1 you learned about the synchronization of your sign-in and other browser data. Please review that chapter.

Ad blocker

Ad blockers are extensions that can be added to stop the constant stream of ads one encounters on the web. AdGuard AdBlocker is an easy way to block ads in the Microsoft Edge browser. It effectively blocks all types of advertising on all web pages, even on Facebook and YouTube.

Exam essentials

Identify security settings related to the browser.   These include pop-up blockers, clearing browsing data, clearing cache, private-browsing mode, sign-in/browser data synchronization, and using ad blockers.

Review Questions

You can find the answers in the appendix.

1. Which of the following is a series of two doors with a small room between them?
   A. Access control vestibule
   B. Trapdoor
   C. Badgetrap
   D. Safe room

2. Which of the following physical characteristics is used to identify the user?
   A. Hardware tokens
   B. Biometric locks
   C. Smartcards
   D. Badge readers

3. In which filtering is the type of filtering done on a router or firewall?
   A. MAC address filtering
   B. Email filtering
   C. IP address filtering
   D. URL filtering

4. Which of the following is used to ensure integrity?
   A. Rainbow tables
   B. Encryption
   C. Hashing
   D. Serializing

5. Which of the following was created as a first stab at security for wireless devices?
   A. WPA
   B. WPA2
   C. TKIP
   D. WEP

6. Which of the following was used to increase security in WPA?
   A. TKIP
   B. AES
   C. IPSec
   D. SSL

7. Which type of virus covers itself with protective code that stops debuggers or disassemblers from examining critical elements of the virus?

   A. Companion

   B. Macro

   C. Armored

   D. Multipartite

8. What element of a virus uniquely identifies it?

   A. ID

   B. Signature

   C. Badge

   D. Marking

9. Which of the following is the term used for someone being so close to you when you enter a building that they are able to come in right behind you without needing to use a key, a card, or any other security device?

   A. Shadowing

   B. Spoofing

   C. Tailgating

   D. Keyriding

10. Which of the following is the process of masquerading as another user or device?

    A. Shadowing

    B. Spoofing

    C. Duplicating

    D. Masking

11. Which Windows group allows members to install most software but keeps them from changing key operating system files?

    A. Power Users

    B. Guest

    C. Administrators

    D. Users

12. Which NTFS permission is the least required to run a program?

    A. List Folder Contents

    B. Full Control

    C. Read

    D. Write

13. Which of the following passwords is the strongest?

    A. password

    B. pAssword

    C. Pa$$word

    D. P@ssw0rd

14. What principle should drive the granting of permissions?

    A. Separation of duties

    B. Least privilege

    C. Job rotation

    D. Open rights

15. Which type of screen lock uses gestures?

    A. Fingerprint

    B. Face

    C. Swipe

    D. Passcode

16. Which method deletes all content on a lost mobile device?

    A. Remote wipe

    B. Geofencing

    C. Screen lock

    D. Segmentation of data

17. Which of the following involves applying a strong magnetic field to wipe the media?

    A. Degaussing

    B. Incineration

    C. Hammer

    D. Deleting

18. Which method of destroying the data on a hard drive is most effective?

    A. Degaussing

    B. Incineration

    C. Clearing

    D. Deleting

19. Which of the following was a concept that was designed to make it easier for less knowledgeable users to add a new client to the WLAN without manually entering the security information on the client?

    A. SSID

    B. WPS

    C. WEP

    D. WPA

20. Which of the following should always be changed from the default?

    A.   SSID

    B.   WPS

    C.   WEP

    D.   WPA

Chapter

8

Software Troubleshooting

COMPTIA A+ CERTIFICATION EXAM CORE 2 (220-1102) OBJECTIVES COVERED IN THIS CHAPTER:

✓ **3.1 Given a scenario, troubleshoot common Windows OS problems.**

- Common symptoms
  - Blue screen of death (BSOD)
  - Sluggish performance
  - Boot problems
  - Frequent shutdowns
  - Services not starting
  - Applications crashing
  - Low memory warnings
  - USB controller resource warnings
  - System instability
  - No OS found
  - Slow profile load
  - Time drift
- Common troubleshooting steps
  - Reboot
  - Restart services
  - Uninstall/reinstall/update applications
  - Add resources
  - Verify requirements
  - System file check
  - Repair Windows

- Restore
- Reimage
- Roll back updates
- Rebuild Windows profiles

✓ 3.2 Given a scenario, troubleshoot common personal computer (PC) security issues.

- Common symptoms
  - Unable to access the network
  - Desktop alerts
  - False alerts regarding antivirus protection
  - Altered system or personal files
  - Missing/renamed files
  - Unwanted notifications within the OS
  - OS update failures
- Browser-related symptoms
  - Random/frequent pop-ups
  - Certificate warnings
  - Redirection

✓ 3.3 Given a scenario, use best practice procedures for malware removal.

- 1. Investigate and verify malware symptoms
- 2. Quarantine infected systems
- 3. Disable System Restore in Windows
- 4. Remediate infected systems
  - Update anti-malware software
  - Scanning and removal techniques (e.g., safe mode, preinstallation environment)
- 5. Schedule scans and run updates
- 6. Enable System Restore and create a restore point in Windows
- 7. Educate the end user

✓ **3.4 Given a scenario, troubleshoot common mobile OS and application issues.**

- Common symptoms
    - Application fails to launch
    - Application fails to close/crashes
    - Application fails to update
    - Slow to respond
    - OS fails to update
    - Battery life issues
    - Randomly reboots
    - Connectivity issues
        - Bluetooth
        - WiFi
        - Near-field communication (NFC)
        - AirDrop
    - Screen does not autorotate

✓ **3.5 Given a scenario, troubleshoot common mobile OS and application security issues**

- Security concerns
    - Android package (APK) source
    - Developer mode
    - Root access/jailbreak
    - Bootleg/malicious application
    - Application spoofing
- Common symptoms
    - High network traffic
    - Sluggish response time
    - Data-usage limit notification
    - Limited Internet connectivity
    - No Internet connectivity

- High number of ads
- Fake security warnings
- Unexpected application behavior
- Leaked personal files/data

This chapter focuses on the exam topics related to software troubleshooting. It follows the structure of the CompTIA A+ 220-1002 exam blueprint, objective 3, and it explores the five subobjectives that you need to master before taking the exam.

3.1 Given a scenario, troubleshoot common Windows OS problems

Because it's software and there are so many places where things can go wrong, the operating system can be one of the most confusing components to troubleshoot. Sometimes it seems a miracle that operating systems even work at all, considering the hundreds of files that work together to make the system function. In this section common operating system issues and their solutions are covered.

Common symptoms

What follows in this section can seem like a daunting list of symptoms the operating system can exhibit. But with a proper plan of action and good backup (always have a backup!), you can approach any of these problems with confidence. In many cases today, technicians have ceased to spend significant amounts of time chasing operating system issues, since the most important data is kept on servers and computers can be reimaged so quickly that trouble-shooting doesn't warrant the effort. Nevertheless, you should know these basic symptoms and the approach to take when they present themselves

Blue screen of death (BSOD)

You learned about Blue screens of death in Chapter 5. Once a regular occurrence when working with Windows, blue screens (also known as the blue screen of death, or BSOD) have become less common. Occasionally, systems will lock up; you can usually examine the log files to discover what was happening when this occurred and take steps to correct it. Remember, when dealing with a blue screen, always ask yourself, "What did I just install or change?" In many cases, the change is involved in the BSOD. Also keep in mind that (as the instructions on the blue screen will tell you) a simple reboot will often fix the problem. Retaining the contents of the BSOD can help troubleshoot the issue. In most instances, you can find the BSOD error in Microsoft's knowledge base to help with troubleshooting.

Sluggish performance

Slow system performance can come from many issues. For the purposes of this discussion, I will focus on performance that deteriorates after being acceptable, as opposed to system performance that is poor from the outset (which could be a matter of insufficient resources such as RAM). Here is a list of possibilities:

- The first thing to check is the presence of a virus. If the system seems to have an over-abundance of disk activity, scan it for viruses using a virus program that resides externally on a CD/DVD, memory stick, or USB drive.

- Defragment the hard drive. The more fragmented it is, the slower the disk access will be.

- Check the space on the hard drive. When the partition or volume where the operating system is located becomes full, performance will suffer. This is why it is a good idea to store data and applications on a different partition from that holding the system files.

- Ensure that the latest updates are installed. In many cases, updates help to solve performance problems, so make sure they are current.

- Use Task Manager to determine whether a process is using too much memory or CPU or is simply locked up (not responding), and if necessary, end the process.

Boot problems

Booting problems can occur with corruption of the boot files or missing components. Common error messages include an invalid boot disk, inaccessible boot drive, missing NTLDR file, or missing BOOTMGR (some of which are discussed in more detail later in this section). Fortunately, during the installation of the operating system, log files are created in `C:\Windows`. If you have a puzzling problem, look at these logs and see whether you can find error entries there.

You can configure problems with system failure to write dump files (debugging information) for later analysis when they occur by clicking Start ➢ Control Panel ➢ System and then clicking the Advanced System Settings option. The Advanced tab of the System Properties dialog box should open. Then click the Settings button in the Startup And Recovery section. Here, in addition to choosing the default operating system, you can configure whether events should be written to the system log, whether an alert should be sent to the administrator, and what type of memory dump should be written.

Slow bootup

Slow bootups can be caused by a number of issues. First, it could be that the system is struggling for resources. This might indicate a memory or hard drive issue. It also can slow down the startup if many programs are set to start at bootup.

In cases where the computer belongs to a domain, it could also be having trouble locating the domain controller and perhaps performing policy updates.

Finally, it could be that the device is set to access a Distributed File System (DFS) share or other type of remote drive and locating it is the issue. (DFS is a system used to provide connections to shared folders without known their physical location.) The cause could also be the next issue in the list.

Frequent shutdowns

It doesn't get any more obvious that something is wrong than when the computer just shuts down on its own. In some cases, a blue screen on the display with a lot of text precedes this shutdown. If that occurs, the problem is related to the operating system and may not involve a hardware issue. Operating system issues related to the Blue Screen of Death was covered in the section "Proprietary crash screens (BSOD/pinwheel)" earlier in this chapter.

One common reason for shutdowns is overheating. Often when that is the case, however, the system reboots itself rather than just shutting down. Reboots are covered later in this section.

Always check the obvious, such as the power cable and the source of power. Check to see whether a circuit breaker flipped in the electrical panel as well. Checking these items is an example of starting the process at the physical layer. If the computer is plugged into a power strip or UPS that has a fuse or breaker, check to see whether the fuse blew or the breaker flipped because of a power surge.

Services not starting

Sometimes when the system is started, you receive a message that tells you a service failed to start. When that occurs, use the event log to determine the service that failed. Then, to interact with the service, access the Administrative Tools section of Control Panel and choose Services. This starts the Services console. You can right-click any service and choose to start, stop, pause, resume, or restart it. You can also double-click the service to access its properties and configure such things as the startup type, dependencies, and other variables.

If the service refuses to start, it could be that a service on which it depends will not start. To determine what services must be running for the problem service to start, select the Dependencies tab of the service's Properties dialog box, as shown in Figure 8.1.

In the figure you can see that the Remote Desktop service depends on both the RPC and Terminal Device Driver services to function. Try starting these services first. In some cases, you may need to trace the dependencies up several levels to get things going.

Applications crashing

Another possible symptom of a malware infection is the crashing of applications. While this will occur from time to time for other reasons, when it is occurring repeatedly, you should suspect malware. When the application that is crashing is your antivirus software, this is an even stronger indication of malware because disabling or damaging your antivirus protection is the first thing that some types of malware attempt to do.

FIGURE 8.1   Service dependencies

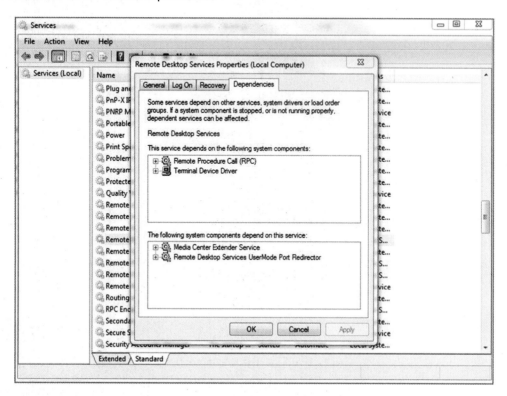

Low memory warnings

Another key indicator of a compromised host is increased memory consumption. Many times it is an indication that additional programs have been loaded into RAM so they can be processed. Then once they are loaded, they use RAM in the process of executing their tasks, whatever they may be. You can monitor memory consumption by using the same approach you use for CPU consumption. If memory usage cannot be accounted for, you should investigate it. (Review what you learned about buffer overflows, which are attacks that may display symptoms of increased memory consumption.)

USB controller resource warnings

Although it was mostly an issue with older Microsoft operating systems, you may encounter the error message shown in Figure 8.2.

FIGURE 8.2   USB controller resource warnings

There are three major situations that can cause this:

- USB Controller limit is exceeded—You've exceeded the available number of endpoints. USB 3.0 controllers have a limit of 96 endpoints per controller on Intel XHCI controllers whereas AM4 controllers support 254 endpoints.

- The USB port endpoints usage exceeded the limit—Most USB controllers are capped at 16 IN and 16 OUT endpoints.

- Power being drawn from the USB devices exceeds the maximum capacity.

System instability

System instability can arise from issues with the OS or with applications. Specifically these issues might be:

- Malware infection
- Damage due to shutdown during updates
- Damage to Registry keys
- Unstable third-party applications
- Unstable hardware

No OS found

The "no operating system found" message can result from a number of issues. Among them are the following:

- Incorrect boot device order in the BIOS
- Corrupted or missing boot sector
- Corrupted boot files

In short, the operating system is not actually missing; the system is missing the file that can either locate it or load it.

In Windows 10, if using Startup Repair does not work you may need to create a bootable disc to boot the device. The directions for this vary between the systems but can be found on the Microsoft site.

Slow profile load

Remote profiles are loaded from remote servers, and when location issues like the ones discussed in the previous section are present, this will hold up the startup process.

Time drift

When a system time keeps drifting, it is usually an issue with the CMOS battery.

The CMOS chip must have a constant source of power to keep its settings. To prevent the loss of data, motherboard manufacturers include a small battery to power the CMOS memory. On modern systems, this is a coin-style battery, about the diameter of a U.S. dime and about as thick. Figure 8.3 shows the location of the CMOS battery.

FIGURE 8.3 CMOS battery

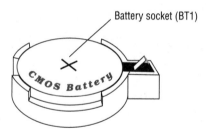

The CMOS clock is located on the computer's motherboard and keeps time when the computer is off. The operating system gets its time from the BIOS clock at boot time. This clock can be set using the BIOS if it is not correct. Figure 8.4 shows the time setting.

FIGURE 8.4 Setting the CMOS clock in the BIOS

Common troubleshooting steps

The following are common approaches to addressing the issues described in the previous section.

Reboot

You would be surprised how many system issues can be solved by a simple reboot. Therefore, the first step in many guides is a reboot. Always try this first.

Restart services

In some cases, it may not be necessary to kill the service—it may be advisable to simply restart the service. See the earlier section "Services not starting."

Uninstall/reinstall/update applications

To repair an application, consult the application vendor website. Most applications allow for a repair function if you attempt to reinstall the application when it is already installed.

Although updates sometimes cause issues, in most cases they solve issues. When an issue involves possible driver problems, check to see whether any of the devices involved have new updates available. You can try this using Windows Update or by going to the vendor website. Sometimes they have tools that can scan your entire system for potential driver updates.

Add resources

In some cases there will no escaping the fact that the system does not have the resources to handle the workload. Adding the following resources will address performance issues related to insufficient resources:

- Memory
- CPU

Adding disk resources will only be beneficial when the partition where the operating system is located is full. In that case, adding disk resources and extending that partition to give it extra room will help.

Adding network interfaces will only be beneficial when a performance issue is due to slow in-out performance on the current interface(s).

Verify requirements

Some issues are related to not reading the instructions. All operating systems and applications require a minimum of each compute resource to function. In most cases you will be alerted to the fact you don't meet the minimums during the installation, but not always. If you have issues, always consider the possibility that you need more resources. Even better, read the documentation before installation.

System file check

Some issues are caused by damaged or corrupted system files. In Chapter 6 you learned about the Windows tool System File checker (SFC), which you can use to both verify system files and repair those that are damaged or corrupted.

Repair/Restore Windows

In some cases, the easiest way to repair an issue is to completely reinstall the operating system. This is one of the biggest reasons you should encourage users to store data on servers rather than the workstation. However, operating system vendors are beginning to offer some options that are less drastic. They have also made it easier to perform various recovery types with no media.

For example, in Windows 10, there are several options presented when you choose to repair the computer:

Refresh   This reinstalls Windows and keeps your personal files and settings. It also keeps the apps that came with your PC and the apps you installed from the Windows Store.

Reset   This reinstalls Windows but deletes your files, settings, and apps—except for the apps that came with your PC.

Restore   This is a way to undo recent system changes you've made by returning the system configuration to a previous point in time. It does not delete any files or applications, unless the application was installed after the restore point was taken.

To access these options, follow these steps:

1. Swipe in from the right edge of the screen, tap Settings, and then tap Change PC Settings. (If you're using a mouse, point to the upper-right corner of the screen, move the mouse pointer down, click Settings, and then click Change PC Settings.)

2. Tap or click Update And Recovery and then tap or click Recovery.

3. You will now see the three options shown in Figure 8.5.

FIGURE 8.5   Recovery

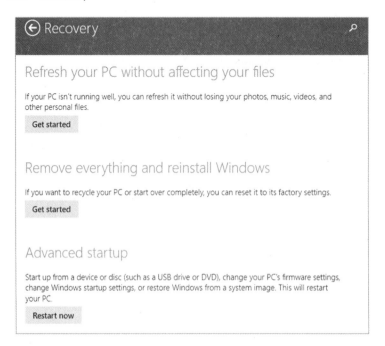

Reimage

In some cases, especially in the case of a serious malware infection, it is simpler to just reimage the device and start over with a clean installation. For this reason, always encourage users to *not* save data on the local hard drive, as this will complicate the issue. If they insist, at least convince them to perform their own data backups.

Roll back updates

Vendors test updates before rolling them out, but it is impossible for them to anticipate every scenario in which the update may be introduced. For this reason, an update might break something. In that case, the issues should occur soon after the update. It's always worth the attempt to roll back the update, since it is simple to do. Just locate the update in the list of installed updates and select to remove the update.

Roll back devices drivers

It's rare for a driver update to fail, but sometimes they do. If you install a new driver and there is an issue, you can use the Rollback Driver feature to revert to the old driver. The Rollback Driver option is found in Device Manager on the Driver tab of the device.

Rebuild Windows profiles

To fix a corrupted user profile on a Windows 10 computer, follow these steps:

1. Go to Control Panel.
2. Go to User Accounts (or Accounts And Family Safety ➤ User Accounts).
3. Click Manage Another Account.
4. Click Create A New Account (Add A New User in the PC settings in Windows 11) to create a new account on your computer.
5. Type a name and choose an account type.
6. Click Create Account.
7. Choose Account Type For New User.
8. Open File Explorer or My Computer.
9. Click Tools. If you don't see the Tools item at the top of the window, press the Alt key.
10. Click Folder Options.
11. Select the View tab.
12. Check the Show Hidden Files And Folders option.
13. Deselect the Hide Protected Operating System Files option.
14. Click Apply.
15. Click OK.
16. Go to C:\Users*OLD_USERNAME*, where C:\ is where your Windows is installed and *OLD_USERNAME* is the username that has the corrupted profile error.

17. From this folder (*OLD_USERNAME*), select all files except `ntuser.data`, `ntuser.data.log`, and `ntuser.ini`.

18. Right-click these files (except the files mentioned in the previous step) and click Copy.

19. Go to `C:\User\`*NEW_USERNAME*, where *NEW_USERNAME* is the username you created as new.

20. Paste all files in this folder, `NEW_USERNAME`.

21. Restart the computer and log in with the new username you've created.

Exam essentials

Identify the most common symptoms of operating system and system boot problems.   These include BSODs, boot failures, problems from improper shutdowns, spontaneous shutdowns/restarts, devices that fail to start, slow system performance, files that fail to open, missing items (NTLDR, `boot.ini`, operating system, GUI), and invalid boot disk.

Identify the most common solutions to operating system issues.   These include but are not limited to defragmenting the hard drive, rebooting, killing tasks, restarting services, updating network settings, reimaging/reloading the OS, rolling back updates, rolling back devices drivers. and applying updates

3.2 Given a scenario, troubleshoot common personal computer (PC) security issues

System issues in many cases have security breaches at the root of the cause. It has become almost a given that any problem that cannot be traced to any other cause should be attacked by first scanning for viruses and malware. This section discusses common symptoms of security-related failures and tools that can be used to mitigate the damage.

Common symptoms

Systems can display many symptoms when something is amiss. Not all are malware related, but crazy things start to happen when malware is introduced to a computer. This section discusses some of the strange behaviors of computers that are infected as well as issues unrelated to malware.

Unable to access the network

When network connectivity is an issue, you should ensure the following about your configuration:

- Is the IP address in the same network as the default gateway address?
- Is the subnet mask correct?
- Is the default gateway address correct?
- If this is all correct, has the interface been enabled?
- If this is all correct, it's time to check the settings on the router.

Some malware will affect your Internet access. It may block you from accessing certain sites, or it may allow access to only a small number of sites. It has been reported that viral programs block access for certain programs and browsers while still allowing others to function. When access is denied, a message like the following is generated:

```
Unable to connect to HTTP Proxy. Your proxy may be misconfigured or
offline. -336
```

Moreover, this occurred even after the virus was supposedly cleaned from the system.

Desktop alerts

Sometimes you can tell by security warnings that the site you are on is attempting to attack your computer. This is true if you have a personal firewall such as Windows Firewall. It can also occur when you have the phishing filter enabled in Bing. You will know when the system asks you whether you want to allow access to your machine from the site. Unless you initiated a download, don't allow it.

False alerts regarding antivirus protection

If you receive messages (again, usually at a suspect website) warning you that your system is infected, it will also usually offer to clean the system. At a minimum, they are trying to sell you antimalware software through the bogus warning.

Worse, though, is that executing the "cleaning" sometimes results in the introduction of malware to the system—which was the whole point of the message to begin with. In general, pay no attention to these messages and try to close them and exit the website that generated them as quickly as possible.

Altered system or personal files

Malware can also make changes to files and to the operating system itself. Many viruses delete key files in your system to render it inoperable. This could be one of the ways it renders any existing antivirus programs inoperable. It also can be part of disabling Internet access either completely or selectively.

Missing/renamed files

Many viruses will rename system files and adopt the name of the system file. This can help the virus escape detection when scanning occurs since most virus definitions identify the virus by the name of the file that introduced the virus. This renaming of the system file can cause big problems when the file is required and the virus file is incapable of providing the required functionality.

Unwanted notifications within the OS

The operating system can generate a lot of messages called notifications that are designed to keep you informed about the health and security of the system. In some cases you aren't really interested in all these messages. You can control the notifications that you review.

In System settings, as shown in Figure 8.6, you can allow or disallow any types of notifications. Before you go too crazy, keep in mind you probably want to get some of the notifications.

FIGURE 8.6   Notification settings

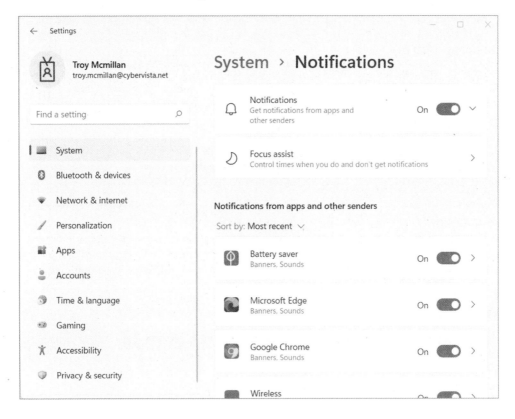

OS update failures

Malware may take certain measures to protect itself. One of these is to block you from accessing operating system update sites like Windows Update. You never notice this because these updates can be set to run automatically, so when they fail, it may not be obvious that they did.

Another action the malware can take along the same lines is to disable your antivirus software. For this reason, any time your antivirus program notifies you that it is not functional or cannot update itself, you should consider this possibility and get it back up and running (if you can) as soon as possible.

Browser-related symptoms

Some issues are related to the browser. In this section you'll learn about browser-related problems.

Random/frequent pop-ups

Although relatively benign when compared with malware in general, pop-ups are annoying to users. They also use system resources since they open and in some cases can introduce additional malware when they open.

Fortunately, most browsers now contain pop-up blockers that can prevent unwanted pop-ups. In some cases, users want pop-ups to be allowed—in fact, some website functions fail when a pop-up blocker is enabled. For that reason, users can use the Pop-Up Blocker Settings of Bing to allow pop-ups for certain websites, as shown in Figure 8.7. Other browsers usually have a similar setting.

FIGURE 8.7   The Pop-Up Blocker Settings dialog box

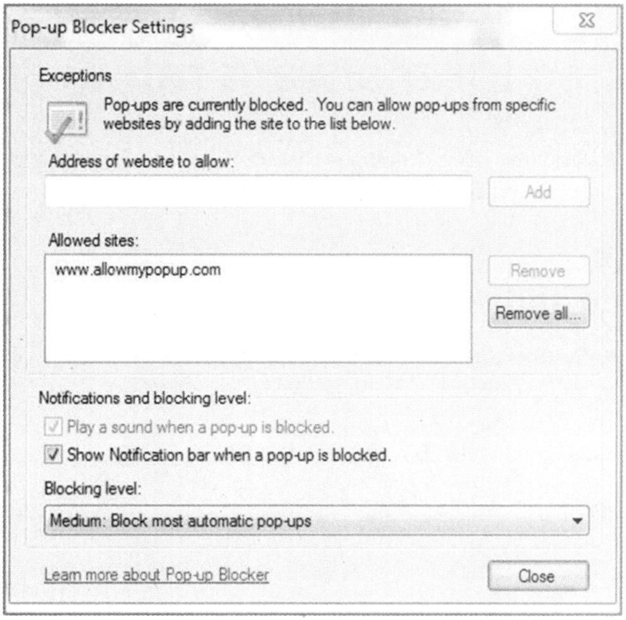

Certificate warnings

When you are bombarded with certificate error messages at every website you visit, it's another sign of malware. Some types of malware interface with the certificate authentication process.

Redirection

A browser redirection is one of the most serious security problems. Browser hijacking software is external code that changes your Bing settings. It may include changing your home page or adding or removing items from your favorites. Some sites will be added that point to dubious content. In most cases, the home page will revert to the unwanted destination even if you change it manually because the hijacker made Registry changes to your system. To prevent this from occurring, remember these tips:

- Avoid suspect sites.
- Use and update an antivirus program regularly.
- Tighten your browser security settings.

Once you are a victim, you may have to apply antivirus software from an external source.

Exam essentials

Identify the most common symptoms displayed from security issues.   These include but are not limited to pop-ups, browser redirection, security alerts, slow performance, Internet connectivity issues, OS updates failures, rogue antivirus, and renamed system files.

3.3 Given a scenario, use best practice procedures for malware removal

Over time best practices have been developed through trial and error that help minimize the chances of getting viruses and reduce the effort involved in getting rid of malware. Some of these practices are discussed in this section

1. Investigate and verify malware symptoms

First, identify the symptoms the malware is producing as clearly as you can. This can help identify the exact virus in some cases. In many scenarios, identifying the symptoms can help establish the severity of the infection, which is good to determine when IT resources are stretched thin and battles must be chosen.

2. Quarantine infected systems

The infected system should be quarantined—removed from the network to prevent a spread of the infection to other systems. This is why it is a good practice to keep data on servers so that when user systems need to be quarantined, a new machine can be quickly imaged for the user to reduce the impacts on productivity while the infected machine is cleaned.

3. Disable System Restore in Windows

System Restore is a useful tool in many cases, but when a virus infection occurs, it can be an ally of the virus. Virus scanners cannot clean infections from restore points, making reinfection possible. If a system restore is performed after running an antispyware utility, viral objects may reappear. Disable System Restore before attempting to clean a system. When you do this, you will delete all restore points in the system, including any that may have an infection.

4. Remediate infected systems

Once the infected system has been quarantined, you must take steps to clean it. This two-step process is discussed in this section.

Update anti-malware software

Before scanning the system with antivirus software, update the software and the engine if necessary. Definition files can change daily, and the virus may be so new that it is not contained in your current definitions file even if it is only a week old.

Scanning and removal techniques (e.g., safe mode, preinstallation environment)

Although you can run the scan and removal from the GUI, it is a best practice to do this either after booting to safe mode or from a preinstallation environment like Windows PE. Viruses that evade detection in the GUI cannot do so as easily in either of these environments.

5. Schedule scans and run updates

The antivirus software can be scheduled to perform a scan of the system. You should set this up to occur when the system is not in use, like at night. The scanning process will go faster then and will not affect users. Also, set the software to automatically check for and install any updates to the definition files and to the engine when available.

6. Enable System Restore and create a restore point in Windows

Although it is recommended that you disable System Restore before cleaning an infection, it is a good idea to create a restore point after an infection is cleaned. This gives you a clean restore point going forward in case the system becomes infected again at some point. For non-Windows systems, a backup should be performed at this time.

7. Educate the end user

In many cases, users are partly responsible for the virus infection. After an infection occurs is a great time to impress on users the principles of secure computing. They should be reminded that antivirus software and firewalls can go only so far in protecting them and that they should exercise safe browsing habits and refrain from opening any attachments in email from unknown sources, regardless of how tempting.

Exam essentials

Identify the steps to remove malware. According to best practices, the steps to address malware removal are as follows:

1. Identify malware symptoms.
2. Quarantine infected system.
3. Disable System Restore.
4. Remediate infected systems, including updating antivirus software.
5. Scan and remove the malware.
6. Enable System Restore and create a restore point.
7. Educate end users.

3.4 Given a scenario, troubleshoot common mobile OS and application issues

Mobile devices have their own unique sets of issues that may not be encountered with desktop computers. In this section I'll discuss common issues and their solutions.

Common symptoms

Not all mobile device issues are unique to mobile devices. They suffer from many of the same issues as desktop machines. However, some problems are unique to mobile devices or at least more prone to occur with them, as you will learn in this section.

Application fails to launch

When applications will not launch, there are several possible explanations:

- Malware has infected the system and is using all the resources.
- Too many applications are open at the same time.
- There is a lack of storage space to open the application file.
- There is an unstable Internet connection when opening the app on a remote server.

Application fails to close/crashes

Application crashes or lockups (won't shut down) can also have a variety of causes, some of which also cause launch failures. Causes include:

- Inadequate testing before launch by developer
- Memory issues that are robbing the system of resources
- Malware infection
- Unstable network connection
- Corrupted cache files, which have not been cleared in a long time

Application fails to update

Although vendors have attempted to make updates as trouble-free as possible, sometimes updates still fail. Some possible reasons for this include the following:

- No room—Updates must be downloaded before they can be executed. When there is a lack of space to hold the update, the process will fail.
- Multiple updates in the queue in the wrong order—Updates build on one another, and you may not be able to apply one until another has been applied. If updates are out of order in the queue and you are attempting to apply one that has a prerequisite update that has not been run, the process will fail.
- Drive conflicts—Bad drivers and driver conflicts can cause all sorts of issues—among them, failed updates.
- Corrupted system files—Updates may require the operation of a system file to complete. If system files are corrupted, it can cause an update to fail.
- Update system failure—Sometimes it's the fault of the application managing the updates. For example, there have been a number of occasions when the Windows Update system itself has caused updates to fail.

Slow to respond

When malware is present and running in the background, it is using resources as well as running down your battery. That means when you are downloading or uploading data, the process is competing with the malware for resources. Therefore, slow data speeds or latency in the response may also be a sign of a malware infection.

OS fails to update

Operating system updates, like any type of update, can fail. Earlier in this chapter you learned why updates can fail. Please review that section.

Battery life issues

One of the biggest complaints users lodge against their mobile devices is short battery life. When a battery is nearing the end of its life cycle, it will begin to fail to hold a charge, so it could be you need a new battery. However, there are a number of other things you can do to mitigate the problem:

- Change the location and brightness settings, because these components really eat power.
- Turn off Bluetooth and WiFi when not needed. These also take power.
- Disable push notifications for nonessential apps.
- Close apps not in use.
- Prevent the device from overheating, which is bad for the battery.

Randomly reboots

As you learned in Chapter 3, "Hardware," one of the biggest causes of random reboots is overheating of the system. A mobile device can overheat when you are doing too many things at once or when you keep running the system when the battery is low. Reboots can also be caused by a malware infection and by failing updates that require reboots.

Connectivity issues

Some issues are related to the network connection of the device. In this section you'll see some variations on this theme.

Bluetooth

In Chapter 1, "Mobile Devices," you learned that unattended Bluetooth connections can be a serious issue. You also learned what issues can prevent a Bluetooth connection. Please review that chapter.

WiFi

When there is no wireless connectivity, it is usually because of one of two things:

- The wireless capability is disabled (usually with a key combination or a function key); it is easy to disable inadvertently. There can also be a hardware switch on the side, front, or back of the case.

- The wireless antenna is bad or the cable needs to be reseated.

Try the following steps when troubleshooting a lack of wireless connectivity:

1. Power-cycle the AP or wireless router.
2. Power-cycle the device.
3. On a laptop, check the hardware wireless button (if the laptop has one).
4. On a smartphone or tablet, check your wireless settings to ensure that Wi-Fi is on. Also make sure that Airplane mode is off.
5. Disconnect and reconnect.
6. Verify that the wireless device is using the correct password.

Near-field communication (NFC)

In Chapter 1 you learned about near-field communication (NFC). If NFC is not working on a mobile device, check the following:

- Ensure that it is NFC compatible—there should be an NFC logo on the device if so.
- Remove the case or skin—in some cases these may be blocking the transmission.
- When touching the NFC device or the mobile device to the top of the retail unit, check the connection status of the mobile device. The mobile device may not be recognized if you touch the wrong area of the unit or touch it too quickly.
- NFC sensitivity may not be strong enough to connect the unit.

AirDrop

AirDrop transfers files among supported Mac computers and iOS devices by means of close-range wireless communication. When it is not working, reasons include:

- The device doesn't support AirDrop—not all Mac systems support this function.
- Missing updates—yes, this can cause issues with AirDrop.
- Ensure your visibility is set properly to allow you to be seen by the destination device.
- Ensure Do Not Disturb is *not* enabled.
- Version incompatibility—some older devices run a different version, which may be incompatible.
- Ensure "Block all incoming connections" is *not* enabled.
- Are Bluetooth and Wi-Fi enabled? They must be for functionality.

Screen does not autorotate

Autorotate rotates the desktop to landscape or portrait mode automatically depending on the orientation of the screen. When it is not working, check the following:

- Check for updates.
- Try restarting.

- Disconnect peripherals.
- Ensure Rotation Lock is off.
- If this is Windows, try running the Sensors troubleshooter.
- Update the motion sensor driver.
- As a *last resort only*, edit the Registry key.

  Specifically, do the following:

1. Navigate to: `HKEY_LOCAL_MACHINE\SOFTWARE\Microsoft\Windows\CurrentVersion\AutoRotation`.
2. Double-click `Enable` dword and make sure the value is set to 1. Click OK.
3. Double-click the `LastOrientation` dword and make sure the value is set to 0. Click OK.
4. Double-click the `SensorPresent` dword and make sure the value is set to 1. Click OK.
5. Double-click the `SlateEnable` dword and make sure the value is set to 1. Click OK.
6. Save the settings.

Exam essentials

Identify common mobile device issues.   These include but are not limited to intermittent wireless, no wireless connectivity, no Bluetooth connectivity, random reboots, and battery issues

3.5 Given a scenario, troubleshoot common mobile OS and application security issues

Mobile devices may use different operating systems than desktop systems, and their applications may be packaged a bit differently, but they still can suffer from security issues. It logically follows that they must be secured as well. In this final section of Chapter 8, I'll talk about the symptoms of security issues and describe some tools you can use in the struggle to protect these devices and their data.

Security concerns

Just as desktop systems do, mobile devices can suffer security issues. In this section you'll learn about some of the issues.

Android package (APK) source

Android Application Package (APK) is a file format that is used by the Android operating system. Android uses this file format for the distribution and installation of Android applications, which can be mobile apps or mobile games. Proper APKs can access only a limited range of system resources.

Security issues can arise when APKs are obtained from questionable sources. Application signatures play an important role in device security and are used for permissions checks as well as software updates. Best practices with regard to developing applications to run on Android include:

- Review source code.
- Use automated testing.
- Sign system images.
- Sign applications.

Developer mode

Developer mode in Windows 11 is a mode that can be used to test apps more easily, to use the Ubuntu Bash shell environment, and to change a variety of developer-focused settings. The Developer Mode setting is available in the Settings app. To access it, head to Settings > Update & Security, select For Developers, and select Developer Mode.

The security issues arise from the fact that if you select Developer Mode you can install UWP (Universal Windows Platform) apps from outside the Windows Store, even if they're not signed. For this reason applications developed using this tool should undergo a robust security assessment.

Root access/jailbreak

While rooting or jailbreaking a device enables the user to remove some of the restrictions of the device, it also presents security issues. Jailbreaking removes the security restrictions on your iPhone or iPad. This means apps are given access to the core functions of the device, which normally requires the user's consent. It also allows the installation of apps not found in the App Store. One of the reasons those apps are not in the App Store is that they are either insecure or malware masquerading as a legitimate app. Finally, a rooted or jailbroken device receives no security updates, making it even more vulnerable.

Bootleg/malicious application

Unsigned applications represent code that cannot be verified to be what it purports to be or to be free of malware. While many unsigned applications present absolutely no security issues, most enterprises wisely chose to forbid their installation. Mobile device management (MDM) software and security settings in the devices themselves can be used to prevent this.

System apps are those that come preinstalled on the device. While these apps probably present no security issue, some of them run all the time, so it might be beneficial to remove them to save space and improve performance. The organization also might decide that removing some system apps is necessary to disable features in these apps that can disclose information about the user or the device that could lead to a social engineering attack. By following the instructions on the vendor site, these apps can be removed.

Application spoofing

Mobile application spoofing is an attack where a malicious mobile app mimics the visual appearance of another one. A great example of this is when a social engineering attack leads you to a fake website that looks just like a legitimate one. While you can't stand over users and advise them at every turn, instilling users with a healthy dose of suspicion through security awareness training can certainly help.

Common symptoms

Just as desktop systems do, mobile devices will exhibit certain symptoms when security issues manifest themselves. This section surveys some common symptoms of a security issue with a device.

High network traffic

In any case where the device appears to be utilizing CPU and memory at a rate that is not consistent with the activities of the user, it is a sign that malware is possibly at work on the device. A good example of this is lots of network activity not initiated by the user. Malware will utilize resources in the process of performing whatever functions it has been designed to perform. When there is unexplained excessive resource usage, it is another indication that the device has been compromised. With respect to network traffic, the malware could be attempting to connect to the hacker.

Sluggish response time

Whenever a device is sluggish, it means there is a struggle for resources in the system. While this could be due to attempting to do too many things at once (such as running too many apps), it can also be a sign of malware. Malware requires resources to operate, so again, when there is unexplained excessive resource usage, it is another indication that the device has been compromised.

Data-usage limit notification

When certain types of malware begin to operate on a mobile device, they may transmit data from the device to the hacker, or vice versa. Since this uses your data plan without your knowledge, you may suddenly find yourself over your data limit. You may not find this out until you receive a data bill that exceeds your mortgage payment. In any cases such as this, the device should be immediately scanned for malware.

Limited Internet connectivity/No Internet connectivity

Whenever a device cannot access the Internet or can only access certain sites on the Internet, it is another sign of malware. Some malware creates entries in the host file and prevents the system from using DNS to obtain the IP address of a site. This results in one only being able to access sites with these host file entries. In other cases it simply prevents Internet access altogether.

High number of ads

When the system suddenly seems to be getting a lot of unsolicited ads, it is…you guessed it—a sign of malware, in this case, a type called adware. In Chapter 7, "Security," you learned about spyware, which tracks your activity. Sometimes the spyware is not trying to steal data but is trying to learn your interests so that it can target ads to those interests.

Fake security warnings

Users can be motivated to do things they shouldn't if they are alarmed or if they have been convinced that a situation is urgent. These two principles are what make social engineering attacks successful. When users receive warnings that their system has been compromised and that they need to install a software "solution," in a fit of fear they might disregard what you've taught them and install the software (thus installing the malware). Users should be taught to never install these tools that are offered and to report any notices about a system compromise to the administrator.

Unexpected application behavior

Whenever applications are exhibiting odd behavior, it's a sign that application is corrupted at the least and that malware is present at the worst. If reinstalling the app does not solve the issue, it's time to suspect and look for malware.

Leaked personal files/data

Obviously, if personal files located on a mobile device suddenly are gone or suddenly are found to be leaked, it is also a clue that the device has been compromised through either malware or social engineering.

Exam essentials

Describe common mobile device issues.　　Some of the symptoms include high network traffic, sluggish response, slow data speeds, high network traffic, and leaked personal files/data.

Review Questions

You can find the answers in the appendix.

1. Which of the following is the first thing to check when system performance is sluggish?
   A. Malware
   B. Fragmentation
   C. Lack of space
   D. Missing update

2. When having issues accessing the network, what should you check last?
   A. IP address
   B. Subnet mask
   C. Default gateway
   D. Router settings

3. What is the third step in malware removal?
   A. Quarantine infected systems.
   B. Remediate infected systems.
   C. Disable System Restore in Windows.
   D. Investigate and verify malware symptoms.

4. The "no operating system found" message can result from a number of issues. Which of the following is *not* among them?
   A. Corrupted boot files
   B. Incorrect boot device order in the BIOS
   C. Missing boot sector
   D. Lack of permissions

5. Which of the following is *the least likely* sign of a malware infection?
   A. Slow performance
   B. High network traffic
   C. Data limit messages
   D. Overheating

6. What is external code that changes your browser settings?
   A. On-path attack
   B. Browser redirection
   C. SYN flood
   D. Fraggle

7. Which of the following is not a symptom of malware?

   A. Increase in performance

   B. Internet connectivity issues

   C. Browser redirection

   D. Pop-ups

8. Which of the following is the first step in malware removal?

   A. Remediate the infected systems.

   B. Quarantine the infected systems.

   C. Educate the end user.

   D. Identify and research malware symptoms.

9. What Windows service should be disabled before cleaning an infection?

   A. NAT

   B. System Restore

   C. Windows Firewall

   D. Antivirus

10. Which of the following does *not* negatively impact mobile battery life?

   A. Low brightness setting

   B. Location services

   C. Enabled Bluetooth

   D. Overheating device

11. Which of the following does not cause overheating of a mobile device?

   A. Excessive gaming

   B. Leaving phone on

   C. Old battery

   D. Continuous online browsing

12. Which of the following is *not* an indication of a security issue with a mobile device?

   A. Power drain

   B. Weak signal

   C. Slow speeds

   D. Low resource utilization

13. Which of the following is an indication of a security issue with a mobile device?

   A. Low resource utilization

   B. Disabled microphone

   C. Enabled camera

   D. Authorized account access

Chapter

9

Operational Procedures

COMPTIA A+ CERTIFICATION EXAM CORE 2 (220-1002) OBJECTIVES COVERED IN THIS CHAPTER:

✓ **4.1 Given a scenario, implement best practices associated with documentation and support systems information management.**

- Ticketing systems
    - User information
    - Device information
    - Description of problems
    - Categories
    - Severity
    - Escalation levels
    - Clear, concise written communication
        - Problem description
        - Progress notes
        - Problem resolution
- Asset management
    - Inventory lists
    - Database system
    - Asset tags and IDs
    - Procurement life cycle
    - Warranty and licensing
    - Assigned users
- Types of documents
    - Acceptable use policy (AUP)
    - Network topology diagram

- **Regulatory compliance requirements**
    - **Splash screens**
    - **Incident reports**
- **Standard operating procedures**
    - **Procedures for custom installation of software package**
- **New-user setup checklist**
- **End-user termination checklist**
- **Knowledge base/articles**

✓ **4.2 Explain basic change-management best practices.**

- **Documented business processes**
    - **Rollback plan**
    - **Sandbox testing**
    - **Responsible staff member**
- **Change management**
- **Request forms**
    - **Purpose of the change**
    - **Scope of the change**
    - **Date and time of the change**
    - **Affected systems/impact**
    - **Risk analysis**
        - **Risk level**
    - **Change board approvals**
    - **End-user acceptance**

✓ **4.3 Given a scenario, implement workstation backup and recovery methods.**

- **Backup and recovery**
    - **Full**
    - **Incremental**

- Differential
- Synthetic
- Backup testing
  - Frequency
- Backup rotation schemes
  - On site vs. off site
  - Grandfather-father-son (GFS)
  - 3-2-1 backup rule

✓ 4.4 Given a scenario, use common safety procedures.

- Electrostatic discharge (ESD) straps
- ESD mats
- Equipment grounding
- Proper power handling
- Proper component handling and storage
- Antistatic bags
- Compliance with government regulations
- Personal safety
  - Disconnect power before repairing PC
  - Lifting techniques
  - Electrical fire safety
  - Safety goggles
  - Air filtration mask

✓ 4.5 Summarize environmental impacts and local environmental controls.

- Material safety data sheet (MSDS)/documentation for handling and disposal
  - Proper battery disposal
  - Proper toner disposal
  - Proper disposal of other devices and assets

- Temperature, humidity-level awareness, and proper ventilation
  - Location/equipment placement
  - Dust cleanup
  - Compressed air/vacuums
- Power surges, under-voltage events, and power failures
  - Battery backup
  - Surge suppressor

✓ 4.6 Explain the importance of prohibited content/activity and privacy, licensing, and policy concepts.

- Incident response
  - Chain of custody
  - Inform management/law enforcement as necessary
  - Copy of drive (data integrity and preservation)
  - Documentation of incident
- Licensing/digital rights management (DRM)/end-user license agreement (EULA)
  - Valid licenses
  - Non-expired licenses
  - Personal use license vs. corporate use license
  - Open-source license
- Regulated data
  - Credit card transactions
  - Personal government-issued information
  - PII
  - Healthcare data
  - Data retention requirements

✓ **4.7 Given a scenario, use proper communication techniques and professionalism.**

- Professional appearance and attire
  - Match the required attire of the given environment
    - Formal
    - Business casual
- Use proper language and avoid jargon, acronyms, and slang, when applicable
- Maintain a positive attitude/project confidence
- Actively listen, take notes, and avoid interrupting the customer
- Be culturally sensitive
  - Use appropriate professional titles, when applicable
- Be on time (if late, contact the customer)
- Avoid distractions
  - Personal calls
  - Texting/social media sites
  - Personal interruptions
- Dealing with difficult customers or situations
  - Do not argue with customers or be defensive
  - Avoid dismissing customer problems
  - Avoid being judgmental
  - Clarify customer statements (ask open-ended questions to narrow the scope of the problem, restate the issue, or question to verify understanding)
  - Do not disclose experience via social media outlets
- Set and meet expectations/time line and communicate status with the customer
  - Offer repair/replacement options, as needed
  - Provide proper documentation on the services provided

- Follow up with customer/user at a later date to verify satisfaction
- Deal appropriately with customers' confidential and private materials
  - Located on a computer, desktop, printer, etc.

✓ 4.8 Identify the basics of scripting.

- Script file types
  - Match the required attire of the given environment
    - .bat
    - .ps1
    - .vbs
    - .sh
    - .js
    - .py
- Use cases for scripting
  - Basic automation
  - Restarting machines
  - Remapping network drives
  - Installation of applications
  - Automated backups
  - Gathering of information/data
  - Initiating updates
- Other considerations when using scripts
  - Unintentionally introducing malware
  - Inadvertently changing system settings
  - Browser or system crashes due to mishandling of resources

✓ **4.9 Given a scenario, use remote access technologies.**

- ▪ Methods/tools
  - ▪ RDP
  - ▪ VPN
  - ▪ Virtual network computer (VNC)
  - ▪ Secure Shell (SSH)
  - ▪ (RMM)
  - ▪ Microsoft Remote Assistance (MSRA)
  - ▪ Third-party tools
    - ▪ Screen-sharing software
    - ▪ Video-conferencing software
    - ▪ File transfer software
    - ▪ Desktop management software
- ▪ Security considerations of each access method

This chapter will focus on the exam topics related to daily procedures. It will follow the structure of the CompTIA A+ 220-1102 exam blueprint, objective 4, and it will explore the nine subobjectives that you need to master before taking the exam.

4.1 Given a scenario, implement best practices associated with documentation and support systems information management

If you ever heard the adage "the job isn't done until the paperwork is done," then you may grasp the importance of documentation. In this section we'll talk about some of documentation you should be generating and updating.

Ticketing systems

When network and security issues arise, organizations need some way to collect and store the details of each incident and a system to address each issue in a time frame that is appropriate for each incident based in the incident priority. In this section you'll learn about the types of information that a ticketing system needs to collect to be able to accomplish this goal.

User information

A ticketing system must be capable of recording the user involved in the incident. This could be the person who reported the issue, but it might not. In some cases, one user may report an issue that impacts another user more directly, like when one user discovers that a file owned by another user is suddenly gone. In other cases, a user may report an incident that could have been caused by another user. The system should be capable of colleting all user involvement.

Device information

All information about the devices that are involved should also be collected. This includes device name, IP address, MAC address, subnet mask, and default gateway. In cases where device spoofing is involved, collecting all the data may make it possible to verify that someone is masquerading as a legitimate device.

Description of problems

A complete description of the incident should be generated. Keep in mind that as an investigation proceeds, the description might change as more information becomes available. Don't allow the team to get locked into the first impression of the event, which may cause a discounting of new evidence.

Categories

Not all incidents require the same sense of urgency. Categories should be created to organize incidents by their potential impact. For example, a data breach requires a greater sense of urgency than a password reset.

Severity

Utilizing the assignment of incidents to severity categories, incidents should be dealt with not in the order they are received but by utilizing a system somewhat like a triage in an emergency room, where they are treated based on the severity of their issue. This means that, just as sometimes occurs in the emergency room, a brand-new issue may require dropping efforts on other issues to address the new, more serious issue.

Escalation levels

Escalation procedures are created to prevent technicians from spending too much time on an issue they don't completely understand. Creating levels or tiers of technicians with an increasing amount of knowledge and experience is a best practice. This offers two benefits. It encourages a faster solution by preventing issues remaining unresolved from a lack of skill by the responding technician, and it frees up more experienced technicians to deal with more serious issues. There should be a hard time limit placed on the solution of issues before an escalation is required.

Clear, concise written communication

While technicians are not required to be professional writers, they do need to be able to create clear and concise written communications regarding an incident or issue. In this section you'll see what is included in a clear and concise issue statement.

Problem description

The problem description should describe what evidence caused the issue to be reported, what systems are affected, and what causes might be initially suspected. Keep in mind the problem description may change over time as more data is collected. The documentation should reflect these changes to the description.

Progress notes

The progress notes should reflect every effort that has been made to resolve the issue and the results of each operation. These progress notes make a great reference when similar issues arise in the future. Placing them in a searchable database is a great idea.

Problem resolution

Once the issue is resolved, the solution must be recorded with great detail. This information should also be placed in a searchable database and should be used to generate a lessons learned document to initiate actions to prevent the same issue in the future.

Asset management

Asset or inventory management includes knowing what you have. You can't know that something is missing until you take an inventory, so this should be done on a regular basis. In this section you'll learn about tools and methods used to maintain an inventory-tracking system.

Inventory lists

The basis of any robust asset management system is the inventory list itself. If it's incorrect, then the whole system will fail. Inventory counts and recounts should be performed regularly to catch errors and identify thefts and other losses. What type of information is useful to record in these inventories? You may choose to record more, but three items should certainly be included.

Make

The manufacturer of the device should be recorded and the name they give the device should as well.

Model

The exact model number should be recorded in full, leaving nothing out. Sometimes those dangling letters at the end of the model number are there to indicate how this model differs from another or could indicate a feature, so record *all* of it.

Serial number

The serial number of the device should be recorded. This is a number that will be important to you with respect to the warranty and service support. You should be able to put your hands on this number quickly.

Database system

Certainly, organizations were capable of maintaining proper inventory systems long before the advent of database systems, but these systems do have advantages. They can increase consistency and accuracy, which will help cut down on erroneous supply and stock records and lost items. It can also help create more dependable records for shipments and returns and better product relevancy. So as you can see, these database systems can help with the entire asset procurement life cycle (covered in a moment).

Asset tags and IDs

If your organization places asset tags on the devices, it probably means you have your own internal numbering or other identification system in place. Record that number and any other pertinent information that the organization deems important enough to place on the asset tag such as region, building, and so on.

Barcodes

One popular method of tagging devices is with barcodes that can be read by scanners when performing an inventory. If these are RFID tags, they can even be read from a short distance.

Procurement life cycle

The asset procurement life cycle consists of the steps in the process of obtaining an asset, using the asset, and disposing of the asset. It is important to track the asset throughout each stage in the life cycle. The major steps in this life cycle are:

- Acquisition
- Operations and maintenance
- Disposal and replacement

Warranty and licensing

Especially with respect to digital assets such as operating systems and applications, maintaining the proper number of licenses is critically important. Later in this chapter you'll learn much more about licensing issues, but for now realize that tracking the proper number of licenses per software package is an important part of asset management.

With respect to physical asserts, such as devices, vehicles, and heating systems, the warranty information is also critical. This is why maintaining the serial number of each device is important because that is how you will access your warranty services when needed. With some devices and systems, the warranty coverage may be so important to ensuring you have a fault-tolerant environment that you may want to be alerted when devices are coming off warranty so that you can replace them or extend the warranty.

Assigned users

Assets don't just sit in an asset safe somewhere. They are assigned to users for them to use. This creates two problems. First, they are out of your control. Making matter worse, the individual to whom you have turned the asset over may be careless, both from a physical security and from a logical security perspective. While we just have to accept these dangers and try to mitigate them with training as best we can, it *is* in our power to know who has been issued what assets. This becomes very important when a user leaves the organization and we need to get those assets back.

Types of documents

You learned earlier in this chapter that "the job isn't done until the paperwork is done," so you should grasp the importance of documentation. In this section we'll talk about documentation you should be generating and updating.

Acceptable use policy (AUP)

The most effective method of preventing viruses, spyware, and harm to data is education. Teach your users not to open suspicious files and to open only those files that they're reasonably sure are virus-free. They need to scan every disc, email, and document they receive before they open it. You should also have all workstations scheduled to be automatically scanned on a regular basis.

While education is important, in most cases you must also attempt to control what users do. An acceptable use policy (AUP) is a document that specifies what users can and cannot do, and it should be signed by all during the hiring process. This creates a contract that can be used later to form the basis for disciplinary measures. These measures or consequences for noncompliance should be spelled out ahead of time. The AUP should be reviewed at least annually, and if changes are made, personnel should have to re-sign the agreement.

Network topology diagram

All network diagrams should be kept in both hard-copy and digital format. Moreover, this document must be closely integrated with the change management process. The change management policy should specifically call for updating this document at the conclusion of any network change that impacts the network diagram. It should also emphasize that no change procedure be considered complete unless the update has occurred.

There are two types of network topologies: physical and logical. The physical diagram focuses on the cabling, connections, and locations of devices. The logical diagram illustrates data flows that may or may not follow the physical diagram.

Figure 9.1 shows a physical diagram, while Figure 9.2 illustrates a logical diagram.

Regulatory compliance requirements

As an administrator and professional, it is your responsibility to know (or learn) the regulations that exist for dealing with safety. You should know them from the local level to the federal level and be familiar with the reporting procedures for incidents you are faced with.

FIGURE 9.1   A physical diagram

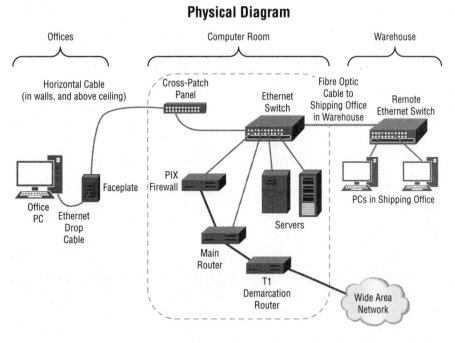

FIGURE 9.2   A logical diagram

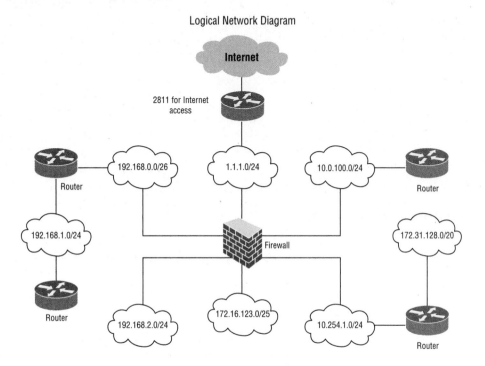

If employees are injured, for example, you may need to contact the Occupational Safety and Health Administration (OSHA). On its website (`www.osha.gov`), you can find links to information about issues of compliance, laws and regulation, and enforcement.

The U.S. Environmental Protection Agency (EPA) offers basic information here:

`www.epa.gov/osw/conserve/materials/ecycling/index.htm`

Splash screens

A splash screen, also known as a launch screen, is the first screen that a user sees when opening your app, and it stays visible while the app is loading. Password-protected lock screens, a related concept, can be used to prevent access to the desktop when a user steps away from the system. Many regulations, such as NIST, PCI DSS, and ISO 27001, require that organizations implement some sort of screen lock timer to promote security. If you are required to comply with one of these standards and a lock screen is not implemented, you will be considered out of compliance.

Incident reports

Just as you should keep all technical articles that help to solve an issue, all incidents should be recorded in detail for future reference. This helps to identify recurring issues for which the root cause has yet to be determined. With regard to security incidents, your incident-handling policy should support this effort.

Standard operating procedures

While policies are broad statements of intent, procedures are step-by-step instructions of how something is done in an organization. They are especially relevant in scenarios where users may have performed an operation in a different manner in another organization. These standard operating procedures (SOPs) serve to maintain consistency of operations.

Procedures for custom installation of software package

When software packages are to be installed in a very specific manner, perhaps in a manner that is unusual, the exact procedures must be defined and communicated to all who might be installing such packages. This is a scenario where a scripted installation might be advisable to ensure the installation is performed correctly.

New-user setup checklist

A new-user checklist is used to ensure that when a user is provisioned an account upon hiring, everything is taken care of. Examples of configuration items that might be on this list are:

- Username and password
- Group memberships
- Assignment of right and permissions
- Signing of all new user documents (AUP, NDA, etc.)

End-user termination checklist

An end-user termination checklist is used to ensure that when a user leaves the company that certain tasks are taken care of. They include:

- The return of all devices

- The removal of all permissions

- Disabling or deleting of the account

- Exit interview

Knowledge base/articles

Often in the process of troubleshooting an issue, you may find useful information in a knowledge base article. Vendors share these documents to assist technicians. You should keep these articles and tie them to the issue they solved. This will help solve future instances of the same issue.

Exam essentials

Explain the importance of asset management and documentation.   List what should be included when creating an asset inventory. Understand the importance of organizing and maintaining documentation. Describe some of the types of sensitive documents that require special treatment.

4.2 Explain basic change-management best practices

There is an old saying that "too many cooks spoil the broth," and when it comes to managing networks, it certainly applies. When technicians make changes to the servers that are not centrally managed and planned, chaos reigns. In that environment, changes might be made that work at cross purposes to one another. All organizations need a change management process whereby all changes go through a formal evaluation process before they are implemented.

This process ensures that all changes support the goals of the organization and that the impact of each change is anticipated before the change is made. There should be a change management board (sometimes called a *change control board*) to which all changes are submitted for review. Only when the change has been approved should it be made.

Documented business processes

As organizations grow and develop, they generate business processes they follow. Sometimes these processes become almost ingrained in users, but over time methods utilized may "drift" away from the original process. For this reason, all key business processes should be recorded and followed, and any change to such processes must undergo the change management examination to ensure that it is beneficial to the entire organization and supports all of its goals.

Rollback plan

In Chapter 5, "Hardware and Network Troubleshooting," you learned that you must have a clear understanding of the potential impact of any change you make and always ensure that a rollback plan has been established in advance. Whenever you determine that a change has the potential to cause widespread issues, try to make the change in a test environment or on a small, low-impact section of the network. Please review that chapter.

Sandbox testing

A sandbox is a virtual environment, disconnected from your physical and virtual production network, where changes to the environment might be tested without suffering the consequences of a bad outcome in the production network. This type of testing is becoming commonplace as more organizations embrace virtual networking.

Responsible staff member

Organizations find it beneficial to establish a process owner for each established business process. This person is responsible for establishing (through the change management process discussed in the next section), monitoring, and identifying needed changes in the process. This ensures that outdated and inefficient processes are discontinued or altered to improve the process.

Change management

Changes to any process, including changes to the network environment, should be managed by a formal process called *change management*. While in some instances this process may impede changes that need to be made quickly, the benefit is that it tends to avoid drastic changes that are not well thought out. In this section you'll learn about the change management process.

Request forms

The process begins with a formal written request to make the change. This form is submitted to a change control board (covered later in this section) that will consider the change in light of many of the considerations in this section, such as its potential impact and what improvement it could bring. Finally, the potential risk of the change must be considered.

Purpose of the change

When any change is suggested, the proposed benefit derived from the change must be identified. Otherwise, there is no reason for the change. During the change management process, the relative costs and benefits to the overall organization will be weighed by a change management board or team.

Scope of the change

In some cases, a change may be beneficial for some users or groups but not others. In that case, we may limit the change (called *scoping*) to only those it will benefit. While scoping is not possible with some changes (cases where all must share any changes), it can be utilized in some specific cases where a change can be segregated to only a set of users.

Date and time of the change/Affected systems/impact

Once a change has been approved, the timing of the change and its implementation must be carefully planned so as not to disrupt operations. Affected parties should be notified of the change and when it will occur. Any disruptions to service must be announced ahead of time so that users can plan for doing without service for the specified period of downtime.

Risk analysis

Sometimes changes bring risk, and these risks must be identified. All changes should undergo a risk analysis process to identify such risks and any controls or countermeasures that can be implemented. The goal of such countermeasures may be either to reduce the risk to a level the organization is comfortable with or to eliminate it entirely.

Risk level

While somewhat of an estimation at this point, the change should be assigned a *risk level*, which could be either descriptive (red, yellow, and green colors, for example) or a numerical metric. It may be beneficial to bring in subject matter experts to help assign these values, which will be used by the less technically inclined members of the change control board to assess the risk of each change.

Change board approvals

The change management or change control board should contain a cross-section of representatives from the company. In this way each change can be assessed by each stakeholder group in the organization. The process should follow these steps:

1. All changes should be formally requested.

2. Each request should be analyzed to ensure that it supports all goals and polices.

3. Prior to formal approval, all costs and effects of the methods of implementation should be reviewed.

Approvals

After they're approved, the change steps should be developed.

End-user acceptance

The change management board should include regular users so any proposed changes can be assessed for end-user acceptance. This can help avoid widespread user dissatisfaction after the change.

Exam essentials

Describe the steps in change management.

These steps are as follows:

- All changes should be formally requested.
- Each request should be analyzed to ensure it supports all goals and polices.
- Prior to formal approval, all costs and effects of the methods of implementation should be reviewed.
- After they're approved, the change steps should be developed.
- During implementation, incremental testing should occur, relying on a predetermined fallback strategy if necessary.
- Complete documentation should be produced and submitted with a formal report to management.

4.3 Given a scenario, implement workstation backup and recovery methods

Preventive maintenance is more than just manipulating hardware; it also encompasses backing up systems on a regular basis to prevent loss of data. These procedures can include scheduled backups, backup testing, and maintenance of backup media rotation schemes.

Backup and recovery

Backups are duplicate copies of key information, ideally stored in a location other than the one where the information is currently stored. Backups include both paper and computer records. Computer records are usually backed up using a backup program, backup systems, and backup procedures.

The primary starting point for disaster recovery involves keeping current backup copies of key data files, databases, applications, and paper records available for use. Your organization must develop a solid set of procedures to manage this process and ensure that all key information is protected. A security professional can do several things in conjunction with systems administrators and business managers to protect this information. It's important to think of this problem as an issue that is larger than a single department.

Image level

An image-level backup is also sometimes called a *bare-metal* backup. It is a backup in which the entire system is saved, including operating system, applications, configuration data, and files. It rapidly speeds up the recovery process because there is no need to reinstall the operating system and the applications or to configure the server again before restoring the data. It is called *bare metal* because this type of backup can be restored to a system with no operating system.

Full

A *full backup* is a complete, comprehensive backup of all files on a disk or server. The full backup is current only at the time it's performed. Once a full backup is made, you have a complete archive of the system at that point in time. A system shouldn't be in use while it undergoes a full backup, because some files may not get backed up. Once the system goes back into operation, the backup is no longer current. A full backup can be a time-consuming process on a large system.

Incremental

An *incremental backup* is a partial backup that stores only the information that has been changed since the last full or incremental backup. If a full backup were performed on a Sunday night, an incremental backup done on Monday night would contain only the information that changed since Sunday night. Such a backup is typically considerably smaller than a full backup. This backup system requires that each incremental backup be retained until a full backup can be performed. Incremental backups are usually the fastest backups to perform on most systems, and each incremental tape is relatively small, as you are only backing up data that has changed since the last backup.

Differential

A differential backup is similar in function to an incremental backup, but it backs up any files that have been altered since the last full backup. If a full backup was performed on Sunday night, a differential backup performed on Monday night would capture the information that was changed on Monday. A differential backup completed on Tuesday night would record the changes in any files from Monday and any changes in files on Tuesday. As you can see, during the week each differential backup would become larger; by Friday or Saturday night, it might be nearly as large as a full backup. This means the backups in the earliest part of the weekly cycle will be very fast, and each successive one will be slower.

Synthetic

A synthetic backup is a full backup performed by synthesizing the data from the previous full backup (either a regular full backup for the first backup, or the previous synthetic full backup) and the periodic incremental backups. The incremental backups are the only files that need to be transferred during replication, greatly reducing the bandwidth needed for offsite replication.

Backup testing

While many backup utilities offer a "verification process," nothing beats actually attempting to restore the data. While test restorations may not be appropriate after every backup, they should be done often to ensure that you have not been creating corrupted backups for days on end.

Frequency

The frequency of backup testing should depend on the sensitivity and value of the data involved. For example, extremely mission-critical data might be tested after every backup, whereas the successful backup of less critical data might only be verified once every four backups.

Backup rotation schemes

When backups are performed, the data being backed up will be committed to some sort of media (tape, CD, DVD, remote hard drive in the cloud, etc.). The backup media can be reused but not forever. Also, the media must be rotated so that wear on the tapes is even. In this section you'll learn not only about backup media rotation schemes but also about storage location issues with the media.

On site vs. off site

The information you back up must be immediately available for use when needed. If a user loses a critical file, they won't want to wait several days while data files are sent from a remote storage facility. Two types of storage mechanisms are available for data storage:

On-Site Storage   *On-site storage* usually refers to a location on the site of the computer center that is used to store information locally. On-site storage containers are available that allow computer cartridges, tapes, and other backup media to be stored in a reasonably protected environment in the building.

On-site storage containers are designed and rated for fire, moisture, and pressure resistance. These containers aren't *fireproof* in most situations, but they're *fire-rated*: a fireproof container should be guaranteed to withstand damage regardless of the type of fire or temperatures, whereas fire ratings specify that a container can protect the contents for a specific amount of time in a given situation.

If you choose to depend entirely on on-site storage, make sure the containers you acquire can withstand the worst-case environmental catastrophes that could happen at your location. Make sure as well that those containers are in locations where you can easily find them after the disaster and access them (near exterior walls, for example).

Off-Site Storage   *Off-site storage* refers to a location away from the computer center where paper copies and backup media are kept. Off-site storage can involve something as simple as keeping a copy of backup media at a remote office, or it can be as complicated as a nuclear-hardened high-security storage facility. The storage facility should be bonded, insured, and inspected on a regular basis to ensure that all storage procedures are being followed.

Determining which storage mechanism to use should be based on the needs of the organization, the availability of storage facilities, and the budget available. Most off-site storage facilities charge based on the amount of space you require and the frequency of access you need to the stored information.

Grandfather-father-son (GFS)

In the grandfather/father/son scheme (GFS), three sets of backups are defined. Most often these three definitions are daily, weekly, and monthly. The daily backups are the sons, the weekly backups are the fathers, and the monthly backups are the grandfathers. Each week, one son advances to the father set. Each month, one father advances to the grandfather set.

Figure 9.3 displays a typical 5-day GFS rotation using 21 tapes. The daily tapes are usually differential or incremental backups. The weekly and monthly tapes must be a full backup.

3-2-1 backup rule

The 3-2-1 rule is a best practice for backup and recovery. It is quite simple, which means that when you build your backup and recovery strategy you should:

- Keep at least three copies of your data.
- Keep the backed-up data on two different storage types.
- Keep at least one copy of the data off-site.

Exam essentials

List three backup types.   Three methods exist to back up information on most systems: full, differential, and incremental. A full backup backs up everything. An incremental backup is a partial backup that stores only the information that has been changed since the last full or incremental backup. A differential backup is similar in function to an incremental backup, but it backs up any files that have been altered since the last full backup.

FIGURE 9.3   GFS scheme

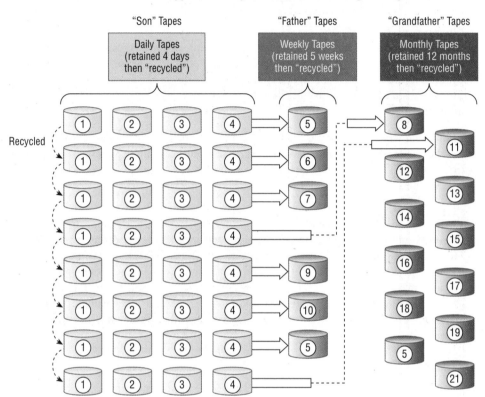

Typical 5-Day GFS Rotation Using 21 Tapes

4.4 Given a scenario, use common safety procedures

This objective deals with potential hazards, both to you and to the computer system. It focuses on protecting humans from harm due to electricity and on protecting computer components from harm due to electrostatic discharge

Electrostatic discharge (ESD) straps

There are measures you can implement to help contain the effects of ESD. The easiest one to implement is the *antistatic wrist strap*, also referred to as an *ESD strap*. You attach one end of the ESD strap to an earth ground (typically the ground pin on an extension cord), or to the metal case, and wrap the other end around your wrist. This strap grounds your body and keeps it at a zero charge. Figure 9.4 shows the proper way to attach an antistatic strap.

FIGURE 9.4   Proper ESD strap connection

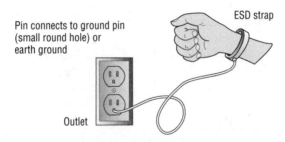

Pin connects to ground pin
(small round hole) or
earth ground

ESD strap

Outlet

If you do not have a grounded outlet available, you can achieve partial benefit simply by attaching the strap to the metal frame of the PC case. Doing so keeps the charge equalized between your body and the case so that there is no electrostatic discharge when you touch components inside the case.

> An ESD strap is a specially designed device to bleed electrical charges away *safely*. It uses a 1 megaohm resistor to bleed the charge away slowly. A simple wire wrapped around your wrist will not work correctly and could electrocute you!

> Do not wear the antistatic wrist strap when there is the potential to encounter a high-voltage capacitor, such as when working on the inside of a monitor or power supply. The strap could channel that voltage through your body.

ESD mats

It is possible to damage a device simply by laying it on a bench top. For this reason, you should have an *ESD mat* (also known as an *antistatic mat*) in addition to an ESD strap. This mat drains excess charge away from any item coming in contact with it (see Figure 9.5). ESD mats are also sold as mouse/keyboard pads to prevent ESD charges from interfering with the operation of the computer.

FIGURE 9.5   Proper use of an ESD mat

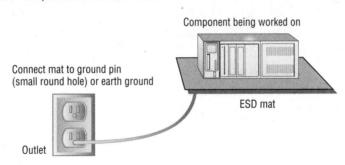

Component being worked on

Connect mat to ground pin
(small round hole) or
earth ground

ESD mat

Outlet

You can also purchase ESD floor mats for technicians to stand on while performing computer maintenance. These include a grounding cord, usually 6 to 10 feet in length.

Vendors have methods of protecting components in transit from manufacture to installation. They press the pins of ICs into antistatic foam to keep all the pins at the same potential, and circuit boards are shipped in antistatic bags, discussed later. However, keep in mind that unlike antistatic mats, antistatic bags do not drain the charges away—they should never be used in place of antistatic mats.

Equipment grounding

Electrostatic discharge (ESD) is one of the most dangerous risks associated with working with computers. Not only does ESD have the potential to damage components of the computer, but it can also injure you. Failing to understand the proper way to avoid it could cause you great harm.

The ESD that we are speaking about here does not have the capability to kill you since it doesn't have the amperage. What does represent a threat, though, is using a wrist strap of your own design that does not have the resistor protection built into it and then accidentally touching something with high voltage while wearing the wrist strap. Without the resistor in place, the high voltage would be grounded through you!

ESD is the technical term for what happens whenever two objects of dissimilar charge come in contact—think of rubbing your feet on a carpet and then touching a light switch. The two objects exchange electrons to equalize the electrostatic charge between them. If the device receiving the charge happens to be an electronic component, there is a good chance it can be damaged.

The likelihood that a component will be damaged increases with the use of complementary metal-oxide semiconductor (CMOS) chips because these chips contain a thin metal-oxide layer that is hypersensitive to ESD. The previous generation's transistor–transistor logic (TTL) chips are more robust than the CMOS chips because they don't contain this metal-oxide layer. Most of today's integrated circuits (ICs) are CMOS chips, so ESD is more of a concern lately.

The lowest static voltage transfer that you can feel is around 3,000 volts (it doesn't electrocute you because there is extremely little current). A static transfer that you can *see* is at least 10,000 volts! Just by sitting in a chair, you can generate around 100 volts of static electricity. Walking around wearing synthetic materials can generate around 1,000 volts. You can easily generate around 20,000 volts simply by dragging your smooth-soled shoes across a carpet in the winter. (Actually, it doesn't have to be winter to run this danger; it can occur in any room with very low humidity. It's just that heated rooms in wintertime generally have very low humidity.)

It would make sense that these thousands of volts would damage computer components. However, a component can be damaged with as little as 80 volts. That means if your body has a small charge built up in it, you could damage a component without even realizing it.

Just as you can ground yourself by using a grounding strap, you can ground equipment. This is most often accomplished by using a mat or a connection directly to a ground.

Proper power handling

You should never attempt to remove a case, open a case, or work on any element that is carrying electricity without first disconnecting it. If removing power to the device you are working on is more complicated than just unplugging it (requiring circuit breakers to be thrown, fuses to be removed, and so forth), then use a voltmeter to make sure the current is off at the device before proceeding.

Proper component handling and storage

When handling computer components, such as motherboards, network cards, and such, it is easy to damage the delicate circuitry with the static electricity that builds up in your body in certain environments. In the next section, we'll talk about how you can protect these components and how you should store them when not in use.

Antistatic bags

When working with components and when storing them, it is a good idea to store them in antistatic bags. Although you can buy these bags, replacement parts usually come in antistatic bags, and if you keep these bags, you can use them later. These bags also can serve as a safe place to lay a component temporarily while working on a device.

Compliance with government regulations

It is your responsibility, as an administrator and a professional, to know (or learn) the regulations that exist for dealing with safety. You should know them from the local level to the federal level and be familiar with the reporting procedures for incidents you are faced with.

Personal safety

There is nothing on a computer, a server, a router, and so on that cannot be replaced or repaired. The same, however, is not true for you. It is imperative that you protect yourself from harm and follow safety procedures when working with computers.

Disconnect power before repairing PC

Earlier in this section you learned that power should always be disconnected when working in a system. Please review the section on proper power handling.

Lifting techniques

An easy way to get hurt is by moving equipment in an unsafe or improper way. Here are some safe lifting techniques to always keep in mind:

- Lift with your legs, not your back. When you have to pick something up, bend at the knees, not at the waist. You want to maintain the natural curve of the back and spine when lifting.

- Be careful to not twist when lifting. Keep the weight on your centerline.

- Keep objects as close to your body as possible and at waist level.

- Where possible, push instead of pull.

The goal in lifting should be to reduce the strain on lower back muscles as much as possible, since muscles in the lower back aren't nearly as strong as those in the legs or other parts of the body. Some people use a back belt or brace to help maintain the proper position while lifting.

Electrical fire safety

Repairing a computer is not often the cause of an electrical fire. However, you should know how to extinguish such a fire properly. Three major classes of fire extinguishers are available, one for each type of flammable substance: A for wood and paper fires, B for flammable liquids, and C for electrical fires. The most popular type of fire extinguisher today is the multipurpose, or ABC-rated, extinguisher. It contains a dry chemical powder that smothers the fire and cools it at the same time. For electrical fires (which may be related to a shorted-out wire in a power supply), make sure the fire extinguisher will work for Class C fires. If you don't have an extinguisher that is specifically rated for electrical fires (Class C), you can use an ABC-rated extinguisher.

Safety goggles

In any environment where you may get dust or harmful materials in your eyes, you should wear safety goggles. For example, when working in a dusty shop area where a computer is located, this might be advisable. Another example might be when you are cleaning up printer toner.

There are also safety glasses that can be used when spending long hours staring at a computer screen that will reduce the eyestrain that comes with this type of activity.

Air filtration mask

While safety goggles will protect your eyes from dust and other harmful particulates, they will do nothing to protect your lungs. Air filter masks should always be available, and technicians should be encouraged to wear them in any situation where safety goggles are called for or in any scenario where you have reason to believe that the surrounding air may contain harmful compounds.

Exam essentials

Understand ESD.   Electrostatic discharge occurs when two objects of unequal electrical potential meet. One object transfers some charge to the other one, just as water flows into an area that has a lower water level.

Understand how to use an antistatic wrist strap.   The antistatic wrist strap is also referred to as an ESD strap. To use the ESD strap, you attach one end to an earth ground (typically the ground pin on an extension cord) and wrap the other end around your wrist. This strap grounds your body and keeps it at a zero charge, preventing discharges from damaging the components of a PC.

4.5 Summarize environmental impacts and local environmental controls

Environmental harm can come from many sources. Not only are there temperature and humidity elements that must be controlled, but administrators also need to carefully monitor power, air, and particulates that can harm humans and computers. Not understanding environmental impact and controls can cause great harm.

Material safety data sheet (MSDS)/documentation for handling and disposal

It is important that you know the potential safety hazards that exist when working with computer elements and how to address them. It is imperative that you understand such issues as *material safety data sheets* (MSDSs) and know how to reference them when needed. OSHA calls these Safety Data Sheets. Any type of chemical, equipment, or supply that has the potential to harm the environment or people has to have an MSDS associated with it. These are traditionally created by the manufacturer, and you can obtain them from the manufacturer or from the Environmental Protection Agency at www.epa.gov.

These sheets are not intended for consumer use but are aimed at emergency workers and employees who are exposed to the risks of the particular product. Among the information they include are such things as boiling point, melting point, flash point, and potential health risks. They also cover storage and disposal recommendations and the procedures to follow in the case of a spill or leak.

Proper battery disposal

Batteries can contain a number of compounds and materials that should not make their way into landfills. The following are some examples:

- Rare earth metals
- Lead
- Cadmium
- Lithium
- Alkaline manganese
- Mercury

You should make battery recycling a standard procedure and follow local regulations for battery disposal when the time comes to dispose of the batteries.

Proper toner disposal

Toner cartridges are another item that should not be thrown away. They should be recycled. Moreover, in any case where toner has been spilled you should clean up with a special vacuum made for that purpose. If you use a regular vacuum, the metal toner will damage the vacuum.

Proper disposal of other devices and assets

There may be other devices and physical assets that require special handing when disposing of them. In this section you'll see several examples.

CRT

While most CRT monitors have been disposed of already, you may find yourself with a number of them that you need to get rid of. These cannot be thrown in the trash. The contents of the device are under pressure, and if something breaks the glass screen, there will be glass and other materials sprayed out with a force that could injure someone.

The monitor uses a lot of power as it directs electrons on the screen via a strong magnet. The electrons and magnet require a considerable amount of voltage to be able to do their task. Like power supplies, monitors have the ability to hold their charge a long time after the power has been disconnected.

You should never open a power supply or a monitor for the reasons discussed here. The risk of electrocution with these two devices is significant.

If you are not sure whether electricity is present, or its voltage, use a voltmeter. Figure 9.6 shows a simple voltmeter capable of working with both AC and DC currents.

Many states have laws that govern the disposal of monitors since they are often classified as hazardous. CRT monitors contain high amounts of lead and other harmful materials such as arsenic, beryllium, cadmium, chromium, mercury, nickel, and zinc. To dispose of a monitor, contact a computer recycling firm and let them get rid of the monitor for you. CRT monitors must be disposed of according to the environmental regulations.

FIGURE 9.6   A simple voltmeter

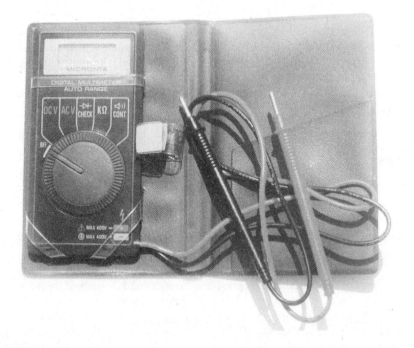

Cell phones

Cell phones should not be thrown away, as they contain many of the same compounds found in laptops and desktops. Since the majority of the time the device is still perfectly functional (the user simply wanted a new phone), it should be sold or donated so that someone else can make use of the phone.

Tablets

Treat tablets in the same way you would cell phones and sell, recycle, or donate.

Temperature, humidity-level awareness, and proper ventilation

Three items closely related to an environmentally friendly computing environment are temperature, humidity, and ventilation. We will cover the most important elements with all three.

Temperature   Heat and computers don't mix well. Many computer systems require both temperature and humidity control for reliable service. The larger servers, communications equipment, and drive arrays generate considerable amounts of heat; this is especially true of mainframe and older minicomputers. An environmental system for this type of equipment is a significant expense beyond the actual computer system costs. Fortunately, newer systems operate in a wider temperature range. Most new systems are designed to operate in an office environment.

Humidity Level   Another preventive measure you can take is to maintain the relative humidity at around 50 percent. Be careful not to increase the humidity too far—to the point where moisture starts to condense on the equipment! It is a balancing act keeping humidity at the right level since low humidity causes ESD and high humidity causes moisture condensation. Both extremes are bad but have completely different effects.

Also, use antistatic spray, which is available commercially, to reduce static buildup on clothing and carpets. In a pinch, a solution of diluted fabric softener sprayed on these items will do the same thing.

At the least, you can be mindful of the dangers of ESD and take steps to reduce its effects. Beyond that, you should educate yourself about those effects so you know when ESD is becoming a major problem.

Ventilation   Rounding out temperature and humidity is ventilation. It is important that air—clean air—circulate around computer equipment to keep it cool and functioning properly. Server rooms require much more attention to ventilation than office spaces but are the subject of other exams (Server+, for example) and not test fodder for A+.

What is test fodder is the topic of ventilation within the computer itself—an inadequate flow of internal air within a computer is a common cause of overheating. To prevent this, know that all slot covers should remain in place and be replaced if a card is removed from the system. Know as well that internal fans should be periodically cleaned to ensure proper airflow. A missing slot cover or malfunctioning fan can lead to inadequate flow of internal air.

Location/equipment placement

If the computer systems you're responsible for require special environmental considerations, you'll need to establish cooling and humidity control. Ideally, systems are located in the middle of the building, and they're ducted separately from the rest of the heating, ventilation, and air conditioning (HVAC) system. It's a common practice for modern buildings to use a zone-based air conditioning environment, which allows the environmental plant to be turned off when the building isn't occupied. A computer room will typically require full-time environmental control.

Dust cleanup

One of the most harmful atmospheric hazards to a computer is dust. Dust, dirt, hair, and other airborne contaminants can get pulled into computers and build up inside. Because computer fans work by pulling air through the computer (usually sucking it in through the case and then pushing it out the power supply), it's easy for these items to enter and then become stuck. Every item in the computer builds up heat, and these particles are no exception. As they build up, they hinder the fan's ability to perform its function, and the components get hotter than they would otherwise. Figure 9.7 shows the inside of a system in use for only six months in an area with carpeting and other dusty surroundings.

FIGURE 9.7   Dust builds up inside the system.

Compressed air/vacuums

You can remove dust and debris from inside computers with *compressed air* blown in short bursts. The short bursts are useful in preventing the dust from flying too far out and entering another machine, as well as in preventing the can from releasing the air in liquid form. Compressed air cans should be held 2–3 inches from the system and always used upright so the content is released as a gas. If the can becomes cold to the touch, discontinue using it until it heats back to room temperature.

WARNING   It's possible to use an air compressor instead of compressed-air cans when you need a lot of air. If you take this approach, make sure you keep the pounds per square inch (PSI) at or below 40, and include measures on the air compressor to remove moisture.

Vacuums

Dust can build up not just within the computer but also in crevices on the outside. Figure 9.8 shows USB ports on the back of a system that have become a haven for small dust particles. These ports need to be blown out with compressed air, or cleaned with an electronic *vacuum*, before being used, or degradation with the device connected to them could occur.

FIGURE 9.8   Dust collects in unused ports as well.

Power surges, brownouts, and blackouts

A number of power-related threats can harm computers. An *uninterruptible power supply* (UPS) is a solution to a number of power-related threats that can harm computers. Among them are the following:

Blackout   This is a complete failure of the power supplied.

Brownout   This is a drop in voltage lasting more than a few minutes.

Sag   This is a short-term voltage drop.

Spike   The opposite of a sag, this is a short (typically less than one second) increase in voltage that can do irreparable damage to equipment.

Surge   This is a long spike (sometimes lasting many seconds). Though a surge is typically a less intense increase in power, it can also damage equipment.

The two solutions to know for the power issues on the exam are battery backups and surge suppressors.

Battery backup

A battery backup, or UPS, keeps the system up and running when the normal power is removed (because of blackout, brownout, and so on). Even in installations that use generators to keep the systems running, battery backups are usually still used so they can keep the machines running while the generators come up to speed.

Most UPS units come with software that can be used to configure the actions to take when the battery backup is active. The software, for example, can be configured to shut down the connected devices when the battery begins to get low. Always ensure that the UPS provides the required voltage for all devices.

Surge suppressor

A surge suppressor keeps a spike from passing through it and onto the equipment that could be damaged. *Tripping* occurs when the breaker on a device such as a power supply, surge protector, or UPS turns off the device because it received a spike. If the device is a UPS, when the tripping happens, the components plugged into the UPS should go to battery instead of pulling power through the line. Under most circumstances, the breaker is reset, and operations continue as normal. Figure 9.9 shows a surge-protector power strip, with the trip button to reset at the top.

FIGURE 9.9   The reset button on the top of a surge-protector power strip

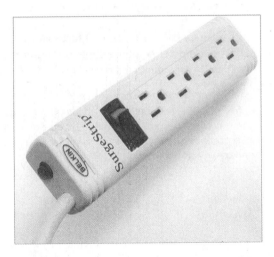

Nuisance tripping is the phrase used if tripping occurs often and isn't a result of a serious condition. If this continues, you should isolate the cause and correct it, even if it means replacing the device that continues to trip.

Surge suppressors (also known as *surge protectors*), either stand-alone or built into the UPS, can help reduce the number of nuisance trips. If your UPS doesn't have a surge protector, you should add one to the outlet before the UPS to keep the UPS from being damaged if it receives a strong surge. Figure 9.10 shows an example of a simple surge protector for a home computer.

FIGURE 9.10   A simple surge protector

All units are rated by Underwriters Laboratories (UL) for performance. One thing you should never do is plug a UPS or computer equipment into a ground fault circuit interrupter (GFCI) receptacle. These receptacles are intended for use in wet areas, and they trip easily.

WARNING   Don't confuse a GFCI receptacle with an isolated ground receptacle. Isolated ground receptacles are identifiable by orange outlets and should be used for computer equipment to avoid their picking up a surge passed to the ground by any other device.

Exam essentials

Know that you may need to report incidents.   When incidents happen, you must always document them, and every attempt should be made to do so both fully and truthfully. Depending on the type of incident, you may also need to report it to other authorities, such as the EPA.

Know what components are not suitable for a landfill.   Batteries, CRTs, and circuit boards are all examples of items that should not be thrown away normally because of the elements used in them. Batteries contain metals such as lead and nickel, circuit boards contain lead solder, and CRTs contain phosphors.

Know the safety procedures to follow when working with computers.   Be careful when moving computers or working around any electrical components. Know that liquids and computers don't mix, and keep the systems as clean and dust-free as possible to ensure optimal operation.

4.6 Explain the importance of prohibited content/activity and privacy, licensing, and policy concepts

Working in the IT profession, it is entirely plausible that you will encounter a situation where you find proof of a user, or a number of users, engaging in activities that are prohibited. Those activities can include any number of things, and the prohibition may range from a company policy (you cannot use social media during working hours) all the way up to a federal law (you cannot traffic in child pornography). You have an obligation to respond appropriately and accordingly.

Regardless of whether you agree with a prohibition, when you encounter instances wherein activities are in violation of it, you must respond in a professional and legal manner.

Incident response

The extent to which a security event causes harm to your network largely depends on the speed and quality of your response to the incident. By following a structured incident response policy, you greatly enhance the chances of minimizing the damage and the likelihood that you will be able to bring parties to justice in the case of illegal activity. The following sections cover some important guidelines regarding the incident response process.

Chain of custody

An important concept to keep in mind when working with incidents is the *chain of custody*.

Tracking of evidence/documenting process

When you begin to collect evidence, you must keep track of that evidence at all times and show who has it, who has seen it, and where it has been, known as the *chain of custody*. The evidence must always be within your custody, or you're open to dispute about whether it has been tampered with.

Inform management/law enforcement as necessary

A part of identifying the problem involves identifying what policy or law prohibits such an action. Prohibited content generally falls within the following categories (this list should not be considered to represent everything prohibited, because many companies have other policies):

- Exploiting people (in any way, such as sexually, violently, and so on)
- Promoting harassment of any person or group
- Containing or promoting anything illegal or unauthorized

- Promoting racism, hatred, bigotry, or physical harm
- Containing adult content involving nudity or sexual acts
- Violating privacy rights, copyrights, contract rights, or defamation rights
- Viruses or malware of any sort
- Impersonation
- Soliciting information from anyone younger than 18
- Involving pyramid schemes, junk mail, chain letters, spamming, or the like

Report through proper channels

Once you have identified prohibited content or activity, you must report it through the proper channels. If the violation is one only of company policy, then usually the company's human resources department is the proper channel. If the violation is of a law, then often you must contact legal authorities—notifying the appropriate internal resources as well. If the violation is of a federal law and you tell only an internal resource (HR manager, for example), it does not absolve you of the responsibility if that person does not continue to report it up the appropriate chain.

Law enforcement personnel are governed by the rules of evidence, and their response to an incident will be largely out of your control. You need to carefully consider involving law enforcement before you begin. There is no such thing as dropping charges. Once they begin, law enforcement professionals are required to pursue an investigation.

Copy of drive (data integrity and preservation)

You have as well an obligation to preserve the content found until it is turned over to the appropriate authority. Doing so may require commandeering anything from a flash drive up to a network server. Until someone in a position of authority relieves you of the responsibility, you must preserve the data or device in the state in which you discovered it. If you are ever unsure of how to proceed, you should immediately contact your supervisor.

Because knowing what to do when something is discovered is something that may not come naturally, it is a good idea to include the procedures you'll generally follow in an *incident response plan* (IRP). The IRP outlines what steps are needed and who is responsible for deciding how to handle a situation.

Your policies should clearly outline who needs to be informed in the company, what they need to be told, and how to respond to the situation.

Documentation of incident

During the entire process, you should document the steps you take to identify, detect, and report the problem. This information is valuable and will often be used should the problem escalate to a court of law. Many help-desk software systems provide detailed methods you can use to record procedures and steps.

Licensing/digital rights management (DRM)/end-user license agreement (EULA)

While many in the IT community would like to think that software, music files, and movie files should be free, that is not the case. Using any of these items without paying for them is *illegal*. Operating systems, application software, and many third-party utilities require a license to legally use the software. It also requires that you accept an end-user license agreement (EULA) whereby you agree to use the software as described in that agreement.

Music and movie files, on the other hand, are protected by digital rights management (DRM). This is a system that maintains control over these files and ensures that they are installed only on devices that belong to the person who purchased the file, with the end goal being to prevent users from sharing and giving these files away without paying for them.

Not all software requires a license. In the next sections we'll talk about software that doesn't require a license and also discuss the differences between personal and enterprise licenses.

Valid licenses

Software licenses must be purchased for each instance of the software you plan to deploy. Software piracy is the unauthorized reproduction or distribution of copyrighted software. Although software piracy is a worldwide issue, it is much more prevalent in Asia, Europe, Latin America, and Africa/Middle East. Part of the problem with software piracy stems from the cross-jurisdictional issues that arise. Obtaining the cooperation of foreign law enforcement agencies and government is often difficult or impossible. Combine this with the availability of the hardware needed to create pirated software and the speed with which it can be made, and you have a problem that will only increase over the coming years.

Security professionals and the organizations they work with must ensure that the organization takes measures to ensure that employees understand the implications of installing pirated software. In addition, large organizations might need to utilize an enterprise software inventory application that will provide administrators with a report on the software that is installed.

Non-expired licenses

Pay attention to how long the license lasts. A perpetual license doesn't expire. Once you purchase it, you have rights to use the software for as long as you like. A term license expires after a specified period of time (often one year) and must be periodically renewed. An expired license is just as bad as no license at all.

Personal use license vs. corporate use license

Whereas an individual software license entitles a single user to install and use a piece of commercial software, an enterprise license purchase is based on a number of seats or devices on which the software can be legally installed. Also, while each individual license will come with installation media, the purchase of an enterprise license comes with a single version of the installation media, which can be installed on the number of devices specified in the license agreement.

Open-source license

Open source software is software that is free and available to all. Commercial software, on the other hand, requires the purchase of a license to legally use the software. While there is the obvious monetary advantage to using open source software, the organization or user must typically have a deeper understanding of the software than may be required to use commercial software successfully. Another advantage of commercial software is the ongoing support the vendor can provide in using the software, while a user of open source software is pretty much on their own when issues arise. The good news is that open source software has large, active user communities, though it may be that their information can't be as authoritative as manufacturer support.

Regulated data

Some data types require special attention because they are regulated. This means their proper handling is specified by regulation. In this section we'll look at some of these types of data.

Credit card transactions

Credit card data is some of the most sensitive data there is and users and customers depend on organizations to protect it. PCI-DSS v4.0 was released in Q1 of 2022. It encourages and enhances cardholder data security and facilitates the broad adoption of consistent data security measures globally.

Personal government-issued information

Information such as driver license numbers, Social Security numbers, and other government-issued identifiers must be kept confidential because when used together these pieces of information can be used to steal an identity. These values are also considered PII (covered in Chapter 7).

PII

Personally identifiable information (PII) was covered in Chapter 7, "Security." Please review that chapter.

Healthcare data

Protected health information (PHI), also referred to as *electronic protected health information* (EPHI or ePHI), is any individually identifiable health information. NIST SP 800-66 provides guidelines for implementing the Health Insurance Portability and Accountability Act (HIPAA) Security Rule.

Data retention requirements

Once data has reached the end of the life cycle, you should either properly dispose of it or ensure that it is securely stored. Some organizations must maintain data records for a certain number of years per local, state, or federal laws or regulations. This type of data should be archived for the required period. In addition, any data that is part of litigation should be retained as requested by the court of law, and organizations should follow appropriate chain of custody and evidence documentation processes. Data archival and destruction procedures should be clearly defined by the organization.

All organizations need procedures in place for the retention and destruction of data. Data retention and destruction must follow all local, state, and government regulations and laws. Documenting proper procedures ensures that information is maintained for the required time to prevent financial fines and possible incarceration of high-level organizational officers. These procedures must include both retention period and destruction process.

Exam essentials

Report prohibited content and activities.   You have an obligation to report prohibited activities and content to the appropriate authorities when you uncover them. You must ascertain which authority is prohibiting the actions and notify them.

Document and preserve the evidence.   It is imperative that the evidence be documented and preserved until turned over to the appropriate authority. In some cases, this can include commandeering a removable drive, a computer, or even a server. Failure to do so can leave you facing fines and other punishments.

4.7 Given a scenario, use proper communication techniques and professionalism

It's possible that you chose computers as your vocation instead of public speaking because you want to interact with people on a one-on-one basis. As unlikely as that possibility may be, it still exists.

Some have marveled at the fact that CompTIA includes questions about customer service on the A+ exam. A better wonder, however, is that there are those in the business who need to know these items and don't. Possessing a great deal of technology skill does not immediately endow one with great people skills. A bit more on appropriate behavior as it relates to the IT field follows.

Professional appearance and attire

You cannot change a first impression, and if you make a bad first impression it can be difficult to recover and gain the customer's trust. In this section we'll talk about appearance and how you present yourself to the customer.

Match the required attire of the given environment

When deciding the right appearance to present to the customer, it is useful to consider the environment in which you will meeting the customer and performing the work. There are two basic approaches to this.

Formal

If you are going into an environment where the prevailing custom regarding proper dress is formal or is unknown, you should assume that you need to wear formal business attire. This will ensure the best possible first impressions.

Business casual

Never assume this is the case but, if you can identify the prevailing custom regarding work attire to be business casual, then by all means go that route, but what does that mean? Business casual options differ from company to company.

Use proper language and avoid jargon, acronyms, and slang, when applicable

Avoid using jargon, abbreviations, slang, and acronyms. Every field has its own language that can make those from outside the field feel lost. Put yourself in the position of someone not in the field, and explain what is going on using words they can relate to.

Be honest and fair with the customer, whoever that is, and try to establish a personal rapport. Tell them what the problem is, what you believe is the cause, and what can be done in the future to prevent it from recurring.

Alert your supervisor if there is a communication barrier with the customer (for example, the customer is deaf or does not speak the same language as you do). This is particularly important if the barrier will affect the problem resolution or the amount of time it will take.

If you're providing phone support, do the following:

- Always answer the telephone in a professional manner, announcing the name of the company and yourself.
- Make a concentrated effort to ascertain the customer's technical level, and communicate at that level, not above or below it.

Maintain a positive attitude/project confidence

Maintain a positive attitude. Your approach to the problem, and the customer, can be mirrored back. Moreover, project confidence in dealing with the issue because that engenders more cooperation and patience from the customer, both of which have a direct impact on the success of your troubleshooting efforts.

Actively listen, take notes, and avoid interrupting the customer

Good communication includes listening to what the user, manager, or developer is telling you and making certain that you understand completely what they are trying to say. Just because a user or customer doesn't understand the terminology, syntax, or concepts that you do doesn't mean they don't have a real problem that needs addressing. You must, therefore, be skilled not only at listening but also at translating. Professional conduct encompasses politeness, guidance, punctuality, and accountability. Always treat the customer with the same respect and empathy you would expect if the situation were reversed. Likewise, guide the customer through the problem and the explanation. Tell them what has caused the problem they're currently experiencing and offer the best solution to prevent it from recurring.

Listen intently to what your customer is saying. Make it obvious to them that you're listening and respecting what they're telling you. If you have a problem understanding them, go to whatever lengths you need to in order to remedy the situation. Look for verbal and nonverbal cues that can help you isolate the problem. Avoid interrupting the customer because that implies that what they have to say is not important enough to listen to.

Be culturally sensitive

It is important as well to be culturally sensitive—not everyone enjoys the same humor. Moreover, be mindful of the differences in the way business is conducted in different cultures and be flexible in your approach based on this. When you sense that the customer prefers a more formal relationship with you, try to reflect that in your approach.

Use appropriate professional titles, when applicable

While many folks are not put off at all when you address them by their first name, in many cultures it is considered rude to do so, and you should also address the customer using the appropriate title when applicable. Not all cultures are as informal as what you may have become accustomed to. Again, sensitivity to the customer's approach to you can be a valuable clue to how the customer would prefer to interact with you.

Be on time (if late, contact the customer)

Punctuality is important and should be part of your planning process before you ever arrive at the site. If you tell the customer you'll be there at 10:30, you need to make every attempt to be there at that time. If you arrive late, you have given them false hope that the problem would be solved by a set time. That false hope can lead to anger when you arrive late and appear to not be taking their problem as seriously as they are. Punctuality continues to be important throughout the service call and doesn't end with your arrival. If you need to leave to get parts, tell the customer when you'll be back, and then be there at that time. If for some reason you can't return at the expected time, alert the customer and inform them of your new return time.

In conjunction with time and punctuality, if a user asks how much longer the server will be down and you respond that it will be up in five minutes only to have it remain down for five more hours, you're creating resentment and possibly anger. When estimating downtime, always allow for more time than you think you'll need, just in case other problems occur. If you greatly underestimate the time, always inform the affected parties and give them a new time estimate. Here's an analogy that will put it in perspective: if you take your car to get the oil changed and the counter clerk tells you it will be "about 15 minutes," the last thing you want is to be sitting there four hours later.

Avoid distractions

It is important that you avoid distractions while working on a customer's or user's problem. Those distractions can come in the form of personal calls, talking to co-workers, or personal interruptions.

If you arrive at the site to troubleshoot a problem and you encounter distractions there of the customer's making (children present, TV on, and so on), you should politely ask the customer to remove the distractions if possible. If the area you will be working in is cluttered with personal items (mementos from the state fair, stuffed animals, and so on), ask the customer to relocate the items as needed or ask them if it is okay to do so before you relocate the items.

Personal calls

Taking personal calls while working with a customer can make the customer feel as if their problem is being minimized. Spend time solving the problem and interacting with the customer and then attend to the personal calls when you leave.

If you are anticipating an important call that cannot be avoided, let the customer know beforehand so that they will understand this interruption is coming.

Texting/social media sites

Keep in mind that when you are supporting a customer, you are working on their time and not your own. You are also using their equipment, not your own. Consequently, avoid any use of the customer's equipment or time for personal texts or visits to social media sites. It is allowable to use the time and the equipment for legitimate research or other activities that are directly related to solving the customer's issues.

Talking to co-workers while interacting with customers

Just as taking personal calls can seem to minimize the importance of interacting with the customer, so too can talking to co-workers. The customer needs to be the focus of your attention until their problems have been addressed, and then you can attend to other matters.

If you must contact someone else while troubleshooting, always ask the customer's permission.

Personal interruptions

The broad category of personal interruptions includes anything that takes you away from focusing on the customer and is not job-related. Spend your time dealing with the customer first and solving their problems before attending to personal issues.

Dealing with difficult customers or situations

Handle complaints as professionally as possible. Accept responsibility for errors that may have occurred on your part, and never try to pass the blame. Remember, the goal is to keep them as a customer, not to win an argument.

Do not argue with customers and/or be defensive

Avoid arguing with a customer, because doing so serves no purpose; resolve their anger with as little conflict as possible. Moreover, don't be defensive when the customer questions your approach and thought process. While they may clueless about troubleshooting, they deserve to understand why you are doing what you are doing.

Avoid dismissing customer problems

Just as personal calls and interruptions can make it seem as if you are not taking the customer seriously enough, so too can dismissing their problems as less important than they believe they are. It is important to put yourself in their shoes and see the issue from their perspective. What may seem trivial to you may be a vital issue for them.

Avoid being judgmental

It is important not to minimize their problem or appear to be judgmental.

Clarify customer statements (ask open-ended questions to narrow the scope of the problem, restate the issue, or question to verify understanding)

The most important skill you can have is the ability to listen. You have to rely on the customer to tell you the problem and describe it accurately. They can't do that if you're second-guessing them or jumping to conclusions before the whole story is told. Ask questions that are broad and open-ended at first and then narrow them down to help isolate the problem. This is particularly necessary when you are trying to solve the problem remotely. For example, start with questions like these:

- What were you doing before the problem occurred?
- What application were you using when the problem occurred?

It's also your job to help guide the user's description of the problem. Here are some examples:

- Is the printer plugged in?
- Is it online?
- Are any lights flashing on it?

Restate the issue to the customer to make sure that you correctly understand what they are telling you (for example, "There is only one green light lit, correct?"). Ask questions as needed that verify your understanding of the problem. The questions you ask should help guide you toward isolating the problem and identifying possible solutions.

Do not disclose experiences via social media outlets

Although it might make you feel better about a particularly trying experience with a customer to vent about it on social media, don't do that. Not only is it remotely possible that the post may somehow find its way to the attention of the customer, it reflects poorly on you as someone who shares their business dealings with the world.

Set and meet expectations/time line and communicate status with the customer

Customer satisfaction goes a long way toward generating repeat business. If you can *meet* the customer's expectations, you'll almost assuredly hear from them again when another problem arises. If you can *exceed* the customer's expectations, you can almost guarantee that they will call you the next time a problem arises.

Customer satisfaction is important in all communication media—whether you're on-site, providing phone support, or communicating through email or other correspondence.

Share the customer's sense of urgency. What may seem like a small problem to you can appear to the customer as if the whole world is collapsing around them.

Offer repair/replacement options, as needed

If there are multiple solutions to the problem the customer is encountering, offer options to them. Those options often include repairing what they already have or replacing it. If the repair could lead to a recurrence of the situation but the replacement will not, then that should be explained to them clearly.

The ramifications of each choice should be clearly explained along with costs (estimates, if necessary) so that they can make the decision they deem in their best interest.

If you are unable to resolve the issue, explain to the customer what to do and be sure to follow up properly to forward the issue to appropriate personnel.

Provide proper documentation on the services provided

Document the services you provided so there is no misunderstanding on the part of the customer. Supply them with the documentation and keep a copy handy to refer to should any questions arise. Explain clearly the cause of the problem and how to avoid it in the future.

It is important that the documentation be complete so that if you do not refer to it for quite some time (years), you will still be able to understand and explain what was done.

Follow up with customer/user at a later date to verify satisfaction

When you finish a job, notify the user you're done. Make every attempt to find the user and inform them of the resolution. If it's difficult to find them, leave a note for them to find when they return, explaining the resolution. You should also leave a means by which they can contact you, should they have a question about the resolution or a related problem. In most cases, the number you leave should be that of your business during working hours and your pager, where applicable, after hours.

If you do not hear back from the customer, follow up with them at a later date to verify that the problem is resolved and they are satisfied with the outcome. One of the best ways to keep customers is to let them know that you care about their success and satisfaction.

Deal appropriately with customers' confidential and private materials

The goal of *confidentiality* is to prevent or minimize unauthorized access to files and folders and disclosure of data and information. In many instances, laws and regulations require specific information confidentiality. For example, Social Security records, payroll and employee records, medical records, and corporate information are high-value assets. This information could create liability issues or embarrassment if it fell into the wrong hands. Over the last few years, there have been several cases in which bank account and credit card numbers were published on the Internet. The costs of these types of breaches of confidentiality far exceed the actual losses from the misuse of this information.

Confidentiality entails ensuring that data expected to remain private is seen only by those who should see it. Confidentiality is implemented through authentication and access controls.

Just as confidentiality issues are addressed early in the design phase of a project, you as a computer professional are expected to uphold a high level of confidentiality. Should a user approach you with a sensitive issue—telling you their password, asking for assistance obtaining access to medical forms, and so on—it's your obligation as part of your job to make certain that information passes no further.

Located on a computer, desktop, printer, etc.

Technicians may come into contact with confidential information in the course of performing their job duties. That information could come in the form of data stored on a computer, information on a desktop, data (in any form) on a printer, and many other locations. When that possibility exists, ask users to remove such confidential information or close the application that displays it (saving their work before they close).

If the area where you will be working is cluttered with personal information (such as printed customer lists), ask the customer to relocate the items if possible. No confidential information should ever be disclosed to outside parties.

Exam essentials

Use good communication skills.   Listen to the customer. Let them tell you what they understand the problem to be and then interpret the problem and see whether you can get them to agree to what you're hearing them say. Treat the customer, whether an end user or a colleague, with respect, and take their issues and problems seriously.

Deal appropriately with confidential data.   You—as a computer professional—are expected to uphold a high level of confidentiality. No confidential information should ever be disclosed to outside parties.

4.8 Identify the basics of scripting

Scripts are used to automate anything that can be accomplished at the command line. It prevents having to manually type in the commands and also allows you to schedule a script file to run at a certain time.

Script file types

Script files can come in various file types. In this section we'll look at these file types.

.bat   Batch file or files with a .bat extension are used to automate a command or set of commands each time you execute the batch file.

.ps1   Files with this extension are used to script tasks in PowerShell, a powerful scripting.

.vbs   These are Visual Basic script files. The VBScript scripting language contains code that can be executed within Windows or Bing via the Windows-based script host.

.sh   Files that have the .sh file extension are self-extracting files. The SH file contains selected files and a shell script along with instructions on how to extract the contents of the SH file archive.

.js   A JS file is a text file containing JavaScript code that is used to execute JavaScript instructions in web pages.

.py   A .py file is one written in the Python language. Python runs on Windows, macOS, and Linux/Unix.

Use cases for scripting

Scripting makes the scheduling and automation of any function possible. In this section you'll learn about some of the use cases for creating and scheduling scripts to run.

Basic automation

Any task can be automated by creating a script that performs the function and then scheduling it to run at the proper time. For example, you can use the at command to schedule a command, a script, or a program to run at a specified date and time.

Restarting machines

Many systems benefit from a restart from time to time. Rather than putting this task on a checklist and dedicating a technician's time to walking over to the machine and manually restarting the system, you can schedule the process to occur on a regular basis.

Remapping network drives

Users need easy access to network systems and network locations where they can safely save data. Mapping network drives makes this much easier for users. This can be done from the command line so that it can be automated. Using the at command you can schedule the following command to map a network drive:

```
net use DRIVE: PATH
```

Installation of applications

Applications use special file types to install the application. A good example is a Microsoft MSI file. Regardless or the installation file types (EXE, BAT), the installation can be scheduled by using the at command. This is especially useful when you are installing to multiple systems—you can do so with a single command if you reference the systems correctly.

Automated backups

Many backup tools and utilities allow for the scheduling of backups. So why would you use a script? Customization. Scripts offer much more granular control over how the backup is performed than using the scheduling in backup software. For example, if you need to pull information from your backup software and put it into a spreadsheet to generate a special report, you can only do this with a script.

Gathering of information/data

Sometimes you need to gather information on a system(s) such as the software currently installed or the types of CPU in use. Doing this on a large scale manually can be overwhelming, but scripts can be created that will interrogate the system and return an answer for each.

Initiating updates

Many organizations automate the installation of updates through tools such as Windows Update, but sometimes you have an update that you do *not* want widely installed. Maybe you only want it installed on certain systems. In that case you could use a script to install it on the system that requires it.

Other considerations when using scripts

While scripting is an amazing tool, there are some issues to be mindful of. In this section you'll learn some of these issues.

Unintentionally introducing malware

One of the ways you can introduce malware when scripting is when you reference a file to execute that *is* malware. This can happen if you haven't verified the integrity of the file you are referencing. Any time you download an installation file of any type, always check its integrity by verifying its hash value. If a hash value is not provided, that is a red flag and you need to go elsewhere for that file.

Inadvertently changing system settings

When constructing your script be very careful that the script does *only* what you want and does not make other unwanted changes. This can happen when you copy scripts from websites that you don't fully understand.

Browser or system crashes due to mishandling of resources

Sometimes poorly written scripts can cause resource issues that can lead to a browser crash or even a complete system crash. For example, if a script is written in such a way that you're specifying that you only want one byte to be read from the Universal Synchronous Asynchronous Receiver Transmitter (USART) hardware buffer, and if there isn't a byte to be read, the script might wait for data that never comes, causing your program to freeze.

Exam essentials

Identify script file types.   These include BAT, PS1, VBS, SH, JS, and PY.

4.9 Given a scenario, use remote access technologies

As an A+ technician, there will be times when you need to make a remote connection to another device for the purpose of managing the device. In this section we'll look at some options for doing this and the security issues related to each.

Methods/tools

First, let's look at some of the options available for remote access, and in the following section you'll learn about the security considerations.

RDP

Developed by Microsoft, Remote Desktop Protocol (RDP) allows you to connect to remote computers and run programs on them. When you use RDP, you see the desktop of the computer you've signed into on your screen. When you use RDP, the computer at which you are seated is the client and the computer you're logging into is the server.

The server uses its own video driver to create video output and sends the output to the client using RDP. All keyboard and mouse input from the client is encrypted and sent to the server for processing. RDP also supports sound, drive, port, and network printer redirection. You learned about Remote Desktop Protocol in Chapter 4, "Virtualization and Cloud Computing." Please review that chapter.

VPN

You learned about VPNs in Chapter 2, "Networking." Please review that chapter.

Virtual network computer (VNC)

Virtual network computing (VNC) operates much like RDP but uses the Remote Frame Buffer (RFB) protocol. Unlike RDP, VNC is platform independent. For example, it could be used to transmit between a Linux server and a macOS laptop. The VNC system contains the following components:

- The VNC server is the program on the machine that shares its screen.
- The VNC client (or viewer) is the program that watches, controls, and interacts with the server.
- The VNC protocol (RFB) is used to communicate between the VNC server and client.

Secure Shell (SSH)

You learned about Secure Shell in Chapter 2, "Networking." Please review that chapter.

Remote monitoring and management (RMM)

Remote monitoring and management is not a product but rather a process that can be performed by many different tools. It is the process of supervising and controlling IT systems with locally installed agents that can be accessed by a management service provider. Some products are:

- Atera RMM
- SuperOps RMM
- NinjaRMM by NinjaOne
- N-able RMM

Microsoft Remote Assistance (MSRA)

MSRA is a tool that allows you to connect to a remote computer to provide assistance to another user currently logged into that computer. When you connect through MSRA, you do not have to log into that computer; instead, invitations are sent from the host computer to you so that you can take over the computer. You can use the remote computer (the host computer) as if you are sitting in front of it. The user on the other end can watch your activities on-screen. At any time, either user can terminate the session. To configure this feature, follow these steps:

1. Enter **Remote** in the desktop search box.
2. Click Settings under the search box.
3. Click Allow Remote Assistance Invitations To Be Sent From This Computer. The System Properties dialog box appears, with the Remote tab selected.
4. Click Allow Remote Assistance Connections To This Computer, as shown in Figure 9.11.
5. Click OK.

FIGURE 9.11   Enabling Remote Assistance in Windows 10

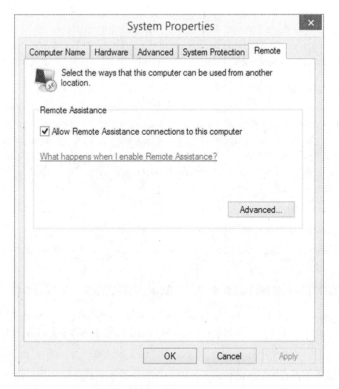

A user on the host computer can now send an invitation to you to allow you to connect to that computer for repair or training purposes.

Third-party tools

There are also third-party tools that sometimes include screen- and file-sharing features. Let's briefly discuss these capabilities.

Screen-sharing software

Many of the collaboration or meeting software packages such as Go To Meeting, Webex, and Adobe Connect offer a screen sharing option. These are also possible in third-party remote access software such as Go To My PC, LogMeIn, and Remote PC.

Video-conferencing software

With the increasing use of remote work, videoconferencing and virtual meetings have become commonplace. Tools like Zoom and Google Hangout allow groups of users to meet, share screens, work on common documents, and continue to get work done as if they are in the office.

File transfer software

Many of the collaboration or meeting software packages such as Go To Meeting, Webex, and Adobe Connect also offer a file-sharing option. In many collaboration solutions, multiple users can even edit a document at the same time. These options are also available in third-party remote access software such as Go To My PC, LogMeIn, and Remote PC.

Desktop management software

Desktop management software is designed to allow for control of what is available to users on their desktops as well as other settings. It allows IT departments to find, manage, and control endpoints, such as desktop computers or mobile devices, on local and remote sites without the need for physical access to these devices. Also called endpoint management software, it has many of the same features as Windows Group Policy but is vendor neutral. Examples include:

- Tivoli Endpoint Manager
- ManageEngine Desktop Central
- Symantec Client Management Suite

Security considerations of each access method

Except for Telnet, which is completely insecure, RDP and third-party methods are generally secure and encrypted. However, you should ensure the following about the solution you select:

RDP   Ensure that all passwords are complex and that rights are restricted to the minimum to do the job.

VPN   Ensure that the most secure protocols (such as IPsec) are in use and that all passwords are complex.

SSH   Ensure that all passwords are complex and that rights are restricted to the minimum to do the job.

RMM   Select the most secure tool available. Ensure that all passwords are complex and that rights are restricted to the minimum to do the job.

MSRA   Strictly control the process of soliciting help and ensure that helpers do not take advantage of users while they have control of the user's system.

Third-Party Methods   Ensure that you understand the security capabilities and the shortcomings of the specific method under consideration.

Exam essentials

Describe common remote access tools.   These include Telnet, RDP, SSH, and third-party screen- and file-sharing tools such as LogMeIn and Go To My PC.

Review Questions

You can find the answers in the appendix.

1. Which of the following is the least important piece of information to record about each device for proper asset inventory?

   A. Make

   B. Model

   C. Serial number

   D. Operating system

2. Which of the following is false with respect to change management?

   A. All changes should be formally requested.

   B. Each request should be analyzed to ensure it supports all goals and policies.

   C. After formal approval, all costs and effects of the methods of implementation should be reviewed.

   D. After changes are approved, the change steps should be developed.

3. What is the process called that ensures all configuration changes are beneficial?

   A. Change management

   B. Acceptable use

   C. Separation of duties

   D. Risk analysis

4. Which of the following are created to prevent technicians from spending too much time on an issue they don't completely understand?

   A. Escalation levels

   B. Phased deployments

   C. Scenario triage

   D. Runbooks

5. If you use incremental backups every day except Monday, when you do a full backup, how many backup tapes will be required if there is a drive failure on Wednesday after the backup has been made?

   A. 4

   B. 3

   C. 2

   D. 1

6. If you use differential backups every day except Monday, when you do a full backup how many backup tapes will be required if there is a drive failure on Wednesday after the backup has been made?

    A. 4

    B. 3

    C. 2

    D. 1

7. Which of the following is *not* a safe lifting technique to keep in mind?

    A. Lift with your back, not your legs.

    B. Be careful to not twist when lifting.

    C. Keep objects as close to your body as possible.

    D. Where possible, push instead of pull.

8. What class of fire extinguisher is used for paper fires?

    A. A

    B. B

    C. C

    D. D

9. Any type of chemical, equipment, or supply that has the potential to harm the environment or people has to have what document associated with it?

    A. SOW

    B. MSDS

    C. SLA

    D. MOU

10. What humidity level should be maintained for computing equipment?

    A. 50 percent

    B. 40 percent

    C. 60 percent

    D. 30 percent

11. Which of the following is *not* part of the first response to an incident?

    A. Shut down the affected system.

    B. Identify the issue.

    C. Report through proper channels.

    D. Preserve the data/device.

12. Which of the following is a secure substitute for Telnet?

    A. RDP

    B. SSH

    C. SSL

    D. VPN

13. Which of the following is false regarding dealing with customers?

    A. Always answer the telephone in a professional manner, announcing the name of the company and yourself.

    B. Make a concentrated effort to ascertain the customer's technical level, and communicate above it.

    C. Use proper language (avoid jargon, acronyms, and slang when applicable).

    D. Maintain a positive attitude/project confidence.

14. Which of the following should the IT professional do when dealing with customers?

    A. Use appropriate professional titles, when applicable.

    B. Take personal calls.

    C. Use the customer's equipment for personal messages.

    D. Talk to co-workers while interacting with customers.

15. Which of the following files is written in Python?

    A. PSI

    B. VBS

    C. SH

    D. PY

16. How is the warranty status of a device determined?

    A. By model number

    B. By serial number

    C. By date of deployment

    D. By device name

17. Which of the following is a command-line tool?

    A. RDP

    B. Screen sharing

    C. File sharing

    D. SSH

18. Which of the following is the least secure remote access technology?

    A. RDP

    B. Screen sharing

    C. Telnet

    D. SSH

Appendix

Answers to the Review Questions

Chapter 1: Mobile Devices

1. B. Yahoo recommends using IMAP as an email client.

2. B. Many laptop manufacturers will consider a warranty void if an unauthorized person opens a laptop case and attempts to repair it.

3. B. Many laptop manufacturers will consider a warranty void if an unauthorized person opens a laptop case and attempts to repair it. Some models of notebook PCs require a special T-8 Torx screwdriver. Most PC toolkits come with a T-8 bit for a screwdriver with interchangeable bits, but you may find that the T-8 screws are countersunk in deep holes so that you can't fit the drive in the hole.

4. B. As you can imagine, setting up iCloud email on an iOS device is simple because the applications all reside in the Apple ecosystem. First set up an iCloud email account. If you have an email address that ends with *@mac.com* or *@me.com*, you al-ready have an equivalent address that's the same except that it ends with *@icloud.com*.

5. C. When removing the connector attached to the old drive's signal pins and attaching it to the new drive, make sure it's right side up and do not force it. Damaging the signal pins may render the drive useless.

6. C. Starting with Windows Vista, ActiveSync has been replaced with the Windows Mobile Device Center, which is included as part of the operating system.

7. B. The advantage of solid-state drives is that they are not as susceptible to damage if the device is dropped, and they are generally faster because no moving parts are involved. They are, however, more expensive, and when they fail, they don't typically display any advanced warning symptoms like a magnetic drive will do.

8. C. Authenticator applications, such as Google Authenticator, make it possible for a mobile device to use a time-based one-time password (TOTP) algorithm with a site or system that requires such authentication.

9. D. In-plane switching (IPS) is a newer technology that solves the issue of poor quality at angles other than straight on. It also provides better color quality. However, it has much slower response time and is more expensive than the other options.

10. B. You will need the following information to complete this setup:

    The FQDN of your POP3 server or IMAP server (this server receives the emails sent to you, so it's sometimes called incoming)

    The FQDN of your SMTP server (this server sends your email to the recipient's email server, so it's sometimes called outgoing)

    The port numbers used for both server types

    The security type used (if any)

11. C. Laptops can support plug and play at three levels, depending on how dynamically they're able to adapt to changes:

Cold docking: The laptop must be turned off and back on for the change to be recognized.

Warm docking: The laptop must be put in and out of suspended mode for the change to be recognized.

Hot docking: The change can be made and is recognized while running normal operations.

12. C. It is important to understand that using two or more of the same type of factors (such as a password and a PIN, both something you know) is not multifactor authentication.

13. A. A global positioning system (GPS) uses satellite information to plot the global location of an object and uses that information to plot the route to a second location.

14. A. Mobile device management (MDM) policies can be created in AD, or they can be implemented through MDM software. This software allows you to exert control over the mobile devices, even those you do not own if they have the software installed.

15. A. Many external devices will ask for a PIN when you select the external device from the list of discovered devices. In many cases, the PIN is 0000, but you should check the manual for the external device.

16. C. POP3 uses port 110 by default.

17. C. Hybrid storage products have a magnetic disk and some solid-state memory. These drives monitor the data being read from the hard drive, and they cache the most frequently accessed bits to the high-speed flash memory.

18. D. Most mobile devices now offer the option to incorporate biometrics as an authentication mechanism. The two most common implementations of this use fingerprint or facial scans or facial recognition technology.

Chapter 2: Networking

1. D. POP3 uses port 110. SSH uses port 22, FTP uses ports 20 and 21, and Telnet uses port 23.

2. A. FTP uses ports 20 and 21. POP3 uses port 110, SSH uses port 22, and Telnet uses port 23.

3. B. SSH uses port 22, POP3 uses port 110, FTP uses ports 20 and 21, and Telnet uses port 23.

4. B. Switches operate at layer 2. Routers operate at layer 3. Repeaters and hubs operate at layer 1.

5. D. Hubs operate at layer 1. Switches and bridges operate at layer 2. Routers operate at layer 3.

6. B. Switches operate at layer 2. Routers operate at layer 3. Hubs and repeaters operate at layer 1.

7. B. The class B range is 172.16.0.0–172.31.255.255. The other ranges are correct.

8. A. Symmetric DSL (SDSL) offers an upload equal to the download speed. The other versions all have slower upload speed than download speed.

9. C. Industrial control systems (ICSs) is a general term that encompasses several types of control systems used in industrial production. The most widespread is supervisory control and data acquisition (SCADA). SCADA is a system operating with coded signals over communication channels so as to provide control of remote equipment.

10. A. 802.11a operates in the 5.0 GHz range. The other standards all operate in the 2.4 GHz range.

11. D. 802.11a and 802.11g have a maximum rate of 54 MB, 802.11b has a maximum of 11 MB, and 802.11 has a maximum of 2 MB.

12. C. 802.11g has a distance that is the cell size of 125 ft. The others have a distance of 115 ft.

13. B. DNS servers resolve IP addresses to hostnames. HTTP servers are web servers. DHCP servers provide automatic IP configurations. SQL is a database server.

14. C. DHCP servers provide automatic IP configurations. DNS servers resolve IP addresses to hostnames. HTTP servers are web servers. SQL is a database server.

15. D. A SQL server is a database server. DNS servers resolve IP addresses to hostnames. HTTP servers are web servers. DHCP servers provide automatic IP configurations.

16. C. The Class B range is 128–191. The class A range is 1–126. The Class C range is 192–223.

17. B. The Class A range is 1–126. The class B range is 128–191. The Class C range is 192–223.

18. A. The Class C range is 192–223. The Class A range is 1–126. The Class B range is 128–191. The 224 range is for multicasting.

19. C. A personal area network (PAN) is a LAN created by personal devices. A wide area network (WAN) is a collection of two or more LANs, typically connected by routers and dedicated leased lines. Occasionally, a WAN will be referenced as a metropolitan area network (MAN) when it is confined to a certain geographic area, such as a university campus or city. Wireless mesh networks (WMNs) are a form of an ad hoc WLAN that often consists of mesh clients, mesh routers, and gateways.

20. B. Metropolitan area network (MAN) is the term occasionally used for a WAN that is confined to a certain geographic area, such as a university campus or city. A personal area network (PAN) is a LAN created by personal devices. A wide area network (WAN) is a collection of two or more LANs, typically connected by routers and dedicated leased lines. Wireless mesh networks (WMNs) are a form of an ad hoc WLAN that often consist of mesh clients, mesh routers, and gateways.

21. D. Wireless mesh networks (WMNs) are a form of an ad hoc WLAN that often consists of mesh clients, mesh routers, and gateways. A personal area network (PAN) is a LAN created by personal devices. A wide area network (WAN) is a collection of two or more LANs, typically connected by routers and dedicated leased lines. Occasionally, a WAN will be referenced as a metropolitan area network (MAN) when it is confined to a certain geographic area, such as a university campus or city.

22. A. Wire crimpers look like pliers but are used to attach media connectors to the ends of cables. A cable stripper is used to remove the outer covering of the cable to get to the wire pairs within. A multimeter combines a number of tools into one. There can be slight variations, but a multimeter always includes a voltmeter, an ohmmeter, and an ammeter (and is sometimes called VOM as an acronym). A toner probe has two parts: the tone generator (called the *toner*) and the tone locator (called the *probe*). The toner sends the tone, and at the other end of the cable, the probe receives the toner's signal. This tool makes it easier to find the beginning and end of a cable.

23. C. A multimeter combines a number of tools into one. There can be slight variations, but a multimeter always includes a voltmeter, an ohmmeter, and an ammeter (and is sometimes called VOM as an acronym). Wire crimpers look like pliers but are used to attach media connectors to the ends of cables. A cable stripper is used to remove the outer covering of the cable to get to the wire pairs within. A toner probe has two parts: the tone generator (called the *toner*) and the tone locator (called the *probe*). The toner sends the tone, and at the other end of the cable, the probe receives the toner's signal. This tool makes it easier to find the beginning and end of a cable.

24. D. A toner probe has two parts: the tone generator (called the *toner*) and the tone locator (called the *probe*). The toner sends the tone, and at the other end of the cable, the probe receives the toner's signal. This tool makes it easier to find the beginning and end of a cable. Wire crimpers look like pliers but are used to attach media connectors to the ends of cables. A cable stripper is used to remove the outer covering of the cable to get to the wire pairs within. A multimeter combines a number of tools into one. There can be slight variations, but a multimeter always includes a voltmeter, an ohmmeter, and an ammeter (and is sometimes called VOM as an acronym).

Chapter 3: Hardware

1. C. Twisted pair is commonly used in office settings to connect workstations to hubs or switches. It comes in two varieties: unshielded (UTP) and shielded (STP). Fiber-optic, serial, and coaxial do not come in shielded and unshielded versions.

2. B. Cat 5 transmits data at speeds up to 100 Mbps and was used with Fast Ethernet (operating at 100 Mbps) with a transmission range of 100 meters. It contains four twisted pairs of copper wire to give the most protection. Although it had its share of popularity (it's used primarily for 10/100 Ethernet networking), it is now an outdated standard. Newer implementations use the Cat 5e or Cat6 standard. Cat 4 transmits at 16 Mbps, and Cat 6 transmits at 1 Gbps.

3. A. Fiber-optic cabling is the most expensive type of those discussed for this exam. Although it's an excellent medium, it's often not used because of the cost of implementing it. It has a glass core within a rubber outer coating and uses beams of light rather than electrical signals to relay data. None of the other options uses glass in its construction.

4. A. An RJ-11 is a standard connector for a telephone line and is used to connect a computer modem to a phone line. It looks much like an RJ-45 but is noticeably smaller. The RJ-45 is used for networking. RS-232 is a serial connector. BNC is a coaxial connector.

5. C. The RS-232 standard had been commonly used in computer serial ports. A serial cable (and port) uses only one wire to carry data in each direction; all the rest are wires for signaling and traffic control. An RJ-11 is a standard connector for a telephone line and is used to connect a computer modem to a phone line. It looks much like an RJ-45 but is noticeably smaller. The RJ-45 is used for networking.

6. D. Bayonet Neill–Concelman (BNC) connectors are sometimes used in the place of RCA connectors for video electronics, so you may encounter these connectors, especially when video equipment connects to a PC. In many cases, you may be required to purchase an adapter to convert this to another form of connection because it is rare to find one on the PC. An RJ-11 is a standard connector for a telephone line and is used to connect a computer modem to a phone line. It looks much like an RJ-45 but is noticeably smaller. The RJ45 is used for networking. RS-232 is a serial connector.

7. B. Portable computers (notebooks and subnotebooks) require smaller sticks of RAM because of their smaller size. One of the two types is a small outline DIMM (SODIMM), which can have 72, 144, or 200 pins. DIMM is a full-size RAM type. Rambus is a type of RAM but is not used in laptops, and BNC is a connector for coaxial cabling.

8. D. DDR SDRAM is Double Data Rate 2 (DDR2). This allows for two memory accesses for each rising and falling clock and effectively doubles the speed of DDR. DDR2-667 chips work with speeds at 667 MHz and are also referred to as PC2-5300 modules. DDR3 is the higher-speed successor to DDR and DDR2. Portable computers (notebooks and subnotebooks) require smaller sticks of RAM because of their smaller size. One of the two types is a small outline DIMM (SODIMM), which can have 72, 144, or 200 pins.

9. B. DDR4 SDRAM is an abbreviation for Double Data Rate fourth-generation synchronous dynamic random access memory. DDR4 is not compatible with any earlier type of random access memory (RAM). The DDR4 standard allows for DIMMs of up to 64 GB in capacity, compared to DDR3's maximum of 16 GB per DIMM. DDR3 and DDR2 are backward compatible, and there is no DDR5.

10. B. Compact Disc-ReWritable (CD-RW) media is a rewritable optical disc. A CD-RW drive requires more sensitive laser optics. It can write data to the disc but also has the ability to erase that data and write more data to the disc. CD, DVD, and CD-ROM are all read-only.

11. A. M.2, formerly known as the Next Generation Form Factor (NGFF), is a specification for internally mounted computer expansion cards and associated connectors. It replaces the mSATA standard. M.2 modules are rectangular, with an edge connector on one side, and a semicircular mounting hole at the center of the opposite edge. Non-Volatile Memory

Host Controller Interface Specification (NVME) is an open logical device interface specification for accessing nonvolatile storage media attached via a PCI Express (PCIe) bus. Serial ATA and serial ATA 2.5 are computer bus interfaces that connect host bus adapters to mass storage devices such as hard disk drives, optical drives, and solid-state drives.

12. C. At 10,000 rpm, the latency will decrease to about 3 ms. Data transfer rates also generally go up with a higher rotational speed but are influenced by the density of the disk (the number of tracks and sectors present in a given area). Latency at 5400 rpm will be 5.56 ms. At 7200 it will be 4.17, and at 15000 it will drop to 2.

13. A. Laptops and other portable devices utilize an expansion card called the miniPCI. It has the same functionality as the PCI but a much smaller form factor. PCI and PCIe are used in desktops. SATA is a drive connector.

14. A. Unified Extensible Firmware Interface (UEFI) is a standard firmware interface for PCs, designed to replace BIOS. NVRAM is RAM that retains its data during a reboot. CMOS is a battery type found on motherboards, and CHS is a drive geometry concept.

15. A. The pins in the printhead are wrapped with coils of wire to create a solenoid and are held in the rest position by a combination of a small magnet and a spring. To trigger a particular pin, the printer controller sends a signal to the printhead, which energizes the wires around the appropriate print wire. This turns the print wire into an electromagnet, which repels the print pin, forcing it against the ink ribbon and making a dot on the paper.

16. B. The heating element for a thermal printer is what generates the heat and does the actual printing. It is often the most expensive component.

17. C. When a printer gets out of calibration, the print quality will decline. When a new cartridge is loaded, the printer will usually perform a calibration, but you may need to do this manually from time to time, especially on printers that are not used often enough to require a cartridge change as often as a calibration may be required.

18. D. There can be damage to the drum or charging roller, and if there is, replacing the cartridge will help with the problem.

19. C. In 2004, the ATX 12V 2.0 (now 2.03) standard was passed, changing the main connector from 20 pins to 24. The additional pins provide +3.3V, +5V, and +12V (the fourth pin is a ground) for use by PCIe cards. When a 24-pin connector is used, there is no need for the optional four- or six-pin auxiliary power connectors.

20. A. Explanation: Work done by the CPU for a component or application is called a process, and these processes are subdivided into threads of work.

21. C. The SATA power connector consists of 15 pins, with 3 pins designated for 3.3V, 5V, and 12V and with each pin carrying 1.5 amps. This results in a total draw of 4.95 watts + 7.5 watts + 18 watts, or about 30 watts.

22. A. Verify that there is toner in the cartridge. If it's an old cartridge, you can often shake it slightly to free up toner once before replacing.

23. B. The steps in order are:

1. Processing
2. Charging
3. Exposing
4. Developing
5. Transferring
6. Fusing
7. Cleaning

24. B. A DC power supply applies a uniform positive charge (about +600V) to the paper. When the paper rotates past the drum, the toner is pulled off the drum and onto the paper. Then the paper passes through a static eliminator that removes the positive charge from it. Some printers use a transfer corona wire; others use a transfer corona roller.

25. B. Print jobs can also be submitted through the SMB protocol. The SMB printing function is used to print data by directly specifying this machine on the computer.

26. C. In some cases you are printing a document that is so secure that you don't want random users visiting the printer to pick up their print jobs to see it. Many printers have the ability to hold the print job until you enter a PIN that releases the job to be printed while you physically monitor the process. These are called secure prints.

27. C. When printing with a Bluetooth-enabled device (like a mobile phone) and a Bluetooth-enabled printer, all you need to do is get within range of the device (that is, move closer), select the print driver from the device, and choose Print.

28. A. When you install a printer driver for the printer you are using, it allows the computer to print to that printer correctly (assuming you have the correct interface configured between the computer and printer). Also, keep in mind that drivers are specific to the operating system, so you need to select the one that is both for the correct printer and for the correct operating system.

29. B. An optional component that can be added to printers (usually laser but also inkjet) is a duplexer. This can be an optional assembly added to the printer, or built into it, but the sole purpose of duplexing is to turn the printed sheet over so that it can be run back through the printer and allow printing on both sides.

30. C. The orientation of a document refers to how the printed matter is laid out on the page. In the landscape orientation, the printing is written across the paper turned on its long side, whereas in portrait the paper is turned up vertically and printed top to bottom. The driver is the software that talks between the printer and the operating system. Duplexing makes it possible to print on both sides. To collate is to create multiple copies with all sets in correct page order.

31. A. Continuous-feed paper feeds through the printer using a system of sprockets and tractors. Sheet-fed printers accept plain paper in a paper tray. Dot matrix is continuous feed; everything else is sheet fed.

32. B. Never reuse paper in a laser printer that has been through the printer once. Although it may look blank, you're repeating the charging and fusing process on a piece of paper that most likely has something already on it.

33. A. A printer controller is a large circuit board that acts as the motherboard for the printer. It contains the processor and RAM to convert data coming in from the computer into a picture of a page to be printed. The imaging drum is the drum where the toner is placed on the correctly charged area. The toner cartridge is the container holding the toner. The maintenance kit contains items that should be changed periodically.

Chapter 4: Virtualization and Cloud Computing

1. B. Software as a service (SaaS) involves the vendor providing the entire solution. This includes the operating system, the infrastructure software, and the application. Infrastructure as a service (IaaS) provides only the hardware platform to the customer. Platform as a service (PaaS) provides a development environment. Security Information and Event Management (SIEM) is a system that aggregates all log files and analyzes them in real time for attacks.

2. A. When a company pays another company to host and manage a cloud environment, it is called a public cloud solution. If the company hosts this environment itself, it is a private cloud solution. A hybrid cloud solution is one in which both public and private clouds are part of the solution. A community cloud is one in which multiple entities use the cloud.

3. B. One of the advantages of a cloud environment is the ability to add resources as needed on the fly and release those resources when they are no longer required. This makes for more efficient use of resources, placing them where needed at any particular point in time. These include CPU and memory resources. This is called rapid elasticity because it occurs automatically according to the rules for resource sharing that have been deployed. On-demand refers to the ability of the customer to add resources as needed. Virtual sharing and stretched resources are not terms used when discussing the cloud.

4. A. There are three models for implementing VDI:

- **Centralized model:** All desktop instances are stored in a single server, requiring significant processing power on the server.

- **Hosted model:** Desktops are maintained by a service provider. This model eliminates capital cost and is instead subject to operation cost.

- **Remote virtual desktops model:** An image is copied to the local machine, making a constant network connection unnecessary.

    There is no local model.

5. C. Platform as a service (PaaS) involves the vendor providing the hardware platform and the software running on the platform. This includes the operating systems and infrastructure software. The company is still involved in managing the system. Software as a service (SaaS) involves the vendor providing the entire solution. This includes the operating system, the infrastructure software, and the application. Infrastructure as a service (IaaS) provides only the hardware platform to the customer. Security Information and Event Management (SIEM) is a system that aggregates all log files and analyzes them in real time for attacks.

6. A. Some virtualization products require that the motherboard support hardware-assisted virtualization. The benefit derived from using hardware-assisted virtualization is that it reduces overhead and improves performance. It does not improve security, lower power consumption, or ease troubleshooting.

7. B. The hypervisor is the software that allows the VMs to exist. Dual inline memory module (DIMM) is a type of memory. There is no software called Azureware, and network address translation (NAT) is a service that translates private IP addresses to public ones.

8. A. XP Mode is a free emulator from Microsoft that you can download and use as a virtual emulator. A number of others are also available. In most cases, the motherboard and associated BIOS settings need no modification to provide services to these VMs.

9. A. Virtual desktop infrastructures (VDIs) host desktop operating systems within a virtual environment in a centralized server. Users access the desktops and run them from the server.

10. D. Sandboxing is the segregation of virtual environments for security proposes. Sandboxed appliances have been used in the past to supplement the security features of a network. These appliances are used to test suspicious files in a protected environment.

Chapter 5: Hardware and Network Troubleshooting

1. B. The steps are as follows:
    1. Identify the problem.
    2. Establish a theory of probable cause (question the obvious).
    3. Test the theory to determine cause.
    4. Establish a plan of action to resolve the problem and implement the solution.
    5. Verify full system functionality and, if applicable, implement preventive measures.
    6. Document findings, actions, and outcomes.

2. D. The steps are as follows:

    1. Identify the problem.

    2. Establish a theory of probable cause (question the obvious).

    3. Test the theory to determine cause.

    4. Establish a plan of action to resolve the problem and implement the solution.

    5. Verify full system functionality and, if applicable, implement preventive measures.

    6. Document findings, actions, and outcomes.

3. A. The most common reason for shutdowns is overheating. Often when that is the case, however, the system reboots itself rather than just shutting down.

4. D. A bad NIC driver would cause the NIC not to work but would not cause a system lockup.

5. B. Once a regular occurrence when working with Windows, blue screens (also known as the blue screen of death [BSOD]) have become much less frequent.

6. A. While Microsoft users have the BSOD to deal with, Apple users have also come to have the same negative feelings about the Pinwheel of Death. This is a multicolored pinwheel mouse pointer that signifies a temporary delay while the system "thinks."

7. A. Pixels are the small dots on the screen that are filled with a color; as a group they present the image you see on the screen.

8. B. Artifacts are visual anomalies that appear on the screen. They might be pieces of images left over from a previous image or a "tear in the image" (it looks like the image is divided into two parts and the parts don't line up).

9. A. The backlight is the light in the device that powers the LCD screen. It can go bad over time and need to be replaced, and it can also be held captive by the inverter. The inverter takes the DC power the laptop is providing and boosts it up to AC to run the backlight. If the inverter goes bad, you can replace it on most models (it's cheaper than the backlight).

10. B. TouchFLO is a user interface feature designed by HTC. It is used by dragging your finger up and down or left and right to access common tasks on the screen. This movement is akin to scrolling the screen up and down or scrolling the screen left and right.

11. B. With laser printers, streaks usually indicate that the fuser is not fusing the toner properly on the paper. It could also be that the incorrect paper is being used. In laser printers, you can sometimes tell the printer that you are using a heavier paper. For dot-matrix, you can adjust the platen for thicker paper.

12. C. In laser printers, faded output usually indicates that the toner cartridge is just about empty. You can usually remove it, shake it, and replace it and then get a bit more life out of it before it is completely empty, but it is a signal that you are near the end.

13. B. You may be able to ping the entire network using IP addresses, but most access is done by name, not IP address. If you can't ping resources by name, DNS is not functional, meaning either the DNS server is down or the local machine is not configured with the correct IP address of the DNS server.

14. C. If the computer cannot connect to the default gateway, it will be confined to communicating with devices on the local network. This IP address should be that of the router interface connecting to the local network.

Chapter 6: Operating Systems

1. D. Windows 10 Home is the only system listed that cannot be a member of a domain.

2. A. The md command is the shorthand version of the mkdir command and is used to create a new folder. Its syntax is md [<drive>:]<path>.

3. B. Task Manager lets you shut down unresponsive applications selectively in all Windows versions. In current versions of Windows, it can do much more. Task Manager allows you to see which processes and applications are using the most system resources, view network usage, and see connected users, among other things.

4. C. As the name implies, from this tab you can configure connections for an Internet connection, a dial-up or VPN connection, and LAN settings.

5. D. The Recovery section of Update & Security contains settings to reset the PC and to boot to advanced options when there are boot issues.

6. A. In Windows 10 when you make a new connection, you are asked to identify whether it is a private or a public network. If you choose the first, Network Discovery is on by default, allowing you to see other computers and other computers to see you. If you choose Public, Network Discovery is turned off.

7. B. The dir command is used to view a listing of the files and folders that exist within a directory, subdirectory, or folder.

8. C. The change directory (cd) command is used to move to another folder or directory. It is used in both Unix and Windows.

9. A. Device Manager shows a list of all installed hardware and lets you add items, remove items, update drivers, and more.

10. B. Every program and process theoretically could have its own logging utility, but Microsoft has come up with a rather slick utility, Event Viewer, which, through log files, tracks all events on a particular Windows computer.

11. D. Force Quit can be used on a Mac to stop an unresponsive application. To use this function, follow these steps:

   1. Choose Force Quit from the Apple menu or press Command+Option+Esc.

   2. Select the unresponsive app in the Force Quit Applications window, and then click Force Quit.

12. B. Differences between 64-bit and 32-bit systems include their hardware requirements and the types of applications you can run on them. You can run a 32-bit application on either a 64-bit or a 32-bit operating system, but you can only run 64-bit applications on a 64-bit system.

13. A. The minimum of RAM required should be viewed as just that, a minimum. Make sure you have more than required for satisfactory performance.

14. C. Outside of the enterprise most installations occur by using the CD that came with the software or by placing these same files on a USB stick and accessing them from the USB drive.

15. C. Many proprietary operating systems that reside on devices such as access points, switches, routers, and firewalls are Linux-based. Linux systems also predominate in the software development area.

16. A. `net use` can also be used to connect to a shared printer: `net use lpt1: \\`*printername*.

17. A. In Linux, a shell is a command-line interface.

18. B. In Apple, Mission Control provides a quick way to see everything that's currently open on your Mac.

Chapter 7: Security

1. A. An access control vestibule is a series of two doors with a small room between them. The user is authenticated at the first door and then allowed into the room. At that point, additional verification will occur (such as a guard visually identifying the person), and then the person is allowed through the second door. A trapdoor is a doorway that is usually hidden. A safe room is a room that is impenetrable from the outside, and badgetrap is not a term used when discussing doorway systems.

2. A. Biometric devices use physical characteristics to identify the user. Such devices are becoming more common in the business environment. Biometric systems include hand scanners, retinal scanners, and, possibly soon, DNA scanners. Hardware tokens are devices that contain security credentials. Smartcards are cards that contain a chip and credentials. Badge readers are devices that read the information on a card and allow or disallow entry.

3. C. IP address filtering is the type of filtering done on a router or firewall, based on IP addresses. Email filtering is the filtering of email addresses from which a user is allowed to receive. URL filtering restricts the URLs that can be reached with the browser.

4. C. Hash values, also referred to as message digests, are calculated using the original message. A hash function takes a message of variable length and produces a fixed-length hash value. If the receiver calculates a hash value that is the same, then the original message is intact. If the receiver calculates a hash value that is different, then the original message has been altered.

5. D. Wired Equivalent Privacy (WEP) is a standard that was created as a first stab at security for wireless devices. Using WEP-encrypted data to provide data security has always been under scrutiny for not being as secure as initially intended. Wi-Fi Protected Access (WPA) and WPA2 are later methods that came after WEP. Temporal Key Integrity Protocol (TKIP) is the encryption method used in WPA.

6. A. WPA was able to increase security by using a Temporal Key Integrity Protocol (TKIP) to scramble encryption keys using a hashing algorithm. Advanced Encryption Standard (AES) is the encryption used in WPA2. IPSec is an industry-standard encryption method, and Secure Sockets Layer (SSL) is an encryption method used in many VPNs.

7. C. An armored virus is designed to make itself difficult to detect or analyze. Armored viruses cover themselves with protective code that stops debuggers or disassemblers from examining critical elements of the virus. A companion virus is one that attaches to a file or adopts the name of a file. A macro virus is one that hides in macros, and a multipartite virus is one that has multiple propagation methods.

8. B. A signature is an algorithm or other element of a virus that uniquely identifies it. Because some viruses have the ability to alter their signature, it is crucial that you keep signature files current, whether you choose to manually download them or configure the antivirus engine to do so automatically. An ID is any type of identifying badge or marker. A badge is something worn to provide identification. Marking is not a word typically used when discussing algorithms or attacks.

9. C. Tailgating is the term used for someone being so close to you when you enter a building that they are able to come in right behind you without needing to use a key, a card, or any other security device. Many social engineering intruders needing physical access to a building will use this method of gaining entry. Shadowing is when one user monitors another for training. Spoofing is the adoption of another's email address, IP address, or MAC address. Keyriding is not a word typically used when discussing social engineering.

10. B. Spoofing is the process of masquerading as another user or device. It is usually done for the purpose of accessing a resource to which the hacker should not have access or to get through a security device such as a firewall that may be filtering traffic based on source IP address. Shadowing is when one user monitors another for training. Duplication is the creation of a matching object. Masking is not a term used when discussing impersonation.

11. A. The Power Users group is not as powerful as the Administrators group. Membership in this group gives read/write permission to the system, allowing members to install most software but keeping them from changing key operating system files. This is a good group for those who need to test software (such as programmers) and junior administrators. The Guest group is used to allow restricted access to the device. The Administrators group allows full access to the device. The rights held by the Users group are a compromise between Admin and Guest.

12. D. Write combines the permissions of Read with those of List Folder Contents and adds the ability to run executables. List Folder Contents allows you to view what items are in a folder. Full Control allows everything, and Read only allows you to read documents.

13. D. Although length is now considered the most important password security factor, complexity is also a factor, and these examples are all the same length. The password P@ssw0rd contains four character types, the most of any of the options, which increases the strength of the password. Password and pAssword contain only two types of characters. Pa$$word contains three types.

14. B. When assigning user permissions, follow the principle of least privilege by giving users only the bare minimum they need to do their job. Separation of duties prescribes that any operation prone to fraud should be broken up into two operations with different users performing each. Job rotation has the same goal but accomplishes it by requiring users to move around from job to job. Open rights is not a term used when discussing permission and rights.

15. C. Swipe locks use a gesture or series of gestures, sometimes involving the movement of an icon to open the screen. In some cases, they require only knowledge of the mobile platform in use; they offer no security to the process because no authentication of the user is occurring. Fingerprint locks open when the correct fingerprint is presented. Facial locks require a matching face scan to open. Passcode locks require the configured passcode to unlock.

16. A. Remote wipe gives you the ability to delete all content when a device is stolen or lost. Geofencing allows you to restrict use of the device to a geographic area. Screen locks prevent access to the home screen on the device. Segmentation of data is the separation of personal data from enterprise data on a device.

17. A. Degaussing involves applying a strong magnetic field to wipe the media (this is also referred to as disk wiping). This process helps ensure that information doesn't fall into the wrong hands. Incineration is the burning of the storage device. Hammers can be used to destroy the device. Deleting is the least effective way of removing information.

18. B. Physically destroying the drive involves rendering the component no longer usable.

19. B. Wi-Fi Protected Setup (WPS) was a concept that was designed to make it easier for less knowledgeable users to add a new client to the WLAN without manually entering the security information on the client. One method involves pushing a button on the AP at the same time a client is attempting to join the network so that the settings are sent to the client. Other methods involve placing the client close to the AP, and near-field communication is used for the process. Service set identifier (SSID) is the name of the WLAN. Wired Equivalent Privacy (WEP) and Wi-Fi protected Access (WPA) are wireless security protocols.

20. A. Every wireless AP or wireless router on the market comes with a default SSID. Cisco models use the name *tsunami*, for example. You should change these defaults and create a new SSID to represent your WLAN. Wi-Fi Protected Setup (WPS) was a concept that was designed to make it easier for less knowledgeable users to add a new client to the WLAN without manually entering the security information on the client. Wired Equivalent Privacy (WEP) and Wi-Fi Protected Access (WPA) are wireless security protocols.

Chapter 8: Software Troubleshooting

1.   A. Although all of these can cause sluggish performance, the first thing to check is the presence of a virus. If the system seems to have an overabundance of disk activity, scan it for viruses using a virus program that resides externally on a CD/DVD, memory stick, or USB drive.

2.   D. When network connectivity is an issue, you should ensure the following about your configuration:

   ▪   Is the IP address in the same network as the default gateway address?

   ▪   Is the subnet mask correct?

   ▪   Is the default gateway address correct?

   ▪   If this is all correct, has the interface been enabled?

   ▪   If this is all correct, it's time to check the settings on the router.

3.   C. The steps in order are:

   1.   Investigate and verify malware symptoms.

   2.   Quarantine infected systems.

   3.   Disable System Restore in Windows

   4.   Remediate infected systems.

   5.   Schedule scans and run updates.

   6.   Enable System Restore and create a restore point in Windows.

   7.   Educate the end user.

4.   D. Lack of permissons will not generate this error. The following issues can:

   ▪   Incorrect boot device order in the BIOS

   ▪   Corrupted or missing boot sector

   ▪   Corrupted boot files

5.   D. Overheating is usually a hardware issue rather than a malware issue.

6.   B. Browser redirection is one of the most serious security problems. Browser hijacking software is external code that changes your browser settings. It may include changing your home page or adding or removing items from your favorites. An on-path attack is when malicious individuals position themselves between two communicating systems, receiving all data. A SYN flood is a form of a DoS attack. Fraggle is an attack using UDP packets.

7.   A. Malware never increases performance.

8. D. The steps are as follows:

  1. Identify and research malware symptoms.

  2. Quarantine the infected systems.

  3. Disable System Restore (in Windows).

  4. Remediate the infected systems.

  5. Schedule scans and run updates.

  6. Enable System Restore and create a restore point (in Windows).

  7. Educate the end user.

9. B. Although it is recommended that you disable System Restore before cleaning an infection, it is a good idea to create a restore point after an infection is cleaned. This gives you a clean restore point going forward in case the system becomes infected again at some point. Network address translation, the Windows Firewall, and your antivirus should not be disabled.

10. A. A low brightness setting does not negatively impact battery life. A high setting, however, does. Location services, Bluetooth, and overheating do not negatively affect battery life.

11. B. While leaving the phone on will run down the battery, it will not alone cause it to overheat. Excessive gaming, using an old battery, and continuous online browsing will cause overheating.

12. D. On the contrary, evidence of malware or other issues is usually accompanied by very high resource utilization. Unusual loss of power, slow speeds, and a weak signal are all signs of security issues.

13. C. When cameras have been enabled when they weren't previously, it is an indication of compromise. Low resource utilization, a disabled microphone, and authorized use of the device are not symptoms of a security issue.

Chapter 9: Operational Procedures

1. D. While the OS may be important, for warranty issues the make, model, and serial number are more important.

2. C. All costs and effects of the methods of implementation should be reviewed prior to formal approval. The other statements are true.

3. A. During the change management process, the relative costs and benefits to the overall organization will be weighed by a change management board or team. Acceptable use is a policy that defines what users can and cannot do. Separation of duties is a concept that says that any operation prone to fraud should be broken into two jobs and assigned to two people. Risk analysis is a process that identifies risks and mitigations.

4. A. Creating levels or tiers of technicians with an increasing amount of knowledge and experience is a best practice. This approach offers two benefits. It encourages a faster solution by preventing issues from remaining unresolved because of a lack of skill of the responding technician, and it frees up experienced technicians to deal with more serious issues.

5. B. Since an incremental backup backs up everything that has changed since the last backup of any type, each day's tape is unique, so you will need the Monday full backup and the incremental tapes from Tuesday and Wednesday.

6. C. Since a differential backup backs up everything that has changed since the last full backup, each day's incremental tape contains what was on the previous day's tape. So, you only need the last differential and the last full backup.

7. A. Lift with your legs, not your back. When you have to pick something up, bend at the knees, not at the waist. The other options are all safety recommendations.

8. A. Class A is for wood and paper fires, Class B is for flammable liquids, Class C is for electrical fires, and Class D is for metal fires.

9. B. Any type of chemical, equipment, or supply that has the potential to harm the environment or people has to have a material safety data sheet (MSDS) associated with it. These are traditionally created by the manufacturer, and you can obtain them from the manufacturer or from the Environmental Protection Agency. A statement of work (SOW) is a document that indicates the work to be performed. A service level agreement is a document that indicates what is being paid and what the service consists of. A memorandum of understanding (MOU) is a document that indicates the intent of two parties to do something together.

10. C. Another preventive measure you can take is to maintain the relative humidity at around 50 percent. Be careful not to increase the humidity too far—to the point where moisture starts to condense on the equipment!

11. A. You should not shut down the system until evidence such as memory contents is gathered.

12. B. Secure Shell is an encrypted alternative when connecting to a device from the command line.

13. B. If you're providing phone support, make a concentrated effort to ascertain the customer's technical level, and communicate at that level, not above or below it.

14. A. You should use appropriate professional titles, when applicable, and never take personal calls, use the customer's equipment for personal messages, or talk to co-workers while interacting with customers.

15. D. A PY file is written in the Python language. Python runs on Windows, macOS, and Linux/Unix. A VBS file is a Visual Basic file. An SH file is a script programmed for Bash, a type of Unix shell.

16. B. This is why maintaining the serial number of each device is important, because that is how you will access your warranty services when needed.

17. D. When you don't need access to the graphical interface and you just want to operate at the command line, you have two options: Telnet and SSH. While Telnet works just fine, it transmits all of the data in clear text, which obviously would be a security issue. Remote Desktop and screen sharing are graphical concepts, and file sharing is not a command-line utility.

18. C. Telnet transmits all of the data in clear text, which obviously is a security issue. Remote Desktop and screen sharing are graphical concepts and can be secured, while Secure Shell (SSH) is an encrypted technology.

Index

Note: Page numbers in *italics* refer to tables or figures.

G

Q

R

S

Online Test Bank

Register to gain one year of FREE access after activation to the online interactive test bank to help you study for your CompTIA A+ certification exams—included with your purchase of this book! All of the chapter review questions and the practice tests in this book are included in the online test bank so you can practice in a timed and graded setting.

Register and Access the Online Test Bank

To register your book and get access to the online test bank, follow these steps:

1. Go to www.wiley.com/go/sybextestprep.
2. Select your book from the list.
3. Complete the required registration information, including answering the security verification to prove book ownership. You will be emailed a pin code.
4. Follow the directions in the email or go to www.wiley.com/go/sybextestprep.
5. Find your book on that page and click the "Register or Login" link with it. Then enter the pin code you received and click the "Activate PIN" button.
6. On the Create an Account or Login page, enter your username and password, and click Login or, if you don't have an account already, create a new account.
7. At this point, you should be in the test bank site with your new test bank listed at the top of the page. If you do not see it there, please refresh the page or log out and log back in.

SYBEX®

A Wiley Brand